Steppingstones

Steppingstones

Ways to Better Reading

Patt McDermid
California Maritime Academy

Mayfield Publishing Company
Mountain View, California
London ■ Toronto

Library of Congress Cataloging-in-Publication Data

McDermid, Patt Craig
    Steppingstones : ways to better reading / Patt McDermid.
      p.   cm.
    Includes index.
    ISBN 1-55934-163-7
    1. Reading (Higher education)—United States. 2. Developmental
reading.   I. Title.
LB2365.R4M3   1993
428.4'071'1—dc20
                    92–33024
                    CIP

Manufactured in the United States of America
10 9 8 7 6 5 4 3 2 1

Mayfield Publishing Company
1240 Villa Street
Mountain View, California 94041

Sponsoring editor, James Bull; production editor, Sondra Glider;
manuscript editor, Mark Gallaher; art director, Jeanne M. Schreiber;
art editor, Jean Mailander; illustrator, Marilyn Kreiger; text and cover
designer, MaryEllen Podgorski; cover photograph, James Bull;
manufacturing manager, Martha Branch.

The text was set in 10½/12 Bembo by G & S Typesetters and printed on
50# Finch Opaque by R. R. Donnelley & Sons Company.

Text credits appear on a continuation of the copyright page, p. 379.

For our daughter Maire Esther Bacon Gutiérrez-McDermid, who wasn't around yet at the last book:

". . . hearing the sweetness of her voice, the tunefulness of her words, the melody of her singing and playing on instruments . . ."

—Baldassare Castiglione,
from *Il Cortegiano,* 1528

Contents

■ CHAPTER 3
THE PEOPLE SECTION 56

CHAPTER 5
THE EDITORIAL SECTION 137

■   CHAPTER 6
THE SPORTS SECTION   175

■ CHAPTER 7
THE COMICS SECTION

Readings from the College Curriculum   243   PART III

■ CHAPTER 8
ARCHAEOLOGY

■ CHAPTER 9
RELIGIOUS STUDIES

Preface

The purpose of this book is to help students develop essential academic reading skills. These skills are first defined and demonstrated. Then students are asked to apply them to a variety of stimulating reading material chosen to encourage class discussion and the thoughtful engagement necessary for critical thinking. The apparatus is designed to spark such individual response, while at the same time providing exercises in the more traditional essentials of vocabulary and reading comprehension development.

The readings in *Steppingstones* are not ordinary "developmental reader" fare because this book does not have ordinary objectives. Some of the material from newspapers and magazines in Part II focuses on serious issues, posing difficult questions that may occasionally raise eyebrows. In Part III, entire chapters from several challenging undergraduate textbooks provide a realistic basis for applying and testing the reading skills developed in Part II. In spite of this unorthodoxy of content, however, the variety of subject matter in *Steppingstones*—in both the news articles and textbook selections—appeals to a wide range of interests and has proven extremely effective for both instructors and students.

Pedagogically, *Steppingstones* is divided into three parts:

Part I introduces basic strategies for effective reading comprehension, including analysis of the material's organization, visual mapping of its ideas, outlining, and the application of critical reading and thinking skills. Basic expository patterns are defined and illustrated through visual maps, and students are encouraged to "map" readings in Parts II and III on their own, based on the models in Part I. These reading strategies provide the foundation for students to comprehend and remember what they read, abilities essential to academic success.

Part II provides twenty-six readings from the print media, organized after the model of a typical newspaper or newsmagazine. Within each of the first five chapters ("The Front Page," "The People Section," "The Science Section," "The Editorial Section," and "The Sports Section"), readings increase in difficulty so that students move from easier to more challenging material. Each news article is accompanied by a pre-reading essay that can be read aloud, raising issues for class discussion and the interactive exchange of ideas; a follow-up "exploded view" of the article that highlights fifteen target vocabulary terms; reading comprehension questions; a set of vocabulary exercises, including a cloze exercise; and finally a set of critical thinking problems ("Critical Reading Practice/Topics for Discussion") that ask students to expand their responses to the topic of the article. Part II ends with a Comics Section, focusing on political cartoons, to spark further critical thinking and response.

Part II allows for the development of increasingly abstract reading and thinking skills and offers instructors a clear way to chart individual student progress.

Part III, which includes chapters from five undergraduate textbooks in different disciplines, provides an opportunity for students to apply these skills to the demands of college-level work. Here the functions of effective "highlighting," more sophisticated mapping techniques, and the fusing of reading and critical thinking to form creative "reading notes," are all explained and illustrated. Students can then practice these techniques as they read the sample textbook selections (all annotated with specific guidelines for reading), allowing a highly accurate assessment of student preparedness for successful undergraduate study.

Steppingstones is intended to help a lot of people: those who have arrived at college with reading skills unequal to the demands of undergraduate study, those who wish to prepare themselves for successful entrance into a post-secondary environment, those for whom English is a second language, and, perhaps as important as any of these, those who teach developmental reading.

There is no higher or more demanding calling, in any time and at any place, than transmitting the gift of powerful reading skills. Great wonder lies behind that door, and it is my sincere hope that *Steppingstones* will help to open it for many.

Please allow me a word of thanks for four groups of people who have made this book possible. The first, of course, is made up of my family, who have put up with deadlines, travel, late nights, and Macintosh pigging on a regular basis for more than a year. No man has ever had better life companions.

The second group are my editors and friends at Mayfield Publishing Company, particularly James R. Bull, who played Moses, our remarkable production editor Sondra Glider, permissions editor Pamela Trainer, copy editor Mark Gallaher, Julianne Rovesti, Tom Broadbent, Jean Mailander, MaryEllen Podgorski, Margaret Moore, and a host of other talented and witty people. They, at least, always knew what was going on.

The schools where I have studied and taught, and my colleagues and students there, come next, particularly Stanford, San Francisco State, Keio University in Tokyo, Nankai University in the PRC, the University of Southern California, Southern Illinois University at Carbondale, the California Maritime Academy, Lassen College, Santa Rosa Junior College, the Nichibei Kaiwa Language Institute (also Tokyo). Gladly would they learn and gladly teach . . .

And thanks also to those thoughtful enough to lend advice and direction in this project as it evolved, including Barbara Henry, West Virginia State College; Steve Lucas, Phoenix College; Tim Rasinski, Kent State University; and Barry Selinger, Northern Virginia Community College.

Introduction

This first section of *Steppingstones* defines and illustrates the basic forms of expository writing. Used either individually or in combination with one another, these forms are the elemental building blocks of exposition. Your ability to understand and retain print information is directly related to your skill at identifying these forms and their relationships, so that is where we begin.

This section also explains and demonstrates the main idea/subtopic structure common to all expository forms. Identifying these components is crucial both to the comprehension and critical thinking skills you'll practice in Part II and to the more sophisticated forms of note-taking you'll encounter in Part III. Part I will also introduce you to the techniques of mapping, outlining, and note-taking, as well as to the concepts of critical reading and thinking.

CHAPTER 1

On Reading, Expository Architecture, and Using What You Read

■ A BRIEF OVERVIEW

Learning involves the transfer, exchange, or discovery of ideas. When the ideas are in print, reading becomes the medium of learning and the reader's ability to recognize, reassemble, and judge written ideas becomes absolutely essential.

Fortunately, for all of its seriousness and importance, the process of reading carefully is fun; for many people, in fact, such reading is more fun than any other intellectual activity. Since there are clearly defined skills involved, and steps to be taken, in order to master critical reading, this book's purpose is to identify and explain each of those components. In the pages that follow, examples and exercises designed to illustrate the basic techniques of careful reading will teach stronger, more effective reading skills in an organized, increasingly challenging, program of study.

Steppingstones has three parts. This section identifies the elements common to all expository writing, defines them, explains their structures or functions, and then shows ways of storing and using what is read. The second section provides readings, analyses of those readings, and exercises that reinforce critical reading skills. The third section provides opportunities to work with still more challenging college-level text material in order to apply the skills learned in section two. Collectively, the three general units should give a clear picture of both how and why reading functions as the most important of all the academic learning tools.

■ READING FOR THE MAIN IDEA

Whatever their form, all written things are *constructions*. Like houses, shoes, horse trailers, and tables, written things are *built* things, and the first step in understanding written things well is understanding how they are built and why.

Houses, we know, give shelter. Shoes protect feet. Horse trailers carry horses. Tables give a surface to hold things. And writing, too, has a basic function or intention. From news stories to anthropology texts, writers build their work in order to transmit a basic, or "main," idea. Traditionally, this main idea was called the "thesis" of a work, from the Greek word *tithenai,* which means "to place or put down" the most important idea being discussed.

For any piece of writing the first thing a careful reader must identify is the main idea. Usually the main idea of a piece is stated directly. Often, for example, it can be identified in a sentence and underlined or highlighted because the author wants the writing's objective to be clear, unquestionably understood. Most writers try to give this one-sentence statement of the "heart" of the writing within the first few sentences or paragraphs. Journalists are particularly trained to do this in their first, or "lead," sentence or paragraph. When writing is constructed in this way, the reader can usually identify the main idea quickly and then move on to see how the main idea is developed, explained, or explored.

But main ideas can also be presented indirectly for various reasons, and readers must then define what they consider to be the main idea for themselves. When this is the case, writers *want* reader participation and involvement. Sometimes, especially when they are creating works of art (like a story, a poem, a song, or a novel), writers can't summarize a single "main idea" without damaging the idea or making it smaller than it truly is. This is not because they are incompetent but because the most important part of the main idea in works of art is the reader's participation.

At other times, the main idea of a piece lies "between the lines" of the actual writing. Aside from works of art, then, the reader can almost always summarize the main idea of such a piece by asking "What is the *most* basic message in this?" or "What is the *most* important idea here?" An answer to either question will identify the main idea, and the reader can then proceed to analyze other elements of the construction.

■ READING FOR SUBTOPICS AND MAPPING

For each main idea explained or explored in a piece of expository prose, there are several (usually three or more) *subtopics* that clarify and define the main idea. The nature of any subtopic depends on its purpose within the written piece, but a subtopic always concerns some aspect of the main idea. By noting the content and arrangement of subtopics, careful readers can produce a "map" of the progression of ideas within the writing.

Writers are very careful about constructing subtopics, so readers must take care to understand *what* the subtopics say and *why* they are arranged in a particular order. This is sometimes made clear by the basic expository intention of the main idea. For example, if the intention is primarily to show a cause/effect relationship, the subtopics are naturally going to be causes and/or effects. If the intention is comparison, the subtopics are very likely to be the ways in which two or more things are being compared or contrasted. If the intention is critical, the subtopics will almost always be reasons to explain why the writer liked or did not like something.

Consider the following "Periodic Table of Expository Elements" as a brief, easily remembered description of the most common intentions of writers. Each determines, in a general way, the nature of the subtopics required for the particular form of writing those intentions will take. With these in mind you can quickly map subtopics and store them.

Periodic Table of Expository Elements

	SUMMARY			ANALYSIS	
CRITICISM		CAUSALITY		COMPARISON	
		PERSUASION			

A *summary,* of course, simply condenses ideas or information. An *analysis* breaks a process or structure into its components. *Criticism* makes a judgment. *Causality* explains why things happened, are happening, or may happen. *Comparison* deals with two or more subjects simultaneously, in three or four ways. *Persuasion* is the attempt to convince readers to accept an opinion or pursue a particular course of action. Each of these forms, from left to right, from top to bottom, increases in complexity and relies on the organizational skills of the forms that come before it. Each also may include techniques from forms that come later on the table. Criticism, for example, can easily contain comparisons, but using comparisons in this case would be optional, based on the writer's choices, rather than mandated by the form. On the other hand, critical judgments *are* mandatory in comparisons.

Once a reader can identify the writer's general intention in a piece, mapping the written material becomes much easier. Very often this basic structure is revealed quite directly in a title. Further, when the writer's general intention or intentions seem difficult to find or understand, mapping can often help the reader work backward from the subtopics in order to identify the nature of the work's main idea.

Few writers use only one of the expository forms in any given piece. In fact, the way writers mix and alternate these basic elements is one of the things that careful readers come to admire most about writers they like. But just about every piece of expository writing will have a definite main idea, and that idea will fit one of these forms.

The following are some simple "mapping" diagrams for each of the six expository forms. The "clusters" include ideas *usually* found in the same paragraph but occasionally gathered from different paragraphs and grouped together by type in the reader's notes.

The purpose of such maps is to organize print information visually both to understand it better and to see relationships among ideas more clearly. Mapping is particularly useful to help identify reasons to believe or question what you read.

The maps below chart a series of hypothetical newspaper reports about a city scandal. Each report corresponds to a basic expository form and is mapped in order to illustrate the form's organizational principles.

Every reader develops his or her own style of mapping and note-taking, as we will discuss in Part III. The following maps are illustrations of an extremely useful reading technique, but they represent only a few of the ways that mapping can be done.

Summary

Main Idea	The city's water supply is low
Subtopic 1	Municipal reservoir only 35% of normal
Subtopic 2	City engineer says problem is serious
Subtopic 3	Fire chief calls shortage dangerous

Map:

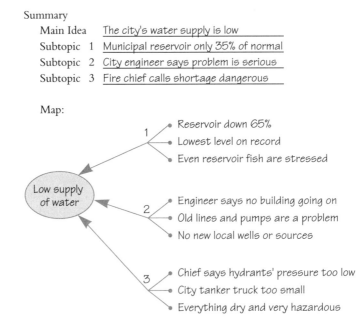

Analysis

Main Idea   There are four basic sources of city's H₂0

Subtopic 1   Rainfall and run-off to reservoir

Subtopic 2   City wells, pumps, and water towers

Subtopic 3   Experimental desalinization plant

Subtopic 4   Home rain-collectors and irrigation systems

Map:

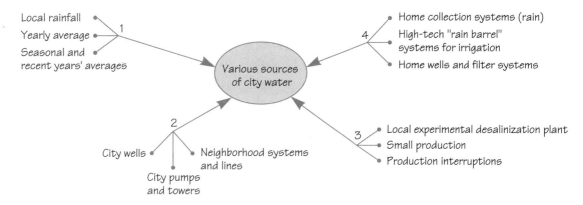

Criticism

Main Idea   Low water supply is the mayor's fault

Subtopic/reason 1   Three new mini golf courses (54 holes)

Subtopic/reason 2   Mayor's brother has all landscaping contracts

Subtopic/reason 3   Mayor built 2 city pools, one of her own, and 19 fountains

Subtopic/reason 4   Mayor put water slides in city hall

Map:

Causality (Causes)

Main Idea   <u>Causes of city water crisis</u>

Subtopic/cause 1   <u>Existing demands—commercial & residential & municipal</u>

Subtopic/cause 2   <u>Drought conditions and low rainfall</u>

Subtopic/cause 3   <u>Golf courses, pools, fountains, & water slides</u>

Map:

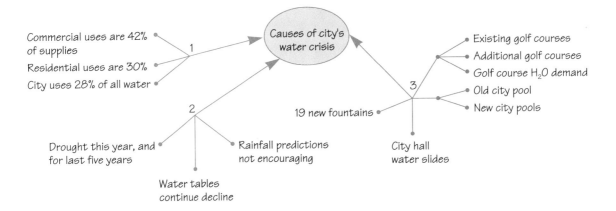

Causality (Effects)

Main Idea   <u>City faces tough times ahead for water supply</u>

Subtopic/effect 1   <u>No new building or commercial expansion</u>

Subtopic/effect 2   <u>Declining tax base—business and residential flight</u>

Subtopic/effect 3   <u>Increased insurance costs because of fire dangers</u>

Map:

Causality (Chain of Causes and Effects)

Main Idea		Mayor Fosstor washed away in recall
Subtopic/cause	1	Water crisis precipitated political downfall
Subtopic/effect	1	Recall petitions in every business qualify vote, lay political base
Subtopic/cause	2	Community unified against Fosstor
Subtopic/effect	2	New long-term plan in effect now—projects cancelled
Subtopic/effect	2	Mayor hired as water consultant by state government

Map:

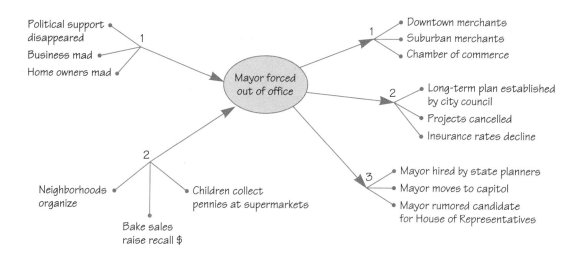

Comparison

Main Idea		Mayor Fosstor and Caligula: style & vision
Area of Comparison/contrast	1	Obligations of power not their business: sufferings of the governed
Area	2	Long-term welfare sacrificed for personal benefits now
Area	3	Caligula assassinated, Fosstor groomed for governorship?

Map:

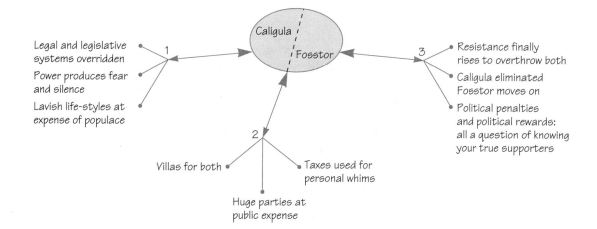

Persuasion
    Main Idea   <u>City should recall mayor and try her as a criminal</u>
    Reason to Agree 1   <u>Abused public trust, oath of office, to enrich family</u>
    Reason to Agree 2   <u>Should be liable for damages</u>
    Reason to Agree 3   <u>Put her in jail as a lesson to other officials</u>

Map:

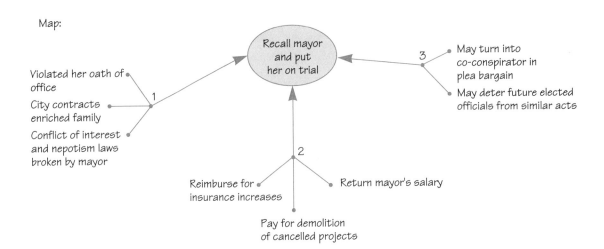

■ STORING AND USING WHAT YOU READ: OUTLINING AND TAKING NOTES

    All main ideas and subtopics of expository writing depend on *specific information, data,* or *examples* for clarity. Recording these elements and their relationships in "reading notes" allows a reader to store such writing in a condensed form for later use.

    In the previous section, the general, skeletal structures of several types of writing were mapped and numbered. Rearranged, these identified parts can also form outlines. Consider, for example, the outline form that the elements of the third example of Causality (Chain of Causes and Effects) might take:

Mayor forced from office (*Main Idea*)
    Water crisis became political crisis (*Cause #1*)
        Political support evaporated, bad PR
        Business community angry
        City voters furious
    Community unites against mayor (*Cause #2*)
        Neighborhoods organize

> Bake sales raise recall money
>
> Children collect pennies at supermarkets
>
> Businesses now organized and involved (*Effect #1*)
>
>> Downtown and suburban merchants cooperate
>>
>> Chamber of Commerce forms political watch committee of its own
>
> Long-term city plan is now in effect (*Effect #2*)
>
>> City council regains true authority
>>
>> Earlier projects cancelled
>>
>> Insurance rates tumble
>
> Mayor hired as water use consultant (*Effect #3*)
>
>> State-level planning commission likes the mayor's style
>>
>> New home in capitol has indoor pool, 3 spas
>>
>> Mayor rumored to be candidate for U.S. House of Representatives

Outlines like the one above can describe intentions and content in a general way, but they are not truly academically useful until we add *specific, detailed* information of particular importance or interest to the reader. Specifics, in this case, would probably be direct quotes ("I've known Fosstor for twenty years," said local merchant Henrietta Mitchell, owner of Mitchell's Mighty Malts, "and I don't think she could tell the truth if you gave her sixteen tries") or objective data (city water use increased 385% in the fourteen months following Mayor Fosstor's most recent reelection). Such details, when added to the outline, provide a much more thorough and useful set of notes for you as a reader.

Specific data can be added to general outlines very easily, as in this section from the previous outline.

> Community unites against mayor (*Cause #2*)
>
> Neighborhoods organize
>
>> 73 Westview Acres residents meet at Ann Samson's garage on Tuesday, July 28th, form "Committee to Fry Fosstor" (CFF) and collect $422.63
>>
>> CFF and "Easthills Voters Association" (EVA) hold joint planning meeting, Aug. 2nd, in Baptist Church, map ad campaign for mayor's recall
>
> Bake sales raise recall money
>
>> $1,000 for radio ads, $3,250 for tv ads, and $1,200 for billboards, raised by Aug. 17th through weekly bake sales, "Great Pie Auction," and "Let Them Eat Cake" fundraising dessert in city park

Children collect pennies at supermarkets

Few actual pennies donated, many larger coins, lots of dollar bills of several denominations, all collected by 243 elementary school volunteers at supermarkets and two shopping malls

Total from "Children's Crusade" is $2,230.11 by Aug. 30th

Money presented to CFF and EVA Steering Committee by Teresa Alvarez, 8, on steps of City Hall (extensive media coverage)

■ READING AND THINKING CRITICALLY

Even after a careful reader has understood, analyzed, and stored a piece of writing in the form of reading notes, one important task still remains: judging what has been read.

This critical reading process involves personal judgments of several kinds. Try answering the following questions in order to arrive at such judgments:

Do you believe what you have just read? Identify elements which seem true or which seem false in the work you have just read. If the writer is an expert or authority on the subject, consider whether the writer personally may have anything to gain or lose, depending on readers' reactions.

In general, if what you have read *seems* and *feels* like the truth, then go ahead with that judgment. But if a "suspicion alarm" ever sounds, whether arising from unanswered questions or doubts as to accuracy or truthfulness, listen to it very carefully. Try to figure out what triggered the alarm. Put the reason into words, and be sure to include this in any sort of notes you may be taking.

When we read the following, we can only sigh:

Mayor Fosstor today became the subject of a grand jury investigation.

Our reaction might be a bit different, however, if we were to read this:

Sources, who spoke on condition of anonymity, claimed that Fosstor has actually embezzled millions over the years, owns an estate in the south of France, a string of polo ponies, and a huge collection of stolen Meso-American art, and has business ties with "many" organized crime figures in this country and abroad.

How does what you have just read compare to other works on the same or a related subject? How does the writing compare to other writing (on any subject)? If the work contradicts or expands upon what you may have already read or otherwise learned about this topic, figure out the nature of the contradiction or expansion. When ideas seem to conflict, decide whether you want to resolve them, choose one, or live with the ambiguity.

Note the ways in which the writing style of the work compares to the styles of other works. Pay close attention to techniques of the writer that you find particularly effective.

When you finish reading the work, what questions do you have about it? What would you like to see added to the work and why? If an argument, discussion, or demonstration seems somehow incomplete, try to identify what needs to be added for you to accept it. If your experience or common sense raises questions about the work's believability in whole or in part, determine as closely as possible what bothers you about the work in terms of your background or judgment.

All in all, do you trust what you have read enough to use it as fact in your own work? Do you believe it strongly enough to act on its information, should that ever be a choice facing you? Would you present what you have just read as the truth to a close friend? Taking everything into consideration, including the questions above, decide how much faith you have in the work's author, information, and integrity. If your faith is considerable, there must be reasons for that. If, on the other hand, you are skeptical of what you've read in large ways or small, there are almost always solid reasons for that reaction, as well.

Critical reading and critical thinking will help you articulate both sets of reasons for yourself and perhaps for others. Careful reading in this fashion adds both to your skills and to your enjoyment of any work you read.

News from the World About Us

This second section of *Steppingstones* asks you to apply the skills discussed and illustrated in Part I to a variety of articles and essays from several daily newspapers. By striving for full comprehension as you analyze, discuss, and judge each of these articles, you'll have a chance to develop the reading and critical thinking skills required for success in college.

Each article is introduced by a brief introductory essay, intended to stimulate class discussion and encourage a lively exchange of views on a challenging topic. Following the introductory essay, the article is presented as it originally appeared in print, with the paragraphs numbered for reference and for convenience when reading aloud. The article is then reprinted in an "exploded view," with fifteen "target" vocabulary terms or phrases highlighted so that you can study and discuss them in context.

This "exploded view" of the article is followed by reading comprehension questions, a series of exercises to help you master the target vocabulary, and a Reading Practice/Topics for Discussion section that encourages critical thinking, as well as personal expression, creativity, and ingenuity in responding to the topic of the article.

CHAPTER 2

The Front Page

Sam Richards and the Great War

This section focuses on the subject of war, specifically on the "Great War," World War I. Also, the last member of a WWI Marine aviation tontine, Sam Richards—the subject of the news article—contributes a few thoughts on life and luck. You may find yourself agreeing or disagreeing with the positions taken in the pre-reading essay and in the news article itself.

Both essay and article provide opportunities for identification of the main idea, and subtopics, as well as ample material for mapping exercises.

PRE-READING FOR DISCUSSION

War is ugly, sad, and usually stupid, but it is sometimes an effective way for one group or country to get what it wants from another.

And sometimes war is the *only* way for a particular group or country to get what it wants from another.

For these reasons, wars are fought over all sorts of things: natural resources such as water and oil, concepts such as freedom or independence, desires to make others believe in certain gods or values, and at least once over a guy's wife who ran off with a younger, better-looking man.

Wars will be around as long as people want something enough to risk dying for it. Even if humankind eliminates all weapons of mass destruction and even if all the firearms and swords and knives in the world are melted down into swing sets and merry-go-rounds, people will simply go back to using rocks and sticks, if enough of them want something badly enough to risk death for it.

In the recent past—about the last 7,000 years or so—whole societies and nations have made war against each other. Instead of two fairly small tribal groups fighting over, for example, a really good fishing spot, entire countries have fought each other for control of lands, seas, people, and ideas. They kept getting more efficient at it, too, inventing all sorts of clever and imaginative ways to kill larger and larger armies. Swords and javelins were replaced by pistols, muskets, and cannon. Then came machine guns, submarines, poison gas, airplanes, aircraft carriers, missiles, and finally, on August 6th and 9th of 1945, the first use of atomic weapons on Hiroshima and Nagasaki, the cities that may have saved the world.

Ordinary citizens become involved in national wars largely by chance: if a war comes along and you are the right age, physically normal, and male (or even female in some countries) generally either you join the military or your government puts you in jail.

The following article is about a remarkable man named Sam Richards, who was a United States pilot in The First World War, or WWI, as it is usually written. For two decades WWI was called "The Great War," and as wars go, WWI was particularly bloody, horrible, wasteful, and tragic. The war began in August of 1914, was fought until the 11th hour of the 11th day of the 11th month of 1918, took millions of lives, and solved nothing.

The United States did not enter the war until the last year of the fighting, at that point joining France, Great Britain, and Italy in opposing Germany and Austria. (It was British writer H. G. Wells, by the way, who coined the phrase regarding the end of the war, quoted in paragraph 8 of the reading. He wrote a book published in 1914 titled *The War That Will End War,* and the idea caught on. Unfortunately, even great thinkers like Wells make mistakes: twenty years later "WWI" had to be changed to "WWII.")

Sam Richards is remarkable for several reasons. At least 21 pieces of metal had a chance to kill him in 1917, and none did, even figuring two holes for every piece of metal mentioned in the reading. Also, of his 1,000-man unit, Sam Richards will forever be the longest survivor. But perhaps most remarkable of all, after a war, a career as a stockbroker, and then another war, Sam Richards was wise enough to spend the rest of his working days with the United States Forest Service, which was about as far from both military and economic wars as it was possible to get.

Members of the U.S. 1st Marine Aviation Force agreed to save a bottle of wine for the last surviving member to drink. Here Sam Richards, the last remaining vet, displays the bottle.

WWI Flier Finally Gets to Pop Cork

Oakland vet last remaining 'devil dog' given 1918 wine

Associated Press

1　SAN FRANCISCO A veteran pilot the Marine Corps believes is its last World War I "devil dog of the air" will pop the cork on a bottle of 1918 wine Saturday night and toast the passing of his buddies.

2　"Actually, I'd prefer brandy," said 95-year-old Sam Richards of Oakland. "It has a stronger kick."

3　As prestigious a figure as the commandant of the Marine Corps, Gen. Carl Mundy, will join the ceremony at the annual Marine Corps Aviation Association convention in San Francisco.

4　A bottle of Cos d'Estournel was presented to the First Marine Aviation Force on Nov. 27, 1918, while the leathernecks stood in ranks in front of their hangars near Bois-en-Ardres, France.

5　The Marines, fresh from victory over the Germans in the war that ended on Nov. 11, received the gift from the wife of the town's mayor. They vowed to form a Last Man Club in which the last man would open the wine.

6　Unfortunately, the bottle of wine won't be the same one. It might have been expecting too much for such a tempting pleasure to have survived all that time.

7　"The original was misplaced over the years and, knowing Marines, I'm pretty sure I know how it got misplaced," said a laughing Col. Don Treichler, the convention chairman.

8   "We have an exact duplicate. Same kind of wine, same year," said the colonel, who believes Richards is the last Marine pilot from the "war to end all wars."

9   "Could be," agreed Richards, who said he lost touch with his old buddies years ago.

10   "I was head of our veterans organization from 1969 to 1970 but everybody started dying off," said Richards.

11   The Marine infantrymen of World War I were so fearless that the Germans dubbed them "devil dogs." It didn't take long for the moniker to get off the ground and reach the air arm.

12   Richards, a native of Bryn Mawr, Pa., and the other 1,000 men of the force arrived in France on July 31, 1918.

13   The outfit was in action less than four months before the war ended. Nevertheless, the unit earned 30 Navy Crosses, four Dis-tinguished Flying Crosses and two Medals of Honor.

14   Richards learned what it's like to be on the receiving end of gunfire during the war. Then a second lieutenant, he was shot down by anti-aircraft fire while returning from a raid in a de Havilland fighter aircraft.

15   Uninjured, he crash landed in sand dunes but "42 bullet and shrapnel holes in the fuselage and wings had to be sealed." Richards has a piece of the plane's engine that was recovered after the crash.

16   Richards, who returned home and became a stockbroker, also served in World War II. That stint was with the Army, flying C-47 transports out of Australia.

17   He was a lieutenant colonel at war's end and "didn't want to go back to stocks."

18   So he joined the U.S. Forest Service in California and retired in 1963.

■   **EXPLODED VIEW FOR STUDY**

Each of the highlighted words should be mastered in the following exercises.

WWI Flier Finally Gets to Pop Cork

Oakland vet last remaining 'devil dog' given 1918 wine

Associated Press

1   SAN FRANCISCO   A veteran pilot the Marine Corps believes is its last World War I "devil dog of the air" will pop the cork on a bottle of 1918 wine Saturday night and toast the passing of his buddies.

2   "Actually, I'd prefer brandy," said 95-year-old Sam Richards of Oakland. "It has a stronger kick."

3   As prestigious a figure as the commandant of the Marine Corps,

Gen. Carl Mundy, will join the ceremony at the annual Marine Corps Aviation Association convention in San Francisco.

4   A bottle of Cos d'Estournel was presented to the First Marine Aviation Force on Nov. 27, 1918, while the leathernecks stood in ranks in front of their hangars near Bois-en-Ardres, France.

5   The Marines, fresh from victory over the Germans in the war that ended on Nov. 11, received the gift from the wife of the town's mayor. They vowed to form a Last Man Club in which the last man would open the wine.

6   Unfortunately, the bottle of wine won't be the same one. It might have been expecting too much for such a tempting pleasure to have survived all that time.

7   "The original was misplaced over the years and, knowing Marines, I'm pretty sure I know how it got misplaced," said a laughing Col. Don Treichler, the convention chairman.

8   "We have an exact duplicate. Same kind of wine, same year," said the colonel, who believes Richards is the last Marine pilot from the "war to end all wars."

9   "Could be," agreed Richards, who said he lost touch with his old buddies years ago.

10   "I was head of our veterans organization from 1969 to 1970 but everybody started dying off," said Richards.

11   The Marine infantrymen of World War I were so fearless that the Germans dubbed them "devil dogs." It didn't take long for the moniker to get off the ground and reach the air arm.

12   Richards, a native of Bryn Mawr, Pa., and the other 1,000 men of the force arrived in France on July 31, 1918.

13   The outfit was in action less than four months before the war ended. Nevertheless, the unit earned 30 Navy Crosses, four Distinguished Flying Crosses and two Medals of Honor.

14   Richards learned what it's like to be on the receiving end of gunfire during the war. Then a second lieutenant, he was shot down by anti-aircraft fire while returning from a raid in a de Havilland fighter aircraft.

15   Uninjured, he crash landed in sand dunes but "42 bullet and shrapnel holes in the fuselage and wings had to be sealed." Richards has a piece of the plane's engine that was recovered after the crash.

16   Richards, who returned home and became a stockbroker, also served in World War II. That stint was with the Army, flying C-47 transports out of Australia.

17   He was a lieutenant colonel at war's end and "didn't want to go back to stocks."

18   So he joined the U.S. Forest Service in California and retired in 1963.

■ READING COMPREHENSION QUESTIONS

1.   During World War I, Sam Richards was a pilot stationed in
(a) Germany (b) Austria (c) France (d) the United States

2.   The commandant of the Marine Corps attended the ceremony honoring Richards out of a sense of (a) obligation (b) respect
(c) decency (d) guilt

3.   In just four months, Richards' unit received *many* decorations: 30 Navy Crosses, four Distinguished Flying Crosses, and two Medals of Honor. These decorations suggest that (a) the pilots had very influential relatives in the military (b) decorations were awarded more easily in WWI than in later wars (c) the unit had a terrific Public Relations officer (d) Richards and his comrades were very brave men

4.   Marine infantrymen were so ferocious in combat that German soldiers nicknamed them (a) "leathernecks" (b) "fighting fools"
(c) "devil dogs" (d) "The Four Horsemen"

5.   Sam Richards also flew planes in World War II, 25 years after his service in Europe. In that war, however, instead of being based in France, he was in (a) Australia (b) Burma (c) North Africa (d) China

6.   The Last Man Club's original bottle of wine disappeared over the years: "'Knowing Marines,' Col. Don Treichler laughed, 'I'm pretty sure I know how it got misplaced.'" He was probably implying that
(a) the wine had been donated to charity (b) the wine had been used at

a wedding (c) the wine had been lost to the Navy in a card game
(d) former Marines drank it

■ TARGET VOCABULARY

veteran	**hangar**	**shrapnel**
pilot	**vowed**	**fuselage**
prestigious	**duplicate**	**stockbroker**
commandant	**infantrymen**	**stint**
in ranks	**moniker**	**transports**

Dictionary Practice

Use each word in a sentence of your own.

1. veteran _____

2. pilot _____

3. prestigious _____

4. commandant _____

5. in ranks _____

6. hangar _____

7. vowed _____

8. duplicate _____

9. infantrymen _____

10. moniker _____

11. shrapnel _____

12. fuselage _____

13. stockbroker _____

14. stint _____

15. transports _____

Cloze Practice

Fill in each blank with an appropriate term from the target vocabulary list.

Sam Richards, a _____ of both world wars, served as a _____ in France and in the Pacific. During WWI, standing _____ with his fellow fliers beside the _____ for their planes, the airmen _____ that their last survivor would drink a particular bottle of wine.

Following his career as a _____ between the wars, Richards served a _____ flying _____ in WWII.

In his final career, with the U.S. Forest Service, Richards pioneered the use of aircraft in fighting forest fires, modifying a plane's _____ to carry and "bomb" flames with fire-retardant chemicals.

■ CRITICAL READING PRACTICE/TOPICS FOR DISCUSSION

1. What sort of a guy does Sam Richards seem to be to you, based on what you have just read? Why do you feel as you do?

2. What war, throughout history, do you know the most about? Why do you think that this is so?

3. Is it useful to study something as *awful* as war? Is it necessary? Why or why not?

4. In your family, who has military experience and what kind of military experience did they have? Do they ever talk about it? Do they seem to enjoy talking about it? Do you like to hear about their experiences?

Why do you think you feel as you do about listening to family members discuss their time in the military?

5. What do you think about Sam Richards not returning to his career as a stockbroker following WWII? How do you feel about his having joined the United States Forest Service? Why do you think he might have made that career choice?

Sample Map for "WWI Flier Finally Gets to Pop Cork" (AP)

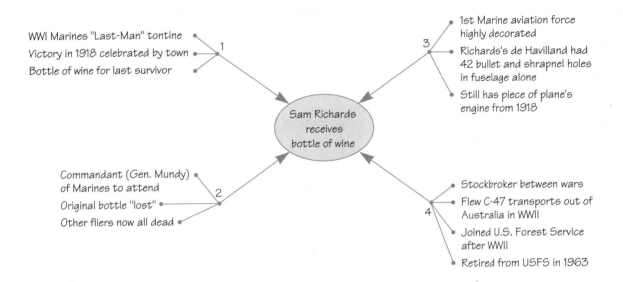

Note: For each of the following readings in this chapter you are encouraged to draw maps of your own like this one, applying the mapping skills you learned in Part I.

■ *Drugs, People, and Money*

This section focuses on drugs: why people have abused them over the centuries, some consequences of that abuse, and the particular case of an Andean poppy farmer named "Edgar."

As you discuss the pre-reading essay and the subsequent article from the New York Times *with your classmates, feel free to agree or disagree with any of the ideas presented here.*

Both the pre-reading essay and the article lend themselves to identifying main idea and subtopics, as well as to mapping work.

■ PRE-READING FOR DISCUSSION

Drugs chemically change the way people's minds work, and consequently the way people feel about their lives and how they perceive reality. For these reasons, drugs have always been used and will always be used, although different drugs will be unacceptable in different societies. Every drug, however, comes with a physical price tag: whether alcohol, heroin, nicotine, caffeine, amphetamines, or LSD, each extracts its cost from our bodies and frequently from the lives of those around us.

Throughout history, and in all cultures, drugs have been used specifically to alter people's realities. From heightening awareness during religious ceremonies and rituals to escaping miserable lives, drugs have been part of human society from time immemorial, and with increases in drug use have come social problems. In Rome, in England, in Russia, in Mexico, in China, and in the United States—in fact all around the world—drugs have been the cause of death, destruction, and waste for centuries.

So long as people are willing to pay the physical price for them, including death, drugs will be used. So long as governments try to stop the flow of certain drugs, there will be a lot of money involved in selling them. The type of drug and the society involved don't really matter, in these cases. If people want gin in an Islamic society or hashish in Chicago, they will be willing to pay for them, and pay a lot. In both cases, of course, what they seek to buy is an alternative reality, and they get it, for good or ill.

The following article is about the economic and distributive aspects of the heroin market, and it also has an interesting observation by Edgar, a Colombian poppy farmer. When asked about what people do with the product of his crops—that is, how he felt about producing the raw material used to make heroin, a very dangerous and often fatal drug—Edgar replies that it does not concern him.

Tobacco and alcohol companies pay law firms and advertising agencies enormous amounts of money to convince people that the companies are not responsible for the misuse of their products. It seems only fair that we give the same consideration to a hard-working farmer high in the Andes.

But if the tobacco and beer and liquor companies (and Edgar) are not responsible for the terrible effects of drugs, then who is? Is it the government, either here or in Colombia? Are the laws and the courts and the prisons the problem? Is life truly so horrible that people have to get doped up to stand it? Or are there always going to be a certain number of people who use drugs in all societies in all times and places?

Should we find the answers to such questions, we will be the first people, and the first society, ever to do so.

Colombia Turns on to Heroin

Drug traffickers tap into new vein

New York Times

1   PITAYO, COLOMBIA On a craggy hillside here in the Andean foothills of Cauca state, an Indian farmer is tending his two-acre poppy crop, a raging palette of reds, purples and pinks. It is his first harvest and he is pleased with the results.

2   The plants, he says, are much hardier than corn or potatoes and bring in about 20 percent more income.

3   He says the same men who first brought him the seeds and encouraged him to grow the crops are now regular customers, coming monthly to buy every drop of the milky paste he and his workers extract from the plants' ripened pods.

4   "They say they'll buy everything I can produce," the farmer said, identifying himself only as Edgar. Asked if he realized that the extract was used to make heroin, Edgar said that did not concern him.

5   Narcotics experts say they have known of the existence of small isolated poppy plots, like Edgar's, since 1984. The plots were always considered to be experiments by Colombia's drug traffickers, who have produced most of the world's cocaine since the 1970s.

6   But this summer, raids on about 3,000 acres of poppy plants by the Colombian police, including 2,300 acres in a single raid in southwestern Huila state, signaled that poppy production might have left the experimental stage.

7   "The operation really opened people's eyes," a United States official in Bogota said of the Huila raid. He said one harvest from the raided area could have produced 2,000 pounds of heroin.

8   But official concern centers less on actual production levels than on Colombian drug traffickers' ability to apply to the heroin trade skills learned producing and smuggling cocaine.

9   "They have a cocaine distribution network and money-laundering scheme already established in the United States," said Felix Jimenez, chief heroin investigator for the Drug Enforcement Administration. "It wouldn't be that hard to change from cocaine to heroin."

10   Certainly, there is a great financial incentive to expand into heroin. One kilo of high-grade heroin sells wholesale in New York City for $160,000—nearly 10 times the asking price for the same amount of cocaine.

11   Jimenez said he believes that most Colombian heroin was destined for the United States, where there are about 500,000 heroin addicts.

12   While law-enforcement officials are hoping to learn more about Colombia's heroin by seizing a processing laboratory, that goal has so far eluded them.

13   "We know the labs exist," the U.S. official said, "but they're so hard to find. You could set one up in a small room in the middle of a city and no one would ever know."

14   The poppy fields are only slightly easier to discover. Colombian police say most are hidden away in the mountainous southwestern states of Huila and Cauca, where constant cloud cover makes them difficult to detect from planes.

15   No roads lead to the fields, and officials say many are guarded by armed leftist guerrillas employed by the drug barons.

16   The small, inaccessible plots, tended by Paez Indians like Edgar, cannot be seized by the police without permission from the Indian leaders.

■ **EXPLODED VIEW FOR STUDY**

Each of the highlighted words should be mastered in the following exercise.

Colombia Turns on to Heroin
Drug traffickers tap into new vein

New York Times

1   PITAYO, COLOMBIA   On a craggy hillside here in the Andean foothills of Cauca state, an Indian farmer is tending his two-acre poppy crop, a raging palette of reds, purples and pinks. It is his first harvest and he is pleased with the results.

2   The plants, he says, are much hardier than corn or potatoes and bring in about 20 percent more income.

3   He says the same men who first brought him the seeds and encouraged him to grow the crops are now regular customers, coming monthly to buy every drop of the milky paste he and his workers extract from the plants' ripened pods.

4   "They say they'll buy everything I can produce," the farmer said, identifying himself only as Edgar. Asked if he realized that the extract was used to make heroin, Edgar said that did not concern him.

5   Narcotics experts say they have known of the existence of small isolated poppy plots, like Edgar's, since 1984. The plots were always considered to be experiments by Colombia's drug traffickers, who have produced most of the world's cocaine since the 1970s.

6   But this summer, raids on about 3,000 acres of poppy plants by the Colombian police, including 2,300 acres in a single raid in southwestern Huila state, signaled that poppy production might have left the experimental stage.

7   "The operation really opened people's eyes," a United States official in Bogota said of the Huila raid. He said one harvest from the raided area could have produced 2,000 pounds of heroin.

8   But official concern centers less on actual production levels than

on Colombian drug traffickers' ability to apply to the heroin trade skills learned producing and smuggling cocaine.

9   "They have a cocaine distribution network and money-laundering scheme already established in the United States," said Felix Jimenez, chief heroin investigator for the Drug Enforcement Administration. "It wouldn't be that hard to change from cocaine to heroin."

10   Certainly, there is a great financial incentive to expand into heroin. One kilo of high-grade heroin sells wholesale in New York City for $160,000—nearly 10 times the asking price for the same amount of cocaine.

11   Jimenez said he believes that most Colombian heroin was destined for the United States, where there are about 500,000 heroin addicts.

12   While law-enforcement officials are hoping to learn more about Colombia's heroin by seizing a processing laboratory, that goal has so far eluded them.

13   "We know the labs exist," the U.S. official said, "but they're so hard to find. You could set one up in a small room in the middle of a city and no one would ever know."

14   The poppy fields are only slightly easier to discover. Colombian police say most are hidden away in the mountainous southwestern states of Huila and Cauca, where constant cloud cover makes them difficult to detect from planes.

15   No roads lead to the fields, and officials say many are guarded by armed leftist guerrillas employed by the drug barons.

16   The small, inaccessible plots, tended by Paez Indians like Edgar, cannot be seized by the police without permission from the Indian leaders.

■ READING COMPREHENSION QUESTIONS

1.   According to Felix Jimenez, of the Drug Enforcement Administration, the number of people in the United States addicted to heroin is about (a) 200,000 (b) 2,000,000 (c) 500,000 (d) 75,000

2. The farmer in the article, named Edgar, began cultivating opium poppies after (a) he read a newspaper article about the enormous profits to be made (b) some men brought him poppy seeds and promised to buy his crop (c) he received a research grant (d) he rented a video of *The Wizard of Oz*

3. Officials are concerned that former cocaine suppliers will now begin supplying the U.S. market with heroin because (a) it is easier to produce (b) cocaine use is declining in the U.S. (c) the laws are not as strict (d) the profits are ten times as great

4. The country which seems likely to produce most of the opium crop, and consequently most of the heroin, is (a) Colombia (b) Peru (c) Albania (d) Chile

5. Law-enforcement officials have been unable to stop the flow of heroin because (a) they can't find all of the poppy fields (b) the smugglers are too clever (c) they can't find the processing labs (d) all of the above

6. Small opium poppy plots have been in existence in this area of the Andes for years but until now they were considered to be (a) private mini-plantations for local use (b) accidental and uncultivated (c) too small to bother with (d) scientific research experiments conducted by drug barons

■ TARGET VOCABULARY

to turn on to	**to smuggle**	**processing**
poppies	**network**	**laboratory**
palette	**to launder**	**to elude**
to extract	**(money)**	**guerrillas**
heroin	**incentive**	**drug baron**
traffickers	**addict**	

Dictionary Practice

Use each word in a sentence of your own.

1. to turn on to _____

2. poppies _____

3. palette _____

4. to extract _____

5. heroin _____

6. traffickers _____

7. to smuggle _____

8. network _____

9. to launder (money) _____

10. incentive _____

11. addict _____

12. processing laboratory _____

13. to elude _____

14. guerrillas _____

15. drug baron _____

Cloze Practice

Fill in each blank with an appropriate term from the target vocabulary list.

Flowers known as opium _____ produce a milky paste, which is further refined to produce _____, an extremely powerful and addictive drug. People who are _____ will do anything to get the money necessary to acquire the drug. These people are at the end of a long line of transportation extending from powerful _____ all around the world. Drugs are _____ across borders almost at will and the huge profits are then _____ through legitimate banks and businesses. Even the CIA and heads of state have been known to act as _____ in such commodities when it suited their purposes.

■ CRITICAL READING PRACTICE/TOPICS FOR DISCUSSION

1. What has been your worst personal experience with drugs— including alcohol—in terms of their effect either on you or on someone close to you? What have you learned from the experience that might help somebody else deal with a drug-related problem?

2.   What do you consider the most dangerous drug to you or to your friends? Why do you consider it more dangerous than other drugs? What effects have you seen produced by this drug?

3.   Our representatives in the government make the laws which govern drug use and drug control. What advice would you have for them if they asked you what we should do to make the drug situation better in your neighborhood or community?

4.   Do you think that Edgar, the Andean farmer, is doing something evil by growing poppies instead of corn and sweet potatoes? Why or why not?

5.   Some people contend that because of the effects on law enforcement, the judicial system, and prison populations, drugs should simply be legalized along the lines of the British system. How do you feel about this proposal, and why?

■ *Individuals and Their Governments*

Exactly how much power should the state have to control drugs (as in the last section)? If you answered "Quite a bit," are you then willing to grant the state equal power in telling you what to look at, think, read, say, or write?

On the other hand, if you answered "As little as possible," some very grim vistas open up regarding public safety and social stability.

Currently, in the People's Republic of China and in many other countries around the world, the government has virtually absolute power to determine the actions and choices of its people. What interesting situations result, then, when a member of the government takes his own state and party to court over individual liberties!

Such conflicts between liberty and social stability have been around forever and show no signs of disappearing soon.

■ **PRE-READING FOR DISCUSSION**

Governments which frequently tell their people what to do and how to act are called "repressive." Governments which have total control over what their people can and cannot do are called "totalitarian." In fact, good or bad, every government must have different types and degrees of control over its people in order for the society to work, so everybody will drive on the same side of the road, for instance, or even have public roads to begin with.

This relationship between a citizen and the government is called the "social contract." Like all contracts, this one is an agreement to exchange things: tax dollars for schools and space shuttles and those roads, for example, or military service in times of genuine emergency for military protection the rest of the time. The citizen and the government each has rights and responsibilities under the social contract, but they don't always agree about who owes what to whom. This disagreement is what causes governments to change and evolve, for better or worse.

The sad part of all this is that people have to abide by the terms of the existing contract in the country where they are born. There are some pretty rotten contracts out there, and nobody gets to choose where they are born, so a lot of people want their social contracts rewritten. This idea is seldom popular with the government.

Religion, art, and learning are all far more important than any government, and all three die very quickly when government touches them. These truly important things can only live outside of the social contract, and so they make governments nervous. When a government gets *really* nervous about any or all of these three, it tries to mess with them and the things die.

When they die this way, they do not entirely disappear, of course, but the remaining zombies are even worse than extinction: religion becomes small, art becomes tame, and learning becomes shallow. No matter what society tries this, it always fails, always has, and always must.

In the following unusual case, an artist has decided to fight his government's attempt to control art by suing his government in the government's own governmentally controlled court system. What he is really asking, of course, is that the government allow people to make up their own minds and allow artists more freedom.

Historically, people like Wang Meng usually wind up being silenced; or executed.

Historically, the rest of us have called them "heroes," because making up our own minds has always sounded pretty good.

(In Asia, by the way, a person's *family* name comes first and the *given* name or names come after, the reverse of the European pattern. In this article, for example, Wang Meng is "Mr. Wang," but Linda Jaivin is "Professor Jaivin.")

Chinese Writer Sues Over 'Persecution'

Former culture minister takes rare action against Communist-controlled journal

Lena H. Sun

1   BEIJING In an unusual act of defiance, a Chinese culture minister who was removed from office after the 1989 crackdown on democracy demonstrators is launching a public counteroffensive against orthodox Marxists who he says are trying to discredit him and to consolidate socialist control over the arts.

2   The former minister, Wang Meng, has filed suit in Beijing's Intermediate People's Court against a cultural journal controlled by Communist Party hardliners.

3   His suit accuses the weekly Arts and Literature Newspaper, and its chief editor, of political persecution and of publishing a libelous letter last month about a short story of his that the newspaper printed. The letter implied that the story was an attack on the reform programs of Chinese leader Deng Xiaoping. Chinese newspapers customarily do not comment on internal matters.

4   The story that provoked the controversy, "Hard Porridge," centers on a traditional family headed by a patriarch in his 80s. It pokes fun at the difficulties the family faces in trying to change its breakfast from the traditional porridge and pickled vegetables to a meal that includes eggs, meat and milk.

5   Wang has said that his allegorical story is meant to show support for the reforms of the 87-year-old Deng rather than attack them. His suit seeks a public apology and unspecified damages for what he calls harm to his reputation.

CULTURAL REVOLUTION

6   Wang's case is significant for several reasons. China's most intense political battles often have been staged in the cultural arena. During the disastrous Cultural Revolution of 1966 to 1976, hundreds of thousands of artists and intellectuals were purged and dissidents were persecuted for their political beliefs.

7   Wang, one of the country's best-known establishment writers, has long been a powerful symbol in China. Forced into exile during the Cultural Revolution, his rise to government power in 1986 as minister of culture was seen as a negation of that era's repression.

8   What Wang says are personal attacks on him are now causing a great stir in cultural circles because writers and artists fear that they could lead to another purge in literary and artistic circles.

RESURGENCE OF ARTS

9   After the 1989 democracy movement was crushed, cultural life in China sank into the doldrums. Wang was replaced as culture minister by an orthodox Marxist poet. Party conservatives, eager to purge the influences of political and cultural pluralism, ordered strict ideological control of the arts.

10   But in the past year, liberal Chinese writers have gone outside the major journals and newspapers to publish their work in minor provincial journals and in publications in Hong Kong and Taiwan.

11   Wang's case also is significant because

of the way he has chosen to fight back. While more and more Chinese have turned to civil litigation in recent years to seek redress for wrongs, it is highly unusual for individuals, particularly of Wang's rank, to file suit charging political persecution.

12   "I think it's indicative of a growing tendency by thinking people to take their legal right seriously," said Linda Jaivin, a specialist on contemporary Chinese culture at Australian National University.

■ **EXPLODED VIEW FOR STUDY**

Each of the highlighted words should be mastered in the following exercises.

Chinese Writer Sues Over 'Persecution'

Former culture minister takes rare action against Communist-controlled journal

Lena H. Sun

1   BEIJING   In an unusual act of defiance, a Chinese culture minister who was removed from office after the 1989 crackdown on democracy demonstrators is launching a public counteroffensive against orthodox Marxists who he says are trying to discredit him and to consolidate socialist control over the arts.

2   The former minister, Wang Meng, has filed suit in Beijing's Intermediate People's Court against a cultural journal controlled by Communist Party hardliners.

3   His suit accuses the weekly Arts and Literature Newspaper, and its chief editor, of political persecution and of publishing a libelous letter last month about a short story of his that the newspaper printed. The letter implied that the story was an attack on the reform programs of Chinese leader Deng Xiaoping. Chinese newspapers customarily do not comment on internal matters.

4   The story that provoked the controversy, "Hard Porridge," centers on a traditional family headed by a patriarch in his 80s. It pokes fun at the difficulties the family faces in trying to change its breakfast from the traditional porridge and pickled vegetables to a meal that includes eggs, meat and milk.

5   Wang has said that his allegorical story is meant to show support for the reforms of the 87-year-old Deng rather than attack them. His suit seeks a public apology and unspecified damages for what he calls harm to his reputation.

6   Wang's case is significant for several reasons. China's most intense political battles often have been staged in the cultural arena. During the disastrous Cultural Revolution of 1966 to 1976, hundreds of thousands of artists and intellectuals were purged and dissidents were persecuted for their political beliefs.

7   Wang, one of the country's best-known establishment writers, has long been a powerful symbol in China. Forced into exile during the Cultural Revolution, his rise to government power in 1986 as minister of culture was seen as a negation of that era's repression.

8   What Wang says are personal attacks on him are now causing a great stir in cultural circles because writers and artists fear that they could lead to another purge in literary and artistic circles.

9   After the 1989 democracy movement was crushed, cultural life in China sank into the doldrums. Wang was replaced as culture minister by an orthodox Marxist poet. Party conservatives, eager to purge the influences of political and cultural pluralism, ordered strict ideological control of the arts.

10   But in the past year, liberal Chinese writers have gone outside the major journals and newspapers to publish their work in minor provincial journals and in publications in Hong Kong and Taiwan.

11   Wang's case also is significant because of the way he has chosen to fight back. While more and more Chinese have turned to civil litigation in recent years to seek redress for wrongs, it is highly unusual for individuals, particularly of Wang's rank, to file suit charging political persecution.

12   "I think it's indicative of a growing tendency by thinking people to take their legal right seriously," said Linda Jaivin, a specialist on contemporary Chinese culture at Australian National University.

■ READING COMPREHENSION QUESTIONS

1. In the People's Republic of China, intense political battles often take the form of arguments over (a) sporting events, particularly soccer (b) foreign trade and the balance of payments (c) the arts (d) influential figures' relatives

2. Wang Meng's suit charges that the letter published in *Arts and Literature Newspaper* was "libelous," which means that the letter (a) misinterprets his story (b) is badly written (c) is stupid (d) tells lies about him and harms his reputation

3. Taking legal action against a newspaper is considered extremely unusual and dangerous in China because (a) the government controls the press and does not welcome criticism (b) newspapers have powerful legal staffs and may ruin the claimant with a countersuit (c) newspaper editors are known to be violent, short-tempered people (d) other newspapers may refuse to publish a trouble-maker.

4. The ten-year period in recent Chinese history during which hundreds of thousands of artists, teachers, and dissidents were persecuted is known as the (a) Great Awakening (b) Romantic Revolution (c) New Deal (d) Cultural Revolution

5. Wang Meng's story "Hard Porridge" centers on a family's attempt to substitute Western, high-protein foods such as milk, eggs, and meat for the traditional Chinese breakfast of (a) fish and rice (b) muffins, buns, and tea (c) fruit and cheese (d) pickled vegetables and gruel

6. Since the Tiananmen Square massacre (June 4th, 1989), many Chinese writers have refused to publish in major government-controlled periodicals, preferring to publish instead in (a) the U.S. and Europe (b) Taiwan, Hong Kong, and small Chinese periodicals (c) Japan and Korea (d) underground newspapers and newsletters

■ TARGET VOCABULARY

persecution	orthodox	to purge
defiance	to consolidate	dissidents
crackdown	journal	democracy
demonstrators	libelous	ideological
counteroffensive	to imply	indicative

Dictionary Practice

Use each word in a sentence of your own.

1. persecution _____
2. defiance _____
3. crackdown _____
4. demonstrators _____
5. counteroffensive _____
6. orthodox _____
7. to consolidate _____
8. journal _____
9. libelous _____
10. to imply _____
11. to purge _____
12. dissidents _____
13. democracy _____
14. ideological _____
15. indicative _____

Cloze Practice

Fill in each blank with an appropriate term from the target vocabulary list.

The _____ of people who do not hold _____ views, whether those views are political, religious, or artistic, is a regrettable universal constant. In especially repressive societies, when _____ become public _____ in open _____ of particular _____ values or standards, a swift and ruthless _____ can occur, which is _____ of the lack of tolerance for divergent views within the government itself.

■ **CRITICAL READING PRACTICE/TOPICS FOR DISCUSSION**

1.   What cases of censorship have you experienced or observed? How did you react to the censorship at the time, and how do you feel about it now?

2.   Do you think that the Chinese government has the right to control the press in order to protect certain social standards and attitudes? Why, or why not?

3.   Do you think that the U.S. government has the right to fund artists and artistic projects of which it approves and not to fund artists and artistic projects of which it does not approve? How does this response relate to your response to question 2?

4.   If an artist in the United States were to sue the National Endowment for the Arts, charging that the rejection of her work was libelous and politically motivated (in roughly the same way that Wang Meng has sued the *Arts and Literature Newspaper*), what do you think public reaction would be? How would you feel about such a suit? What differences or similarities do you see between the two?

5.   In what cases, if any, do you think that government should censor books, movies, newspapers, or other forms of the arts and the press? Why do you feel that censorship is justified in these cases?

■ *A Time to Live and a Time to Die*

The concept of personal rights is at the heart of the next pre-reading discussion and article, and one might naturally assume that taking a stand for personal rights would be automatic and easy; but the issue is by no means a simple one.

Should a physician, under any circumstances, assist a patient in ending his or her life? Do patients in fact have the "right" to suicide at all, and, if so, does the physician then have a responsibility to help them carry out their deaths in a painless way? The Hippocratic Oath forbids this, but it isn't really much help: this ancient oath also forbids physicians from charging other physicians' children for medical training, seducing either male or female slaves, and ever repeating information that could harm anybody, whether a patient or not.

There is yet another issue to deal with here: What attitude should the law reflect regarding these questions? And should law conflict with conscience, then what?

These personal rights things get tricky. . . .

■   **PRE-READING FOR DISCUSSION**

Suicide is a painful thing to think about and it becomes more painful the closer it approaches us in time and experience. Almost everybody has known, or known about, someone who committed suicide and as a result is aware of the hole such a death leaves in the fabric of the lives of those who knew the person.

From the outside, the reasons people have for killing themselves often seem small or unimportant: an unhappy love affair, family problems, disappointments or failures on the road of life. But from the inside, what things are really more important than these? In many ways, each of us is our own world, and when our whole world hurts, it is tough to live from hour to hour, let alone from day to day.

It all comes down to a question of the future. If the future looks impossibly bleak, then one might consider suicide in order to avoid all that infinite, awful unhappiness and pain. But if the future holds even the slightest possibility of things getting better, then it makes sense to work through the tough times (which *often* isn't easy) in order to check it out.

From the outside, we almost always wonder why people who commit suicide couldn't wait for the futures we can imagine for them. The reason, of course, is that they couldn't imagine those positive futures which seem so possible to us. There is a deep sadness to lives in which the future seems hopeless, and it is sadder still that the world causes so many people to reach this conclusion.

The following article tells of two women—Sherry Miller and Marjorie Wantz—who reached the conclusion that things simply were not going to get any better for them under any circumstances, and in fact were almost certain to get worse. The sheer physical suffering each had to endure led these women to take their lives. But, unlike most suicides, they were indirectly "assisted" in doing so by a physician, a person whose usual duty is preserving life.

The resulting furious debate over who is right and who is wrong in this case will be talked about by politicians, argued about by attorneys, voted on in legislatures throughout the land, interpreted variously by a lot of judges, and finally ruled on, probably, by the Supreme Court.

But who is right and who is wrong in this case, and others like it, will finally and truly only be decided in each of our hearts.

Some questions are too big even for the law, and this is one of them.

The bodies of two women were found in this cabin in a remote area near Pontiac, Mich. Dr. Jack Kevorkian called police Wednesday to tell them he had assisted the suicides of Marjorie Wantz, center, and Sherry Miller, right. In 1990, Kevorkian helped Alzheimer's patient Janet Adkins of Portland, Ore., die by hooking her up to a suicide machine he built.

Suicide Doctor Helps 2 to Die

Inventor present when bodies found, hooked up to devices

Associated Press

1   PONTIAC, MICH.   Two more deaths facilitated by the inventor of a suicide machine drew praise yesterday from a right-to-die organization and threats from officials to revoke his medical license and charge him in the deaths.

2   Dr. Jack Kevorkian, 63, who in 1990

helped Alzheimer's disease patient Janet Adkins die by hooking her up to a suicide machine he built, called authorities Wednesday night to report another "physician-assisted suicide."

3   Kevorkian, a pathologist, directed police to a cabin about 40 miles north of Detroit. There, they were met by him and found the bodies of two women, both connected to devices apparently used to end their lives.

4   Sherry Miller, 43, of Roseville had multiple sclerosis. Marjorie Wantz, 58, of Sodus suffered from a painful but nonterminal pelvic disease.

5   "I bless the doctor, I really do. I've seen the woman in so much pain," Millie Gast, a neighbor of Wantz, told the Herald-Palladium of Benton Harbor. "I hope they don't do anything to him."

6   Wantz received a lethal injection using a device similar to the one Adkins used, said Geoffrey Fieger, Kevorkian's lawyer. The device allows the patient to push a button that delivers a lethal injection. Miller inhaled carbon monoxide through a mask, Fieger said.

7   "He was present. He provided the expertise. He provided the equipment," Fieger said. But, he said, Kevorkian "did not assist in the deaths at all."

8   The Hemlock Society, a right-to-die organization, praised Kevorkian but said the suicides underscored a need for specific laws governing physician-assisted suicides for terminally ill patients.

9   "Clearly, these women were suffering and wanted to die," the Eugene, Ore. based organization said in a statement. "Kevorkian's motive was purely humanitarian."

10   But Hemlock Society staff attorney Cheryl K. Smith added: "This type of ad hoc assistance in suicide for the dying is wide open to abuse because there are no ground rules and no criteria."

11   A judge dismissed a murder charge against Kevorkian in the Adkins case after ruling that Michigan has no law against assisting suicide. But Kevorkian was barred from helping people commit suicides in Oakland County and could face contempt charges if he is found to have violated the court order.

12   Sheriff's Captain Glenn Watson said it could take two weeks to determine whether to file charges.

13   State Senator Fred Dillingham, the sponsor of a bill to outlaw assisted suicide, said he had spoken with the county prosecutor and state Attorney General Frank Kelley about revoking Kevorkian's medical license.

14   "My feeling is we need to punch Kevorkian's lights out right now," Dillingham said. "He's proven himself to be a danger."

15   Twenty-five states have laws against assisting suicide: A measure on the November ballot in Washington state would allow doctor-assisted suicide.

■ **EXPLODED VIEW FOR STUDY**

Each of the highlighted words should be mastered in the following exercises.

Suicide Doctor Helps 2 to Die
Inventor present when bodies found, hooked up to devices

Associated Press

1   PONTIAC, MICH.   Two more deaths facilitated by the inventor of a suicide machine drew praise yesterday from a right-to-die organization and threats from officials to revoke his medical license and charge him in the deaths.

2   Dr. Jack Kevorkian, 63, who in 1990 helped Alzheimer's disease patient Janet Adkins die by hooking her up to a suicide machine he built, called authorities Wednesday night to report another "physician-assisted suicide."

3   Kevorkian, a pathologist, directed police to a cabin about 40 miles north of Detroit. There, they were met by him and found the bodies of two women, both connected to devices apparently used to end their lives.

4   Sherry Miller, 43, of Roseville had multiple sclerosis. Marjorie Wantz, 58, of Sodus suffered from a painful but nonterminal pelvic disease.

5   "I bless the doctor, I really do. I've seen the woman in so much pain," Millie Gast, a neighbor of Wantz, told the Herald-Palladium of Benton Harbor. "I hope they don't do anything to him."

6   Wantz received a lethal injection using a device similar to the one Adkins used, said Geoffrey Fieger, Kevorkian's lawyer. The device allows the patient to push a button that delivers a lethal injection. Miller inhaled carbon monoxide through a mask, Fieger said.

7   "He was present. He provided the expertise. He provided the equipment," Fieger said. But, he said, Kevorkian "did not assist in the deaths at all."

8   The Hemlock Society, a right-to-die organization, praised Kevorkian but said the suicides underscored a need for specific laws governing physician-assisted suicides for terminally ill patients.

9   "Clearly, these women were suffering and wanted to die," the
Eugene, Ore. based organization said in a statement. "Kevorkian's
motive was purely humanitarian."

10   But Hemlock Society staff attorney Cheryl K. Smith added:
"This type of ad hoc assistance in suicide for the dying is wide open
to abuse because there are no ground rules and no criteria."

11   A judge dismissed a murder charge against Kevorkian in the
Adkins case after ruling that Michigan has no law against assisting
suicide. But Kevorkian was barred from helping people commit suicides in Oakland County and could face contempt charges if he is
found to have violated the court order.

12   Sheriff's Captain Glenn Watson said it could take two weeks to
determine whether to file charges.

13   State Senator Fred Dillingham, the sponsor of a bill to outlaw assisted suicide, said he had spoken with the county prosecutor and
state Attorney General Frank Kelley about revoking Kevorkian's
medical license.

14   "My feeling is we need to punch Kevorkian's lights out right
now," Dillingham said. "He's proven himself to be a danger."

15   Twenty-five states have laws against assisting suicide: A measure
on the November ballot in Washington state would allow doctor-
assisted suicide.

■   READING COMPREHENSION QUESTIONS

1.   Although many states have laws against assisting suicide, there
was no such law where Dr. Kevorkian assisted Sherry Miller and Marjorie Wantz in (a) Minnesota (b) Wisconsin (c) North Dakota
(d) Michigan

2.   The Hemlock Society derives its name from the poisonous weed
"hemlock," which is related to the carrot family rather than the tree.

This was the type of slowly numbing poison the great teacher Socrates drank when he was forced to commit suicide by the city-state of Athens. The Hemlock Society's name suggests that suicide can be (a) very quick (b) a private matter (c) ordered by the government (d) painless

3.   Although no law forbade Dr. Kevorkian from assisting the women, State Senator Fred Dillingham wanted the authorities to take action against the physician by (a) charging him with another crime (b) making him leave the state (c) revoking his medical license (d) buying him a one-way ticket to Eugene, Oregon

4.   Dr. Kevorkian's first assisted-suicide, several years before the one reported here, involved a patient suffering from (a) cancer (b) multiple sclerosis (c) heart disease (d) Alzheimer's disease

5.   It is perhaps grimly ironic that Dr. Kevorkian's medical specialty is (a) dermatology (b) podiatry (c) pathology (d) proctology

6.   Certain legal and ethical questions are raised by the fact that although the physician constructs the "machines" and instructs the patients in how to activate them in order to commit suicide, the actual act which ends the patient's life is performed by (a) hospital staff (b) a relative (c) a court-appointed nurse (d) the patient

■ TARGET VOCABULARY

right-to-die	**Hemlock Society**	**to bar**
Alzheimer's disease	**humanitarian**	**contempt charges**
multiple sclerosis	**ad hoc**	**prosecutor**
lethal	**ground rules**	**Attorney General**
to inject	**criteria**	**to revoke**

Dictionary Practice

Use each word in a sentence of your own.

1. right-to-die _____

2. Alzheimer's disease _____

3. multiple sclerosis _____

4. lethal _____

5. to inject _____

6. Hemlock Society _____

7. humanitarian _____

8. ad hoc _____

9. ground rules _____

10. criteria _____

11. to bar _____

12. contempt charges _____

    _____

13. prosecutor _____

14. Attorney General _____

15. to revoke _____

Cloze Practice

Fill in each blank with an appropriate term from the target vocabulary list.

Many people believe, with the organization known as the _____, that individuals have _____ choices which should be firmly protected by law. Other people believe equally as strongly that no condition or disease, even _____ or _____, justifies such a choice. At present, in Michigan there are no legal _____ regarding physician-assisted suicide, though some public _____, including the state's _____, wish to change that situation and _____ the practice altogether. If it is declared illegal, an assisting physician's license could be _____ and the physician's career destroyed.

■ CRITICAL READING PRACTICE/TOPICS FOR DISCUSSION

1. Do you feel that a person ever has the right to end his or her life? If so, under what conditions? Based on your responses, how do you feel about the decisions of the two women described in the article?

2. Do you think that the physician, Dr. Kevorkian, was right or wrong in helping the two women to end their lives? Why do you feel as you do?

3. Since what Kevorkian did was not against any law, do we have any reason to judge whether his actions were "right" or "wrong," both personally and professionally?

4. Do you agree with the Hemlock Society's opinion that Dr. Kevorkian's actions were "humanitarian"? Why or why not?

5. Would you favor or oppose proposed legislation that would outlaw physician-assisted suicide? Would such an opinion held by a candidate, one way or the other, influence the way you would vote?

■ *Prayer, Schools, and the Constitution*

The following pre-reading essay and news article examine the controversy over prayer in public schools, in this case a high school in Rhode Island. The school, of course, could be anywhere, and the question would be the same: Is there a clear separation of church and state in the public schools, and should there be such a separation?

In discussing this issue, keep in mind that the Supreme Court has already ruled in this case that the use of prayer is unconstitutional. But there will be more and more such cases, as there always have been. The question of religious freedom (including freedom from religion) is a classic American issue, debated anew in each generation and each court.

■ PRE-READING FOR DISCUSSION

Before the American Revolution, some of the colonies along the eastern seaboard of what is now the United States were anything *but* tolerant of religious differences, particularly colonies in what is now New England.

In fact, many of these colonies were established specifically to provide a safe place in the New World for religious groups that were too radical, unpopular, or threatening for Europe. And once they arrived, these sects quickly established political and legal systems that mirrored their religious beliefs. Each community sought to fit worldly action to the will of God for the eternal benefit of everyone's soul (and certainly there could be no more admirable goal).

When an outsider arrived with different religious ideas or a community member moved away from the established group's way of thinking, that person conformed, was punished, or was driven out of the community.

The problem, of course, is that good people can have honest differences of opinion regarding the exact nature of God's will and the shaping of worldly actions to conform to that will. Pass any law regarding religion or any law based only on a religious belief, and you offend somebody's sense of what is right or wrong, in terms of either theology or personal liberty.

The only good solution to the problem was the ancient Roman solution: worship as you please, don't fight with each other, and be sure to pay your taxes on time.

After our revolution, the Constitutional Convention pretty much decided the same thing as the Romans. "Freedom of religion" meant not only that you were free to worship as you pleased, but that nobody could make you worship any other way or even worship at all. That seemed like the only sensible solution at the time, and it still does to many people, including Daniel Weisman, the subject of the following article.

There is great historical irony to the fact that Mr. Weisman lives in Rhode Island. During the colonial period, Rhode Island was for many years the most tolerant of all the colonies regarding religious opinion. In fact, because it was so enlightened Rhode Island was frequently where religious exiles, radicals, and occasional whackos went for refuge.

Perhaps it is fitting that after two centuries we return to New England to again debate the oldest issue of American society: "How are we to best worship God, and how may this affect our neighbors?"

Thomas Jefferson stands with Daniel Weisman.

We shall see over the years, who stands with Joseph Rotella and Vincent McWilliams.

R.I. Test Case on Prayer in School

High court to review 'Lemon' ruling

Ellen Uzelac

1　PROVIDENCE, R.I. It all started in 1986, when Daniel Weisman, a Jew, heard the Baptist minister extol the wondrous ways of Jesus Christ at his older daughter's middle school graduation. Even school board officials politely concede now that the minister did get "carried away."

2　In Daniel Weisman's book, there are some things that just don't mix, school and prayer being examples.

3　So, when a rabbi offered prayers at his younger child's graduation from the same public school in Rhode Island three years later, Weisman sued—triggering a major constitutional confrontation between church and state that will reach the Supreme Court next month.

4　In the most direct attack this term on a constitutional precedent, the justices will be asked in legal arguments Nov. 6 to lower the wall separating church and state.

5　If Rhode Island school officials—supported by the Bush administration—win their appeal, courts in the future could find it easier to approve such things as a moment of silence for classroom prayer, Nativity scenes on government property and government assistance to parochial schools.

6　Unlikely as it may have seemed when Weisman and his daughter, Deborah, 16, filed suit against the Providence school board in 1989, their case now is being used to try to scuttle a court ruling used since 1971 to bar government from aiding or encouraging religion in American public life. The ruling is known as the "Lemon test" after the Supreme Court appeal, Lemon vs. Kurtzman.

7　"Just because someone mentions God, is that tantamount to endorsing a certain religion?" asked Joseph A. Rotella, an attorney for the Providence School Board. "Every day, by state law, Rhode Island school kids are required to say the Pledge of Allegiance and every day, these kids buy lunch with dollar bills that say 'In God We Trust.' So what are you going to do? Censor the Pledge of Allegiance? Reprint the money?"

8　"That's the essence of the case: Where do you draw the line? We think the Lemon test should be revisited," Rotella said. "When you get criticized for using the word 'God,' it's time to revisit a lot of things."

9　At Deborah Weisman's graduation from Nathan Bishop Middle School in 1989, Rabbi Leslie Gutterman opened his invocation with the words: "God of the Free, Hope of the Brave." In the benediction at the conclusion of the commencement, attended by about 600 people at the school, he made two direct references to a deity.

10　"I clearly gave a prayer," he said.

11　Last year, in response to the Weismans' suit, the U.S. District Court for the District of Rhode Island ruled that a benediction or invocation that invokes a deity and is delivered by clergy at an annual public school graduation ceremony runs afoul of the Lemon test because it advances religion.

12　Under the three-tiered Lemon standard, a law or governmental action is considered constitutional if it has secular purpose, has a primary effect that neither advances nor inhibits religion, and does not involve excessive entanglement between church and state.

13　In the District Court ruling on the Weisman case, later upheld by a federal appeals court, Judge Francis J. Boyle noted that school-sponsored prayer is prohibited "on every other school day at every other school function. . . . If the students cannot be led in prayer on all of those other days, prayer on graduation day is also inappropriate."

14   School officials in Providence, which has 22,000 public school students, maintain that graduation prayers are strictly ceremonial, and part of an American tradition that stretches nearly two centuries. They note that Congress and even the Supreme Court open their sessions with prayer.

15   "A lot of people looked to it for tradition," school board chairman Vincent McWilliams said. "We're not talking about school prayer here, but graduation invocations and benedictions, traditions for time immemorial."

16   As a result of an injunction issued by the federal court, Providence schools now are forbidden to offer graduation prayers.

17   Religious groups have come down on both sides of the case. The Baptist Joint Committee, for instance, supports the Weismans, but the U.S. Catholic Conference argues that "the circumstances of this case demand scrupulous protection, not suppression of religious exercise."

■   **EXPLODED VIEW FOR STUDY**

Each of the highlighted words should be mastered in the following exercises.

R.I. Test Case on Prayer in School

High court to review 'Lemon' ruling

Ellen Uzelac

1   PROVIDENCE, R.I.   It all started in 1986, when Daniel Weisman, a Jew, heard the Baptist minister extol the wondrous ways of Jesus Christ at his older daughter's middle school graduation. Even school board officials politely concede now that the minister did get "carried away."

2   In Daniel Weisman's book, there are some things that just don't mix, school and prayer being examples.

3   So, when a rabbi offered prayers at his younger child's graduation from the same public school in Rhode Island three years later, Weisman sued—triggering a major constitutional confrontation between church and state that will reach the Supreme Court next month.

4   In the most direct attack this term on a constitutional precedent, the justices will be asked in legal arguments Nov. 6 to lower the wall separating church and state.

5   If Rhode Island school officials—supported by the Bush administration—win their appeal, courts in the future could find it easier to approve such things as a moment of silence for classroom prayer, Nativity scenes on government property and government assistance to parochial schools.

6   Unlikely as it may have seemed when Weisman and his daughter, Deborah, 16, filed suit against the Providence school board in 1989, their case now is being used to try to scuttle a court ruling used since 1971 to bar government from aiding or encouraging religion in American public life. The ruling is known as the "Lemon test" after the Supreme Court appeal, Lemon vs. Kurtzman.

7   "Just because someone mentions God, is that tantamount to endorsing a certain religion?" asked Joseph A. Rotella, an attorney for the Providence School Board. "Every day, by state law, Rhode Island school kids are required to say the Pledge of Allegiance and every day, these kids buy lunch with dollar bills that say 'In God We Trust.' So what are you going to do? Censor the Pledge of Allegiance? Reprint the money?"

8   "That's the essence of the case: Where do you draw the line? We think the Lemon test should be revisited," Rotella said. "When you get criticized for using the word 'God,' it's time to revisit a lot of things."

9   At Deborah Weisman's graduation from Nathan Bishop Middle School in 1989, Rabbi Leslie Gutterman opened his invocation with the words: "God of the Free, Hope of the Brave." In the benediction at the conclusion of the commencement, attended by about 600 people at the school, he made two direct references to a deity.

10   "I clearly gave a prayer," he said.

11   Last year, in response to the Weismans' suit, the U.S. District Court for the District of Rhode Island ruled that a benediction or invocation that invokes a deity and is delivered by clergy at an

annual public school graduation ceremony runs afoul of the Lemon test because it advances religion.

12   Under the three-tiered Lemon standard, a law or governmental action is considered constitutional if it has secular purpose, has a primary effect that neither advances nor inhibits religion, and does not involve excessive entanglement between church and state.

13   In the District Court ruling on the Weisman case, later upheld by a federal appeals court, Judge Francis J. Boyle noted that school-sponsored prayer is prohibited "on every other school day at every other school function. . . . If the students cannot be led in prayer on all of those other days, prayer on graduation day is also inappropriate."

14   School officials in Providence, which has 22,000 public school students, maintain that graduation prayers are strictly ceremonial, and part of an American tradition that stretches nearly two centuries. They note that Congress and even the Supreme Court open their sessions with prayer.

15   "A lot of people looked to it for tradition," school board chairman Vincent McWilliams said. "We're not talking about school prayer here, but graduation invocations and benedictions, traditions for time immemorial."

16   As a result of an injunction issued by the federal court, Providence schools now are forbidden to offer graduation prayers.

17   Religious groups have come down on both sides of the case. The Baptist Joint Committee, for instance, supports the Weismans, but the U.S. Catholic Conference argues that "the circumstances of this case demand scrupulous protection, not suppression of religious exercise."

■   READING COMPREHENSION QUESTIONS

1.   According to the Supreme Court ruling in *Lemon v. Kurtzman,* also known as the "Lemon Test," a law or governmental action (in this case a public school-sponsored event such as graduation) is constitutional unless it (a) advocates violence (b) threatens the civil rights of a citizen (c) advances or inhibits religion (d) endorses punctuated evolution

2.   In 1986, Daniel Weisman listened to a Baptist minister at Weisman's eldest daughter's graduation without taking legal action. But three years later, at the graduation of a second daughter, Weisman finally drew the line when he heard a second religious invocation delivered by a (a) Buddhist priest (b) rabbi (c) mullah (d) shaman

3.   Providence school officials and their many supporters believe that prayers at graduation are (a) strictly ceremonial and traditional (b) constitutional rights (c) district policy decisions (d) non-threatening to non-religious students and citizens

4.   Joseph A. Rotella, attorney for the Providence School Board, holds that the real issue at stake in this case is whether or not religion is endorsed by public mention of (a) separation of church and state (b) Old Testament figures such as Noah (c) comparisons between religions (d) God

5.   Providence schools were forbidden to offer graduation prayers when a federal court issued (a) a warning (b) a writ (c) an opinion (d) an injunction

6.   Providence school officials firmly maintain that graduation prayers are strictly (a) informal (b) optional (c) ceremonial (d) agnostic

■ TARGET VOCABULARY

constitutional	commencement	to uphold
precedent	deity	ceremonial
appeal	clergy	injunction
Nativity scene	secular	religious
parochial	entanglement	scrupulous

Dictionary Practice

Use each word in a sentence of your own.

1. constitutional _____

2. precedent _____

3. appeal _____

4. Nativity scene _____

5. parochial _____

6. commencement _____

7. deity _____

8. clergy _____

9. secular _____

10. entanglement _____

11. to uphold _____

12. ceremonial _____

13. injunction _____

14. religious _____

15. scrupulous _____

Cloze Practice

Fill in each blank with an appropriate word from the target vocabulary list.

Most courts, in most cases, follow _____, or "what was decided before." But a revolutionary Supreme Court, like the Warren Court, hears _____ on _____ issues and often overturns earlier rulings rather than _____ them. We seem to be in such a period now regarding social issues, but no one can tell yet what is going to happen when _____ and _____ interests collide in the high court. Sorting out such an emotional _____ of passions and rights will demand _____ care by the justices of the Supreme Court.

■ CRITICAL READING PRACTICE/TOPICS FOR DISCUSSION

1. The law says that everybody has to go to school. If the law were to permit public schools to have religious prayers, ceremonies, or rituals, would that force religion on people? Why, or why not?

2. As we have noted, it is ironic that this is happening in Rhode Island. Why is it also ironic that this is happening in a city named "Providence"?

3.   Only Judaism and Protestant Christianity are mentioned in the article. If there are Hindu, Moslem, Catholic, Greek Orthodox, and Buddhist students, students who worship trees, students who think that all formal religions are pretty much the same, and students who don't care or think about God one way or the other, how can a balance be struck so that each has equal religious rights and freedoms?

4.   Why do you think that Mr. Weisman waited to file his suit until after the rabbi spoke at Deborah's commencement, instead of filing suit when the Baptist minister spoke at the commencement of Deborah's older sister three years before?

5.   How do you feel about this whole issue of prayer in school? How do you feel about the separation of church and state as a concept? Why do you feel as you do about each?

CHAPTER 3

■ *The People Section*

■ *"We Will, We Will . . . ROCK YOU!!!!"*

At all times and in all places, humanity has been faced with fatal diseases that come in deadly waves: smallpox, cholera, measles, scarlet fever, and a dozen other plagues (including plague itself) have killed more millions than all the many, many wars.

In our time, due to modern preventative science, most such diseases are no longer a threat if medical services are available. For a time it actually seemed that the days of helplessness in the face of such deadly illnesses were over.

The following pre-reading essay and news article demonstrate how wrong we were to think ourselves beyond the reach of such forces. In your class discussion you'll probably wind up debating cause-and-effect issues when considering Freddie Mercury's death and subsequent developments regarding the social impact of AIDS.

■   PRE-READING FOR DISCUSSION

In the year 1347 a terrible plague called The Black Death arrived in Europe. The greatest doctors were powerless, the greatest politicians were helpless, and many people said that the millions of deaths were judgments from God. More than a third of Europe's population died in twenty years. Rich and poor, good and evil, strong and weak, healthy and infirm, they died faster than the living could bury them.

All of the health care systems and many of the basic social systems, such as the legal system and public works, simply collapsed. In many cases people lived in towns and cities that were ruled by the strongest and the best armed.

You can probably imagine what that led to. . . .

About 150 years later, Europeans arrived in the New World, with roughly the same results. Once again, millions of people (particularly native Americans) died from illnesses that defied their medicine, rocked their societies, and raised new questions of "Why? Why?"

An *acronym* is a word made up of the first letters of other words, such as UPS for United Parcel Service or USFS for the United States Forest Service. AIDS stands for Acquired Immune Deficiency Syndrome, and AIDS is the plague of our time, the invasion, the killer we have yet to understand and thereby stop. Now, we are the ones—of all colors and ages and sexual preferences—who are dying without answers to our modern "Why? Why?"

The following article is about musician Freddie Mercury, who died from complications of AIDS. Before he died, though, his art reached across all boundaries, touching the lives of many millions of people and influencing hundreds of other artists.

Scientists make advances every day in showing us the interdependence of the elements in the physical world: acid rain, the ozone layer, and smog all have their origins in people's choices. Artists have long understood this interdependence because they have seen art reach across boundaries and through time in ways that most other people do not notice.

Problems, tragedies, and disasters also reach across time, and if there is any good at all in them, perhaps it is that they make each of us a bit more aware of our common humanity and the common problems each of us faces in our life. And they give us an appreciation of dignity under pressure, as well—even the final test of dying (like so many before, in so many places) with grace and honor.

ASSOCIATED PRESS

Queen lead singer Freddie Mercury performs at a concert in Sydney, Australia. Mercury, 45, died Sunday night, the day after announcing that he had AIDS.

British Star's AIDS Battle

One of rock's great eccentrics

Bruce Britt

1   LOS ANGELES   With the exception of David Bowie, Freddie Mercury was the most flamboyant of all the 1970s rockers.

2   The vocalist for the British rock band Queen pranced about the stage in ballerina outfits that made him look like a moustached Tinkerbell. In the process he out-glamorized such pioneering pop music peacocks as the New York Dolls' David Johansen and Roxy Music's Bryan Ferry.

3   Mercury died Sunday of complications from AIDS. On Saturday the singer disclosed he had contracted the disease, ending months of media speculation. In a statement, he explained that he had kept mum about his ailment "in order to protect the privacy of those around me."

4   "He had that style and grace that put him totally above the usual music types," said producer Roy Thomas Baker. "Working with him was a dream."

5   Winning a reputation for being one of rock's leading eccentrics was no mean feat—after all, the 1970s were pop music's decade of outrageous androgyny. But as is sometimes the case in pop culture, Mercury's larger-than-life image sometimes obscured his prodigious talent.

6   Most Queen fans are quick to recall the rock and roll aria "Bohemian Rhapsody" or the stomping "We Will Rock You," which is such a convincing expression of competitiveness that it has become a universal sports anthem.

7   But what was most memorable about Queen was Mercury's remarkably pliant voice. In the '60s and early '70s, most rock singers seemed too dispassionate or full of histrionics to compare with R&B singers such as Wilson Pickett, Aretha Franklin, and Sam and Dave.

8   All of which made Queen's 1973 debut album, "Queen," such a surprise. Even today the disc's mix of metallic melody and religious lyricism sounds fresh and exotic. It remains the band's most ethereal record, and Mercury's voice figured largely in its creative success.

9   In order to endear themselves to the masses, Queen was forced to master more concise pop music forms, and on subsequent albums the band became masters of the three-minute hit. During its evolution, Queen experimented with McCartneyesque show tunes, funk, rockabilly, heavy metal and even gospel, and it was Mercury's voice .that made all these experiments sound less like eccentric whims and more like loving homages.

10   In fact, Mercury's elastic voice could embrace the most ridiculous concepts. Imagine the look on most singers' faces if you presented them with a song requiring a heart-rending falsetto, operatic warbling and hard-rock snarling.

11   But Mercury effortlessly juggled all of these tricky turns on Queen's memorable 1976 hit, "Bohemian Rhapsody." It's no wonder peers as diverse as Michael Jackson, Vanilla Ice, Guns N' Roses and Metallica have paid homage to Mercury.

■   **EXPLODED VIEW FOR STUDY**

Each of the highlighted words should be mastered in the following exercises.

British Star's AIDS Battle

One of rock's great eccentrics

Bruce Britt

1   LOS ANGELES   With the exception of David Bowie, Freddie Mercury was the most flamboyant of all the 1970s rockers.

2   The vocalist for the British rock band Queen pranced about the stage in ballerina outfits that made him look like a moustached Tinkerbell. In the process he out-glamorized such pioneering pop music peacocks as the New York Dolls' David Johansen and Roxy Music's Bryan Ferry.

3   Mercury died Sunday of complications from AIDS. On Saturday the singer disclosed he had contracted the disease, ending months of media speculation. In a statement, he explained that he had kept mum about his ailment "in order to protect the privacy of those around me."

4   "He had that style and grace that put him totally above the usual music types," said producer Roy Thomas Baker. "Working with him was a dream."

5   Winning a reputation for being one of rock's leading eccentrics was no mean feat—after all, the 1970s were pop music's decade of outrageous androgyny. But as is sometimes the case in pop culture, Mercury's larger-than-life image sometimes obscured his prodigious talent.

6   Most Queen fans are quick to recall the rock and roll aria "Bohemian Rhapsody" or the stomping "We Will Rock You," which is such a convincing expression of competitiveness that it has become a universal sports anthem.

7   But what was most memorable about Queen was Mercury's remarkably pliant voice. In the '60s and early '70s, most rock singers seemed too dispassionate or full of histrionics to compare with R&B singers such as Wilson Pickett, Aretha Franklin, and Sam and Dave.

8   All of which made Queen's 1973 debut album, "Queen," such a surprise. Even today the disc's mix of metallic melody and religious lyricism sounds fresh and exotic. It remains the band's most ethereal record, and Mercury's voice figured largely in its creative success.

9   In order to endear themselves to the masses, Queen was forced to master more concise pop music forms, and on subsequent albums the band became masters of the three-minute hit. During its evolution, Queen experimented with McCartneyesque show tunes, funk,

rockabilly, heavy metal and even gospel, and it was Mercury's voice that made all these experiments sound less like eccentric whims and more like loving homages.

10   In fact, Mercury's elastic voice could embrace the most ridiculous concepts. Imagine the look on most singers' faces if you presented them with a song requiring a heart-rending falsetto, operatic warbling and hard-rock snarling.

11   But Mercury effortlessly juggled all of these tricky turns on Queen's memorable 1976 hit, "Bohemian Rhapsody." It's no wonder peers as diverse as Michael Jackson, Vanilla Ice, Guns N' Roses and Metallica have paid homage to Mercury.

■ READING COMPREHENSION QUESTIONS

1.   Like many other musicians, and indeed like many artists working in other media, Freddie Mercury's lifestyle was considered by the general public to be (a) staid (b) conservative (c) eccentric (d) middle class

2.   Mercury did not disclose the nature of his illness until just before his death because (a) the British typically do not discuss illnesses (b) he wished to protect the privacy of those around him (c) his parents asked him not to (d) he did not wish to harm sales of Queen's recordings

3.   Music critic Bruce Britt identifies the 1970s as the decade in which pop music was dominated by (a) social consciousness and civil rights (b) pacifism and the anti-war movement (c) the "Delta Blues" (d) androgyny

4.   One of Queen's best-known compositions, which thunders in gymnasiums and sports arenas at every level of athletics, is the pounding song (a) "Born in the U.S.A." (b) "Frank's Wild Years" (c) "Great Balls of Fire" (d) "We Will Rock You"

5.   Male vocalists can greatly increase their singing range and artistic scope by using their voice above its natural notes through the technique called (a) vibrato (b) falsetto (c) primavera (d) fettuccine

6.   In addition to producing an impressive body of his own work, Freddie Mercury will also be remembered because of the tremendous influence his work had on (a) other musicians (b) British domestic policy (c) Prime Minister Margaret Thatcher (d) compact disc technology

■ TARGET VOCABULARY

rock	prodigious	histrionic
eccentric	Bohemian	lyricism
flamboyant	anthem	elastic
vocalist	pliant	falsetto
androgyny	dispassionate	peers

Dictionary Practice

Use each word in a sentence of your own.

1. rock _____

2. eccentric _____

3. flamboyant _____

4. vocalist _____

5. androgyny _____

6. prodigious _____

7. Bohemian _____

8. anthem _____

9. pliant _____

10. dispassionate _____

11. histrionic _____

12. lyricism _____

13. elastic _____

14. falsetto _____

15. peers _____

Cloze Practice

Fill in each blank with an appropriate word from the target vocabulary list.

Musicians who play _____ music often have _____ lifestyles considered _____ by society at large. Rock singers, or _____, are especially _____ on stage since part of rock music's power is the ability to shock. One such method of artistic surprise is the physical _____ of some male performers,

singing in a high _____ that demands a truly _____

vocal range. Such performers, Freddie Mercury among them, had a

_____ effect on international styles and standards, both

personal and artistic.

◼ CRITICAL READING PRACTICE/TOPICS FOR DISCUSSION

1.   Have you ever heard anyone say that AIDS is a punishment for sin? Do you agree or disagree, and why? If you agree, why do you think unborn babies contract the disease and die during early childhood? If you disagree, how do you respond to those who would say that people who engage in practices that put them at risk of contracting the AIDS virus are the cause of their own death?

2.   Do you think that the government of the United States would have funded more AIDS research if the majority of early victims of the disease had been white, rich, and heterosexual? Why or why not?

3.   In the 14th century people did not know how the Bubonic Plague was spread. We believe that we know, at least, how AIDS is transmitted. In light of this, if someone knowingly infects someone else, is that an act of murder? Why or why not?

4.   What is your personal reaction upon hearing that someone has died of AIDS? What assumptions do you make, and how valid are those assumptions?

5.   If you have ever heard Queen's music, do you like it? If you have not heard the group, has reading the article on Freddie Mercury's death produced any interest on your part in listening to Queen? Why or why not?

Sample Map for "One of Rock's Great Eccentrics"—Bruce Britt

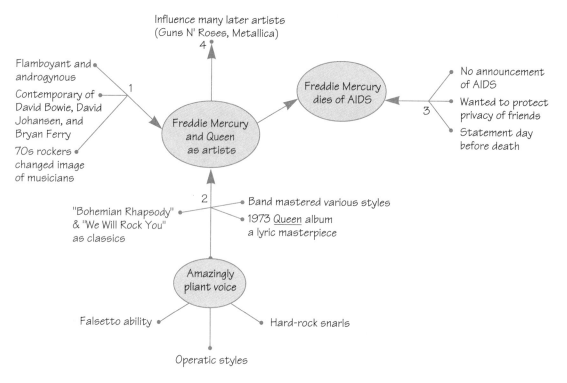

Note: For each of the following readings in this chapter, you are encouraged to draw maps of your own like this one, applying the mapping skills you learned in Part I.

■ *"Listen . . . Do You Want to Know a Secret?"*

Sexism is discrimination based on gender and a lively topic in any society, not only our own. Once, for example, while teaching in China, which has an annual "Women's Day," I asked my brilliant female colleague at Nankai University, Professor Gu, if China had a "Men's Day," as well. She replied unhesitatingly, "All the rest of the year is 'Men's Day'." Her husband, the equally brilliant Professor Liu, raised his eyebrows slightly and remained silent as a stone.

The following pre-reading essay on discrimination and language and the accompanying article on the creation of a "secret language" in response to sexism, should get you thinking about the past, present, and future of gender equality.

■ PRE-READING FOR DISCUSSION

The first weapon of resistance to oppression is language. From South Africa to South Carolina, from the streets of the *barrio* to the streets of Bombay and Beijing, language which frustrates the oppressor is the first step toward freedom.

In the next article, however, the usual language of resistance takes a very unusual form. Unlike "slang," which is language understood by particular groups (such as teenagers) or "jargon," which is specialized language used by professionals (jazz musicians, brain surgeons), the secret language called *nushu* was "secret" because it could not be *read* rather than because it could not be understood when it was heard.

Even more unusual is the fact that *nushu* was phonetic; that is, the written characters represented sounds rather than words. In China at the time, such a language was revolutionary. Perhaps this "women's language" was the first phonetic alphabet in Asia. Perhaps it is even the origin of the phonetic Japanese *hiragana* alphabet, which is used along with the picture "ideographs" of written Japanese.

One fact, however, is as solid as a rock: the creation of *nushu* was an amazing act of scholarship. Denied access to learning in a male-dominated society, the genius of half of humanity literally had to invent its own voice.

Throughout history and throughout the world, women of intelligence and courage have been called "witches" by men who felt threatened in the presence of nonmasculine courage and intelligence. In most such cases the women were persecuted. In some cases, such as those in New England only a few hundred years ago, the women were killed.

Strangely, while oppression of any kind shows mankind at its worst, resistance to oppression shows us at our very best, as the Chinese students and professors (many of them women) who were slaughtered at Tiananmen Square demonstrated in 1989.

Such resistance burns brightly for thousands of years, in *nushu* as well as in less secret languages.

Oppression itself seems to be a disease which we have only imperfectly learned how to treat and almost never can cure.

Fortunately, research continues . . . in all the languages of the earth.

A Secret Language for Women

Now, men are trying to save ancient Chinese 'nushu'

Andrew Quinn

1   BEIJING   On paper fans and in delicate, cloth-bound diaries, women in the heart of ancient China once transcribed their secrets in a written language that no man could understand.

2   Called everything from "the witches' script" to the first language of women's liberation, the flowing ideographs were passed from mother to daughter in a secret literary tradition that defied China's male-dominated establishment.

3   The script, known as "nushu" or "women's calligraphy," has all but disappeared, surviving only among a dwindling handful of elderly women in one county of mountainous Hunan province.

4   Now a team of male scholars has embarked on a sweeping research project to analyze the writing and preserve it for its historical and linguistic value.

5   "Women don't seem interested in it any more. It's just a few of us men who are doing the research," said Chen Qiguang, a professor at Beijing's Central Institute of Nationalities who has been the driving force behind efforts to save the script.

6   Nushu, made up of 2,000 individual characters, has been used by women in Hunan for at least 1,000 years, Chen said.

7   "Some people say it is at least 6,000 years old, but I don't believe it is that ancient," he said.

8   Lovingly written on the frail paper pages of crumbling diaries, the characters of nushu are simpler and more fluid than the complex ideographs of standard Chinese.

9   Made up of a cryptic collection of strokes and dashes, looking rather like chicken scratches, the characters flowing down the page resemble Arabic more than Chinese.

10   While Chen believes nushu may originally have been adapted from common Chinese characters, he said the two languages have significant differences.

11   "Chinese characters represent individual meanings, but nushu characters represent only sounds," Chen said. "It is really quite complicated on its own."

12   Research into the origins of the language has centered on Yang Huanyi, an 83-year-old resident of Jiangyong county in Hunan who Chen believes may be the last woman left in China fully literate in nushu.

13   Yang, who had not practiced her nushu in almost four decades, has helped visiting scholars compile dictionaries of nushu characters and decipher older nushu writings, Chen said.

14   "She is also teaching nushu to her friend, who is only in her mid-70s, so there will be someone else who can write it," Chen said. "There are a few more women who can read it, but they are all also old."

15   Chen's research has been primarily linguistic, but he said the nushu writings are equally valuable because they shed light on a secret woman's world that received little space in China's official histories.

16   In their books of nushu, women discussed their views of such events as the 1840–42 Opium War with Britain and the Japanese invasion of China in the 1930s, Chen said.

17   "They would describe how the bombs fell from planes and how people died on the ground," Chen said. "Some of these are valuable historical documents."

18   The women also used nushu to write

about their own private tribulations in a world run by men.

19 Nushu booklets and songs were traditional gifts between women before marriage, offering advice on how to manage if a husband leaves on a long trip and how to cope with your mother-in-law, as well as lamenting the fact that marriage effectively cut a woman's ties with her friends and family. "The women would get together and sing songs written in nushu," Chen said. "They had powerful feelings of sisterhood."

20 The tradition of nushu began to fade in the 1930s when women were given more opportunities for formal education, including instruction in standard Chinese, Chen said.

21 "Everyone realized that Chinese was more useful, so they studied that instead," he said.

22 The few women who tried to keep their private language alive ran into serious trouble in the 1950s, when China's new Communist government launched "anti-rightist" campaigns aimed at rooting out feudal traditions.

23 "Men were very suspicious of nushu because they couldn't understand what was written in it. So they called the women witches and labeled nushu "the witches' script," Chen said. He said the fruits of his research with two other scholars would be published early next year as a 900-page book containing original and translated versions of 400 pieces of nushu writing.

24 "Men dare to leave home to brave life in the outside world," one anonymous nushu author wrote in one piece to be included in the collection. "But we women are no less courageous: We can create a language they can't understand."

■ **EXPLODED VIEW FOR STUDY**

Each of the highlighted words should be mastered in the following exercises.

A Secret Language for Women

Now, men are trying to save ancient Chinese 'nushu'

Andrew Quinn

1 BEIJING On paper fans and in delicate, cloth-bound diaries, women in the heart of ancient China once transcribed their secrets in a written language that no man could understand.

2 Called everything from "the witches' script" to the first language of women's liberation, the flowing ideographs were passed from mother to daughter in a secret literary tradition that defied China's male-dominated establishment.

3   The script, known as "nushu" or "women's calligraphy," has all but disappeared, surviving only among a dwindling handful of elderly women in one county of mountainous Hunan province.

4   Now a team of male scholars has embarked on a sweeping research project to analyze the writing and preserve it for its historical and linguistic value.

5   "Women don't seem interested in it any more. It's just a few of us men who are doing the research," said Chen Qiguang, a professor at Beijing's Central Institute of Nationalities who has been the driving force behind efforts to save the script.

6   Nushu, made up of 2,000 individual characters, has been used by women in Hunan for at least 1,000 years, Chen said.

7   "Some people say it is at least 6,000 years old, but I don't believe it is that ancient," he said.

8   Lovingly written on the frail paper pages of crumbling diaries, the characters of nushu are simpler and more fluid than the complex ideographs of standard Chinese.

9   Made up of a cryptic collection of strokes and dashes, looking rather like chicken scratches, the characters flowing down the page resemble Arabic more than Chinese.

10   While Chen believes nushu may originally have been adapted from common Chinese characters, he said the two languages have significant differences.

11   "Chinese characters represent individual meanings, but nushu characters represent only sounds," Chen said. "It is really quite complicated on its own."

12   Research into the origins of the language has centered on Yang Huanyi, an 83-year-old resident of Jiangyong county in Hunan who Chen believes may be the last woman left in China fully literate in nushu.

13   Yang, who had not practiced her nushu in almost four decades, has helped visiting scholars compile dictionaries of nushu characters and decipher older nushu writings, Chen said.

14   "She is also teaching nushu to her friend, who is only in her mid-

70s, so there will be someone else who can write it," Chen said. "There are a few more women who can read it, but they are all also old."

15   Chen's research has been primarily linguistic, but he said the nu-shu writings are equally valuable because they shed light on a secret woman's world that received little space in China's official histories.

16   In their books of nushu, women discussed their views of such events as the 1840–42 Opium War with Britain and the Japanese invasion of China in the 1930s, Chen said.

17   "They would describe how the bombs fell from planes and how people died on the ground," Chen said. "Some of these are valuable historical documents."

18   The women also used nushu to write about their own private tribulations in a world run by men.

19   Nushu booklets and songs were traditional gifts between women before marriage, offering advice on how to manage if a husband leaves on a long trip and how to cope with your mother-in-law, as well as lamenting the fact that marriage effectively cut a woman's ties with her friends and family. "The women would get together and sing songs written in nushu," Chen said. "They had powerful feelings of sisterhood."

20   The tradition of nushu began to fade in the 1930s when women were given more opportunities for formal education, including instruction in standard Chinese, Chen said.

21   "Everyone realized that Chinese was more useful, so they studied that instead," he said.

22   The few women who tried to keep their private language alive ran into serious trouble in the 1950s, when China's new Communist government launched "anti-rightist" campaigns aimed at rooting out feudal traditions.

23   "Men were very suspicious of nushu because they couldn't understand what was written in it. So they called the women witches and labeled nushu "the witches' script," Chen said. He said the fruits of his research with two other scholars would be published early next

year as a 900-page book containing original and translated versions of 400 pieces of nushu writing.

24   "Men dare to leave home to brave life in the outside world," one anonymous nushu author wrote in one piece to be included in the collection. "But we women are no less courageous: We can create a language they can't understand."

■ READING COMPREHENSION QUESTIONS

1.   For at least 1,000 years, tens of thousands of women used *nushu* script in China. Recently, however, scholars have suggested that in China's population of over one billion people the number of women fully literate in *nushu* may be only (a) 7,500 (b) 28,000 (c) 500 (d) 1

2.   What distinguishes *nushu* from other Chinese characters is that whereas characters each have individual meanings, *nushu* characters represent (a) several meanings (b) sounds (c) geometric concepts (d) goddesses

3.   Chinese women developed and perfected their *nushu* script in a society which (a) encouraged intellectual experimentation (b) rewarded new inventions with imperial prizes (c) allowed women no formal educational opportunities (d) was ruled by the woman warrior Hao Churgao

4.   During the many centuries of its use, *nushu* was regarded with great suspicion by *nushu*-illiterate men, some of whom went so far as to accuse women who used *nushu* of being (a) uppity (b) unfeminine (c) feminists (d) witches

5.   In traditional Chinese society, when a woman married she was forced in effect to cut her ties with (a) schoolmates (b) her political party (c) her friends and family (d) her pen-pals

6.   Ironically, both the professor in charge of *nushu* research at the Central Institute of Nationalities and the professor's scholarly colleagues involved in the project are all (a) Brazilian (b) witches (c) women in a still-sexist society (d) men

■   TARGET VOCABULARY

diaries	to dwindle	to lament
transcribe	to embark	to launch
script	cryptic	to root out
ideographs	to compile	feudal
calligraphy	tribulations	anonymous

Dictionary Practice

Use each of the following words in a sentence of your own.

1.   diaries _____

2.   transcribe _____

3.   script _____

4.   ideographs _____

5.   calligraphy _____

6.   to dwindle _____

7.   to embark _____

8.   cryptic _____

9.   to compile _____

10.   tribulations _____

11.   to lament _____

12.   to launch _____

13.   to root out _____

14.   feudal _____

15.   anonymous _____

Cloze Practice

Fill in each blank with an appropriate word from the target vocabulary list.

_____ is the art of writing any language in a beautiful visual form. In Asia, where several languages are written in characters called _____, or "ideas within pictures," this art form is particularly admired. Such characters seem _____ to Westerners until they _____ on the journey of studying the characters' structures and eventually _____ a "visual vocabulary" of the language. Such students often _____ the _____ of such study, but the effort is highly repaid. In addition to ideographs, Japanese also employs a phonetic, or "sound," _____ which can be learned quickly and _____ a student on a voyage of endless discovery.

■ CRITICAL READING PRACTICE/TOPICS FOR DISCUSSION

1. What is your *first* reaction to the article on *nushu,* and why do you think it is your initial response?

2. Name five ways in which women are routinely discriminated against in U.S. society at present. Please be as specific as time allows.

3. Regardless of gender, have you ever been subjected to discrimination? If so, what form did it take? If not, why do you think you have avoided it?

4. Have you ever contributed to discrimination, social or of some other type? If so, why do you think you participated in this?

5. Do you think that women should object to sexist behavior or "just ignore it" because objection may be futile? How do you think people should respond to racist behavior? Why? How do you think one should respond to violent behavior, and why?

■ *"I Grow Old, I Grow Old. . . ."*

The following pre-reading essay and news article treat the twin topics of age and aging. All of us have different ideas, fears, and opinions regarding these topics, and Professor Page Smith offers an articulate and valuable perspective on time and our journeys through it.

As you read, think particularly about the relationship between the elderly and what Smith terms "the accumulation of a lifetime" (paragraph 10).

■ PRE-READING FOR DISCUSSION

Very few people in the United States are satisfied with our society's treatment of old people. (By "old" we usually mean at least seventy and retired from job or profession.)

Unless the old are wealthy themselves or receive ever-increasing amounts of money from their children, it is almost impossible for them to keep up with always-rising costs. Most retired people receive very small, if any, increases in their retirement benefits, and rising health care and insurance costs are particularly difficult for retired people to meet.

Retired professor and historian Page Smith offers some thoughts on aging in the following article, one of his "Coming of Age" series. Specifically, Smith discusses the relationships between aging and memory and between memory and objects.

Most of us acquire objects of special importance to us during our lives: a ring, a dead friend's walking stick, a fountain pen, a picture drawn by a child. Smith argues that as life moves toward its inevitable conclusion, such objects become more than just the triggers of memory. They become, as he puts it, "art and magic" to the old; and yet often the old are separated from these important and powerful sources of emotion and life.

In far too many cases, American society does not appreciate or preserve these relationships for its old. Strange as it may seem to others, American families often give the responsibility of caring for their old to institutions, and in such environments the relationships discussed by Professor Smith cannot exist.

For centuries, Americans have been criticized (often justifiably) for being too materialistic. Perhaps in our treatment of the old, we can find an instance of our not being quite materialistic enough—at least in terms of meeting the needs of those who came before us.

Places, Faces and Things

Coming of age

Page Smith

1   When you get old, familiar places, spaces and faces are a particular comfort. And familiar things. Yet it is often just these consolations that are withdrawn from us when we are old.

2   A beloved place collects associations in layers of sights and sounds and scents—the way the expiring sun catches the tops of redwood trees and filters down through the madrones; the sudden harmonious song of amorous tree frogs, crickets' chorus and the forlorn hoot of an owl; the smell of the pasture after rain—even the odor of steaming horse manure.

3   And then the memories. Above all, the memories, of gatherings of friends and family, the anniversaries, weddings, Christmases, Easters and Thanksgivings. Through such sanctifying occasions the spirit of a place becomes palpable, holy.

4   Spaces are mostly interiors (although there may be a magical redwood cathedral, a sun-drenched deck or patio). Interior spaces become so familiar that one can find one's way about on the blackest night. The hand reaches unerringly for the doorknob, or the light switch, or the refrigerator handle with the confidence born of many nocturnal ramblings. Feet move slowly but surely on stairs and floors.

5   Faces. One searches them for signs of aging, reassured to note that the inevitable tracery of wrinkles still lies lightly. Sometimes we are surprised to observe that a familiar old face suddenly looks younger and brighter, more vivid, as though from a sudden pulse of life, perhaps the visit of a child or grandchild or an old friend. Or, more mundanely, a stiff shot of bourbon.

6   The rate at which (and the way in which) faces age never ceases to fascinate me. Some friends I had not seen for 50 years were instantly recognizable. Their ages are, of course, in their faces, but the passage of time has not substantially altered their basic physiognomy: Time has just slapped some wrinkles on. Other old friends have changed literally beyond recognition (and not, incidentally, always for the worse).

7   It is well known that women suffer more than men from the ravages of time. When my wife went back to her high school's 50th reunion there was not a single feminine face that she recognized, and her closest friends failed to recognize her. On the other hand, she recognized a number of the "boys."

8   Some phases of age make their mark far more deeply on us than others. The physical manifestations of aging are not steady or even: They go, more commonly, by fits and starts. There seems to be heavy aging in the late 50s or early 60s, then a kind of steady state for a decade or so, then an accelerated crumbling—always, as I have noted, allowing for minor reversals of the process and little flare-ups of youthful vitality.

9   Be that all as it may, familiar and beloved old faces are a consolation in old age. As, of course, are familiar and beloved young faces.

10   Then there are things—the accumulation of a lifetime, some of which are, to be sure, merely burdensome, more like unshriven sins than charming consolations. But things, finally, may be the most important elements of all. They are the objects, in the main, that we hold in our hands and that have a special potency for us, hallowed by continual use.

11   They can be as modest as a stone that nestles in the hand or as rare as a jeweled pin passed down through several generations, a piece of crystal, a hand-thrown bowl whose shape gives a kind of visceral pleasure, a tool or tools (I recall especially the beautiful tools of a deceased friend, Hugh DeLacey, who was a skilled carpenter as well as a devoted servant of the public good).

12   My wife has a battered aluminum mixing bowl. Cookie and bread and pie dough beyond calculating have had their origin in its concave form. It has a decided presence and evokes tastes and memories that no new vessel could rival. I suspect she would sooner give me up than the mixing bowl.

13   I cherish a bamboo fly-rod. To be sure, I use a lighter and stronger graphite rod nowadays, but the old bamboo rod is an icon. It serves to remind me of the days when trout fishing was trout fishing, rather than the frantic pursuit of a constantly diminishing stock of fish, many of whom have been caught and released so often that they come to the net with the expression of weary demimondes servicing another john.

14   Strangely, perhaps, I do not worry about our children or grandchildren when we are gone. They, I trust, will do well enough without us. Ideally, though they may miss us and find us sometimes in their dreams and wake with a sense of loss and disappointment as we do with our parents, they will also be released from being our children to being our successors.

15   So they will do well enough. But what about our poor motherless things, orphans too numerous to be absorbed by our progeny? They will have to go off into the world seeking new owners, or in the case of battered old kitchen utensils, consignment to a public dump or a dusty second-hand store in some tenderloin district.

16   And yet for us they were art and magic.

17   Like places and spaces and faces, things are often torn from us by the circumstances of old age long before death; we are often left without our comforters at the time when we need them most. Do we sufficiently attend to this sobering fact? Of course not. This is not our way of thinking in this enlightened age. Kind souls hustle us off to "homes," where we get "professional care," but who needs professional care when the soul languishes and the fires die?

■   EXPLODED VIEW FOR STUDY

Each of the highlighted words should be mastered in the following exercises.

Places, Faces and Things

Coming of age

Page Smith

1   When you get old, familiar places, spaces and faces are a particular comfort. And familiar things. Yet it is often just these consolations that are withdrawn from us when we are old.

2   A beloved place collects associations in layers of sights and sounds and scents—the way the expiring sun catches the tops of redwood trees and filters down through the madrones; the sudden harmonious song of amorous tree frogs, crickets' chorus and the forlorn hoot of an owl; the smell of the pasture after rain—even the odor of steaming horse manure.

3   And then the memories. Above all, the memories, of gatherings of friends and family, the anniversaries, weddings, Christmases, Easters and Thanksgivings. Through such sanctifying occasions the spirit of a place becomes palpable, holy.

4   Spaces are mostly interiors (although there may be a magical redwood cathedral, a sun-drenched deck or patio). Interior spaces become so familiar that one can find one's way about on the blackest night. The hand reaches unerringly for the doorknob, or the light switch, or the refrigerator handle with the confidence born of many nocturnal ramblings. Feet move slowly but surely on stairs and floors.

5   Faces. One searches them for signs of aging, reassured to note that the inevitable tracery of wrinkles still lies lightly. Sometimes we are surprised to observe that a familiar old face suddenly looks younger and brighter, more vivid, as though from a sudden pulse of life, perhaps the visit of a child or grandchild or an old friend. Or, more mundanely, a stiff shot of bourbon.

6   The rate at which (and the way in which) faces age never ceases to fascinate me. Some friends I had not seen for 50 years were instantly recognizable. Their ages are, of course, in their faces, but the passage of time has not substantially altered their basic physiognomy: Time has just slapped some wrinkles on. Other old friends have changed literally beyond recognition (and not, incidentally, always for the worse).

7   It is well known that women suffer more than men from the ravages of time. When my wife went back to her high school's 50th reunion there was not a single feminine face that she recognized, and her closest friends failed to recognize her. On the other hand, she recognized a number of the "boys."

8   Some phases of age make their mark far more deeply on us than others. The physical manifestations of aging are not steady or even: They go, more commonly, by fits and starts. There seems to be heavy aging in the late 50s or early 60s, then a kind of steady state for a decade or so, then an accelerated crumbling—always, as I have noted, allowing for minor reversals of the process and little flare-ups of youthful vitality.

9   Be that all as it may, familiar and beloved old faces are a consolation in old age. As, of course, are familiar and beloved young faces.

10   Then there are things—the accumulation of a lifetime, some of which are, to be sure, merely burdensome, more like unshriven sins than charming consolations. But things, finally, may be the most important elements of all. They are the objects, in the main, that we hold in our hands and that have a special potency for us, hallowed by continual use.

11   They can be as modest as a stone that nestles in the hand or as rare as a jeweled pin passed down through several generations, a piece of crystal, a hand-thrown bowl whose shape gives a kind of visceral pleasure, a tool or tools (I recall especially the beautiful tools of a deceased friend, Hugh DeLacey, who was a skilled carpenter as well as a devoted servant of the public good).

12   My wife has a battered aluminum mixing bowl. Cookie and bread and pie dough beyond calculating have had their origin in its concave form. It has a decided presence and evokes tastes and memories that no new vessel could rival. I suspect she would sooner give me up than the mixing bowl.

13   I cherish a bamboo fly-rod. To be sure, I use a lighter and stronger graphite rod nowadays, but the old bamboo rod is an icon. It serves to remind me of the days when trout fishing was trout fishing, rather than the frantic pursuit of a constantly diminishing stock of fish, many of whom have been caught and released so often that they come to the net with the expression of weary demimondes servicing another john.

14   Strangely, perhaps, I do not worry about our children or

grandchildren when we are gone. They, I trust, will do well enough without us. Ideally, though they may miss us and find us sometimes in their dreams and wake with a sense of loss and disappointment as we do with our parents, they will also be released from being our children to being our successors.

15   So they will do well enough. But what about our poor mother-less things, orphans too numerous to be absorbed by our progeny? They will have to go off into the world seeking new owners, or in the case of battered old kitchen utensils, consignment to a public dump or a dusty second-hand store in some tenderloin district.

16   And yet for us they were art and magic.

17   Like places and spaces and faces, things are often torn from us by the circumstances of old age long before death; we are often left without our comforters at the time when we need them most. Do we sufficiently attend to this sobering fact? Of course not. This is not our way of thinking in this enlightened age. Kind souls hustle us off to "homes," where we get "professional care," but who needs professional care when the soul languishes and the fires die?

■   READING COMPREHENSION QUESTIONS

1.   While some of his friends were instantly recognizable after he had not seen them for half a century, Professor Smith found other friends to have changed (a) slightly more (b) through cosmetic surgery (c) beyond recognition (d) only about the eyes and mouth

2.   Among the objects, the "things," of great emotional value to the author himself, is one particularly cherished item, a (a) photograph of the author with President Franklin Delano Roosevelt (b) "Shoeless" Joe Jackson baseball card (c) sled named "Rosebud" (d) bamboo fly-rod

3.   Professor Smith says that many years of memories render objects very precious to their owners and eventually give the objects a special emotional (a) let-down (b) potency (c) reaction (d) disinterest

4.   His wife's battered aluminum mixing bowl has "a decided presence" to it which is so strong, the author suggests, that—rather than part with the bowl—she would sooner give up (a) him (b) her auto-graphed 8 × 10 photograph of Douglas Fairbanks, Jr. (c) all of her Bessie Smith albums (d) her framed Diego Rivera prints

5.   Professor Smith finds the rate at which, and the ways in which, faces age to be endless sources of (a) fascination (b) disinterested curiosity (c) personal relevance (d) useful column material

6.   When he and his wife are gone, the author does not worry about their children, who will then become the "successors"; he worries instead about (a) their many pets (b) what will happen to the home in which they have lived for many years (c) who will care for their garden (d) their poor motherless things

■   TARGET VOCABULARY

harmonious	**inevitable**	**hallowed**
to sanctify	**vivid**	**to evoke**
palpable	**mundane**	**icon**
unerringly	**physiognomy**	**progeny**
nocturnal	**to accumulate**	**sobering**

Dictionary Practice

Use each word in a sentence of your own.

1.   harmonious _____

2.   to sanctify _____

3.   palpable _____

4.   unerringly _____

5.   nocturnal _____

6.   inevitable _____

7.   vivid _____

8.   mundane _____

9.   physiognomy _____

10.   to accumulate _____

11.   hallowed _____

12.   to evoke _____

13.   icon _____

14. progeny _____

15. sobering _____

Cloze Practice

Fill in each blank with an appropriate word from the target vocabulary list.

The aging process is _____. One's _____ changes, often in _____ and _____ ways, and the _____ reality of death _____ focuses our thoughts on what is truly precious and valuable. Professor Smith suggests that the objects we _____ as we age can be considered _____ only by those unaware that the objects have been _____ by time, love, and life.

■ CRITICAL READING PRACTICE/TOPICS FOR DISCUSSION

1.   Do you have a relative or acquaintance of any age who is particularly attached to some object? If so, why do you think he or she has become so fond of the item in question? Have you ever been especially attached to some object or possession?

2.   Does Professor Smith's essay give you new insights into aging and into the relationships between aging and "places, spaces, and faces," as well as "things"? Explain.

3.   Has a relative or friend who died left you or somebody else any object of special importance? Describe the object, and explain why you believe it came to have special significance for the people involved.

4.   Many people believe, to greater or lesser extents, in "ghosts," a term they generally use to refer to spirits or souls of the dead that are able to interact with the living. Do you think there could be any connection between Professor Smith's "things," the "accumulations of a lifetime," and the feeling people may have when they sense the presence of someone who has died?

5.   If you don't believe in ghosts or spirits, why do you think that so many people in so many times and places have constructed such elaborate traditions and rituals relating to them? Is this some universal myth? Is this some personal wish for immortality? Explain.

■ *The Golden Apples of the Sun*

This section focuses the power of a personal vision. All of us have general objectives in life: happiness, perhaps a career in some field of interest, perhaps a family, maybe some service we wish to perform.

But some people have very particular goals, quite specific in nature: climbing a certain mountain, understanding radiation, figuring out how living things change over time. Such people—like Edmund Hillary, Marie Curie, or Charles Darwin—serve as models for us all and reminders that dedication often produces wonders.

As you read and discuss the following pieces, you might begin by asking if such dedication might be considered a wonder in itself.

■ PRE-READING FOR DISCUSSION

For thousands of years people all over the world have been obsessed by gold. They have crossed oceans and mountains, betrayed families and friends, murdered and prayed, all to possess gold.

For the rings of our loved ones and the temples of our gods, nothing less would do.

This history of humanity's relationship with gold makes Tomoyuki Mizuno, whom we meet in the next article, quite a remarkable man. If he finds the lost golden treasure of the Japanese shoguns (*shogun* is usually translated as "warlord"), he plans to give most of it away to the people of Japan: about one *trillion* dollars altogether, a little over $9,000 for every Japanese citizen. (This is two-thirds the estimated value of the gold Mr. Mizuno is seeking.)

For over a century, the Mizuno family has been searching for the buried Tokugawa treasure, named for Ieyasu Tokugawa, founder of the shogun dynasty in 1603. Three generations of the Mizuno family have been exploring an area north of Tokyo since 1887, carrying out the deathbed command of the first-generation Mizuno's stepfather. But the search is not really about gold; it's about honor.

The Mizuno family are *samurai,* the ancient warrior class of Japanese society. Traditionally, samurai follow the strict code of *bushido,* which treats promises and assigned tasks with sometimes frightening seriousness. Given the job of unearthing the gold in 1866, the family is still at it and presumably will be as long as a Mizuno can use a shovel or puzzle over cryptic clues.

Because the gold came from the earth originally, was reburied in order to hide it, may be dug up again, and then "buried" once more in a bank vault, Tomoyuki Mizuno seems to have his priorities in perfect order: gold might be valuable, but honor is priceless.

Good hunting, Mr. Mizuno.

A Samurai Family's Golden Obsession

Eugene Moosa

1   AKAGI, JAPAN   Engraved maps, cryptic parchment and a golden statue have kept a Japanese samurai family digging for a treasure trove for three generations. The prize could be among the world's richest treasures—the entire stash of gold ingots of the Tokugawa shoguns, feudal overlords who ruled Japan for 265 years until 1868.

2   Nobody really knows how much gold could be waiting to be discovered. Some historians estimate its value at $1.5 trillion.

3   Since 1887, the Mizuno family, whose ancestor worked in the shogun treasury, has been searching for the gold under the barren slopes of Mount Akagi, about 60 miles north of Tokyo.

4   "The gold originally belonged to the Japanese people," said Tomoyuki Mizuno, in his 60s and third in a line of gold-hunters.

5   "So, if I find it, I promise to give every Japanese man, woman and child 1.2 million yen ($9,200), if the larger estimate is true," he said.

6   Last June, after more than a century of fruitless hunting, Mizuno discovered the biggest clue yet—an astonishing labyrinth of tunnels right beneath his own back yard.

7   The passageways, built on at least three levels, run deep under shallow pits first dug in 1887 by his grandfather, Tomoyoshi Mizuno.

8   "The three-tiered tunnels we found this summer could have only been dug by those who originally buried the treasure," Mizuno said in an interview at the site. "I was really excited."

9   Pieces of 150-year-old tableware, cooking knives and lanterns were discovered inside the tunnels, more than 60 feet underground. They were similar in construction to those found in 19th century copper mines dug by convicts.

10   That discovery was thanks to the Tokyo Broadcasting System network, which has featured Mizuno's gold hunt in its program "Give Me a Break." It supplied Mizuno with three power shovels and a 53-man crew.

11   When he began in 1887, grandfather Mizuno encountered all the hallmarks of a classic treasure hunt—mysterious deaths, anagrams and other cryptic clues planted to fool the uninitiated. The stepfather of the original Mizuno was Kurando Nakajima, an official at the shogun treasury. On his deathbed he passed to Mizuno the task of unearthing the gold at the Akagi site.

12   Grandfather Mizuno sold all his Tokyo property and a flourishing real estate business to buy land in Akagi. Building his house there, he soon unearthed an eight-inch golden statue of Ieyasu Tokugawa, founder of the shogun dynasty. He also discovered three bronze plates under a nearby Buddhist temple that were inscribed with vague directions and a map showing the gold's purported hiding place.

13   Later he met the last surviving official who took part in the operation to bury the treasury gold. Before his death, the official gave Mizuno a scroll with details of the burial, written in a cryptic Chinese language.

14   Like other treasure troves, this story starts with the downfall of a dynasty—the Tokugawa shoguns. After the shogun ended Japan's self-imposed isolation in 1854, his chief adviser, Lord Ii, feared a vast outflow of gold from Japan, where the monetary ratio of silver to gold was then 5 to 1, compared with 15 to 1 elsewhere in the world.

15   Foreign merchants, diplomats and even sailors took advantage of this huge difference to make fortunes by exchanging their silver coins for Japanese gold ones. Lord Ii planned to deposit the gold ingots, originally placed in the keep of the Edo castle, now Tokyo's Imperial Palace, in a secret underground tunnel north of the capital. But Lord Ii was assassinated, and the burial plan did not materialize until 1866 when Kozukenosuke Oguri, the shogun's top financial official, secretly moved the gold to Akagi.

16   Hundreds of death-row convicts were mobilized to dig the tunnels and were then beheaded, ostensibly for their crimes, but possibly because they knew where the treasure lay. Oguri's plan was to hide the gold for future use when the shogunate could fight back against the imperial forces. But, in the mid-1860s, the shogun lost a series of battles and in 1868 surrendered the reins of government to Emperor Meiji.

17   Storming into the empty Edo castle, the emperor's generals found nothing in its vast keep. By the time grandfather Mizuno started looking for the gold, there was no longer any possibility of the shogun returning to power. It then became an obsession for him, later his two sons and now his grandson to find the gold.

18   "It's no longer just curiosity or single-mindedness," said grandson Mizuno, when asked about the family obsession. "It's a question of honor and my ability as a samurai to decipher the scroll, and whether or not the heavens will allow me to find the gold."

■ **EXPLODED VIEW FOR STUDY**

Each of the highlighted words should be mastered in the following exercises.

A Samurai Family's Golden Obsession

Eugene Moosa

1   AKAGI, JAPAN   Engraved maps, cryptic parchment and a golden statue have kept a Japanese samurai family digging for a treasure trove for three generations. The prize could be among the world's richest treasures—the entire stash of gold ingots of the Tokugawa shoguns, feudal overlords who ruled Japan for 265 years until 1868.

2   Nobody really knows how much gold could be waiting to be discovered. Some historians estimate its value at $1.5 trillion.

3   Since 1887, the Mizuno family, whose ancestor worked in the shogun treasury, has been searching for the gold under the barren slopes of Mount Akagi, about 60 miles north of Tokyo.

4   "The gold originally belonged to the Japanese people," said To-moyuki Mizuno, in his 60s and third in a line of gold-hunters.

5   "So, if I find it, I promise to give every Japanese man, woman and child 1.2 million yen ($9,200), if the larger estimate is true," he said.

6   Last June, after more than a century of fruitless hunting, Mizuno discovered the biggest clue yet—an astonishing labyrinth of tunnels right beneath his own back yard.

7   The passageways, built on at least three levels, run deep under shallow pits first dug in 1887 by his grandfather, Tomoyoshi Mizuno.

8   "The three-tiered tunnels we found this summer could have only been dug by those who originally buried the treasure," Mizuno said in an interview at the site. "I was really excited."

9   Pieces of 150-year-old tableware, cooking knives and lanterns were discovered inside the tunnels, more than 60 feet underground. They were similar in construction to those found in 19th century copper mines dug by convicts.

10   That discovery was thanks to the Tokyo Broadcasting System network, which has featured Mizuno's gold hunt in its program "Give Me a Break." It supplied Mizuno with three power shovels and a 53-man crew.

11   When he began in 1887, grandfather Mizuno encountered all the hallmarks of a classic treasure hunt—mysterious deaths, anagrams and other cryptic clues planted to fool the uninitiated. The stepfather of the original Mizuno was Kurando Nakajima, an official at the shogun treasury. On his deathbed he passed to Mizuno the task of unearthing the gold at the Akagi site.

12   Grandfather Mizuno sold all his Tokyo property and a flourishing real estate business to buy land in Akagi. Building his house there, he soon unearthed an eight-inch golden statue of Ieyasu Tokugawa, founder of the shogun dynasty. He also discovered three bronze plates under a nearby Buddhist temple that were inscribed with vague directions and a map showing the gold's purported hiding place.

13   Later he met the last surviving official who took part in the op-

eration to bury the treasury gold. Before his death, the official gave Mizuno a scroll with details of the burial, written in a cryptic Chinese language.

14   Like other treasure troves, this story starts with the downfall of a dynasty—the Tokugawa shoguns. After the shogun ended Japan's self-imposed isolation in 1854, his chief adviser, Lord Ii, feared a vast outflow of gold from Japan, where the monetary ratio of silver to gold was then 5 to 1, compared with 15 to 1 elsewhere in the world.

15   Foreign merchants, diplomats and even sailors took advantage of this huge difference to make fortunes by exchanging their silver coins for Japanese gold ones. Lord Ii planned to deposit the gold ingots, originally placed in the keep of the Edo castle, now Tokyo's Imperial Palace, in a secret underground tunnel north of the capital. But Lord Ii was assassinated, and the burial plan did not materialize until 1866 when Kozukenosuke Oguri, the shogun's top financial official, secretly moved the gold to Akagi.

16   Hundreds of death-row convicts were mobilized to dig the tunnels and were then beheaded, ostensibly for their crimes, but possibly because they knew where the treasure lay. Oguri's plan was to hide the gold for future use when the shogunate could fight back against the imperial forces. But, in the mid-1860s, the shogun lost a series of battles and in 1868 surrendered the reins of government to Emperor Meiji.

17   Storming into the empty Edo castle, the emperor's generals found nothing in its vast keep. By the time grandfather Mizuno started looking for the gold, there was no longer any possibility of the shogun returning to power. It then became an obsession for him, later his two sons and now his grandson to find the gold.

18   "It's no longer just curiosity or single-mindedness," said grandson Mizuno, when asked about the family obsession. "It's a question of honor and my ability as a samurai to decipher the scroll, and whether or not the heavens will allow me to find the gold."

■ READING COMPREHENSION QUESTIONS

1. For generations the Mizuno family has been carefully excavating sections of their family's property about 60 miles north of (a) Osaka (b) Kyoto (c) Tokyo (d) Nara

2. Foreign sailors and merchants made huge fortunes in Japan by trading in gold and silver during the 19th century. They were able to amass enormous amounts of money because of the 3-to-1 difference between the international and Japanese (a) languages (b) methods of transportation (c) governmental organization (d) exchange rates for precious metals

3. The Mizuno quest was greatly assisted by power shovels and a 53-man crew provided by (a) the United Nations (b) a Japanese television network (c) Lee Iacocca (d) the Puccini Foundation

4. The Tokugawa shogunate's treasure was originally hidden in Edo Castle (now the Imperial Palace in Tokyo) and was intended at the time to finance (a) the industrialization of 19th-century Japanese industry (b) a rapid modernization of Japan's transportation and communications systems (c) a secret tunnel connecting the islands of Honshu and Hokkaido (d) an uprising against the emperor and the imperial military forces

5. After a century of exploration, the Mizuno family finally discovered a significant clue that they may be on the right track when they found (a) metal plates engraved with burial diagrams (b) strongboxes of the type used by the shogun (c) a labyrinth of tunnels like those used in secret burials (d) Lee Iacocca in a *yukata* robe

6. For over a hundred years the quest to discover the treasure has been slowed because many of the most important and useful written clues have been transcribed in (a) doublespeak (b) Middle English (c) cryptic ideographic script (d) Urdu

■ TARGET VOCABULARY

trove	**fruitless**	**purported**
ingot	**labyrinth**	**scroll**
feudal	**tier**	**dynasty**
ancestor	**uninitiated**	**ratio**
barren	**to flourish**	**to decipher**

Dictionary Practice

Use each word in a sentence of your own.

1. trove _____

2. ingot _____

3. feudal _____

4. ancestor _____

5. barren _____

6. fruitless _____

7. labyrinth _____

8. tier _____

9. uninitiated _____

10. to flourish _____

11. purported _____

12. scroll _____

13. dynasty _____

14. ratio _____

15. to decipher _____

Cloze Practice

Fill in each blank with an appropriate word from the target vocabulary list.

In _____ societies, a powerful family can establish a _____ which may _____ for many generations. Such ancestral "rights" to govern have historically unified societies. Recorded on ancient _____, discovered in buried treasure _____ hidden within complex _____ or beneath many _____ of cleverly engineered stone, these _____ family histories are fascinating. Sometimes the records must be _____ by scholars, and occasionally efforts to understand them prove _____; but the success-to-failure

_____ is high, and such scholars consistently amaze us all with their ingenious work.

◼ CRITICAL READING PRACTICE/TOPICS FOR DISCUSSION

1.   The Mizuno family is said to have an "obsession" with finding the lost gold of the Mizuno shoguns. Do you have knowledge of anyone who could be described as "obsessed" with something? If so, what is the obsession and how do you feel about the person's attitude toward it?

2.   Having read the article, do you think that the gold is really down there where the family thinks it is? If so, why do you think that it has not yet been discovered? If not, how do you explain the objects and tunnels unearthed in the excavations?

3.   To what extent do you consider the stepfather (Nakajima Kurando) of the original Mizuno samurai responsible for the family's three-generations-and-counting quest to find the Tokugawa gold? If the stepfather made the quest "a matter of honor" to his stepson, can the search ever end until the treasure is found?

4.   It has been said that greed (actually "wanting too much") is the source of all evil. Based upon your evidence, do you agree or disagree with this general principle, and why do you feel as you do? Do you think that greed is playing any part in the Mizuno's quest? Explain.

5.   Since the money is not technically theirs, should the Mizuno family eventually find the estimated 1.5 trillion dollars they plan to (a) invest it in Hawaiian real estate (b) build a museum on the Akagi burial site (c) trade in precious metals for old times' sake (d) give most of it away to total strangers

◼ *Reaching Again into the Power of Music*

Since Plato's time, the ability of music to influence society has been acknowledged and hotly debated. Many generations, in many places, have considered the popular music of their time to be a primary cause of moral and social deterioration.

At one time, waltzes caused riots, jazz was thought to promote drug abuse, and swing bands were blamed for promiscuity. More recently, rock has

been criticized as leading to all three, and heavy metal has been said to promote Satanism.

The following pre-reading essay and news article are concerned with this power of music, the censorship that results, and the art of Jamaican poet Muta-baruka. As you read and discuss these pieces, focus on comparisons between censorship of music in the United States and elsewhere in the world, including Jamaica.

■ PRE-READING FOR DISCUSSION

The poetry and music of Mutabaruka has had a powerful, revolutionary effect on the government and the broadcasting industry in his homeland of Jamaica.

Mutabaruka, whose name means "one who is always victorious," writes on themes that have historically made the wealthy and powerful uneasy: poverty, injustice, hypocrisy, racism, and, most disturbing of all, freedom and equality. He also stresses the importance of African traditions for black artists, regardless of those artists' own present-day homelands.

Muta, as he is called, refers in the following article to "world-beat" music ("I prefer to call it black music, y'know"), by which he means the common traditions of American jazz, African and Brazilian music, and reggae. In an age when MTV is almost universal, the term "world-beat" seems especially appropriate.

Also mentioned in the article is Muta's Rastafari religion, which he briefly explains: "It move away from that thinking of making God an elusive God. It make you aware of God in man, rather than God coming out of the sky. . . . God is in man and man cannot love God without him love man."

There is a "world-beat" in those words, which sound rather like the message of that dangerous young rabbi from Nazareth to whom Muta refers in the brief quote from one of his song's lyrics.

Mutabaruka's album *Blakk Wi Blak,* recorded in the United States, may be upsetting to the government of Jamaica, but it is a treasure for the rest of us. When coupled with his poems, read in schools and libraries all over his country and increasingly throughout the world, Muta's art is from the heart of a man who is going to be heard—in spite of government or anything else.

(Note, by the way, the slash marks used in the lyrics in this article: "I am de man/ locks entangled in your nightmares of medusas and gorgons/ unkept religious beliefs/ that pierce. . . ." The slashes indicate the original line endings and allow us to write poetry, song lyrics, or sometimes lines from drama, in a more convenient form.)

Muta's Poetry Stirs Up the Pot

Government upset over political content of Jamaican's new album

Jeff Kaliss

1   Jamaican performance poet Mutabaruka looks forward to visiting the Bay Area, where he can get fresh tofu and nuts at the Berkeley Farmers Market and otherwise feel at home.

2   "That's where we get the biggest audience, really," he notes by phone from a hotel in Springfield, Mo. "Maybe it's because of the thinking of the people on that side of America. . . . It is more musical and political, more conducive to what I am doing."

3   Born Allan Hope in 1953, Muta (he uses a shortened version of his stage name, borrowed from the Kinyarwanda language) speaks in a sonorous, clipped English that transforms "thinking" into "tinkin'." Back home in Kingston, he operates his own health food store and restaurant, along with a bookstore that features his poetry and other written works of black consciousness.

4   His current American tour follows the release of his fifth album on the New Jersey-based Shanachie label, titled "Blakk Wi Blakk." Jamaican radio promptly refused to air one track, "The People's Court," in which an angry Judge "Betta Mus Com" (Muta), with a bubbling reggae chorus and rhythm section behind him, presides over the trial of the current and previous prime ministers (impersonated by actor Gary Saddler) for "sellin' out black people to foreigners."

5   "They said it was libelous," Muta said, laughing. "But the names were changed to protect the 'innocent.' . . . My music is not promoted on the airwaves, because it is seen as upsetting the Jamaican society. It is not seen as the pop reggae."

6   Politically, Muta's messages are more evocative of the reggae of the '70s, when he was in high school and beginning to evolve from his Catholic upbringing to the Rastafari faith of the Kingston ghettos. "Rastafari is the obvious thing outside of the normal Christian thing," he explains. "It move away from that thinking of making God an elusive God. It make you aware of God in man, rather than God coming out of the sky."

7   It also made the budding poet realize "that Africa is very important to the advancement and survival of black people everywhere in the world." While perusing an anthology of African writers, he came across a poem by Jean Batiste of the central African country of Rwanda, who had assumed the name Mutabaruka, meaning "one who is always victorious."

8   "It was very nearly identical to a poem that I wrote, and I found it very strange," Muta muses. "It was great. I was writing like a poet so far away. So the name struck me as a name I should take."

9   The young Muta also absorbed the influence of Malcolm X, Eldridge Cleaver and the Black Panther movement. His own first poems were published during the '70s in Swing, a Jamaican music magazine, and he shared them at community gatherings.

10   But "reading poetry was not really a people thing." With the encouragement of guitarist/producer Earl (Chinna) Smith, Muta recorded his first album in 1981 on Alligator, a Chicago blues label. "I'm not really a musician," he stresses. "I just use the music to bring out musically what the poetry is dealing with."

11   As with all his succeeding albums,

"Blakk Wi Blakk" faces down a variety of issues in a variety of reggae tempi, with creative support from guitar, keyboards, sax and percussion. "We see a neocolonialism taking place, which instead of British, it's really American now," Muta points out. "Jamaica is now run by American investors . . . with junk food and drugs and all the things that combine to make America a healthy place."

12 Some of the album's song titles—"Junk Food" and "Ecology Poem"—are self-explanatory. The lyrics, mainly spoken by Muta, are energized by his searing insight and poetic skill: "I am de man/ locks entangled in your nightmares of medusas and gorgons/ unkept religious beliefs/ that pierce the side of your Jesus in the sky/ your vinegar has turned to blood."

13 "Dispel the Lie" works against the dissolute image created by many reggae performers. "The first thing they tell you about is, 'Light up a spliff, blow your brain with ganga,' " Muta laments. "My poem is trying to just say that Rastafari is much more than smoking marijuana . . . that God is in man and man cannot love God without him love man."

14 As for Muta himself, "I never smoke it yet, y' know, and I don't intend to start. In Jamaica, we have Rastas who been smoking it for years. I don't see it as a negative effect on them." The real drug problems are imported from America, as addressed in his "Letter to Congress": "Now wi gettin u coke and crack/ I wonder/ Is it because wi blakk."

15 Another of his targets is tourism. "It is like whorism, really, the people prostituting themselves for the Yankee dollar," he believes. "It is a situation where the minority run the business, and the profit of the business go back to the pockets of the mi-

nority. . . . It is not really going back to the people, y' know."

16 For his musical inspiration, Muta listens "to a lot of what they call world-beat music. I prefer to call it black music, y' know: from Africa, Brazil, and the old American jazz and things."

17 As a teenager, he'd already been exposed to the best of American exports, Miles Davis and Thelonious Monk on the jazz side and Curtis Mayfield on the pop side. More recently, he's espoused Nigeria's Fela, Mali's Salif Keita, South Africa's Hugh Masekela and Brazil's Milton Nascimento.

18 "They are trying to come to grips with themselves and the tradition," he says of these artists. "You hear the struggle of the people coming out, and their sentiments. This is very similar to what the older type of reggae artists used to sing about."

19 Although he does not consider himself a star of reggae or the raplike Jamaican dub, Muta believes these genres "express the true and genuine feeling of the Jamaican people" and are "the most influential thing musically that is taking place in the world right now."

20 At home, Muta hopes that reggae will help carry his invectives into "the consciousness and the conscience" of his own people, who are hamstrung by an entrenched and unsympathetic two-party political system that more and more mirrors the American model. His collected poems, a beloved standard in schools and libraries, urge Jamaicans to seek inspiration in such revolutionary black leaders as Marcus Garvey, "instead of trying to find out about socialism and communism and capitalism and all these 'isms' that have still not helped the majority."

■ **EXPLODED VIEW FOR STUDY**

Each of the highlighted words should be mastered in the following exercises.

Muta's Poetry Stirs Up the Pot

Government upset over political content of Jamaican's new album

Jeff Kaliss

1   Jamaican performance poet Mutabaruka looks forward to visiting the Bay Area, where he can get fresh tofu and nuts at the Berkeley Farmers Market and otherwise feel at home.

2   "That's where we get the biggest audience, really," he notes by phone from a hotel in Springfield, Mo. "Maybe it's because of the thinking of the people on that side of America. . . . It is more musical and political, more conducive to what I am doing."

3   Born Allan Hope in 1953, Muta (he uses a shortened version of his stage name, borrowed from the Kinyarwanda language) speaks in a sonorous, clipped English that transforms "thinking" into "tinkin'." Back home in Kingston, he operates his own health food store and restaurant, along with a bookstore that features his poetry and other written works of black consciousness.

4   His current American tour follows the release of his fifth album on the New Jersey-based Shanachie label, titled "Blakk Wi Blakk." Jamaican radio promptly refused to air one track, "The People's Court," in which an angry Judge "Betta Mus Com" (Muta), with a bubbling reggae chorus and rhythm section behind him, presides over the trial of the current and previous prime ministers (impersonated by actor Gary Saddler) for "sellin' out black people to foreigners."

5   "They said it was libelous," Muta said, laughing. "But the names were changed to protect the 'innocent.' . . . My music is not promoted on the airwaves, because it is seen as upsetting the Jamaican society. It is not seen as the pop reggae."

6   Politically, Muta's messages are more evocative of the reggae of the '70s, when he was in high school and beginning to evolve from his Catholic upbringing to the Rastafari faith of the Kingston ghettos. "Rastafari is the obvious thing outside of the normal Christian thing," he explains. "It move away from that thinking of making God an elusive God. It make you aware of God in man, rather than God coming out of the sky."

7   It also made the budding poet realize "that Africa is very important to the advancement and survival of black people everywhere in the world." While perusing an anthology of African writers, he came across a poem by Jean Batiste of the central African country of Rwanda, who had assumed the name Mutabaruka, meaning "one who is always victorious."

8   "It was very nearly identical to a poem that I wrote, and I found it very strange," Muta muses. "It was great. I was writing like a poet so far away. So the name struck me as a name I should take."

9   The young Muta also absorbed the influence of Malcolm X, Eldridge Cleaver and the Black Panther movement. His own first poems were published during the '70s in Swing, a Jamaican music magazine, and he shared them at community gatherings.

10   But "reading poetry was not really a people thing." With the encouragement of guitarist/producer Earl (Chinna) Smith, Muta recorded his first album in 1981 on Alligator, a Chicago blues label. "I'm not really a musician," he stresses. "I just use the music to bring out musically what the poetry is dealing with."

11   As with all his succeeding albums, "Blakk Wi Blakk" faces down a variety of issues in a variety of reggae tempi, with creative support from guitar, keyboards, sax and percussion. "We see a neocolonialism taking place, which instead of British, it's really American now," Muta points out. "Jamaica is now run by American investors . . . with junk food and drugs and all the things that combine to make America a healthy place."

12   Some of the album's song titles—"Junk Food" and "Ecology Poem"—are self-explanatory. The lyrics, mainly spoken by Muta,

are energized by his searing insight and poetic skill: "I am de man/ locks entangled in your nightmares of medusas and gorgons/ unkept religious beliefs/ that pierce the side of your Jesus in the sky/ your vinegar has turned to blood."

13   "Dispel the Lie" works against the dissolute image created by many reggae performers. "The first thing they tell you about is, 'Light up a spliff, blow your brain with ganga,'" Muta laments. "My poem is trying to just say that Rastafari is much more than smoking marijuana . . . that God is in man and man cannot love God without him love man."

14   As for Muta himself, "I never smoke it yet, y' know, and I don't intend to start. In Jamaica, we have Rastas who been smoking it for years. I don't see it as a negative effect on them." The real drug problems are imported from America, as addressed in his "Letter to Congress": "Now wi gettin u coke and crack/ I wonder/ Is it because wi blakk."

15   Another of his targets is tourism. "It is like whorism, really, the people prostituting themselves for the Yankee dollar," he believes. "It is a situation where the minority run the business, and the profit of the business go back to the pockets of the minority. . . . It is not really going back to the people, y' know."

16   For his musical inspiration, Muta listens "to a lot of what they call world-beat music. I prefer to call it black music, y' know: from Africa, Brazil, and the old American jazz and things."

17   As a teenager, he'd already been exposed to the best of American exports, Miles Davis and Thelonious Monk on the jazz side and Curtis Mayfield on the pop side. More recently, he's espoused Nigeria's Fela, Mali's Salif Keita, South Africa's Hugh Masekela and Brazil's Milton Nascimento.

18   "They are trying to come to grips with themselves and the tradition," he says of these artists. "You hear the struggle of the people coming out, and their sentiments. This is very similar to what the older type of reggae artists used to sing about."

19   Although he does not consider himself a star of reggae or the rap-

like Jamaican dub, Muta believes these genres "express the true and
genuine feeling of the Jamaican people" and are "the most influential
thing musically that is taking place in the world right now."

20   At home, Muta hopes that reggae will help carry his invectives
into "the consciousness and the conscience" of his own people, who
are hamstrung by an entrenched and unsympathetic two-party political system that more and more mirrors the American model. His
collected poems, a beloved standard in schools and libraries, urge Jamaicans to seek inspiration in such revolutionary black leaders as
Marcus Garvey, "instead of trying to find out about socialism and
communism and capitalism and all these 'isms' that have still not
helped the majority."

■ READING COMPREHENSION QUESTIONS

1.   Jamaican artist Mutabaruka feels more at home on the west coast
of the United States because (a) its conservative lifestyle closely
matches his own (b) he has many relatives there (c) his favorite health
foods are relatively inexpensive (d) he feels that he draws his most
sympathetic audiences there

2.   The name "Mutabaruka" was discovered and adopted by Muta
while reading the poetry of Jean Batiste of Ruwanda, who had also assumed the name. It means (a) "the one who makes great reggae"
(b) "he who can overcome political stupidity" (c) "health foods only"
(d) "one who is always victorious"

3.   The government of Jamaica censored Muta's song "The People's
Court" because it criticized (a) the ambassador from the United
States (b) foreign economic investments in Jamaica (c) former Jamai-
can prime ministers (d) the Rastafarian religion

4.   Speaking for many Jamaicans, Muta claims that the huge Jamaican
tourist industry is (a) the economic salvation of the island (b) an evil
force which hurts Jamaica's people (c) only the beginning of a much
larger influx of tourists (d) very good for local restaurants

5.   Being the owner of a health food store, Mutabaruka feels the
U.S. style "junk food" is (a) a tool of the devil (b) unhealthy and de-
structive (c) amusing (d) conducive to "bulking up" for athletic
events

6.   As a young and developing artist, the original "Allan Hope" listened and learned his craft from artists who were from (a) Senegal (b) South Africa (c) the United States (d) Nigeria

■   **TARGET VOCABULARY**

conducive	**anthology**	**dissolute**
to transform	**to absorb**	**to espouse**
prime minister	**neocolonialism**	**genres**
libelous	**self-explanatory**	**entrenched**
to evolve	**to dispel**	**inspiration**

Dictionary Practice

Use each word in a sentence of your own.

1. conducive _____

2. to transform _____

3. prime minister _____

4. libelous _____

5. to evolve _____

6. anthology _____

7. to absorb _____

8. neocolonialism _____

9. self-explanatory _____

_____

10. to dispel _____

11. dissolute _____

12. to espouse _____

13. genres _____

14. entrenched _____

15. inspiration _____

Cloze Practice

Fill in each blank with an appropriate word from the target vocabulary list.

Like other organisms, political systems can _____ into new forms and _____ new ideas as they grow. However, strongly _____ political forces sometimes resist such change. In fact, they sometimes even move backward to _____ and allow another country to control their economy. When the chief executive, often the _____, of such a country _____ this course of action, he or she can seek to _____ criticism by declaring it _____, or _____ to social unrest. Sooner or later, though, we like to believe that the people themselves can _____ the system and that growth can begin again.

■ CRITICAL READING PRACTICE/TOPICS FOR DISCUSSION

1. Based on your reading of the article, why do you think that Jamaican radio refused to play "The People's Court"? What relationship, if any, do you think exists between the Jamaican government and the radio station in question?

2. In your opinion, what do you think Mutabaruka means when he talks about "the struggle of the people" in Jamaica? Do you think that "the people" he refers to are the same "people" in every country or do they live only in Jamaica? Why do you feel as you do?

3. The "home country" is always the one that makes a profit, in one way or another, from its colonies (usually by importing raw materials and selling finished goods or by exploiting cheap labor). Since Jamaica has historically been associated politically with the United Kingdom, how can the "new colonialism" mentioned in the article involve the United States, as Muta says?

4. How do you feel about Muta's observation that "God is in man and man cannot love God without him love man"? Why do you feel as you do?

5.   "Medusas" and "gorgons" are mentioned in Muta's lyrics. What is your reaction to his use of classical and Christian imagery in his boldly Rastafarian poetry? Does it present a problem for the listener when his lyrics combine elements usually kept quite separate from each other? Why, or why not?

CHAPTER 4

The Science Section

"Being Dumped on," as Idiom and Fact

Environmental pollution is everybody's problem, but not everyone is forced to deal with the problem personally. The following article, "Toxics Often Dumped Where Minorities Live, Conference Told," raises very disturbing questions about who must deal with the most deadly forms of pollution and why.

As you read and discuss the introductory essay and article here, keep in mind that poor communities not populated largely by minorities have suffered the same fate in California, South Carolina, Missouri, and elsewhere. The problem of "environmental racism" is but one part of a larger issue in which social, political, and economic factors collide.

PRE-READING FOR DISCUSSION

As the world becomes more crowded, it becomes dirtier. And as it becomes dirtier, it becomes more dangerous. A *single* garbage incinerator in Florida is said to spew a ton of mercury and seven tons of lead into the atmosphere every year; and there are thousands of such incinerators across the country.

Although it is certainly a huge and growing problem, garbage isn't the only danger to the environment, and therefore to people. "Toxic wastes"—that is, the poisons produced in all sorts of ways by industry, mining, and the pesticides used in farming—are increasingly choking the air, earth, and water. Many forms of sealife (which used to be "seafood") can no longer be eaten, and warnings are common about the safety of freshwater fish, as well.

In fact, water itself, all around the world, is becoming so polluted that it is increasingly dangerous to the people who drink it. The air in many U.S. cities contributes directly to tens of thousands of respiratory diseases every year, many of them permanently damaging to the systems of children. The air of many cities in other countries is often much worse than in cities here; no one knows exactly what the consequences of those conditions might be, since they have not been monitored as closely, but the estimates are grim.

Perhaps worst of all, many of the state and federal agencies that are supposed to protect people from these poisons either cannot or will not do their jobs. The worst polluters make a lot of money by poisoning the earth, and this money quickly becomes political power. Because of the huge profits involved, those who dispose of garbage and toxics also have great political power and frequently prey on communities that are too weak to defend themselves and go undefended by others, as we see in the next article. This situation is particularly disgraceful when the communities are already the victims of economic and social discrimination and exploitation.

Whether such poisonings are defined as "legal" crimes or "moral" crimes or both, public debate tends to focus the issue in terms of two opposing sides. Eventually, however, the whole earth suffers, and every person and every organism will suffer along with it.

We should work hard to avoid that day; if it ever arrives, it will already be too late for any of us. What people have eaten and drunk and breathed for millions of years will be gone, and without those things, so will we.

Money won't mean very much then, to anybody.

Toxics Often Dumped Where Minorities Live, Conference Told

Cox News Service

1   WASHINGTON Sure, the petrochemical companies brought jobs to 80 miles of poverty between New Orleans and Baton Rouge, recalled Pat Bryant. But they also brought so much poisonous waste and early death that the black people who live there have dubbed the corridor "Cancer Alley."

2   Bryant is among some 600 leaders of grassroots groups who have assembled here for the First National People of Color Leadership Summit on the Environment.

3   They believe minority communities are targeted as sites of hazardous waste dumps and polluting industries and therefore suffer most from pollution. Their conference is aimed at ending this "environmental racism."

4   "There is no 'equal protection under the law' in terms of environmental protection," said the Rev. Benjamin Chavis Jr. of the United Church of Christ Commission for Racial Justice.

5   That commission sponsored a landmark study in 1987 that reported that three out of every five black or Hispanic Americans live in areas with uncontrolled toxic waste dumps.

6   The environmental injustices stretch from the back roads of Dixie to the barrios of the Southwest to Indian reservations now proposed as nuclear waste depositories, said leaders of the conference. And the problems are compounded by the lack of minority representation in the leadership of mainstream environmental groups, the leaders added.

7   Although landfills and other waste dumps are often near poor communities, research has shown that race is the key factor in site selection, said Robert Bullard, a sociologist at the University of California, Riverside, and author of "Dumping in Dixie: Race, Class and Environmental Quality."

8   Emelle, Ala., with a population that is 80 percent black, is the site of the nation's biggest toxic waste dump and also home to many middle-class black American families, Bullard noted.

9   Though the focus of the conference is on "environmental racism," leaders of the movement said all Americans—not just minorities—will benefit if their messages are heeded.

10   "We want to force polluters to detoxify," said Toney Anaya, former governor of New Mexico. "We're not asking them to put their dumps into white Anglo neighborhoods. We're saying they shouldn't be put in any neighborhoods."

11   The speakers conceded that many communities with large minority populations try to balance risk and jobs in wooing industries to locate there. But economic arguments do not justify endangering the environment and people, they said.

■ **EXPLODED VIEW FOR STUDY**

Each of the highlighted words should be mastered in the following exercises.

Toxics Often Dumped Where Minorities Live, Conference Told

Cox News Service

1   WASHINGTON   Sure, the petrochemical companies brought jobs to 80 miles of poverty between New Orleans and Baton Rouge, recalled Pat Bryant. But they also brought so much poisonous waste and early death that the black people who live there have dubbed the corridor "Cancer Alley."

2   Bryant is among some 600 leaders of grassroots groups who have assembled here for the First National People of Color Leadership Summit on the Environment.

3   They believe minority communities are targeted as sites of hazardous waste dumps and polluting industries and therefore suffer most from pollution. Their conference is aimed at ending this "environmental racism."

4   "There is no 'equal protection under the law' in terms of environmental protection," said the Rev. Benjamin Chavis Jr. of the United Church of Christ Commission for Racial Justice.

5   That commission sponsored a landmark study in 1987 that reported that three out of every five black or Hispanic Americans live in areas with uncontrolled toxic waste dumps.

6   The environmental injustices stretch from the back roads of Dixie to the barrios of the Southwest to Indian reservations now proposed as nuclear waste depositories, said leaders of the conference. And the problems are compounded by the lack of minority representation in the leadership of mainstream environmental groups, the leaders added.

7   Although landfills and other waste dumps are often near poor

communities, research has shown that race is the key factor in site selection, said Robert Bullard, a sociologist at the University of California, Riverside, and author of "Dumping in Dixie: Race, Class and Environmental Quality."

8   Emelle, Ala., with a population that is 80 percent black, is the site of the nation's biggest toxic waste dump and also home to many middle-class black American families, Bullard noted.

9   Though the focus of the conference is on "environmental racism," leaders of the movement said all Americans—not just minorities—will benefit if their messages are heeded.

10   "We want to force polluters to de-toxify," said Toney Anaya, former governor of New Mexico. "We're not asking them to put their dumps into white Anglo neighborhoods. We're saying they shouldn't be put in any neighborhoods."

11   The speakers conceded that many communities with large minority populations try to balance risk and jobs in wooing industries to locate there. But economic arguments do not justify endangering the environment and people, they said.

■ READING COMPREHENSION QUESTIONS

1.   Since the communities where toxic wastes are often dumped have little established economic or political power, they must rely on support from (a) the United Nations (b) grassroots, community groups (c) the Environmental Protection Agency (d) state pollution-control agencies

2.   Communities that allow—or even encourage—dangerous projects, such as the unsafe incineration of medical wastes, do so because they are (a) generous (b) far-sighted (c) aware that everyone must do their part to get rid of dangerous substances (d) desperate for jobs or unaware of the risks

3.   The Commission for Racial Justice reported in 1987 that the ratio of African-Americans and Hispanic Americans living in areas with uncontrolled toxic waste dumps was (a) 3 in 5 (b) 1 in 15 (c) 1 in 100 (d) 1 in 10,000

4.   So many early deaths attributed to poisonous wastes have been recorded in the "80 miles of poverty" between New Orleans and Baton Rouge that the area has come to be called (a) "The Killing Fields" (b) "Death in the Afternoon" (c) "Dying Inside" (d) "Cancer Alley"

5.   Robert Bullard, a sociologist at the University of California, Riverside, has determined that although waste sites are often located in poor communities, the key factor in site selection is (a) the geography of the region (b) the housing and school opportunities for disposal employees (c) wind and rain patterns (d) racial composition

6.   "Reservations" granted to Native Americans are now being proposed as sites for (a) ecological research (b) spiritual centers for governmental and diplomatic conferences (c) nuclear waste dumps (d) federally subsidized golf course developments

■   TARGET VOCABULARY

petrochemical	**hazardous**	**key factor**
poisonous	**toxic**	**to heed**
to dub	**barrios**	**to de-toxify**
grassroots	**depositories**	**to concede**
targeted	**to compound**	**to woo**

Dictionary Practice

Use each word in a sentence of your own.

1.   petrochemical _____

2.   poisonous _____

3.   to dub _____

4.   grassroots _____

5.   targeted _____

6.   hazardous _____

7.   toxic _____

8.   barrios _____

9.   depositories _____

10.   to compound _____

11.   key factor _____

12.   to heed _____

13.   to de-toxify _____

14. to concede _____

15. to woo _____

Cloze Practice

Fill in each blank with an appropriate word from the target vocabulary list.

Unless we _____ the deadly warning signs, _____ wastes will continue to kill innocent people. Even the _____ industry, the medical community, and other producers of _____ materials _____ that waste dumps and burners hurt people. But poor communities are forced _____ such industry because employment is a _____ in their local economies, as are taxes. This situation has been _____ "environmental racism," when such communities are non-white. It is expensive to _____ sites contaminated with _____ waste, but now lives are at stake. Any community _____ for such a site should at least make the decision a public one, or face violent _____ opposition.

■ CRITICAL READING PRACTICE/TOPICS FOR DISCUSSION

1. If three of five African-Americans and Hispanic-Americans live in areas with uncontrolled toxic waste dumps, do you think that the present system of disposal practices appears to be fair? Why or why not?

2. According to Professor Robert Bullard, the key factor in site selection for toxic waste disposal is race, not economic status. In your opinion, does this situation call for the application of federal civil rights laws in order to protect the health and lives of the people involved?

3. What do you think that poor and minority populations can do to protect themselves from this deadly trend of locating lethal environmental dumps in their communities?

4. What sort of environmental hazards, if any, exist in your community? What do you think will be the long-term effects of these hazards, and whom do you think they will affect most severely?

5.   Federal law protects the habitats of owls, salmon, snail darters, whales, and bighorn sheep. In your opinion, why are the habitats of human beings seemingly given less importance by our government than those of these beautiful animals?

Sample Map for "Toxics Often Dumped
Where Minorities Live, Conference Told" (Cox News Service)

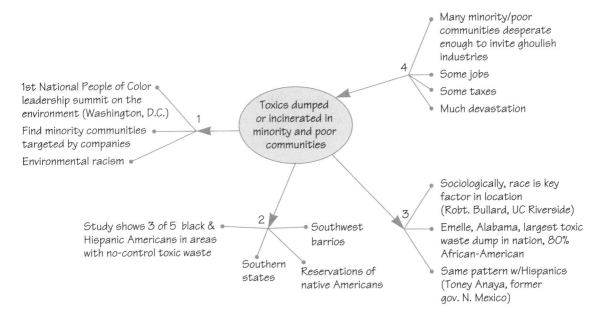

Note: For each of the following readings in this chapter, you are encouraged to draw maps of your own like this one, applying the mapping skills you learned in Part I.

■ *The Search for Intelligent Life Continues Elsewhere*

The possibility of extraterrestrial life—particularly, intelligent life—has been a popular topic of discussion for thousands of years. Now it is a topic of scientific research as well.

NASA's project to search for signs of intelligence on other worlds is the subject of the next pre-reading essay and news article (fittingly, perhaps, from the Baltimore Sun*). Your discussion here might well begin with Metrodorus of Chios, rather than with NASA, SETI, or even E.T. Almost 2500 years later, his opinion that a sown field will produce more than one plant rings clearly, reasonably, and excitingly.*

Some sower. Some field.

◼ PRE-READING FOR DISCUSSION

In the fourth century before the current era, Metrodorus of Chios (who was a pupil of the great father of the atomic theory, Democritus) thought about stars, the earth, life, and common sense. Then he wrote the following: *"To consider the Earth as the only world with life in all of space is as absurd as to believe that in an entire field sown with grain only one plant will grow."*

Almost 2500 years after Metrodorus of Chios, the United States National Aeronautics and Space Administration (NASA) is planning a seven-year attempt, costing $100 million, to find proof that other grains have sprouted. This project, the Search for Extra-Terrestrial Intelligence (SETI), will try to locate radio signals produced artificially by some form of beings outside our solar system. ("Sol," by the way, means "sun"; the "solar system" is our sun and all the planets and other things that whirl around it because of the sun's gravity.)

The SETI project raises interesting questions. First, is this effort worth the money and scientific resources, which could be used in other ways? A lot of school lunches, medical care, or student loans might come from $100 million. Or perhaps NASA ought to get the money but spend it in other ways, on a bigger permanent space station, for example, or on preparations for a manned trip to Mars.

A second serious question is briefly mentioned toward the end of the article: Should SETI locate alien signals, what should our world do about it? If we do not contact the originators of the signals, we remain alone in the darkness. If we do contact "them," we might be viewed as a virus, a threat, or lunch. There's very little evidence that intelligence guarantees compassion here on earth, as the conquest of the New World and a great many other instances amply demonstrate. To expect good will toward all to exist in the stars seems pretty unrealistic.

If NASA proves Metrodorus of Chios right, all we can know for certain is that humanity's views of itself and the universe will both be changed forever.

$100 Million Hunt for Other Life in Universe

Douglas Birch

1   GREEN BANK, W.VA. It could be a crucial moment in human history, the start of a new age of discovery that eclipses Columbus. Or it may be an interstellar wild goose chase.

2   Next Columbus Day [1992], after almost two decades of skepticism and debate, the National Aeronautics and Space Administration plans to launch a seven-year, $100 million effort to scan the heavens for the equivalent of two little words: "Greetings, Earthlings."

3   The program, called the Search for Extra-Terrestrial Intelligence, will be humankind's most ambitious effort so far to pick up radio signals from beings outside our solar system.

4   Success in that quest "would probably be the biggest advance since the birth of language," said astronomer Eric Chaisson, senior scientist at Baltimore's Space Telescope Science Institute, who sat on the panel that helped plan the search.

5   The hunt will begin on Oct. 12 when NASA launches SETI's two phases at separate radio observatories.

6   The so-called "targeted search," directed by NASA's Ames Research Center in Mountain View, Calif., will begin at the world's largest radio telescope—a 1,000-foot-wide dish built into the top of a mountain in Aricebo, Puerto Rico.

7   Using a super fast computer system that monitors 10 million channels at once, scientists will scour the frequency range from 1,000 to 3,000 megahertz from the direction of each of 1,000 stars.

8   All those stars are between about 4 light years and 80 light years from Earth. (A light year is the distance light travels in a year, roughly 6 trillion miles.)

9   SETI's other phase, the all-sky survey, will be run by the Jet Propulsion Laboratory in Pasadena and begin at NASA's Deep Space Network radio observatory in Goldstone, Calif.

10   JPL scientists plan to spend five years aiming NASA's global array of 112-foot Deep Space Network telescopes at broad areas of space, looking for signals in the 1,000- to 10,000-megahertz range.

11   Astronomer Frank Drake hesitantly predicts SETI will achieve success by the end of the century. Others think it will take up to 5,000 years.

12   If an alien signal is detected and verified, scientists say, a massive international effort would probably be launched to study the solar system it came from. And the debate would begin on how, and whether, to answer.

13   However, it would take an answer 500 years to reach a planet 500 light years away—assuming Earthlings could figure out what to say.

■ **EXPLODED VIEW FOR STUDY**

Each of the highlighted words should be mastered in the following exercises.

$100 Million Hunt for Other Life in Universe

Douglas Birch

1   GREEN BANK, W.VA.   It could be a crucial moment in human history, the start of a new age of discovery that eclipses Columbus. Or it may be an interstellar wild goose chase.

2   Next Columbus Day [1992], after almost two decades of skepticism and debate, the National Aeronautics and Space Administration plans to launch a seven-year, $100 million effort to scan the heavens for the equivalent of two little words: "Greetings, Earthlings."

3   The program, called the Search for Extra-Terrestrial Intelligence, will be humankind's most ambitious effort so far to pick up radio signals from beings outside our solar system.

4   Success in that quest "would probably be the biggest advance since the birth of language," said astronomer Eric Chaisson, senior scientist at Baltimore's Space Telescope Science Institute, who sat on the panel that helped plan the search.

5   The hunt will begin on Oct. 12 when NASA launches SETI's two phases at separate radio observatories.

6   The so-called "targeted search," directed by NASA's Ames Research Center in Mountain View, Calif., will begin at the world's largest radio telescope—a 1,000-foot-wide dish built into the top of a mountain in Aricebo, Puerto Rico.

7   Using a super fast computer system that monitors 10 million channels at once, scientists will scour the frequency range from 1,000 to 3,000 megahertz from the direction of each of 1,000 stars.

8   All those stars are between about 4 light years and 80 light years from Earth. (A light year is the distance light travels in a year, roughly 6 trillion miles.)

9   SETI's other phase, the all-sky survey, will be run by the Jet Propulsion Laboratory in Pasadena and begin at NASA's Deep Space
Network radio observatory in Goldstone, Calif.

10   JPL scientists plan to spend five years aiming NASA's global array
of 112-foot Deep Space Network telescopes at broad areas of space,
looking for signals in the 1,000- to 10,000-megahertz range.

11   Astronomer Frank Drake hesitantly predicts SETI will achieve
success by the end of the century. Others think it will take up to
5,000 years.

12   If an alien signal is detected and verified, scientists say, a massive
international effort would probably be launched to study the solar
system it came from. And the debate would begin on how, and
whether, to answer.

13   However, it would take an answer 500 years to reach a planet
500 light years away—assuming Earthlings could figure out what
to say.

■ READING COMPREHENSION QUESTIONS

1.   The National Aeronautics and Space Administration (NASA)
plans to conduct the Search for Extra-Terrestrial Intelligence (SETI)
project for the next (a) 18 months (b) 9 months (c) 2 years (d) 7 years

2.   The first phase of the SETI project will scan 1,000 stars that are
relatively near to the earth, at distances from (a) 500,000 to 1,000,000
miles (b) a light year (about 6 trillion miles) to 2 light years (c) 4 to 80
light years (d) 500 to 1,000 light years

3.   Astronomer Eric Chaisson, senior scientist at Baltimore's Space
Telescope Science Institute, believes that a successful contact with extra-
terrestrial intelligence would be (a) like a cheeseburger contacting a
lumberjack (b) the biggest advance since the birth of language (c) very
important in terms of theology and religious studies in general (d) not
as big a deal as NASA thinks since "a star is a star is a star"

4.   Should SETI contact be made, a world-wide debate would immediately take place regarding (a) how and whether we should answer
(b) what language to use (c) who would receive the honor of commu-
nicating with the other species (d) centuries of unsettled UFO-related
insurance claims

5.   The world's largest radio telescope will be employed in the SETI scan of the skies, operating from a mountaintop in (a) Omaha, Nebraska (b) New Delhi, India (c) Bonn, Germany (d) Aricebo, Puerto Rico

6.   The cost of the SETI project, by national government standards, is not particularly large, estimated at (a) $100 million (b) $5 billion (c) $50 billion (d) $1 trillion

■   TARGET VOCABULARY

crucial	**equivalent**	**phase**
to eclipse	**ambitious**	**observatory**
interstellar	**quest**	**global**
skepticism	**radio telescope**	**array**
to scan	**to monitor**	**to verify**

Dictionary Practice

Use each word in a sentence of your own.

1.   crucial _____

2.   to eclipse _____

3.   interstellar _____

4.   skepticism _____

5.   to scan _____

6.   equivalent _____

7.   ambitious _____

8.   quest _____

9.   radio telescope _____

10.   to monitor _____

11.   phase _____

12.   observatory _____

13.   global _____

14.   array _____

15.   to verify _____

Cloze Practice

Fill in each blank with an appropriate word from the target vocabulary list.

Long, difficult searches, or _____, for prized objects are important parts of all cultural myths. But _____ the depths of _____ space with a _____ in search of other intelligence may be the most _____ such undertaking in history. This is _____ to searching for a literal "new world" and would _____ any physical discovery ever made by humankind. Astronomers will _____ instruments in _____ for years, perhaps centuries, searching for the _____ piece of evidence of other life, then try to _____ their findings in order to overcome certain _____. Whether this would end "human" history or simply be a new _____ of it is a challenging question.

■ CRITICAL READING PRACTICE/TOPICS FOR DISCUSSION

1.   Do you think we are all alone as intelligent creatures, or are there other life forms out there with which we could have a conversation? If you think we have company somewhere, why do you think so? If you think we're all alone, what makes you believe as you do?

2.   Let's assume that the SETI project hits the cosmic jackpot and finds a source of radio waves that could only be produced by technology, that is, by intelligent creatures. Do you think we ought to take steps to get in touch with them? Why, or why not? If you want to get in touch, what would you say? If you don't want to get in touch, are you worried that they may have discovered *our* radio waves and be headed *here*?

3.   We have been transmitting radio waves for about 75 years. Way "out there" we can imagine creatures listening to Buddy Holly, Louis Armstrong, and Glenn Miller. Assume that "they" decipher our languages and keep notes on what they hear. What do you suppose they would think of us, based on our radio broadcasts from the 1920s to the present?

4.   How do you feel about the government spending $100 million on a project such as this, rather than on, say, school lunch programs or student loans? Why do you feel as you do?

5.   The ancient Greeks produced not only Metrodorus of Chios and his theories on the heavens, but also theories of atomic structure (Democritus) and the natural and physical sciences (Aristotle and many others), not to mention political theories that are still functioning in societies all over the world. With practically no scientific technology, how do you think the Greeks were able to create such accurate wonders of scientific thought?

■   *The Great Sphinx's Latest Mystery*

Riddles are fun because they are frustrating until the clever answer is revealed. Scientists in three fields are now struggling with a huge amount of such frustration regarding the Great Sphinx, but so far they have come up with no clever answers, only more riddles. This is not surprising, given the sphinx's personality (discussed in the following pre-reading essay). The sphinx, the greatest riddler of all time, seems to have come out of a brief retirement.

Geology, archaeology, and Egyptology are all able to reveal wonders about the past. Each discipline is absolutely "scientific" in its methods, too, in the broadest sense (that is, each tries to let fact speak for itself rather than conform to some assumption). In this way, rocks and "stuff" can be roughly dated and roughly ordered. Then, patterns and sequences emerge. We begin to understand. . . .

This is just *the right time for the arrival of a sphinx.*

■   **PRE-READING FOR DISCUSSION**

The image of the sphinx, a creature with a lion's body and a human head, has been around for a long, long time. The most famous such image is the "Great Sphinx" at Giza, in Egypt. About 2,550 years before the current era (that is, about 4,500 years ago), King Khafre had his face placed on Giza's giant recumbent sphinx, and it has long been thought that the sphinx was constructed during his reign.

As the following article makes clear, however, there are now serious questions about the age of the sphinx and the means used to construct it. Geologists estimate that the wonderful sculpture may be many thousands of years older than Egyptologists have thought it to be; and if the geologists are correct, archaeologists and Egyptologists have a lot of rethinking to do about a lot of things.

Each science involved in the dispute over the sphinx's age is seeking the truth: geologists want to know the ages of rocks, archaeologists want to know the stages of human development, and Egyptologists want to know the progression of Egyptian society. Each discipline also thinks that it has found a part of the truth, and yet the parts seem to contradict each other . . . if we listen to the rocks.

Only time and study will resolve these fascinating contradictions, and yet it is particularly interesting that this question has arisen over the sphinx.

Western legends from Greece have the sphinx asking a riddle: "What goes on four legs in the morning, two in the afternoon, and three in the evening?" If you could not answer the riddle, the sphinx ate you. It was a well-fed creature for years. Then along came a man named Oedipus, who answered the riddle: "A man. He crawls as a baby, walks as an adult, and uses a cane in old age." The sphinx, being honorable, packed up and left. Oedipus felt quite full of himself . . . for awhile.

Sphinxes are represented as both male and female, sometimes with wings, and have been found in the art of many earlier societies in Europe, Asia, and Africa. The greatest of them all, it seems, has "flown" across time (although the Great Sphinx at Giza has no literal wings) and once again has given us a puzzle which, for all our sciences, we have not yet been able to figure out.

The answer, in a general way, will be the same answer Oedipus gave. The sphinx was conceived in human imagination and built with human hands. To understand the artifact, we will have to understand more about ourselves; and that's a puzzle of considerable complexity, far beyond our present skills or information.

Debate Flares Over Age Of Great Sphinx at Giza

It may be twice as old as previously thought

Lee Dye

1   SAN DIEGO   New evidence that Egypt's Great Sphinx may be twice as old as had been thought has triggered a fierce argument between geologists who say that it must be older and archaeologists who say that conclusion contradicts everything they know about ancient Egypt.

2   Geologists who presented their results at the Geological Society of America convention Tuesday found that weathering patterns on the great monument were characteristic of a period far older than had been believed. But archaeologists and Egyptologists insist that even if the Sphinx is older than they think, it could not be much older because the people who lived in the region earlier could not have built it.

3   Most Egyptologists believe that the Sphinx was built during the reign of the Pharaoh Khafre, also known as Chephren, in approximately 2500 B.C. But scientists who conducted a series of unprecedented studies at the Giza site told their colleagues that evidence shows that the Sphinx was already there long before Khafre came to power.

4   The evidence suggests that Khafre simply refurbished the Sphinx, which may have been several thousand years old, and incorporated it into his funereal complex.

5   Geologist Robert Schoch of Boston University told the meeting that his research suggests that the Sphinx actually dates to between 7000 B.C. and 5000 B.C.

6   "And I'm trying to be conservative," he said. That would double the presumed age of the Great Sphinx and make it the oldest monument in Egypt, he said.

7   Schoch conducted the first seismic studies ever allowed at the site, and that research indicates that the limestone bed that surrounds the monument, part of which was exposed when the Sphinx was first carved, has weathered far longer than had been thought. In addition, erosional differences between the Sphinx and other structures of unambiguous origin also indicate that the Sphinx is much older, Schoch said.

8   But archaeologist Carol Redmount of the University of California at Berkeley, who specializes in Egyptian artifacts, said, "There's just no way that could be true."

9   The people of that region would not have had the technology, the governing institutions or even the will to have built such a structure thousands of years before Khafre's reign, she said.

10   Other Egyptologists who have looked at Schoch's work said that they cannot explain the geological evidence, but they insist that the idea that the Sphinx is thousands of years older than they had thought just simply does not match up with the mountains of archaeological research they have carried out in that region.

■ **EXPLODED VIEW FOR STUDY**

Each of the highlighted words should be mastered in the following exercises.

Debate Flares Over Age Of Great Sphinx at Giza

It may be twice as old as previously thought

Lee Dye

1   SAN DIEGO   New evidence that Egypt's Great Sphinx may be twice as old as had been thought has triggered a fierce argument between geologists who say that it must be older and archaeologists who say that conclusion contradicts everything they know about ancient Egypt.

2   Geologists who presented their results at the Geological Society of America convention Tuesday found that weathering patterns on the great monument were characteristic of a period far older than had been believed. But archaeologists and Egyptologists insist that even if the Sphinx is older than they think, it could not be much older because the people who lived in the region earlier could not have built it.

3   Most Egyptologists believe that the Sphinx was built during the reign of the Pharaoh Khafre, also known as Chephren, in approximately 2500 B.C. But scientists who conducted a series of unprecedented studies at the Giza site told their colleagues that evidence shows that the Sphinx was already there long before Khafre came to power.

4   The evidence suggests that Khafre simply refurbished the Sphinx, which may have been several thousand years old, and incorporated it into his funereal complex.

5   Geologist Robert Schoch of Boston University told the meeting that his research suggests that the Sphinx actually dates to between 7000 B.C. and 5000 B.C.

6   "And I'm trying to be conservative," he said. That would double the presumed age of the Great Sphinx and make it the oldest monument in Egypt, he said.

7   Schoch conducted the first seismic studies ever allowed at the site, and that research indicates that the limestone bed that surrounds the monument, part of which was exposed when the Sphinx was first carved, has weathered far longer than had been thought. In addition, erosional differences between the Sphinx and other structures of unambiguous origin also indicate that the Sphinx is much older, Schoch said.

8   But archaeologist Carol Redmount of the University of California at Berkeley, who specializes in Egyptian artifacts, said, "There's just no way that could be true."

9   The people of that region would not have had the technology, the governing institutions or even the will to have built such a structure thousands of years before Khafre's reign, she said.

10   Other Egyptologists who have looked at Schoch's work said that they cannot explain the geological evidence, but they insist that the idea that the Sphinx is thousands of years older than they had thought just simply does not match up with the mountains of archaeological research they have carried out in that region.

■ READING COMPREHENSION QUESTIONS

1.   For thousands of years the Great Sphinx has silently stared at history across the sands of (a) Karnak (b) Giza (c) Tripoli (d) Aswan

2.   Egyptologists and archaeologists have believed the Great Sphinx to be about 4,500 years old, based on their studies of the reign of the Pharaoh Khafre (whose face may be the one on the present sphinx). Recent studies by geologists, however, suggest that, even conservatively, the sphinx is more likely (a) 5,000 to 7,000 years old (b) 9,000 years old or more (c) 6,246 years old (d) only 3,000 years old

3.   Geologist Robert Schoch, of Boston University, found that the limestone from which the sphinx is carved has weathered far longer than had been thought. In order to establish this, he was allowed to conduct the first tests at the site which gathered (a) seismic data (b) local legends and family histories (c) no moss (d) core samples bored from the interior of the sphinx with lasers

4.   The results of Schoch's research were presented in a scholarly paper delivered at the convention of the (a) North American Society for Egyptology (b) Archaeological Society of America (c) Antony and Cleopatra Association (c) Geological Society of America

5.   Archaeologist Carol Redmount of the University of California at Berkeley, a specialist in Egyptian artifacts, responded to the geological estimate of the sphinx's age by stating, "There's just no way that could be true," because the people of the region (a) didn't have any interest in monuments before Khafre's reign (b) had no design-review process that early in their history (c) lacked the technology and political unity necessary for such a construction (d) were unfamiliar with the legend of the sphinx

6.   Egyptologists and archaeologists insist that the single geological estimate of the Sphinx's age simply can't be true because the estimate contradicts (a) the textbooks they have written (b) what they were taught as students (c) biblical accounts of Egypt (d) mountains of archaeological research in the region

■ TARGET VOCABULARY

to trigger	**characteristic**	**funereal**
fierce	**reign**	**complex**
geologist	**unprecedented**	**seismic**
archaeologist	**colleagues**	**weathered**
to contradict	**refurbished**	**artifacts**

Dictionary Practice

Use each word in a sentence of your own.

1.   to trigger _____

2.   fierce _____

3.   geologist _____

4.   archaeologist _____

5.   to contradict _____

6.   characteristic _____

7.   reign _____

8. unprecedented _____

9. colleagues _____

10. refurbished _____

11. funereal _____

12. complex _____

13. seismic _____

14. weathered _____

15. artifacts _____

Cloze Practice

Fill in each blank with an appropriate term from the target vocabulary list.

Scholars of mankind's past, _____, and scholars of the earth's past, _____, seem to have found information _____ of each field that _____ each other's present beliefs. This _____ debate was _____ by a geologist and his _____, who conducted unique, _____ tests at the extensive _____ site, or _____, of an Egyptian pharoah. The geologists' results are unambiguous: the Great Sphinx is far older than the _____ of the buried pharoah or the burial _____ in the tomb.

The sphinx smiles still.

■ CRITICAL READING PRACTICE/TOPICS FOR DISCUSSION

1. Somebody (or everybody) has to be wrong about the age of the sphinx. The geologists say the archaeologists and Egyptologists are off by at least two or three thousand years. The archaeologists reply that the sphinx simply couldn't have been built any earlier than their estimate, no matter what the rocks seem to say.

What do you think is going on here? Why do you feel as you do? Can you imagine any set of circumstances in which both groups can be right?

2.   Professionals seem confident that the face on the sphinx is that of a "pharaoh," a sort of "super-king-god" ruler of Egypt. His name, they further believe, was Khafre. Still further, they know when Khafre lived because it was written down and they can read it as plain as day.

Does all of this convince you that Khafre was responsible for the construction of the sphinx? If so, why does geology say it's older? If not, why would Khafre want to slap his face on somebody else's tired, old, used sphinx?

3.   If the Egyptologists are correct in saying the people of the region really couldn't have built such a thing before Khafre's time and if the geologist is correct in his estimate of the sphinx's age, there would have to be *some* group of people to build it, and we evidently know nothing about them.

Do you think that such a society could have existed and left absolutely no traces? If so, why didn't other people pick up their technology? If not, then who built that huge, puzzling thing in the desert?

4.   Do you think that studying the past, in Egypt or anywhere else, is a useful thing for us to do? If so, why do you feel as you do? If not, why don't you think such study is valuable?

■ *"You Ain't Seen Nothin' Yet": When the* Real *Volcanoes Erupt*

Human time and geologic time do not meet directly in very many cases, simply because humans haven't been around very long. To the earth a few million years is just a lazy afternoon.

But when seismic or volcanic events occur, the relative importance of our "times" is made very clear. The earth is going about its business regardless of human concerns. Continents drift and collide, magma moves upward, the greatest mountain ranges rise and fall like slow-motion waves.

The recent discoveries that are the subject of the following article relate to "super-volcanoes," huge eruptions that produce immense depressions called calderas (the Spanish word for "caldron" or "very large kettle"). From Wyoming to New Mexico, volcanologists are piecing together the activities of such eruptions in order to understand this huge volcano type in general.

In spite of highways, towns, ski lodges, and National Park sites, the calderas go ahead, unhurriedly, with their important work. In your reading and discussion, you might want to consider these relative time scales.

■   **PRE-READING FOR DISCUSSION**

Human time is as important for human beings as sea turtle time is for sea turtles and mayfly time is for mayflies. The earth itself, however, uses a much larger clock: geologic time. On this clock, if all of our planet's history were represented by the distance from the longest fingernail tip of one of your outstretched arms to the longest fingernail tip of the other, all human history could be erased by one stroke of a fingernail file.

That's a big clock.

It should not be too surprising that, when considered in terms of the Big Clock, a lot of things have happened, and happened regularly, which "recorded" (by humans, that is) history doesn't include. The following article concerns one such type of fairly regular event: volcanic eruptions on a scale so vast that we really have nothing with which to compare them.

The largest recent volcanic eruption in the United States, the Mt. Saint Helens eruption in southern Washington, devastated a huge area, killed several people, affected global weather patterns, and trailed ash (on the jet stream air currents of the atmosphere) all around the earth. The total volume of material spewed out from the Mt. Saint Helens eruption was about a quarter of a "cubic" mile (a "cube" one mile high, one mile wide, and one mile deep).

Volcanologists are now studying "super-volcanoes" that produce *calderas,* giant depressions in the earth's surface. One such caldera producer in Wyoming's Yellowstone National Park is thought to have erupted 240 cubic miles of material into the sky (which is equivalent to 960 Mt. Saint Helens eruptions) at once. As recently as 7,000 years ago—practically this morning in geological time—a "baby" volcano in Oregon (now a peaceful, beautiful, earthen bowl filled with water and known as "Crater Lake") threw about 50 times Mt. Saint Helens' volume of material into the atmosphere.

Hawaii, Japan, and other active volcano sites regularly provide dramatic pictures of lava flows and volcanic activity. And people who live around the Pacific "Ring of Fire" are all accustomed to earthquakes and occasional volcanic eruptions. But never in recorded history has there been anything like the caldera-producing events now under study.

The earth is in no hurry, according to its own clock. We may be one year, or 100,000 or half a million from the next major caldera-producing eruption. But just as the earth does not hurry, neither does it pause or wait or turn aside.

If we know nothing else about the magnificent pulse of the caldera events, we do know that they will continue, with complete indifference toward our concerns and our tiny clock.

2 Western Volcanoes May Blow Anytime in Next 100,000 Years

Charles Petit

1   Two of the biggest dormant volcanoes in western North America, including the region around California's Mammoth Lakes, are primed to go off again on a scale that would dwarf any eruption in recorded history—but that could mean anytime in the next 100,000 years, a leading Berkeley geologist said yesterday.

2   The volcanoes, monsters of a kind that belch 500 or more times as much volcanic ash and lava as exploded from Mount Saint Helens in 1980, leave calderas, tremendous depressions in the ground that may stretch more than 10 miles rim to rim.

3   They include those under Long Valley in the Mammoth Lakes region of eastern California, Yellowstone National Park in Wyoming, and a large, circular feature called Valles Caldera in New Mexico's Jemez Mountains.

4   However, such underground caldrons only go off two or three times over a course of a million years or more, spaced out every few hundred thousand years.

5   Until now, scientists have had no means of telling whether such a caldron is spent or might go off again.

6   "I think we have a way to tell a live one from a dead one," said Donald J. DePaolo, chairman of the department of geology at the University of California at Berkeley, following a presentation yesterday in San Diego at the meeting of the Geological Society of America.

7   He said at the meeting that analysis of ancient deposits around the Yellowstone, Long Valley, and Valles Caldera show that in the 100,000 years before their past, major eruption, the ratio of two isotopes of the element neodymium changes markedly.

8   The shift apparently signals the arrival of magma from deep within the earth, filling a chamber near the surface.

9   Analysis of small volcanoes in the Yellowstone area, and at the Inyo Craters chain of volcanoes near Long Valley, shows that both are in this "precursory" stage and may be building up for another immense eruption. Valles Caldera, by contrast, "looks like a dead one," DePaolo said.

10   The finding is no cause for panic, he said, since it probably takes 100,000 years for enough magma to build up underground to create another true caldera-forming event.

11   The Yellowstone area has had such eruptions three times in the past 2 million years, most recently about 600,000 years ago, when 240 cubic miles of magma erupted.

12   By contrast, Mount St. Helens erupted about one-quarter of a cubic mile, and Crater Lake in Oregon is a relatively small caldera created 6,800 years ago by an eruption of about 12 cubic miles of magma.

13   Long Valley has gone off once, 760,000 years ago, when about 170 cubic miles of magma erupted.

14   The spacing of the immense caldera-forming eruptions is not closely related to smaller, but still dangerous, volcanoes in the region that can erupt much more frequently.

15   For the past decade or so, earthquakes under Long Valley and Mammoth Lakes have indicated movement of enough magma to cause such a smaller eruption, but geologists cannot say if one is on the way soon.

■   EXPLODED VIEW FOR STUDY

Each of the highlighted words should be mastered in the following exercises.

---

2 Western Volcanoes May Blow Anytime in Next 100,000 Years

Charles Petit

1   Two of the biggest dormant volcanoes in western North America, including the region around California's Mammoth Lakes, are primed to go off again on a scale that would dwarf any eruption in recorded history—but that could mean anytime in the next 100,000 years, a leading Berkeley geologist said yesterday.

2   The volcanoes, monsters of a kind that belch 500 or more times as much volcanic ash and lava as exploded from Mount Saint Helens in 1980, leave calderas, tremendous depressions in the ground that may stretch more than 10 miles rim to rim.

3   They include those under Long Valley in the Mammoth Lakes region of eastern California, Yellowstone National Park in Wyoming, and a large, circular feature called Valles Caldera in New Mexico's Jemez Mountains.

4   However, such underground caldrons only go off two or three times over a course of a million years or more, spaced out every few hundred thousand years.

5   Until now, scientists have had no means of telling whether such a caldron is spent or might go off again.

6   "I think we have a way to tell a live one from a dead one," said Donald J. DePaolo, chairman of the department of geology at the University of California at Berkeley, following a presentation yesterday in San Diego at the meeting of the Geological Society of America.

7   He said at the meeting that analysis of ancient deposits around the Yellowstone, Long Valley, and Valles Caldera show that in the

100,000 years before their past, major eruption, the ratio of two isotopes of the element neodymium changes markedly.

8   The shift apparently signals the arrival of magma from deep within the earth, filling a chamber near the surface.

9   Analysis of small volcanoes in the Yellowstone area, and at the Inyo Craters chain of volcanoes near Long Valley, shows that both are in this "precursory" stage and may be building up for another immense eruption. Valles Caldera, by contrast, "looks like a dead one," DePaolo said.

10   The finding is no cause for panic, he said, since it probably takes 100,000 years for enough magma to build up underground to create another true caldera-forming event.

11   The Yellowstone area has had such eruptions three times in the past 2 million years, most recently about 600,000 years ago, when 240 cubic miles of magma erupted.

12   By contrast, Mount St. Helens erupted about one-quarter of a cubic mile, and Crater Lake in Oregon is a relatively small caldera created 6,800 years ago by an eruption of about 12 cubic miles of magma.

13   Long Valley has gone off once, 760,000 years ago, when about 170 cubic miles of magma erupted.

14   The spacing of the immense caldera-forming eruptions is not closely related to smaller, but still dangerous, volcanoes in the region that can erupt much more frequently.

15   For the past decade or so, earthquakes under Long Valley and Mammoth Lakes have indicated movement of enough magma to cause such a smaller eruption, but geologists cannot say if one is on the way soon.

■ READING COMPREHENSION QUESTIONS

1.   Volcanologists are able to estimate the dates of prehistoric volcanic eruptions by (a) studying the rings of trees (b) analyzing ancient volcanic deposits in the surrounding geology (c) estimating erosion rates at crater rims (d) examining the fossil records

2.   During recorded human history, no caldera-forming volcano has ever erupted. However, volcanologists estimate that such an eruption would be many times larger than the greatest known eruptions, in fact, about (a) 10 times as large (b) twice as large (c) 50 times as large (d) 500 times as large

3.   Basically, a volcano is a rupture in the hard surface of the earth which allows the (often quite violent) escape of semi-liquid material from the earth's interior, called (a) steam plumes (b) slip faults (c) iron pyrite (d) magma

4.   The most recent caldera eruption in the Yellowstone National Park area took place about (a) 55,000 years ago (b) 600,000 years ago (c) 150,000 years ago (d) over 1 million years ago

5.   Geologist Donald J. DePaolo says that there is no chance of a "surprise" caldera event. For enough magma to build up for such a titanic eruption takes about (a) 100,000 years (b) 500 to 750 years (c) over a century (d) 30,000 to 40,000 years

6.   Of the three calderas included in DePaolo's study, two seem to still be active, one in the Yellowstone area, the other near Long Valley in the eastern Sierra Nevada Mountains of California. The third, inactive caldera is located in (a) the Portland area (b) Red Deer, Alberta (c) near Ketchum, Idaho (d) the Jemez Mountains of New Mexico

■   **TARGET VOCABULARY**

dormant	**to belch**	**element**
to prime	**circular**	**magma**
to dwarf	**spent**	**immense**
eruption	**analysis**	**by contrast**
recorded history	**isotopes**	**cubic mile**

Dictionary Practice

Use each word in a sentence of your own.

1.   dormant _____

2.   to prime _____

3.   to dwarf _____

4.   eruption _____

5. recorded history _____

6. to belch _____

7. circular _____

8. spent _____

9. analysis _____

10. isotopes _____

11. element _____

12. magma _____

13. immense _____

14. by contrast _____

15. cubic mile _____

Cloze Practice

Fill in each blank with an appropriate word from the target vocabulary list.

Human history, at least our _____, reaches only a short distance into the past (writing is about 6,000 to 7,000 years old). But geologic history, _____, is open to _____ due to the _____ amount of data stored in rocks. The work of geologists ranges from studying tiny amounts of _____ present in basic _____ to the study of mountains, islands, and plates of the earth's surface. Often islands and mountains are formed by the _____ of subterranean _____ which is _____ up by enormous volcanoes. Volcanologists, therefore, use time scales that _____ any such human system. We cannot even tell for certain whether an inactive, or _____, site is truly "inactive" at all.

■ **CRITICAL READING PRACTICE/TOPICS FOR DISCUSSION**

1.   If an eruption of the size to produce a caldera were to occur, what do you think the effects would be on global weather patterns? What effects do you think those weather patterns might then have on, say, food production and social stability? Why do you feel as you do?

2.   Volcanologists say that eruptions of this magnitude occur only two or three times in a million years. They also know that Yellowstone erupted about 600,000 years ago and that Long Valley rocked and rolled about 760,000 years ago. That's two. . . .

But the article only mentions sites in the western United States. Look at a map of the Pacific "Ring of Fire" (that is, the land masses which border the North and South Pacific and are so named because of their seismic and volcanic activity). Do you think that there might be other calderas around the Pacific? If so, how would this change the odds of a huge event taking place? If not, why do you think the article does not note that these are unique to North America?

3.   From a safe distance, of course, would you like to observe a volcano as it erupts? Why or why not? Have you ever visited an area of volcanic activity? If so, what do you remember about it? If not, would you like to? Why or why not?

4.   Should a ready-to-blow volcano capable of producing a caldera somehow be discovered, what steps do you think might be taken to minimize the effects of such an enormous eruption on human societies worldwide?

■ *From the Andes to the Computer to the World: The Amazing Aymara Language*

From the Andean highlands to the floor of the United Nations General Assembly, language is used to communicate; but no two languages "work" in exactly the same way. Endless grief, humor, frustration, and tragedy have resulted from this basic inability to find a common means of expressing ourselves and understanding others.

The problem, like language itself, is probably just about as old as our species.

The following article, reported from Bolivia, stimulates some interesting thought on this issue and suggests that the seemingly remarkable Aymara language may be the translation medium which we have sought for so long. From the General Assembly to the bridge of Captain Kirk's Enterprise, *such a discovery would be most welcome.*

■ PRE-READING FOR DISCUSSION

The 400-year European assault on Latin America was motivated chiefly by a lust for wealth, and the Europeans found what they were looking for. Mountains of gold and silver crossed the Atlantic back to Spain, Portugal, and other powers, and the land itself produced even greater riches for later exploiters, from both Europe and the United States. Coffee, sugar, fruit, minerals, and seemingly endless raw materials were drawn from the area—and still continue to be drawn from it—often bringing great hardship, danger, and almost no benefit to local Latin American populations.

A large and critically important family of medicines is also derived from the plants of the area. Someone in Cleveland, Des Moines, or Baltimore who is taking medication for a heart problem may owe her life to a plant in Brazil, and to those who gather such plants.

Now yet another miraculous Latin American export may be surfacing, thanks to the diligent and imaginative work of Ivan Guzman de Rojas of La Paz, Bolivia.

For many years, attempts at "automatic" or "machine" translation have been stuck on the same problem: languages just don't work like mathematics. They are, as a rule, wild and irresponsible organisms that take delight in breaking their own laws and patterns. They allow us to communicate, of course, but they're also constantly on the lookout for a party or a joke, they quickly establish themselves in new places and then mutate faster than fruitflies, and they positively delight in saying *almost* the same thing in as many ways as possible.

If, however, all of the wild languages could be translated into a language that *does* work like mathematics, then it would be a simple thing to translate from any given language to any other. At present, human interpreters can translate from language A to language B, because the interpreter is fluent in both. But what a miracle it would be if we could translate *any* language into *any* other language simply by going through a "universal mathematical" third language.

In six years, Guzman, his wife, a linguist, and their son, an engineer, have produced a machine that can translate, through the language of the Andean Aymara, nine "wild" languages: French, Spanish, Italian, Dutch, German, Swedish, Hungarian, Portuguese, and the scruffiest of them all, English. All of these are, of course, European languages, made accessible by the language of the Aymara.

More than five centuries after Columbus, the New World may have given one more treasure to the old: instantaneous universal communication. How ironic that a continent which has seen so much tragic misunderstanding may one day provide us with a means of better understanding each other, all around the world.

The Tribal Computer Tongue

Language of the Aymara Indians a bridge to the world

Paul Mylrea

1   LA PAZ, BOLIVIA   Conquered first by the Incas and then by the Spanish, the Aymara Indians kept their language.

2   A thousand years after their complex and mysterious civilization peaked, the guttural Aymara tongue is still spoken by some 2 million Indians, mainly around Lake Titicaca in the Andean highlands.

3   Now a Bolivian mathematician has discovered that Aymara can be used by computers as a bridge to translate books, documents and even newspapers from one language to another.

4   In a cramped apartment in this 12,000-foot-high city, mathematician-inventor Ivan Guzman de Rojas types a trick sentence—one in which verb and noun are the same word in English—into an ordinary personal computer as a test.

5   Moments later, his original English sentence "My friend wants to drink a drink" simultaneously pops up on the screen as "Mon ami veut boire une boisson," "Mein Freund will ein Getraenk trinken" and "Mi amigo quiere beber una bebida."

6   Six years after he produced a prototype, it can translate between Aymara, English, French, Spanish, Italian, German, Dutch, Swedish, Portuguese and Hungarian.

7   Guzman is close to signing a contract with the French computer company Groupe Bull for his invention, which is known as Atamiri, the word for interpreter in Aymara, but he is still not satisfied.

8   "My aim is to make the best multilingual translator in the world. . . . I believe we can reach perfection, where you only have to change the style and there are no grammatical errors in the computer translation," said Guzman, the son of one of Bolivia's most famous painters.

9   He says his system's secret, which solved a problem that has stumped machine translation experts around the world, is the rigid, logical and unambiguous structure of Aymara, ideal for transformation into a computer algorithm.

10   The computer uses the formal representation of Aymara as a bridge. The text to be translated is decoded using the Aymara formula and then recoded into the desired languages.

11   "People saw it (translation) as a linguistic problem, but it is a problem of language engineering, how to translate grammar into logarithms which work in a machine," Guzman said.

12   The idea came to him as he was teaching mathematics to Aymara children, and he began work on a borrowed computer, helped by his wife, Gladys Davalos, a trained linguist, and his son, an engineer.

13   Guzman has faced skepticism despite a contract with the Panama Canal Commission, which used his system between 1985 and 1988 to translate documents between English and Spanish in its first commercial test, and an initial research agreement with Wang Laboratories.

14   The European Community, which spent several million dollars on a computer translation project without producing a working system, canceled a meeting with Guzman after he flew to Brussels with money from Latin American governments to demonstrate Atamiri.

15   "Machine translation has a bad history, so much money has been wasted," says Guzman. "Why pay a mad Bolivian using

Aymara who claims he can solve a problem that 11 European universities can't solve?"

16   To support his family and keep the research going, Guzman has had to continue working as a consultant in computing accounting systems.

17   The long haul may be ending. In July, Bull signed a letter of intent to buy the system and Guzman is negotiating a deal with the firm. But Guzman says his dream is not to get rich by selling his invention.

18   Inspired by the language that gave him his idea, Guzman would like to dedicate himself to helping the Aymaras, most of whom live in poverty on the inhospitable high Andean plain.

19   With enough money coming in from his translation system, he says Atamiri could be used to translate books into Aymara and even form the basis of a newspaper for the Indians.

20   Atamiri could then become the savior of the Aymara language, which, after surviving 4,000 years, is being slowly displaced by Spanish.

■ EXPLODED VIEW FOR STUDY

Each of the highlighted words should be mastered in the following exercises.

The Tribal Computer Tongue

Language of the Aymara Indians a bridge to the world

Paul Mylrea

1   LA PAZ, BOLIVIA Conquered first by the Incas and then by the Spanish, the Aymara Indians kept their language.

2   A thousand years after their complex and mysterious civilization peaked, the guttural Aymara tongue is still spoken by some 2 million Indians, mainly around Lake Titicaca in the Andean highlands.

3   Now a Bolivian mathematician has discovered that Aymara can be used by computers as a bridge to translate books, documents and even newspapers from one language to another.

4   In a cramped apartment in this 12,000-foot-high city, mathematician-inventor Ivan Guzman de Rojas types a trick sentence—one in which verb and noun are the same word in English—into an ordinary personal computer as a test.

5   Moments later, his original English sentence "My friend wants to

drink a drink" simultaneously pops up on the screen as "Mon ami veut boire une boisson," "Mein Freund will ein Getraenk trinken" and "Mi amigo quiere beber una bebida."

6   Six years after he produced a prototype, it can translate between Aymara, English, French, Spanish, Italian, German, Dutch, Swedish, Portuguese and Hungarian.

7   Guzman is close to signing a contract with the French computer company Groupe Bull for his invention, which is known as Atamiri, the word for interpreter in Aymara, but he is still not satisfied.

8   "My aim is to make the best multilingual translator in the world. . . . I believe we can reach perfection, where you only have to change the style and there are no grammatical errors in the computer translation," said Guzman, the son of one of Bolivia's most famous painters.

9   He says his system's secret, which solved a problem that has stumped machine translation experts around the world, is the rigid, logical and unambiguous structure of Aymara, ideal for transformation into a computer algorithm.

10   The computer uses the formal representation of Aymara as a bridge. The text to be translated is decoded using the Aymara formula and then recoded into the desired languages.

11   "People saw it (translation) as a linguistic problem, but it is a problem of language engineering, how to translate grammar into logarithms which work in a machine," Guzman said.

12   The idea came to him as he was teaching mathematics to Aymara children, and he began work on a borrowed computer, helped by his wife, Gladys Davalos, a trained linguist, and his son, an engineer.

13   Guzman has faced skepticism despite a contract with the Panama Canal Commission, which used his system between 1985 and 1988 to translate documents between English and Spanish in its first commercial test, and an initial research agreement with Wang Laboratories.

14   The European Community, which spent several million dollars on a computer translation project without producing a working sys-

tem, canceled a meeting with Guzman after he flew to Brussels with money from Latin American governments to demonstrate Atamiri.

15 "Machine translation has a bad history, so much money has been wasted," says Guzman. "Why pay a mad Bolivian using Aymara who claims he can solve a problem that 11 European universities can't solve?"

16 To support his family and keep the research going, Guzman has had to continue working as a consultant in computing accounting systems.

17 The long haul may be ending. In July, Bull signed a letter of intent to buy the system and Guzman is negotiating a deal with the firm. But Guzman says his dream is not to get rich by selling his invention.

18 Inspired by the language that gave him his idea, Guzman would like to dedicate himself to helping the Aymaras, most of whom live in poverty on the inhospitable high Andean plain.

19 With enough money coming in from his translation system, he says Atamiri could be used to translate books into Aymara and even form the basis of a newspaper for the Indians.

20 Atamiri could then become the savior of the Aymara language, which, after surviving 4,000 years, is being slowly displaced by Spanish.

■ READING COMPREHENSION QUESTIONS

1. The Andean civilization of the Aymara reached its cultural peak about (a) 500 years ago (b) 1,000 years ago (c) 200 to 300 years ago (d) 7,500 years ago

2. Ivan Guzman de Rojas, whose translator prototype can now cross between any of ten languages, is neither a linguist nor a translator but rather a professional (a) musician (b) engineer (c) professor of history (d) mathematician

3. Moments of inspiration sometimes occur in unusual circumstances. Guzman, for example, first conceived of the multilingual translator as

he was (a) shaving before going to work (b) reading the newspaper
(c) teaching math (d) reading an article on Aymara grammar

4.   The multilingual translator is called "Atamiri," which is itself a
word taken from the Aymara language, meaning (a) "bridge over a
canyon" (b) "loud voice" (c) "translator" (d) "peace"

5.   The first commercial use of Atamiri came in the mid–1980s
when the machine was used to translate between Spanish and English
by the (a) U.S. Army central command headquarters in Panama
(b) Mitsubishi Enterprises of Colombia (c) National News Services of
Argentina (d) Panama Canal Commission

6.   To support his family and meet research expenses for the further
development and refinement of Atamiri, Guzman has had to continue
his work (a) as a consultant in computing accounting systems (b) as a
professional Spanish-English translator (c) writing language skills development textbooks (d) teaching at the Bolivian Maritime Academy

■ TARGET VOCABULARY

to conquer	**multilingual**	**long haul**
mysterious	**to stump**	**to inspire**
civilization	**unambiguous**	**inhospitable**
guttural	**linguist**	**savior**
prototype	**commercial**	**to displace**

Dictionary Practice

Use each word in a sentence of your own.

1.   to conquer _____

2.   mysterious _____

3.   civilization _____

4.   guttural _____

5.   prototype _____

6.   multilingual _____

7.   to stump _____

8.   unambiguous _____

9.   linguist _____

10.   commercial _____

11. long haul _____

12. to inspire _____

13. inhospitable _____

14. savior _____

15. to displace _____

Cloze Practice

Fill in each blank with an appropriate word from the target vocabulary list.

A _____ is a scholar who studies how language works and usually has _____ several languages personally in order to become _____. Over the _____ of such study and research, a Bolivian mathematician, Ivan Guzman de Rojas, became _____ to solve a puzzle that has _____ other linguists for years: perfect "parallel" translation, an _____ form identical to the original. Based on the "throaty," or _____, Aymara language, a remnant of their _____ and now-lost _____, Guzman's system may ironically become a _____ success and the financial _____ of today's Aymara tribe.

■ CRITICAL READING PRACTICE/TOPICS FOR DISCUSSION

1. After 4,000 years, we learn from the article, the Aymara language itself is being displaced by Spanish. Why do you suppose that this is happening? Can you think of other languages that have been wiped out? In what ways does this process occur?

2. The languages Atamiri "knows" so far all use the Roman alphabet, the same one we use in English. Some have "diacritical marks," symbols that tell pronunciation, like the ˜ over an ñ in Spanish; but all use the same alphabet. How do you think the Guzman project might deal with languages that use other alphabets (for example Hebrew or Arabic) or that use other systems entirely (such as Chinese)?

3.   Assume that Guzman's project makes a lot of money and that much of it goes to help the Aymara. Do you think that Guzman's efforts, or any efforts, can save the language from extinction? Why, or why not?

4.   Assuming it proves to be completely successful, what effects do you think Atamiri might have in terms of international relations? How about its potential effects on business, education, medicine, and the arts?

5.   If you had access to Atamiri's theoretical translation potential, with whom would you like to speak, in what language, and why? What would you choose as a topic of conversation, and why would you choose it?

CHAPTER 5

■ *The Editorial Section*

■ *We Are What We Eat*

Editorials are designed to give opinions, sometimes shocking ones, but the following editorial by Steve Rubenstein of the San Francisco Chronicle *goes about this job in an unusual way. In "You've Just Had Some Kind of Mushroom," we hear an amused and tolerant voice reflecting indirectly on the attraction of danger in various activities, not just mushroom hunting.*

Interesting issues of liberty and restraint are also raised by Rubenstein's essay, some of which are dealt with in the critical reading questions at the end of the selection.

■ PRE-READING FOR DISCUSSION

The following editorial is really a celebration of human individuality, specifically of people who "hunt" and eat wild mushrooms. There is always a chance, of course, that a wild mushroom can be poisonous and even fatal. But as one participant in the mushroom fair explains, that very fact is what "makes mushrooms interesting."

Many sports and hobbies are dangerous, and that element of danger is often part of the attraction of such activities. People who enjoy such things as hang-gliding, bungee-jumping, surfing in shark-infested waters, and hunting wild mushrooms have all decided that the risks are acceptable to them. And who can disagree with their decisions, since only they may be affected?

A very important principle is defended in this piece: the right of everybody to do what others might think is a little crazy, so long as they place no one else at risk. It is a defense of liberty and what Thomas Jefferson called "the pursuit of happiness."

The title of Steve Rubenstein's column, "You've Just Had Some Kind of Mushroom," is taken from the lyrics of a 1960s song called "White Rabbit" by the rock group Jefferson Airplane and their lead vocalist, Grace Slick. The song is based on one of the truly great books in English literature, Lewis Carroll's *Alice in Wonderland*. In that story, Alice eats a mushroom and . . . well . . . things change for her. While "White Rabbit" is specifically about drug use, none of the mushroom hunters at the mushroom fair are hunting mushrooms that have such effects.

Still, Rubenstein's title raises interesting questions regarding reasonable liberties, rights, restraints, and responsibilities.

You've Just Had Some Kind of Mushroom

Steve Rubenstein

1   With a mushroom, there is scant margin for error. Eat the wrong one and die.

2   "It makes mushrooms interesting, don't you think?" said a man with a sack of mushrooms at the mushroom fair in Golden Gate Park. They were safe mushrooms, he was pretty sure, but just in case he was bringing them to the identify-your-mushroom table. Could he eat them, he asked nonchalantly, without going belly up?

3   The answer was technically yes.

4   "These mushrooms will make you very sick, but they won't kill you," said Harry Thiers, the head mushroom man.

5   Thiers is a retired professor of mushrooms at San Francisco State University. He presides over the identify-your-mushroom table at the Mycological Society of San Francisco's annual fair mainly, it seems, to protect mushroom fans from themselves.

6   The Bay Area is covered with a beautiful wild mushroom called *Amanita phalloides,* for instance. It's a lovely little thing, yellowish white, cute as a button. One bite and you will be pushing up mushrooms.

7   "I don't eat mushrooms myself," said Thiers, perhaps citing the factor that enabled him to reach retirement age in the wild-mushroom field. "I love their structure, their beauty, their appearance. Eating them does not appeal to me."

8   A mushroom fair is a dark, cool, mysterious affair, like most mushroom turf. People with sacks full of mushrooms wander about, flashing them at each other, swapping talk, occasionally swapping mushrooms. At the snack bar is mushroom pizza for $2.50 a slice. The caterer was trying to get into the spirit of the fair, but hardly anyone ate the pizza. The mushroom on it was *Agaricus*

bisporus, which is the common kind of mushroom sold in supermarkets.

9   "They have no taste," said Daniel Knapp of Mill Valley. "They are a flabby mushroom, entirely uninteresting."

10   Knapp got sick on a wild mushroom 50 years ago in Germany. He seemed almost proud. Everyone at the mushroom fair, it appeared, had gotten sick from a wild mushroom.

11   "You don't get to be an expert until you've been poisoned at least once," said Leon Ilnicki, who was staffing the toxicology table. Beside him was a sign that asked the trenchant question: "Is there a test to show which mushrooms are safe and which are poisonous?"

12   And then the answer.

13   "No."

14   Michael Rossman of Berkeley held in his hand an *Agaricus xanthodermus,* which, he said, is a very tasty mushroom until it makes you sick. He didn't eat it, but he did eat a small worm that had crawled from the top of the mushroom. He said the worm was considered by some to be a great delicacy.

15   "It's not all right to eat the mushroom," he said, "but it's all right to eat a worm that has eaten the mushroom. With mushrooms, you learn to be modest about what you know. Mushrooms have a way of punishing the haughty."

16   There were good mushrooms to go with the bad ones, but it was hard work finding out about them. People who find tasty mushrooms play their cards close.

17   "Why do you want to know?" said mushroom hunter Aaron Roland, when I asked where he had found his sack of prized chanterelle mushrooms.

| 18   He studied me as if I were an *Agaricus bisporus*. | 19   "I found them in Marin County," he said. "Under an oak tree. That's all I can say." |

■ EXPLODED VIEW FOR STUDY

Each of the highlighted terms should be mastered in the following exercises.

You've Just Had Some Kind of Mushroom

Steve Rubenstein

1   With a mushroom, there is scant margin for error. Eat the wrong one and die.

2   "It makes mushrooms interesting, don't you think?" said a man with a sack of mushrooms at the mushroom fair in Golden Gate Park. They were safe mushrooms, he was pretty sure, but just in case he was bringing them to the identify-your-mushroom table. Could he eat them, he asked nonchalantly, without going belly up?

3   The answer was technically yes.

4   "These mushrooms will make you very sick, but they won't kill you," said Harry Thiers, the head mushroom man.

5   Thiers is a retired professor of mushrooms at San Francisco State University. He presides over the identify-your-mushroom table at the Mycological Society of San Francisco's annual fair mainly, it seems, to protect mushroom fans from themselves.

6   The Bay Area is covered with a beautiful wild mushroom called *Amanita phalloides,* for instance. It's a lovely little thing, yellowish white, cute as a button. One bite and you will be pushing up mushrooms.

7   "I don't eat mushrooms myself," said Thiers, perhaps citing the factor that enabled him to reach retirement age in the wild-mushroom field. "I love their structure, their beauty, their appearance. Eating them does not appeal to me."

8   A mushroom fair is a dark, cool, mysterious affair, like most mushroom turf. People with sacks full of mushrooms wander about,

flashing them at each other, swapping talk, occasionally swapping mushrooms. At the snack bar is mushroom pizza for $2.50 a slice. The caterer was trying to get into the spirit of the fair, but hardly anyone ate the pizza. The mushroom on it was *Agaricus bisporus,* which is the common kind of mushroom sold in supermarkets.

9   "They have no taste," said Daniel Knapp of Mill Valley. "They are a flabby mushroom, entirely uninteresting."

10   Knapp got sick on a wild mushroom 50 years ago in Germany. He seemed almost proud. Everyone at the mushroom fair, it appeared, had gotten sick from a wild mushroom.

11   "You don't get to be an expert until you've been poisoned at least once," said Leon Ilnicki, who was staffing the toxicology table. Beside him was a sign that asked the trenchant question: "Is there a test to show which mushrooms are safe and which are poisonous?"

12   And then the answer.

13   "No."

14   Michael Rossman of Berkeley held in his hand an *Agaricus xanthodermus,* which, he said, is a very tasty mushroom until it makes you sick. He didn't eat it, but he did eat a small worm that had crawled from the top of the mushroom. He said the worm was considered by some to be a great delicacy.

15   "It's not all right to eat the mushroom," he said, "but it's all right to eat a worm that has eaten the mushroom. With mushrooms, you learn to be modest about what you know. Mushrooms have a way of punishing the haughty."

16   There were good mushrooms to go with the bad ones, but it was hard work finding out about them. People who find tasty mushrooms play their cards close.

17   "Why do you want to know?" said mushroom hunter Aaron Roland, when I asked where he had found his sack of prized chanterelle mushrooms.

18   He studied me as if I were an *Agaricus bisporus.*

19   "I found them in Marin County," he said. "Under an oak tree. That's all I can say."

■ READING COMPREHENSION QUESTIONS

1. According to Leon Ilnicki, who was working at the toxicology table of the Mycological Society, no one can claim to be an expert on mushrooms until they have first (a) eaten at least two dozen species of mushroom (b) passed a rigorous examination on the edible types of mushroom (c) been poisoned by a mushroom at least once (d) gathered and eaten mushrooms for a minimum of ten years

2. Professor Harry Thiers, retired from the faculty of San Francisco State University, is a specialist in mycology and greatly admires mushrooms ("I love their structure, their beauty, their appearance"). As great as his admiration is for mushrooms, however, Professor Thiers never (a) picks and kills them (b) handles them without rubber gloves (c) dissects them (d) eats them

3. At the Mycological Society fair, the caterer's mushroom pizza did not sell well because (a) mushroom hunters disdain common, supermarket mushrooms of the type typically used on pizza (b) most mushroomers are too health-conscious to eat pizza under any circumstances (c) the mushrooms on the pizzas looked suspiciously like a poisonous variety (d) Professor Thiers provided an example for the fairgoers

4. The fact that eating the wrong mushroom can kill you makes mushrooms, in the opinion of one mushroom fair participant, (a) foolhardy (b) idiotic (c) interesting (d) amusing

5. Reporter Steve Rubenstein found that when it comes to revealing the locations of their wild-mushroom spots, mushroomers are extremely (a) secretive (b) eager to share (c) precise in their directions (d) open and cooperative

6. *Agaricus xanthodermus* "is a very tasty mushroom until it makes you sick," so instead of eating the mushroom directly, one can (a) cross it with less toxic species (b) dilute it into a broth (c) use it as a fertilizer for other mushrooms (d) eat a worm which has eaten the mushroom

■ TARGET VOCABULARY

scant	annual	toxicology
margin for error	to cite	trenchant
nonchalant	factor	delicacy
technically	to enable	haughty
to preside	to staff	prized

Dictionary Practice

Use each word in a sentence of your own.

1. scant _____

2. margin for error _____

   _____

3. nonchalant _____

4. technically _____

5. to preside _____

6. annual _____

7. to cite _____

8. factor _____

9. to enable _____

10. to staff _____

11. toxicology _____

12. trenchant _____

13. delicacy _____

14. haughty _____

15. prized _____

Cloze Practice

Fill in each blank with an appropriate word from the target vocabulary list.

Sometimes danger is a _____ in enjoyment, as it seems
to be to those _____ enough to consider the wild mushroom a _____. Although there is only _____ room
for any misidentification, mushroom lovers _____ this
dangerous _____ as part of the attraction. _____, or
"the science of poisons," warns that several wild mushrooms, while
not _____ lethal, can lead to severe illness. For this reason, a
retired professor _____ over the identification booth at
the _____ convention of mushroom lovers as they brought
their _____ specimens for analysis.

■ CRITICAL READING PRACTICE/TOPICS FOR DISCUSSION

1.   Do you enjoy some sport or hobby that others consider dangerous? If so, what is it, and what objections do others have about your participation in it? If not, can you think of a sport or hobby that might interest you if it weren't for the danger involved?

2.   How do you feel about restricting the actions of others in order to protect them from harm? If you are in favor of such restrictions, how do you justify limiting people's freedom, if their actions affect only themselves? If you are opposed to such restrictions, how do you feel about seatbelt laws, motorcycle helmet laws, tobacco laws (or the lack of them), marijuana laws, or pornography laws?

3.   Can you think of activities that seem to be made, as one mushroomer put it, "interesting," *because* of the dangers involved? Does anyone in your family or among your friends engage in activities that strike you as being dangerous? If so, in what ways do you find these activities a threat to your relative's or friend's well-being?

4.   In your opinion, *why* do some people enjoy dangerous sports and activities such as sky diving or collecting and eating wild mushrooms?

Sample Map Exercise For "You've Just Had Some Kind of Mushroom" —Steve Rubenstein

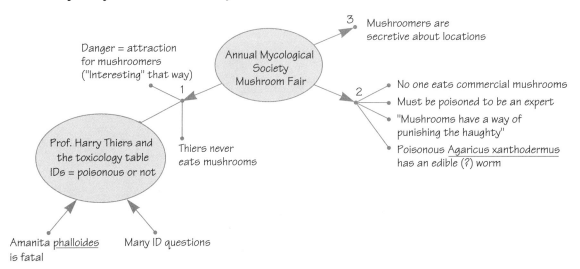

Note: For each of the following readings in this chapter, you are encouraged to draw maps of your own like this one, applying the mapping skills you learned in Part I.

■ *A Distant War with Present Heroes*

Often our closest contacts with history are through family members who lived it. This is the case Marilyn Geewax describes in "Toasting the Heroes Who Fought Fascism."

Historically, veterans have reunited on the anniversaries of important events that occurred during the particular war in which they fought, but in the following editorial they are remembered more generally and, perhaps, made a bit more universal. Do you find any special significance in the fact that the event which brings these veterans together is a wedding?

■ PRE-READING FOR DISCUSSION

History is never truly recorded by facts.

We know that from 1939 to 1945, lives were snuffed out by the tens of millions in World War II.

We know that millions of people lost the precious songs of their existence simply because of their ethnic heritage.

We know that history is a fragile thing, and that all we hold dear in the West was very near extinction during the most horrible war in the history of man, a war ended by the most horrible act ever committed by the hand of man.

History is actually the fossil record of people, how they acted, hoped, and loved—just as we do now.

Marilyn Geewax is keenly aware that history is the record of individual lives, rather than some set of battlefield statistics or data regarding weapons production. Her editorial, "Toasting the Heroes Who Fought Fascism," is a wonderful reminder that the world into which most of us were born would not exist but for the courage, strength, and sacrifice of those who fought and those who died to shape history according to their beliefs.

Neither should we forget or underestimate the heroism of those who fought against the United States and the Allies in World War II. They also did what they believed to be their duty, and they too are part of the terrible fabric of those times which so shaped our century.

People are the stuff of history, but they are not its record. We remember generals and admirals and battles. But the true record of war, any war, is grieving families, lost dreams, and the survivors too wise to celebrate anything but the fact that the madness is over and that they have not lost.

Toasting the Heroes Who Fought Fascism

Marilyn Geewax

1   They sit in small coffee shops and on park benches now, bundled up against the deepening winter.

2   They complain about rising medical costs, laugh over old jokes and show each other pictures of beloved grandchildren.

3   While a few are still working, most of the millions of men whose lives were jolted by the torpedoes at Pearl Harbor are retired. In their lined faces, it's hard to see the young men they once were—skinny guys with sharp eyes and God-given teeth.

4   But under those layers of years lie the boys who, 50 years ago, kissed their moms good-by and boarded ships bound for places they could barely pronounce, let alone imagine.

5   Get them talking today and they can recount five-decade old events in exquisite detail—where they were when they heard about the Japanese bombs, what they ate that first night away from home, how scared they were when the real shooting finally began.

6   Their stories get told and retold. Many times I have heard about how my aunt sat down not long after Pearl Harbor to begin writing the first of hundreds of letters to the young, lank husband she would not see again for years.

7   My father served, along with three brothers and one sister. One day they were gawky teenagers hoping to find work, the next they were in uniforms performing deadly serious jobs.

8   For us postwar babies, it's difficult to imagine the kinds of adjustments our parents were forced to make for the war effort.

9   I have no idea what it's like to save tin, ration sugar or give up driving to save gas.

10   Virtually every member of the World War II generation—male and female—endured personal hardships after that day of infamy in 1941.

11   But certainly the greatest sacrifices were made by the young men who left behind their farms, small towns and city neighborhoods for forbidding foreign lands.

12   Those who survived returned to a country crackling with energy and job opportunities. Those returning men may have been the most blessed generation in the nation's history. Throughout the 1950s, 1960s and 1970s, labor unions and economic growth helped provide them with good-paying jobs, decent benefits and comfortable homes.

13   Today, those veterans, by and large, are out of the workforce. With each passing year, their numbers dwindle and their personal stories fade along with the creased snapshots of boys in crisp uniforms.

14   Recently, at my brother's wedding, I saw my father and many of my uncles. They remain modest about their long-ago lives as soldiers. Ask them what they did in the war, and they'll downplay their own contributions. They say they were just doing what had to be done.

15   But as I look at those good men with their thinning hair and bifocals, I can recognize the heroes who once threw their lean bodies into the fight against fascism. And I will always be grateful to them.

■ **EXPLODED VIEW FOR STUDY**

Each of the highlighted terms should be mastered in the following exercises.

Toasting the Heroes Who Fought Fascism

Marilyn Geewax

1 They sit in small coffee shops and on park benches now, bundled up against the deepening winter.

2 They complain about rising medical costs, laugh over old jokes and show each other pictures of beloved grandchildren.

3 While a few are still working, most of the millions of men whose lives were jolted by the torpedoes at Pearl Harbor are retired. In their lined faces, it's hard to see the young men they once were— skinny guys with sharp eyes and God-given teeth.

4 But under those layers of years lie the boys who, 50 years ago, kissed their moms good-by and boarded ships bound for places they could barely pronounce, let alone imagine.

5 Get them talking today and they can recount five-decade old events in exquisite detail—where they were when they heard about the Japanese bombs, what they ate that first night away from home, how scared they were when the real shooting finally began.

6 Their stories get told and retold. Many times I have heard about how my aunt sat down not long after Pearl Harbor to begin writing the first of hundreds of letters to the young, lank husband she would not see again for years.

7 My father served, along with three brothers and one sister. One day they were gawky teenagers hoping to find work, the next they were in uniforms performing deadly serious jobs.

8 For us postwar babies, it's difficult to imagine the kinds of adjustments our parents were forced to make for the war effort.

9 I have no idea what it's like to save tin, ration sugar or give up driving to save gas.

10　　Virtually every member of the World War II generation—male and female—endured personal hardships after that day of infamy in 1941.

11　　But certainly the greatest sacrifices were made by the young men who left behind their farms, small towns and city neighborhoods for forbidding foreign lands.

12　　Those who survived returned to a country crackling with energy and job opportunities. Those returning men may have been the most blessed generation in the nation's history. Throughout the 1950s, 1960s and 1970s, labor unions and economic growth helped provide them with good-paying jobs, decent benefits and comfortable homes.

13　　Today, those veterans, by and large, are out of the workforce. With each passing year, their numbers dwindle and their personal stories fade along with the creased snapshots of boys in crisp uniforms.

14　　Recently, at my brother's wedding, I saw my father and many of my uncles. They remain modest about their long-ago lives as soldiers. Ask them what they did in the war, and they'll downplay their own contributions. They say they were just doing what had to be done.

15　　But as I look at those good men with their thinning hair and bifocals, I can recognize the heroes who once threw their lean bodies into the fight against fascism. And I will always be grateful to them.

■　READING COMPREHENSION QUESTIONS

1.　After half a century, the veterans at the wedding attended by Marilyn Geewax now recall the events of their World War II experiences (a) incompletely at best (b) only in general ways (c) in exquisite detail (d) without any reluctance

2.　For rapid military deployment, modern armies are usually transported by plane. In World War II, however, the great majority of U.S. troops traveled to military theaters abroad by (a) troop barge (b) dirigible (c) ships (d) the land bridge

3.   Like most Americans, Geewax's family dates the beginning
of World War II from December 7, 1941, the day of the attack on
(a) France's Maginot Line (b) Warsaw (c) Shanghai (d) Pearl Harbor.

4.   Every year, Geewax points out, the numbers of World War II veterans dwindle and with them fade the stories and the (a) memories of
long-ago battles (b) old divisions and hatreds (c) Veterans of Foreign
Wars members (d) snapshots from another time

5.   Geewax noted one complaint common among the veterans gathered for the wedding: (a) the unemployment rate (b) voter apathy
(c) rising medical costs (d) athletes' salaries

6.   Those who survived World War II returned to a United States
which was (a) filled with energy and job opportunities (b) still weak-
ened by the war effort (c) struggling with a huge national debt and
inflation (d) enthusiastically behind President Harry Truman

■ TARGET VOCABULARY

to jolt	**lank**	**forbidding**
torpedoes	**to serve**	**creased**
to board	**gawky**	**crisp**
to recount	**to ration**	**to downplay**
exquisite	**day of infamy**	**bifocals**

Dictionary Practice

Use each word in a sentence of your own.

1. to jolt _____

2. torpedoes _____

3. to board _____

4. to recount _____

5. exquisite _____

6. lank _____

7. to serve _____

8. gawky _____

9. to ration _____

10. day of infamy _____

11. forbidding _____

12. creased _____

13. crisp _____

14. to downplay _____

15. bifocals _____

Cloze Practice

Fill in each blank with an appropriate word from the target vocabulary list.

Wars often begin with an incident that _____ the public.

Perhaps _____ sink a fleet, as on December 7, 1941, which

President Franklin Roosevelt called a _____ at Pearl Harbor.

Or maybe people in the marketplace hear of huge armies gathered in

Turkey _____ Xerxes in his invasion of Greece.

Soldiers often have much in common across time, too. One day

they are _____ and _____ young men, the next

they wear _____, _____ uniforms and are ready

_____ vessels bound for Troy or Vietnam. In later years,

the survivors will _____ their experiences, usually, oddly,

_____ the roles they had in the unreal "fog" of combat.

■ CRITICAL READING PRACTICE/TOPICS FOR DISCUSSION

1. Most veterans of World War II are now in their seventies. If you have a family member who served in that war, in the army of any country, how did you become aware of their service and how do you feel about it?

If your family was unaffected by that war, or affected by it only indirectly, explain where your relatives were living at the time in order to escape most of that war's horror.

2. What war, not necessarily involving the United States, do you think has had the greatest effect on the lives of your family and friends? El Salvador? Vietnam? Iran-Iraq? Korea? What forms did this effect take?

3. Do you think that the history of World War II has been taught to you well? Are you clear about which countries were involved? Are you familiar with any of the political or military leaders of that war? Do you think that it is important for students now to study something that is half a century old? Why, or why not?

4. What elements of history, if any, do you consider the most important things to learn during your student years? If you do not think that learning history is important at all, why do you feel as you do?

5. Personally, under what circumstances do you think it is justified for a nation to go to war? Why do you feel as you do? Can you think of exceptions in history to your criteria? Can you think of specific exceptions in U.S. history?

Some Differences between Learning and Training

Good editorial essays state strong opinions and ignite heated discussion. It is reasonably safe to say that the following editorial on American higher education, by a former community college teacher, will do just that.

In brief, this editorial contends that higher education in the United States is doing more harm than good. It may teach and transmit information, but at the same time it crushes students spiritually and intellectually. Higher education may train and prepare people for the workplace, but it strips them of their souls in the process, dehumanizes them, producing conformity, shallowness, and "small dreams."

You might consider the power of the printed word, especially in such a searing essay as this, as a starting point for class discussion.

■ PRE-READING FOR DISCUSSION

The following editorial argues passionately in defense of learning, rather than simply training, in our post-secondary schools. Its point of view should trigger considerable thought among all students.

Generally speaking, "training" is an end in itself, with a clear, honorable, measurable result. Skills are clearly identified and taught as a means of solving specific problems. Study TV repair and you can repair TVs. Study Motel Management and you can manage motels.

And that's great. A deal is a deal. You do, you earn.

"Learning," though, is a quite different thing, often without measurable results at all beyond the retaining of certain information (which isn't actually learning if it goes no further than remembering stuff). Study literature, for example, and you have nothing material or physical to show for it. Ever. Study sculpture, and while you have physical or conceptual constructions, their existence is all they "do."

Learning, then, may have a general direction or medium, but it has no actual "end."

In "Small School, Dull Dreams," former college instructor Joe Bob Briggs identifies a sobering truth: training is rewarded with money, learning is rewarded only with itself; and money looks more attractive than learning, especially to young people. The young playwright/advertiser Briggs describes hopes to have it both ways by making money and *then* writing plays. That approach doesn't work once in ten million tries.

Student decisions on learning vs. training are important personal choices. Both are equally valid, and let us be thankful that students are free to choose.

But let us also hope that students listen carefully to their minds and hearts: there is no more "practical" or "realistic" advice in the world than the advice from one's soul.

Small School, Dull Dreams

Lower education

Joe Bob Briggs

1   Today's unanswerable question is: What genius invented the following bromide? "Everybody should go to college."

2   We might as well go ahead and stick this one in the Bill of Rights. Everybody in the whole dang country believes this is what you've got to do as soon as you turn 18, and if you don't do it, then the hell with you. You deserve to be selling Amway products.

3   That's why we have the only country in the world that spends more money on so-called higher education than we spend on first graders. We've got places in the Midwest with populations of less than 5,000 that have their own "community college" or "junior college" or "teacher's college" or Southwestern State Agricultural Institute (the more Podunk the college, the longer the name). And we have tax districts supporting these places, and we have weenie math professors who couldn't get hired as the janitor at an Ivy League school, but they can be the head of the department at Struthers County Tech.

4   And we keep building them, and we keep pouring money into them, and they all look like sausage warehouses, because they're designed by government architects, and they all have night schools where guys named Maynard can get their Motel Management degree.

5   And the people in these schools are miserable. They don't want to be there. They don't want to be listening to some nervous assistant professor with dandruff describe the principles of organic chemistry to 38-year-old divorcées and 27-year-old Nigerian exchange students and 19-year-old juvenile delinquents who made a deal with a judge to go to college instead of going to jail.

6   Even the ones who want to be in school are there for some kind of reason normally heard on "infomercials" on late-night TV:

7   "I'm working on a B.S. in real estate management. My goal is to be making $100,000 a year by the time I'm 30."

8   "I chose civil engineering, instead of electrical engineering, because there will be a shortage of civil engineers around 1995, and I'll be able to advance my career twice as fast."

9   You have to wonder about these people. You have to wonder, first of all, why they have such small dreams. People used to dream about being millionaires. Now they dream about making $100,000 a year. People used to dream about designing the next Golden Gate Bridge. Now they dream about working for a company that designs plumbing systems on Donald Trump skyscrapers.

10   What's worse, they don't even believe in their own bullstuff.

11   I know. I used to teach at one of these schools. On the last day of the semester, the students would finish their final exams and turn in their blue books. Before they walked out of my life forever, I would step into the hall with them to say goodbye, and our conversations would always go something like this:

12   "Good luck, Stu. Do you know what you're going to do when you get out of college?"

13   "One of the ad agencies here in town has some entry-level positions. It's not much money, but you get noticed."

14 I notice that Stu doesn't seem too en-thused about this, so I say, "Is that what you *want* to do?"

15 "Oh, yeah, I guess so."

16 "I noticed on your résumé that you did community theater, you wrote for the liter-ary magazine—are those just hobbies or were you serious about the arts?"

17 "I love the theater. I would love to write plays."

18 "Why don't you do that?"

19 "Oh, I will someday."

20 "But not now, huh?"

21 "I can't afford it right now."

22 "I see."

23 "I'll save up some money—write plays in my spare time."

24 And so we part. There's a sadness to it. I'm talking about something that happened not just one time, but over and over and over again. We have a whole generation of people who want to do one thing, but are programmed to do something else.

25 And so the great billion-dollar higher-education system has done its billion-dollar job. It's created a huge workforce of people whose spirits are so crushed they will do anything they've been trained for, no mat-ter how quickly it hastens the death of their minds and hearts.

26 That's what the higher education system has bought.

27 Good job.

■ **EXPLODED VIEW FOR STUDY**

Each of the highlighted words should be mastered in the following exercises.

Small School, Dull Dreams

Lower education

Joe Bob Briggs

1 Today's unanswerable question is: What genius invented the fol-lowing bromide? "Everybody should go to college."

2 We might as well go ahead and stick this one in the Bill of Rights. Everybody in the whole dang country believes this is what you've got to do as soon as you turn 18, and if you don't do it, then the hell with you. You deserve to be selling Amway products.

3 That's why we have the only country in the world that spends more money on so-called higher education than we spend on first graders. We've got places in the Midwest with populations of less than 5,000 that have their own "community college" or "junior college" or "teacher's college" or Southwestern State Agricultural

Institute (the more Podunk the college, the longer the name). And we have tax districts supporting these places, and we have weenie math professors who couldn't get hired as the janitor at an Ivy League school, but they can be the head of the department at Struthers County Tech.

4 And we keep building them, and we keep pouring money into them, and they all look like sausage warehouses, because they're designed by government architects, and they all have night schools where guys named Maynard can get their Motel Management degree.

5 And the people in these schools are miserable. They don't want to be there. They don't want to be listening to some nervous assistant professor with dandruff describe the principles of organic chemistry to 38-year-old divorcées and 27-year-old Nigerian exchange students and 19-year-old juvenile delinquents who made a deal with a judge to go to college instead of going to jail.

6 Even the ones who want to be in school are there for some kind of reason normally heard on "infomercials" on late-night TV:

7 "I'm working on a B.S. in real estate management. My goal is to be making $100,000 a year by the time I'm 30."

8 "I chose civil engineering, instead of electrical engineering, because there will be a shortage of civil engineers around 1995, and I'll be able to advance my career twice as fast."

9 You have to wonder about these people. You have to wonder, first of all, why they have such small dreams. People used to dream about being millionaires. Now they dream about making $100,000 a year. People used to dream about designing the next Golden Gate Bridge. Now they dream about working for a company that designs plumbing systems on Donald Trump skyscrapers.

10 What's worse, they don't even believe in their own bullstuff.

11 I know. I used to teach at one of these schools. On the last day of the semester, the students would finish their final exams and turn in their blue books. Before they walked out of my life forever, I would step into the hall with them to say good-bye, and our conversations would always go something like this:

12   "Good luck, Stu. Do you know what you're going to do when you get out of college?"

13   "One of the ad agencies here in town has some entry-level positions. It's not much money, but you get noticed."

14   I notice that Stu doesn't seem too enthused about this, so I say, "Is that what you *want* to do?"

15   "Oh, yeah, I guess so."

16   "I noticed on your résumé that you did community theater, you wrote for the literary magazine—are those just hobbies or were you serious about the arts?"

17   "I love the theater. I would love to write plays."

18   "Why don't you do that?"

19   "Oh, I will someday."

20   "But not now, huh?"

21   "I can't afford it right now."

22   "I see."

23   "I'll save up some money—write plays in my spare time."

24   And so we part. There's a sadness to it. I'm talking about something that happened not just one time, but over and over and over again. We have a whole generation of people who want to do one thing, but are programmed to do something else.

25   And so the great billion-dollar higher-education system has done its billion-dollar job. It's created a huge workforce of people whose spirits are so crushed they will do anything they've been trained for, no matter how quickly it hastens the death of their minds and hearts.

26   That's what the higher education system has bought.

27   Good job.

■ READING COMPREHENSION QUESTIONS

1.   The author of this impassioned editorial earned the right to his perhaps shocking opinions by (a) conducting a national survey of student interest and perceived reward (b) interviewing instructors throughout the Midwest (c) gathering data from the American Psychological Society (d) teaching

2.   What concerns Briggs most is not that we have too many schools or that instructors are molded by the system in which they work, but, rather, that the "dreams" of the students themselves have become (a) unrealistic (b) totally oriented toward helping others (c) selfish (d) small

3.   Taking the U.S. population as a whole, Briggs also violently disagrees with the general assumption that "everybody" should (a) go to college (b) perform some form of national service (c) register to vote even though they are uninformed (d) attend some form of religious services

4.   According to this editorial, the United States is the only country in the world that spends more money on "so-called higher education" than it spends on (a) drug enforcement (b) political campaigns and lobbying (c) drive-in movies (d) first-graders

5.   Briggs's former student Stu was pursuing a career in advertising even though his real intellectual passion was for (a) painting (b) Greek literature (c) medieval history relating to Italian maritime economic development (d) the theater

6.   This editorial was the result of the author having had essentially the same conversation (a) with another student besides Stu (b) with students from two separate classes (c) with a relative (d) over and over and over again

■   TARGET VOCABULARY

bromide	**semester**	**to program**
higher education	**entry-level**	**workforce**
warehouse	**enthused**	**spirit**
principles	**résumé**	**to crush**
shortage	**theater**	**to hasten**

Dictionary Practice

Use each word in a sentence of your own.

1.   bromide _____

2.   higher education _____

_____

   3. warehouse _____

   4. principles _____

   5. shortage _____

   6. semester _____

   7. entry-level _____

   8. enthused _____

   9. résumé _____

  10. theater _____

  11. to program _____

  12. workforce _____

  13. spirit _____

  14. to crush _____

  15. to hasten _____

Cloze Practice

   Fill in each blank with an appropriate word from the target vocabulary list.

   The United States system of public _____ was never intended _____ the _____ of its students or just to _____ people for a few years. But neither was its purpose ever simply _____ students like robots in order to fill _____ in the economy's _____, particularly in _____ jobs. Briggs argues that "practicality" is fine, except when students who are sincerely _____ about "impractical" fields, such as the arts, must subordinate their personal _____ to meet others' expectations.

■ CRITICAL READING PRACTICE/TOPICS FOR DISCUSSION

1. If you have reached any personal conclusions regarding your educational and/or employment future, what are your decisions and, most importantly, why have you made them? Do you think that Stu, in the editorial, is making the right choice? Why, or why not?

2.   Do you know people who regret having chosen the life they are now leading? What, specifically, don't they like about it? What other, different choices do they wish that they had made? How many of their complaints involve material things or money? How many involve feeling unfulfilled or empty or bored?

3.   Do you consider one choice better than the other in terms of this basic "love" or "money" decision? If so, why do you think that one is preferable? What is gained by choosing each direction? What is lost?

4.   Does Briggs's editorial challenge any of your assumptions regarding your own studies, either now or in the future? If so, in what ways does it challenge them? If not, are you then in agreement with the author?

5.   Do you think that the ideas and values discussed in this piece may help you reach better decisions of your own regarding your academic or personal plans? Why, or why not?

■ *Of Babies and Bathwater, Celibacy and Sexuality*

Our second controversial editorial takes a bold stand regarding sexuality at a time when such an opinion is neither popular nor "officially" accepted, as a result of the widespread AIDS crisis. But the essay raises some extremely thoughtful questions about society, AIDS, personal values, and exactly what it is that makes us members of a community.

Although a hundred points of controversy can be found in "A Few Kind Words for Vulgar Urges," you might begin your discussion with the author's analysis of the "elderly debate" he defines in paragraph 1.

■ PRE-READING FOR DISCUSSION

Just as we all consider our own opinion infallible when it comes to painting, music, and humor, we also secretly consider ourselves infallible in our opinions about sex and morality. And these healthy, honest differences of opinion regarding sexuality often surface—and sometimes explode—when we move from the general principle of freedom to the cold specifics of AIDS transmission.

In the following editorial, Jon Carroll makes a modest proposal: let us not confuse our humanity with wickedness and destruction.

AIDS is now a global tragedy. It has taken the lives of millions and will take the lives of many millions more before science can find, manufacture, and distribute any "magic bullet" to rid us of this plague. Yet since this process will take time, perhaps a long time from start to finish, we are left with the problem of how to conduct ourselves until a "cure" is found. And so are we left with the raised voices at school board meetings, the raised voices in churches, and the raised voices in the halls of governments, all three of which are too often long on certainty and short on the "tenderness . . . charity . . . compassion" expressed in Carroll's editorial.

The third paragraph of the piece may require some explanation. In requesting that someone "take all the modalities in China and put them in a big brown bag for me with all the paradigms in Europe . . . ," Carroll is parodying the lyrics of a beautiful song by Van Morrison titled "Tupelo Honey." His objective is to rid the serious debate at hand of the ridiculous, buzz-word nonsense so dear to the hearts of those who use terms like "modalities" for "methods" and "paradigm" for "pattern" or "system." The issue is difficult enough all by itself; it becomes more difficult still when people fog the discussion with verbal smoke bombs of pretended intelligence.

A Few Kind Words for Vulgar Urges

Jon Carroll

1   It's an elderly debate; you've heard both sides ad nauseam. One side recommends abstinence as the best strategy for preventing the spread of AIDS. If you just don't do it, then you won't get it, and if everybody doesn't do it, then no one will get it.

2   Impractical, says the other side. People are going to have sex one way or another; those crazy teens; those selfish yuppies. Let's face facts: Doing it will never go out of style. So the fight to prevent the spread of AIDS should concentrate on promoting the wearing of condoms and other safe sex practices.

3   Or safe sex "modalities," as I heard someone say on NPR [National Public Radio]. Could you take all the modalities in China and put them in a big brown bag for me with all the paradigms in Europe, and sail it round all the seven oceans, and drop it straight into the middle of the deep blue sea? So kind.

4   Implicitly, both sides agree that it would be best if everyone would just keep their clothes on. One side thinks that's an unwinnable battle; the other side doesn't.

5   Let me suggest another viewpoint: It would not be best if everyone just kept their clothes on. It would be bad if people stopped having sex. Sex is at once liberating and civilizing; sex is life-affirming; sex is fun.

6   If the joy of sex becomes a casualty of the AIDS epidemic, we will have lost an important way of showing love and feeling pleasure. I am in favor of love and pleasure.

7   That's always a controversial viewpoint; this culture has been confusing the denial of pleasure with moral superiority for just about ever. Impulse has managed to hold its own without allies in the past, but maybe now it needs a few friends.

8   I do not quarrel with other people's sexual preferences; if a person wants to remain celibate, that's OK with me. It's also OK with me if a person chooses not to listen to music, or read novels, or walk in meadows in springtime.

9   But I have *opinions*. It is my opinion that celibacy means missing out on an important part of our humanity. It is my opinion that sex promotes communication and harmony between the sexes, and that it bonds people together so they can become effective parents.

10   (That's why I think gay couples should be parents, by the way; they've already done the hard work, let them have the payoff).

11   We are all bundles of vulgar urges; pretending otherwise is sad. (I know some people think it's ennobling; I disagree). Some of the vulgar urges lead us to violence, to cruelty, to indifference. Others lead us to tenderness, to charity, to compassion.

12   I say we have a stake in promoting the latter kind of vulgar urge. I say a society without sex is an arid and nasty place. I say it is a major disservice to our culture to let that aspect of the current medical emergency go unacknowledged.

13   If it were me (and if I did not have to worry about getting funds from the federal government and other founts of prudery), I would urge people to do it safely but also to do it frequently.

14   I would suggest, in delicate but explicit language, the ways to maximize the pleasure of doing it safely. Hell, I would fund *research* into this important area of intellectual inquiry. In short, I would attempt to make sure that the ever-opportunistic neo-puritans are not allowed to hijack sexuality in the name of disease prevention.

15   It's this way: We have the baby, the

marvelous eternal infant of sex. We have the bathwater, a grungy lethal blood-borne virus. Keep the baby; eliminate the bathwater. Thank you.

■ **EXPLODED VIEW FOR STUDY**

Each of the highlighted words should be mastered in the following exercises.

A Few Kind Words for Vulgar Urges

Jon Carroll

1   It's an elderly debate; you've heard both sides ad nauseam. One side recommends abstinence as the best strategy for preventing the spread of AIDS. If you just don't do it, then you won't get it, and if everybody doesn't do it, then no one will get it.

2   Impractical, says the other side. People are going to have sex one way or another; those crazy teens; those selfish yuppies. Let's face facts: Doing it will never go out of style. So the fight to prevent the spread of AIDS should concentrate on promoting the wearing of condoms and other safe sex practices.

3   Or safe sex "modalities," as I heard someone say on NPR [National Public Radio]. Could you take all the modalities in China and put them in a big brown bag for me with all the paradigms in Europe, and sail it round all the seven oceans, and drop it straight into the middle of the deep blue sea? So kind.

4   Implicitly, both sides agree that it would be best if everyone would just keep their clothes on. One side thinks that's an unwinnable battle; the other side doesn't.

5   Let me suggest another viewpoint: It would not be best if everyone just kept their clothes on. It would be bad if people stopped having sex. Sex is at once liberating and civilizing; sex is life-affirming; sex is fun.

6   If the joy of sex becomes a casualty of the AIDS epidemic, we will have lost an important way of showing love and feeling pleasure. I am in favor of love and pleasure.

7   That's always a controversial viewpoint; this culture has been confusing the denial of pleasure with moral superiority for just about ever. Impulse has managed to hold its own without allies in the past, but maybe now it needs a few friends.

8   I do not quarrel with other people's sexual preferences; if a person wants to remain celibate, that's OK with me. It's also OK with me if a person chooses not to listen to music, or read novels, or walk in meadows in springtime.

9   But I have *opinions*. It is my opinion that celibacy means missing out on an important part of our humanity. It is my opinion that sex promotes communication and harmony between the sexes, and that it bonds people together so they can become effective parents.

10   (That's why I think gay couples should be parents, by the way; they've already done the hard work, let them have the payoff).

11   We are all bundles of vulgar urges; pretending otherwise is sad. (I know some people think it's ennobling; I disagree). Some of the vulgar urges lead us to violence, to cruelty, to indifference. Others lead us to tenderness, to charity, to compassion.

12   I say we have a stake in promoting the latter kind of vulgar urge. I say a society without sex is an arid and nasty place. I say it is a major disservice to our culture to let that aspect of the current medical emergency go unacknowledged.

13   If it were me (and if I did not have to worry about getting funds from the federal government and other founts of prudery), I would urge people to do it safely but also to do it frequently.

14   I would suggest, in delicate but explicit language, the ways to maximize the pleasure of doing it safely. Hell, I would fund *research* into this important area of intellectual inquiry. In short, I would attempt to make sure that the ever-opportunistic neo-puritans are not allowed to hijack sexuality in the name of disease prevention.

15   It's this way: We have the baby, the marvelous eternal infant of sex. We have the bathwater, a grungy lethal blood-borne virus. Keep the baby; eliminate the bathwater. Thank you.

■ READING COMPREHENSION QUESTIONS

1.   Jon Carroll makes it clear that he has no quarrel with other people's preferences, whether sexual, musical, literary, or in regard to walking in meadows in springtime. However, Carroll makes it equally clear that he does have (a) a clear sense of universal right and wrong (b) a religious orientation that provides clear moral guidelines (c) opinions (d) an unerring sense of what is best politically

2.   Carroll's opinion concerning common usage of the terms "modality" and "paradigm" is quite outspokenly (a) flattering (b) admiring (c) positive (d) hostile

3.   Since he believes, as have others, that sex "bonds people together so they can become effective parents," the author thinks that (a) sex should take place only after marriage (b) no power on earth can stop sex (c) gay couples should also be parents if they wish (d) restraining sexuality is of the utmost importance

4.   Carroll claims that a society without sex would be (a) a far more orderly system of social organization (b) arid and nasty (c) extremely easy prey for advertisers (d) a model for other nations and for history

5.   Carroll says that one faction in American society loudly favors abstinence as a response to AIDS, while another equally loud element prefers abstinence but sees it as an impractical goal. Carroll adopts a third viewpoint which advocates (a) enthusiastic but responsible sexuality (b) general celibacy punctuated by brief periods of total abandon (c) government control over sexual activity (d) a return to the precepts of medieval courtly love

6.   The author states that if "the joy of sex becomes a casualty of the AIDS epidemic" then we will (a) have actually lost very little (b) be in for some serious labor force problems (c) have fulfilled a centuries-old dream of several traditions (d) have lost an important way of showing love and feeling pleasure

■ TARGET VOCABULARY

ad nauseam	casualty	harmony
abstinence	epidemic	ennobling
implicitly	controversial	arid
liberating	denial	prudery
civilizing	humanity	hijack

Dictionary Practice

Use each word in a sentence of your own.

1. ad nauseam _____

2. abstinence _____

3. implicitly _____

4. liberating _____

5. civilizing _____

6. casualty _____

7. epidemic _____

8. controversial _____

9. denial _____

10. humanity _____

11. harmony _____

12. ennobling _____

13. arid _____

14. prudery _____

15. hijack _____

Cloze Practice

Fill in each blank with an appropriate word from the target vocabulary list.

Arguments about the AIDS _____ began as soon as the _____ disease was identified, and they have continued _____ since. Some voices call for sexual _____ by all, _____ suggesting that non-abstainers get what they deserve. Other voices condemn this viewpoint as dangerous _____, a _____ of reality that contributes to the problem. They argue that sexuality is _____ and _____ and contributes to personal and social _____, thereby _____ us all.

■ **CRITICAL READING PRACTICE/TOPICS FOR DISCUSSION**

1.   What is your basic belief about the best and most practical way to combat the scourge of AIDS? Do you agree with Jon Carroll that "both sides agree that it would be best if everyone would just keep their clothes on"? What have people told or ordered *you* to do in order to avoid placing yourself at risk? How practical do you consider their advice to be?

2.   Carroll argues that "sex promotes communication and harmony" and thereby "bonds people together so they can become effective parents." Do you agree or disagree? Why?
    He then argues that this is no less true for gay couples than for heterosexuals and that consequently "gay couples should be parents," if they so choose. Again, do you agree or disagree, and why?

3.   Our culture "has been confusing the denial of pleasure with moral superiority for just about ever," states the editorial. What examples of this can you think of in our cultural or national history that illustrate this? What examples of this do you see about you in present-day American society? In the educational system? In the government? In the law?

4.   As you were growing up, do you think that issues of sexuality were dealt with well in your family or was the issue perhaps avoided or treated lightly? How do you plan on treating this issue with any children you might have of your own?

■ *The Dollar Is One Thing. . . .*

Our final editorial concerns symbols—in this case military medals, but symbols in a more general sense than that.
    Military decorations are uniquely personal and national at the same time, and David Evans, the military affairs writer for the Chicago Tribune, *has some rather sharp remarks for a Pentagon and a nation that would allow medals to become devalued, even cheapened, to their present low levels.*
    His thoughtful editorial suggests, however, that there may be a lot of the same thing happening in other areas, such as business or education, and that this erosion of worth should concern us as a pattern *even more than it troubles us in terms of devalued decorations.*

■ PRE-READING FOR DISCUSSION

David Evans is an expert on military affairs. He is part historian, part theoretician, part teacher, and part the practical, frank voice of "Willy and Joe," Bill Mauldin's comic strip about a couple of unheroic GI heroes who slogged through World War II. But in the following editorial, Evans is not concerned with long-range strategy, defense preparedness, or what the Pentagon is up to lately.

In "Shutting Down Military Medal Machine," Evans argues that we have gradually allowed a cheapening of our military decorations to occur. Soldiers now receive, as a routine, medals for nothing and medals for very little. Turning the decorations we award our military into "Monopoly money," Evans suggests, results in two disservices: One is to our true heroes, who receive no real reward when decorations are commonplace; the second is to the past, to the millions of soldiers, sailors, airmen, WACS, and WAVES of Vietnam, Korea, World War II, and beyond.

We more or less expect politicians to be superficial, and we are buyers who beware in the marketplace. Skepticism regarding attorneys and the legal system, realtors, and government spokespersons is not entirely unjustified. But we *have* to count on some institutions and their people to tell us the truth: Teachers, cops, journalists, and soldiers seem like reasonable groups with which to begin, even though each has advanced "lies" in the past.

It becomes a question of honesty, finally: the military should make medals truly mean something and quit passing them out "like a pitching machine gone crazy." To do anything less simply isn't fair or honorable.

Shutting Down Military Medal Machine

David Evans

1   WASHINGTON The military awards system is running like a pitching machine gone crazy, pumping out so many medals and decorations that even the recipients sometimes wonder why they're getting them. The final tally from the Persian Gulf war is likely to total 6 million medals.

2   Charles Potempa got one for attending graduate school. The former Marine captain from Chicago spent his last two weeks in the corps, Aug. 2–15, 1990, checking out, packing his gear and driving back to Ohio State University. He received the National Defense Service Medal for simply being in the military in the two-week period following Iraq's invasion of Kuwait.

3   Every one of America's 3½ million active duty and reserve servicemembers in good standing also received this medal—just for being in the military during a period of national emergency.

4   "The system is lost," said Potempa in a telephone interview. "We've got too many medals, so many that it seems hard to stop giving them."

5   Herewith, a few principles that might repair the worst abuses of the system:

6   ▶ Stop giving something for nothing. Eliminate the National Defense Service Medal on the ground that just being in the military doesn't rate a medal. The troops call this medal "the brownie button," suggesting it has zippo prestige anyway.

7   ▶ No clubhouse medals. For the same reason the National Defense medal should be dropped, we might consider eliminating the Air Medal. It's awarded for flying either a certain number of combat missions or flying for so many months in a combat theater (the criteria vary by service). To be sure, there is a special danger in air operations,

but a ground trooper doesn't get a medal for so many combat actions, and walking point on a patrol is the most naked and vulnerable feeling in the world.

8   By the same token, the Distinguished Flying Cross could be eliminated. There is no Distinguished Submarining Cross, for example, so why should the aviators have a unique medal when the Silver Star and other medals exist for rewarding heroism in aerial combat?

9   ▶ No two-fers. Everybody who served in Vietnam received a service medal from the U.S. and a campaign medal from the South Vietnamese government. In the gulf war, every service member will receive at least three campaign medals: one from the U.S., a second from the Saudi government, and a third is in the works from the grateful emir of Kuwait. That's a whole row of participation medals.

10   Give the troops one U.S.-issued campaign medal. Tell the Saudis to hold the medals and send a $100 appreciation check to each of the troops instead. The emir can do likewise.

11   Combat is No. 1. The Medal of Honor and the various service crosses (e.g., Navy Cross) still rank Nos. 1 and 2 in the hierarchy of awards, but the Silver Star and the Bronze Star rank lower in precedence than a brace of medals for consummate staff work.

12   Good staff work can have a decisive impact on the battlefield, but remember what combat awards are all about. A typical citation for battlefield heroism begins with the words, "For action in the presence of an armed enemy. . . ."

13   The words are chilling, but they capture the contest of opposing wills and what war is all about. As a general principle, guts

under fire should rate a higher medal than sterling paperwork under fluorescent lights.

14 The Medal of Honor should be reserved for offensive combat, including counterattacks. Russel Stolfi, a Marine Corps reserve colonel, recalls that this was the German standard in World War II for awarding their highest medal, the Knight's Cross with Oak Leaves, Swords and Diamonds.

15 "The action had to be offensively oriented and have a significant impact on the battle," he said. Under this standard, the Medal of Honor would not be given to the soldier who throws himself on an enemy grenade to save the lives of his buddies. The Silver Star seems a fitting tribute for such bravery.

16 ▶ Real blood for the Purple Heart. Al-though this medal is supposed to be given only for wounds and death in action, in the Panama operation the Army awarded a Purple Heart to a soldier prostrated with heat exhaustion. Try this standard: The wound should break the skin and be severe enough to require evacuation from the unit for 48 hours or more.

17 ▶ Tighten up at the entry level. The debasement of the awards system begins at the cadet level, like the ROTC "colonel" seen wearing a chestful of medals and ribbons.

18 Strip all this stuff off the uniforms of our young Gen. MacArthurs. The overarching message should be that medals aren't like Monopoly money. They're given to real soldiers who fight real wars.

■ **EXPLODED VIEW FOR STUDY**

Each of the highlighted words should be mastered in the following exercises.

Shutting Down Military Medal Machine

David Evans

1 WASHINGTON The military awards system is running like a pitching machine gone crazy, pumping out so many medals and decorations that even the recipients sometimes wonder why they're getting them. The final tally from the Persian Gulf war is likely to total 6 million medals.

2 Charles Potempa got one for attending graduate school. The former Marine captain from Chicago spent his last two weeks in the corps, Aug. 2–15, 1990, checking out, packing his gear and driving back to Ohio State University. He received the National Defense Service Medal for simply being in the military in the two-week period following Iraq's invasion of Kuwait.

3   Every one of America's 3½ million active duty and reserve servicemembers in good standing also received this medal—just for being in the military during a period of national emergency.

4   "The system is lost," said Potempa in a telephone interview. "We've got too many medals, so many that it seems hard to stop giving them."

5   Herewith, a few principles that might repair the worst abuses of the system:

6   ▶ Stop giving something for nothing. Eliminate the National Defense Service Medal on the ground that just being in the military doesn't rate a medal. The troops call this medal "the brownie button," suggesting it has zippo prestige anyway.

7   ▶ No clubhouse medals. For the same reason the National Defense medal should be dropped, we might consider eliminating the Air Medal. It's awarded for flying either a certain number of combat missions or flying for so many months in a combat theater (the criteria vary by service). To be sure, there is a special danger in air operations, but a ground trooper doesn't get a medal for so many combat actions, and walking point on a patrol is the most naked and vulnerable feeling in the world.

8   By the same token, the Distinguished Flying Cross could be eliminated. There is no Distinguished Submarining Cross, for example, so why should the aviators have a unique medal when the Silver Star and other medals exist for rewarding heroism in aerial combat?

9   ▶ No two-fers. Everybody who served in Vietnam received a service medal from the U.S. and a campaign medal from the South Vietnamese government. In the gulf war, every service member will receive at least three campaign medals: one from the U.S., a second from the Saudi government, and a third is in the works from the grateful emir of Kuwait. That's a whole row of participation medals.

10   Give the troops one U.S.-issued campaign medal. Tell the Saudis to hold the medals and send a $100 appreciation check to each of the troops instead. The emir can do likewise.

11   Combat is No. 1. The Medal of Honor and the various service

crosses (e.g., Navy Cross) still rank Nos. 1 and 2 in the hierarchy of awards, but the Silver Star and the Bronze Star rank lower in precedence than a brace of medals for consummate staff work.

12   Good staff work can have a decisive impact on the battlefield, but remember what combat awards are all about. A typical citation for battlefield heroism begins with the words, "For action in the presence of an armed enemy. . . ."

13   The words are chilling, but they capture the contest of opposing wills and what war is all about. As a general principle, guts under fire should rate a higher medal than sterling paperwork under fluorescent lights.

14   The Medal of Honor should be reserved for offensive combat, including counterattacks. Russel Stolfi, a Marine Corps reserve colonel, recalls that this was the German standard in World War II for awarding their highest medal, the Knight's Cross with Oak Leaves, Swords and Diamonds.

15   "The action had to be offensively oriented and have a significant impact on the battle," he said. Under this standard, the Medal of Honor would not be given to the soldier who throws himself on an enemy grenade to save the lives of his buddies. The Silver Star seems a fitting tribute for such bravery.

16   ▶ Real blood for the Purple Heart. Although this medal is supposed to be given only for wounds and death in action, in the Panama operation the Army awarded a Purple Heart to a soldier prostrated with heat exhaustion. Try this standard: The wound should break the skin and be severe enough to require evacuation from the unit for 48 hours or more.

17   ▶ Tighten up at the entry level. The debasement of the awards system begins at the cadet level, like the ROTC "colonel" seen wearing a chestful of medals and ribbons.

18   Strip all this stuff off the uniforms of our young Gen. Mac-Arthurs. The overarching message should be that medals aren't like Monopoly money. They're given to real soldiers who fight real wars.

■ READING COMPREHENSION QUESTIONS

1. David Evans's editorial has one simple point: (a) there are not enough military medals and decorations being granted (b) the number of military decorations and medals being granted is absurdly high (c) Congress has been completely irresponsible in the granting of decorations (d) non-combat personnel receive far less recognition than they deserve

2. The number of servicemembers who received the National Defense Service Medal during the Persian Gulf War was (a) the roughly 1 million direct or indirect participants in that war (b) about 150,000 combat troops (c) all 3.5 million members of the armed forces at the time (d) a few elite combat units and individuals who performed particularly heroic actions under fire

3. Evans is especially critical of the fact that some awards granted to those who perform their duties in safety have become more valued than awards given to those who (a) are actually risking their lives in combat (b) willingly accept the risks of Pentagon politics (c) involve themselves with the current administration (d) testify before congressional budget committees

4. The editorial is firmly opposed to "two-fers," by which the author means (a) two pension or retirement payments received at the same time (b) more than one medal awarded for any given military campaign (c) the use of subsidized military stores by military personnel who do not live on a military base (d) claiming two religions in order to receive two days of release from military duties per week

5. The Purple Heart decoration is awarded for (a) faithful correspondence with a loved one while in the service (b) being physically wounded (c) donating blood while on active duty (d) serving overseas

6. Evans states that the "overarching message" of military decorations should be that they (a) represent gratitude and therefore should be given to as many military personnel as possible (b) are not to be taken seriously by troops (c) ought to be granted only in the field by immediate superior officers and reward heroism on the spot (d) are given to real soldiers who fight real wars

■ TARGET VOCABULARY

to pump out	aerial	under fire
recipient	hierarchy	sterling
to tally	precedence	prostrated
invasion	consummate	debasement
aviators	decisive	overarching

Dictionary Practice

Use each word in a sentence of your own.

1. to pump out _____

2. recipient _____

3. to tally _____

4. invasion _____

5. aviators _____

6. aerial _____

7. hierarchy _____

8. precedence _____

9. consummate _____

10. decisive _____

11. under fire _____

12. sterling _____

13. prostrated _____

14. debasement _____

15. overarching _____

Cloze Practice

Fill in each blank with an appropriate word from the target vocabulary list.

The _____ of any honor should be concerned by the _____ of the award later. If the _____ of an institution decides simply to _____ honors or decorations or degrees, then _____ has been ignored or rejected and the _____ concern of original recipients must be to take firm and _____ action to stop the problem from growing. For military decorations, one's _____ act of courage, particularly _____, is especially appreciated by other citizens and simply cannot be _____ up and equated to hours at a desk.

■   **CRITICAL READING PRACTICE/TOPICS
FOR DISCUSSION**

1.   The general emotional outlook or condition of a military unit, of any size, is called its "morale." What do you suppose the effect of "Monopoly money" decorations is, or may be, on the morale of U.S. armed forces members? Do you think that such an effect is good or bad? Do you think that decorations are intended to produce such an effect?

2.   In what other ways have things like medals lost the value they once had? Can you think of any in education, the economy and money, sports, music, or other types of awards? Be as specific as possible in comparing their past values with their present values.

3.   How do you think we could actually go about taking David Evans's advice and "shut down" this military "medal machine"? What specific, practical steps could be taken by Congress, for example, that might bring such foolishness to a halt? Do you think that such action is likely?

4.   In your opinion, how has it been possible that military decorations, one of the highest and most important honors a nation can give, have become so sadly cheapened? On what do you base your opinion?

CHAPTER 6

The Sports Section

Thousands of Dinosaurs in Buffalo, N.Y.

Few groups of people are so stereotyped as athletes. In all cases stereotyping is unfair, and the most common stereotypes about athletes are particularly misleading since women and men who have been athletes often go on to have interesting and challenging careers in dozens of professions, including law, medicine, politics, and education.

In fact, many sports demand a lot of imagination from their players. The first pre-reading essay and news article in this section look at two professional football players, Ray Bentley and Mike Hamby, who now write and illustrate a series of children's books featuring a baby dinosaur named "Darby."

As you think about athletic stereotypes, you might want to consider how and why other groups—ethnic, religious, and cultural—are stereotyped, as well.

PRE-READING FOR DISCUSSION

Our English word "athlete" has come down to us through several languages from a Greek word, the verb *athlein*, which means "to compete for a prize." Most nonathletes and many athletes (not to mention far too many coaches) assume that the only "prize" is victory; but it's actually much more than that.

The true prize is what we learn about ourselves *through* athletics. Naturally, when we're truly competing, we're trying to win—with every fiber of the body and spark of the mind. But days, years, and decades later, when the victories and losses have faded to insignificance, the lessons learned at third base, as goalie or forward, while running the hurdles, or through playing any position in any sport remain with us forever, advising caution, attack, prudence, and sometimes abandon.

Athletics also teach us an enormous amount about the efforts and skills and struggles of others, both our opponents and our teammates. If we have any native wisdom at all, this knowledge leads to compassion. If we do not, we miss the true lesson of athletics completely, ending up, perhaps, like Ty Cobb, one of the greatest baseball players of all time, who died cold, bitter, and lonely—still confusing winning on the field with the real "prize."

Two supremely successful athletes, Ray Bentley and Mike Hamby, are the subjects of our first sports story. Bentley is an absolute terror as a linebacker for the twice-to-the-Superbowl (at this writing) Buffalo Bills, and Hamby is a former lineman for that team, a man "from the trenches," where muscle, power, and speed are everything.

Bentley is also the author of a series of children's books about a glasses-wearing dinosaur called "Darby." Hamby is an illustrator and brings Darby to life visually through his drawings.

When Bentley and Hamby are old, old men, far from football fields and glory, children will still hold these stories in their hands, memorize them, perhaps learn to read from them, someday share them with their own children.

Nice game, guys.

Nice game.

Darby Has Become a Big Part of Ray Bentley's Playbook

Associated Press

1   Under Christmas trees throughout Buffalo on Christmas morning, little green dinosaurs were greeting happy children.

2   Darby the Dinosaur, the cartoon creation of Buffalo Bills linebacker/children's author Ray Bentley, has jumped off the book pages and become a cuddly toy.

3   "To actually have a fluffy, stuffed Darby is unbelievable," said Bentley, known on the field for his fearless hitting and the black shade that he paints under his eyes.

4   If Bentley has his way, Darby will soon be as beloved around the country as he is in Buffalo. He recently signed a publishing deal with Toronto-based Durkin-Hayes, which will market his books throughout the United States.

5   National distribution was Bentley's aim when he first created Darby with the help of former Bills lineman Mike Hamby, an accomplished artist who is Darby's illustrator.

6   "It has been slow, because I don't have the time or the resources to push it," Bentley said. "I was not only the author but the distributor, the publisher, and it didn't give me time to do it.

7   "Durkin-Hayes has a national sales force, and we're going to go national. They're going to do all that so now I can do what I wanted to do in the first place, which is create new Darby stories and promote Darby, which is what I'm good at."

8   Bentley was a hit during last season's Super Bowl. The thousands of journalists in Tampa, Fla., found the idea of a football player writing children's books too good to pass up, and Bentley was ready with a Darby promotion package.

9   "That probably gave me the impetus to get this publishing deal," he said. "That did a lot, because that's where I got a lot of notoriety. This year it will be even better, because I'll have the publishers behind me as well."

10   While Darby the Dinosaur remains a bespectacled tyke, Darby the concept is a growing concern. T-shirts, sweat shirts, dolls, posters and caps have been spawned from the first book, "Naptime for Darby." The merchandise catalog has grown to the point where Bentley opened a kiosk last month in the Buffalo area's biggest mall.

11   Bentley's three books—the others are "Darby Goes to the Mall" and "Christmas with Darby"—and a companion coloring book have sold 130,000 copies, he said.

12   Bentley said he receives the most enjoyment out of the 50 trips he has made to local schools.

13   "It's such a positive thing, especially with professional athletes," he said. "Everybody likes to dwell on a guy making a mistake, and this is something on the other end of the spectrum. We're trying to do something very positive and something you can have fun with and something that appeals to everyone."

Each of the highlighted words should be mastered in the following exercises.

Darby Has Become a Big Part of Ray Bentley's Playbook

Associated Press

1   Under Christmas trees throughout Buffalo on Christmas morning, little green dinosaurs were greeting happy children.

2   Darby the Dinosaur, the cartoon creation of Buffalo Bills linebacker/children's author Ray Bentley, has jumped off the book pages and become a cuddly toy.

3   "To actually have a fluffy, stuffed Darby is unbelievable," said Bentley, known on the field for his fearless hitting and the black shade that he paints under his eyes.

4   If Bentley has his way, Darby will soon be as beloved around the country as he is in Buffalo. He recently signed a publishing deal with Toronto-based Durkin-Hayes, which will market his books throughout the United States.

5   National distribution was Bentley's aim when he first created Darby with the help of former Bills lineman Mike Hamby, an accomplished artist who is Darby's illustrator.

6   "It has been slow, because I don't have the time or the resources to push it," Bentley said. "I was not only the author but the distributor, the publisher, and it didn't give me time to do it.

7   "Durkin-Hayes has a national sales force, and we're going to go national. They're going to do all that so now I can do what I wanted to do in the first place, which is create new Darby stories and promote Darby, which is what I'm good at."

8   Bentley was a hit during last season's Super Bowl. The thousands of journalists in Tampa, Fla., found the idea of a football player

writing children's books too good to pass up, and Bentley was ready with a Darby promotion package.

9   "That probably gave me the impetus to get this publishing deal," he said. "That did a lot, because that's where I got a lot of notoriety. This year it will be even better, because I'll have the publishers behind me as well."

10   While Darby the Dinosaur remains a bespectacled tyke, Darby the concept is a growing concern. T-shirts, sweat shirts, dolls, posters and caps have been spawned from the first book, "Naptime for Darby." The merchandise catalog has grown to the point where Bentley opened a kiosk last month in the Buffalo area's biggest mall.

11   Bentley's three books—the others are "Darby Goes to the Mall" and "Christmas with Darby"—and a companion coloring book have sold 130,000 copies, he said.

12   Bentley said he receives the most enjoyment out of the 50 trips he has made to local schools.

13   "It's such a positive thing, especially with professional athletes," he said. "Everybody likes to dwell on a guy making a mistake, and this is something on the other end of the spectrum. We're trying to do something very positive and something you can have fun with and something that appeals to everyone."

■ READING COMPREHENSION QUESTIONS

1.   Ray Bentley and Mike Hamby, author and illustrator respectively, made their livings prior to their publishing careers as (a) journalists (b) teachers (c) professional athletes (d) child psychologists

2.   The Darby series created by Bentley and Hamby has already sold (a) 10,000 copies (b) 35,000 copies (c) 85,000 copies (d) 130,000 copies

3.   The title character of the Darby series is a green, glasses-wearing (a) Illinois box turtle (b) six-foot-tall frog (c) dinosaur (d) praying mantis the size of a horse

4.   Author Bentley particularly enjoys his publicity visits to (a) hospitals for the terminally ill (b) prisons (c) colleges and universities in Canada (d) local schools

5.   In addition to being a character in a series of books, Darby has also taken physical shape in the form of a (a) billboard advertising campaign in the Buffalo area (b) popular stuffed toy (c) ceramic planter (d) television series

6.   Through their work and creativity on the Darby books, Bentley and Hamby have gone a long way toward dispelling the common stereotypes of (a) children's literature creators (b) retired businessmen (c) ex-NASA ground controllers (d) football players

TARGET VOCABULARY

throughout	**to promote**	**merchandise**
fearless	**journalists**	**kiosk**
beloved	**impetus**	**to dwell**
to market	**notoriety**	**spectrum**
distribution	**tyke**	**to appeal**

Dictionary Practice

Use each word in a sentence of your own.

1.   throughout _____

2.   fearless _____

3.   beloved _____

4.   to market _____

5.   distribution _____

6.   to promote _____

7.   journalists _____

8.   impetus _____

9.   notoriety _____

10.   tyke _____

11.   merchandise _____

12.   kiosk _____

13.   to dwell _____

14. spectrum _____

15. to appeal _____

Cloze Practice

Fill in each blank with an appropriate word from the target vocabulary list.

To sell, or _____, a product, manufacturers must _____ their _____ so that it will _____ to the greatest possible number of likely consumers. If sales produce too great an _____ for production, however, meeting demand calls for a _____ system _____ the advertising area and a _____ belief that demand will continue. Some ads aim at a broad _____ of potential buyers. Others _____ on points relevant only to a "target" audience, such as parents, for example, for whom the image of a cute little _____ in diapers can be very powerful.

▨ CRITICAL READING PRACTICE/TOPICS FOR DISCUSSION

1. A "stereotype" is literally an image cast in metal, which does not change. When people or groups of people are stereotyped, they are all thought to fit the same "picture" or "profile." This process is both inaccurate and dumb, but it's also widespread, like a universal disease.

Generally speaking, what is the stereotype of professional football players, and how do you think it has been created? In what ways most interesting to you do Ray Bentley and Mike Hamby not fit the usual stereotype of professional football players?

2. What books or stories do you remember most vividly from your own childhood? Who read or told you the stories you remember best? If you were to tell a child a story, what story would you choose and why would you choose it?

3. What part did reading play in your childhood? Did you read only at school, or did you read other books and stories on your own? If you enjoyed a particular type of story or book—for example, science fiction or mysteries or adventure stories—do you still read works of that kind? Why do you think that your reading habits have either remained consistent or changed in this respect?

Sample Map for "Darby Has Become a Big Part of Ray Bentley's Playbook" (AP)

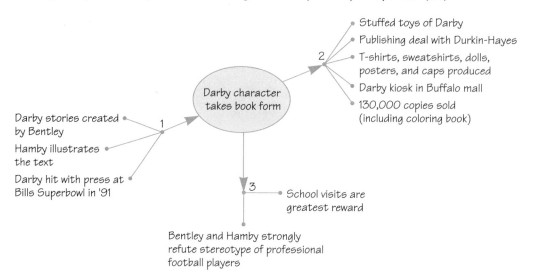

Note: For each of the following readings in this chapter, you are encouraged to draw maps of your own like this one, applying the mapping skills you learned in Part I.

Coach Ernie Kent as Indiana Jones

Sometimes, in sports as in life, it is necessary to approach goals indirectly. Thinking one's strategy through before doing something rash or counterproductive is often a good idea, as well.

The following pre-reading essay and article are about such strategies—self-discipline, sacrifice, and patience—all combined in the career (and career moves) of Ernie Kent, who waited fourteen years to become head coach of a Division I basketball team.

As you read, consider the roles imagination and boldness have played in Coach Kent's career.

■   **PRE-READING FOR DISCUSSION**

Unlike other teachers, coaches often have to wait many years to be completely in charge of their students. Most teachers are "supervised" for a short time during their early training, but coaches often have to wait for decades to get their chance to teach what they know in their own way. Many coaches *never* become head coaches, remaining instead assistant coaches, often with great responsibilities but without the authority to make the ultimate teaching decisions for the teams or individuals in their charge.

The following article concerns the fourteen-year odyssey (four years longer than the original journey by Odysseus) of Coach Ernie Kent, now Head Coach Ernie Kent of St. Mary's College in Moraga, California.

Coach Kent loves basketball. After playing for four years at the University of Oregon, he stayed on at the university as an assistant coach. Quarter by quarter, game by game, season by season, he learned his craft with increasing thoroughness. Over the years, Coach Kent studied hoop the way Mendel studied sweetpeas and Darwin studied orchids.

But then Coach Kent's apprenticeship took an unusual and bold turn. Rather than moving around the country as an assistant coach, acquiring experience and contacts, or staying put in one program, becoming known and waiting for a retirement, Ernie Kent pulled an "Indiana Jones."

He accepted the position of head basketball coach for the *al-Khaleej Club* in Saudi Arabia. For three years, amid minarets and pick-and-rolls, he perfected his craft and learned to move with the new weight of a head coach's responsibilities.

Following his Middle East experience, Coach Kent returned to the U.S. and worked on the coaching staffs at Colorado State and Stanford before becoming the Head Coach at St. Mary's.

All in all, it was 14 years of Teacher Training.

"You do something else for 10 years and can be a hell of a lot more successful if you put in that same time and effort and enthusiasm that we put into this game," observes Coach Kent.

In what sense is the coach using "successful" here? Is doing what you love a form of success? How about earning the respect of your peers, or being asked to teach what you love doing? Are those also forms of success? Few basketball coaches become wealthy, but should wealth be the primary determinant of "success"?

Ernie Kent's passion and his profession are the same. In the X's and O's of life, "success" doesn't get much better.

Go get 'em, Coach Kent.

JANET HOLDEN RAMOS

Ernie Kent has taken giant step from assistant to head coach at St. Mary's.

Head Man Leads a Different Life

St. Mary's Kent Often Feels Like He's Been in a Fight

Frank Blackman

1   Ernie Kent remembers exactly what he thought last spring after learning he was going to be the new St. Mary's men's head basketball coach,

2   "My reaction was: 'Here I go,'" Kent said. "When the call came I felt I was fully ready and fully qualified to go. There was no fear. There was no nervousness."

3   He wouldn't experience that until the next morning.

4   "It really didn't hit me until I walked into the press conference and saw all those people. That's when it hit me—boom, you're a head coach now."

5   Kent had just taken the final giant step. Presumably there will be other big ones in his career, since no one expects him to retire at St. Mary's. But still, you can become a Division I head coach for the first time only once. He now is doing what hundreds of assistants all over the country yearn to do—what he had yearned to do during the 14-year apprenticeship he served in his profession.

6   "I didn't think it would take 14 years," said Kent, a four-year starter at Oregon who began his career as an assistant under his former coach, Dick Harter. "But I enjoyed what I was doing so much, it didn't seem like work. I got so wrapped up in it, it didn't seem such a long period of time.

7   "But you hit it right on the head, you do something else for 10 years and can be a

hell of a lot more successful if you put in that same time and effort and enthusiasm that we put into this game."

8   At age 36, Kent became a head coach later than some, a little earlier than others. Mike Montgomery, his boss at Stanford the previous two years, was 31 when he got the head job at Montana. Cal's Lou Campanelli was 34 when James Madison called. Santa Clara's Carroll Williams was 37.

9   In order to get this opportunity, Kent had to move from Oregon to the Middle-East, where he was the head coach of the al-Khaleej Club in Saudi Arabia for three years, back to the U.S. and a job at Colorado State, then on to Stanford before finally getting the call from St. Mary's.

10   "You need to make moves," Kent said. "Some guys stay at one school for a long time, feeling that they'll take over when that head coach leaves, and they're comfortable with that. But I think that as an assistant the key to this business is you have to move. And it can't be a lateral move. It has to be a move up."

11   Now that he's reached his goal—at least one of them, since what coach doesn't dream of the Final Four, a TV show, and a sneaker contract of his very own?—Kent has been too busy to savor the experience. No matter how ready you are to make that move one seat over, it's still a different ex-

perience when you're the one literally calling the shots.

12   "That's probably the biggest difference," he said. "You're experiencing a different level of pressure during a game as a head coach than as an assistant. I found that out right away. Boyd (Grant, his boss at Colorado State) used to tell me that he felt so drained after a game. And I feel the same way. I come out of a game and, my goodness, it's like you've been in a rock 'em out, slug 'em match. With all the emotion that takes place during the game, the intensity really picks up from being an assistant to being a head coach."

13   And when the game's over, his job isn't finished anymore.

14   "As an assistant, after the game you went home," he said. "As a head, you've got to deal with the media. You have to answer, 'Why did you do this?' and 'Why did you do that?' So you better be out there doing the right things."

15   Kent is the third Gaels head coach in less than a year and inherited a program in turmoil. He must be a stabilizing force while doing enough things right to win some games.

16   His Gaels split their first 10 games. But he thinks the team is improving each time out. It's a start.

■ **EXPLODED VIEW FOR STUDY**

Each of the highlighted words should be mastered in the following exercises.

Head Man Leads a Different Life

St. Mary's Kent Often Feels Like He's Been in a Fight

Frank Blackman

1 Ernie Kent remembers exactly what he thought last spring after learning he was going to be the new St. Mary's men's head basketball coach.

2 "My reaction was: 'Here I go,'" Kent said. "When the call came I felt I was fully ready and fully qualified to go. There was no fear. There was no nervousness."

3 He wouldn't experience that until the next morning.

4 "It really didn't hit me until I walked into the press conference and saw all those people. That's when it hit me—boom, you're a head coach now."

5 Kent had just taken the final giant step. Presumably there will be other big ones in his career, since no one expects him to retire at St. Mary's. But still, you can become a Division I head coach for the first time only once. He now is doing what hundreds of assistants all over the country yearn to do—what he had yearned to do during the 14-year apprenticeship he served in his profession.

6 "I didn't think it would take 14 years," said Kent, a four-year starter at Oregon who began his career as an assistant under his former coach, Dick Harter. "But I enjoyed what I was doing so much, it didn't seem like work. I got so wrapped up in it, it didn't seem such a long period of time.

7 "But you hit it right on the head, you do something else for 10 years and can be a hell of a lot more successful if you put in that same time and effort and enthusiasm that we put into this game."

8   At age 36, Kent became a head coach later than some, a little earlier than others. Mike Montgomery, his boss at Stanford the previous two years, was 31 when he got the head job at Montana. Cal's Lou Campanelli was 34 when James Madison called. Santa Clara's Carroll Williams was 37.

9   In order to get this opportunity, Kent had to move from Oregon to the Middle East, where he was the head coach of the al-Khaleej Club in Saudi Arabia for three years, back to the U.S. and a job at Colorado State, then on to Stanford before finally getting the call from St. Mary's.

10   "You need to make moves," Kent said. "Some guys stay at one school for a long time, feeling that they'll take over when that head coach leaves, and they're comfortable with that. But I think that as an assistant the key to this business is you have to move. And it can't be a lateral move. It has to be a move up."

11   Now that he's reached his goal—at least one of them, since what coach doesn't dream of the Final Four, a TV show, and a sneaker contract of his very own?—Kent has been too busy to savor the experience. No matter how ready you are to make that move one seat over, it's still a different experience when you're the one literally calling the shots.

12   "That's probably the biggest difference," he said. "You're experiencing a different level of pressure during a game as a head coach than as an assistant. I found that out right away. Boyd (Grant, his boss at Colorado State) used to tell me that he felt so drained after a game. And I feel the same way. I come out of a game and, my goodness, it's like you've been in a rock 'em out, slug 'em match. With all the emotion that takes place during the game, the intensity really picks up from being an assistant to being a head coach."

13   And when the game's over, his job isn't finished anymore.

14   "As an assistant, after the game you went home," he said. "As a head, you've got to deal with the media. You have to answer, 'Why did you do this?' and 'Why did you do that?' So you better be out there doing the right things."

15   Kent is the third Gaels head coach in less than a year and inherited a program in turmoil. He must be a stabilizing force while doing enough things right to win some games.

16   His Gaels split their first 10 games. But he thinks the team is improving each time out. It's a start.

■ READING COMPREHENSION QUESTIONS

1.   Ernie Kent began his practical training to be a coach by playing collegiate basketball at (a) Indiana University (b) the University of Oregon (c) UCLA (d) the University of North Carolina

2.   Very few head basketball coaches have had experience coaching overseas, and almost none have Kent's experience of coaching in (a) Peru (b) Sweden (c) Saudi Arabia (d) Australia

3.   One major difference cited by Coach Kent between being an assistant coach and being a head coach is that head coaches (a) never have to count towels (b) don't have to worry about finding a parking space close to their office (c) make enough money to file the long income tax form (d) must deal with the pressures and questions of the media

4.   Like his former boss Boyd Grant, head coach at Colorado State University, Coach Kent feels "drained" after his team plays a basketball game because (a) the level of emotional involvement is so high (b) nobody can watch officials make so many mistakes without it taking a toll (c) keeping track of player and team fouls, shooting percentages, and free throw situations is extremely demanding (d) all of the Gatorade on the bench is reserved for the players

5.   Prior to getting the head coaching job at St. Mary's, Ernie Kent had been a basketball coach for (a) 6 years (b) 8 years (c) 10 years (d) 14 years

6.   Compared with being an assistant coach, Coach Kent "leads a different life" as a head coach basically because of (a) the pressures of recruiting good players (b) a huge increase in responsibility (c) dealing with alumni and boosters (d) the difficulties of scheduling Division I teams

■   TARGET VOCABULARY

fully	**apprenticeship**	**drained**
nervousness	**(to get) wrapped**	**emotion**
press conference	**up (in)**	**intensity**
presumably	**enthusiasm**	**turmoil**
to yearn	**(a) key (to)**	**to stabilize**
	to savor	

Dictionary Practice

Use each word in a sentence of your own.

1. fully _____

2. nervousness _____

3. press conference _____

    _____

4. presumably _____

5. to yearn _____

6. apprenticeship _____

7. (to get) wrapped up (in) _____

8. enthusiasm _____

9. (a) key (to) _____

10. to savor _____

11. drained _____

12. emotion _____

13. intensity _____

14. turmoil _____

15. to stabilize _____

Cloze Practice

Fill in each blank with an appropriate word from the target vocabulary list.

One of the _____ to performing well in any activity is learning to deal with the uneasy _____ of competition. This

_____ can increase in _____ until the competitor is

in _____ and becomes physically _____ even before

the contest begins. Athletes are _____ aware that a certain

excited _____ is a competitive asset, but they also try to

_____ themselves in order to _____ the joy of

competition and its results. _____, even nonathletes could

benefit from this example of dealing with pressure.

■ CRITICAL READING PRACTICE/TOPICS
    FOR DISCUSSION

1.   Coaches, like Ernie Kent, are teachers. But their jobs differ from
the jobs of other teachers in some interesting ways. What do you consider to be the most interesting differences between the teaching of a
sport and the teaching of some other subject? Which do you think is
more difficult? Why?

2.   Athletic teams at St. Mary's are called the "Galloping Gaels,"
which means the "galloping Celts" (the "C" is hard, as in "cool"—
except in Boston). These teams seem to be cousins of the "Fighting
Irish" of Notre Dame. Why do you suppose such schools have names
that refer to Celts (the peoples of Scotland, Wales, Ireland, or the Isle
of Man)?
        Why do you think that the Boston Celtics are called "Celtics"?

3.   What are some of your favorite collegiate team names and why
do they appeal to you? Do you know any particularly unusual or mysterious team names, such as the "Banana Slugs" of the University of
California at Santa Cruz or the "Crimson Tide" of Alabama? What do
you think was the origin of school team names like the "Golden Go-
phers" of Minnesota or the "Hurricanes" of Miami?

4.   To become a head coach takes enormous sacrifice. Do you think
that such a long, tough apprenticeship is worth the effort when, after
all, it's just a game?
        Think carefully, then explain why you feel as you do about the
time it takes to become a head coach, which (even Coach Kent points
out) would bring far greater benefits if spent in another profession. In
light of your answer, how about the time it takes to become a teacher,
and that profession's rewards? How about law? How about business?

A Spirit beyond the Boundaries of Time and Place

Here we turn to the Olympic games, from their origin and eventual death in the Classical Era to their rebirth and growth in modern times. This pre-reading essay and article are particularly concerned with the "spirit" of the games, the "Olympic ideal."

Gigi Fernandez and Mary Joe Fernandez won the gold medal for women's doubles tennis at the Barcelona games of 1992. As you read about them, think about the long history they represent and about the values they embody that have managed miraculously to transcend time, space, and nationalism.

PRE-READING FOR DISCUSSION

For 1,169 years, from 776 years before the current era to 393 years after it began, the Olympic games were held in Greece. The Roman emperor Theodosius I abolished the games in the 4th century (to make it clear that Greece had lost its independence), but for well over a thousand years the Olympics were held at regular intervals to celebrate strength, courage, and beauty.

Wars were interrupted in order to give passage to the games and for competitors to attend them. Olympic champions were honored in life and remembered down through the generations. In many ways the ancient Olympics established the standards and values of all subsequent athletic competition.

Fifteen hundred years after the Games were forbidden, a great teacher and scholar almost single-handedly brought them back to life. The French baron Pierre de Coubertin, who was not an athlete himself but who knew beauty when he saw it, persuaded the king of Greece to revive the games in the country of their birth. In the summer of 1896, the Olympic spirit, now international in scope, was reborn in Athens with the first Olympiad of the modern era.

Under the direction of the International Olympic Committee, these Olympics (and since 1924 the Winter Olympics) have been held regularly in cities all around the world (except during the years of the World Wars; we still don't have the idea quite right). Symbolized by the Olympic flame, ignited from the sun's rays in Greece, the Olympic spirit transcends not just place, now, but time itself.

Gigi Fernandez and Mary Joe Fernandez are Olympic champions from the Barcelona games of 1992. Their names and victories have become part of a tradition that reaches back well over 2,500 years. The following article relates how they achieved this impressive victory, but, perhaps more important, it suggests how ideas transcend borders and how beauty is indeed a joy forever.

Pierre de Coubertin understood that this principle is at the heart of the Olympic spirit.

Perhaps after another 1,070 years of Olympic games, we will be able to demonstrate that our era has understood the principle as well as Coubertin and the Greeks did.

AP/MICHEL LIPCHITZ

Gigi Fernandez, left, lets out a celebratory scream after pairing up with Mary Joe Fernandez to win the gold medal in the women's doubles.

Fernandez Duo Earns Gold for Adopted Country

Associated Press

1 BARCELONA Grander than a Grand Slam.

2 After overcoming a hometown team and a royal rooting section to win the Olympic women's doubles Saturday, Americans Gigi and Mary Joe Fernandez agreed—getting the gold was even better than winning Wimbledon or one of tennis' other major titles.

3 "This is huge," said Mary Joe, who won the 1991 Australian Open doubles with Patty Fendick. "It's hard to describe how happy I am. It's a dream come true."

4 Gigi, who won the French and Wimbledon doubles this year with Natalia Zvereva, said the 7–5, 2–6, 6–2 victory over Arantxa Sanchez Vicario and Conchita Martinez of Spain was the highlight of her career.

5 "This is my most exciting win," said Gigi, who flopped on her back after Mary Joe hit an unreturnable forehand volley on

6   match point. "Playing for your country, playing in front of the king and queen, the atmosphere was special."

Inspired by the entrance of King Juan Carlos and Queen Sofia early in the second set, the top-seeded Spaniards won six straight games to take a 1–0 lead in the final set. But after Sanchez Vicario held serve to even it at 2–2, the second-seeded U.S. pair—who are not related—took four consecutive games to win the match on the slow clay court.

7   "We never got discouraged, even after we lost six games in a row," said Mary Joe, who was born in the Dominican Republic but grew up in Miami. "We regrouped, took a little break and got back on track."

8   It was the second medal for Mary Joe, who shared the bronze with Sanchez Vicario in singles. The victory, combined with Jennifer Capriati's singles title, gave the United States a sweep of the women's gold medals in tennis after the men failed to win a medal of any kind.

9   "It probably doesn't make the men feel any better, but it's a great accomplishment for the women," said U.S. women's coach Marty Riessen.

10   Although Mary Joe and Gigi Fernandez have won Grand Slam doubles titles with other partners, they had only played together in one tournament prior to the Olympics, losing in the semifinals last year at Milan, Italy.

11   The Americans won despite a shaky serving streak by Gigi, who was broken three straight times from the start of the second set to the opening game of the final set. When she finally held serve following a lengthy fifth game in the last set, she let out a scream of relief.

12   "I lost my serve at the worst time," said the native of Puerto Rico, who now lives in Aspen, Colo. "Fortunately, I was able to get some serves in and hold in that (fifth) game. I think that was the difference in the match."

13   The loss was especially disappointing for the Spanish pair because they both come from Barcelona.

14   "We had a chance to win, but we played nervously," Sanchez Vicario said. "But I am very happy to have played in these Games and to be the only Spanish tennis player to win two medals."

■   EXPLODED VIEW FOR STUDY

Each of the highlighted words should be mastered in the following exercises.

Fernandez Duo Earns Gold for Adopted Country

Associated Press

1   BARCELONA   Grander than a Grand Slam.

2   After overcoming a hometown team and a royal rooting section

to win the Olympic women's doubles Saturday, Americans Gigi and Mary Joe Fernandez agreed—getting the gold was even better than winning Wimbledon or one of tennis' other major titles.

3   "This is huge," said Mary Joe, who won the 1991 Australian Open doubles with Patty Fendick. "It's hard to describe how happy I am. It's a dream come true."

4   Gigi, who won the French and Wimbledon doubles this year with Natalia Zvereva, said the 7–5, 2–6, 6–2 victory over Arantxa Sanchez Vicario and Conchita Martinez of Spain was the highlight of her career.

5   "This is my most exciting win," said Gigi, who flopped on her back after Mary Joe hit an unreturnable forehand volley on match point. "Playing for your country, playing in front of the king and queen, the atmosphere was special."

6   Inspired by the entrance of King Juan Carlos and Queen Sofia early in the second set, the top-seeded Spaniards won six straight games to take a 1–0 lead in the final set. But after Sanchez Vicario held serve to even it at 2–2, the second-seeded U.S. pair—who are not related—took four consecutive games to win the match on the slow clay court.

7   "We never got discouraged, even after we lost six games in a row," said Mary Joe, who was born in the Dominican Republic but grew up in Miami. "We regrouped, took a little break and got back on track."

8   It was the second medal for Mary Joe, who shared the bronze with Sanchez Vicario in singles. The victory, combined with Jennifer Capriati's singles title, gave the United States a sweep of the women's gold medals in tennis after the men failed to win a medal of any kind.

9   "It probably doesn't make the men feel any better, but it's a great accomplishment for the women," said U.S. women's coach Marty Riessen.

10   Although Mary Joe and Gigi Fernandez have won Grand Slam doubles titles with other partners, they had only played together in

one tournament prior to the Olympics, losing in the semifinals last year at Milan, Italy.

11   The Americans won despite a shaky serving streak by Gigi, who was broken three straight times from the start of the second set to the opening game of the final set. When she finally held serve following a lengthy fifth game in the last set, she let out a scream of relief.

12   "I lost my serve at the worst time," said the native of Puerto Rico, who now lives in Aspen, Colo. "Fortunately, I was able to get some serves in and hold in that (fifth) game. I think that was the difference in the match."

13   The loss was especially disappointing for the Spanish pair because they both come from Barcelona.

14   "We had a chance to win, but we played nervously," Sanchez Vicario said. "But I am very happy to have played in these Games and to be the only Spanish tennis player to win two medals."

▪ READING COMPREHENSION QUESTIONS

1.   Gigi Fernandez and Mary Joe Fernandez are professional athletes who play tennis for a living. The Olympics award no cash prizes to winners. Both Americans agreed that (a) they might have played harder if money had been involved (b) their Olympic gold medals were better than the prize money or title of any major tennis tournament (c) the Olympics should adopt a prize money system in addition to medals (d) there was little pressure in the Olympics because no purse was at stake

2.   Mary Joe Fernandez and Gigi Fernandez, who are not related, were both born in other countries and are naturalized citizens. They were born, respectively, in (a) Mexico and Argentina (b) Nicaragua and Costa Rica (c) Honduras and Cuba (d) the Dominican Republic and Puerto Rico

3.   The tennis match for the gold medal was interrupted briefly by the entrance of (a) Generalisimo Francisco Franco (b) King Philip II (c) Gabriel García Márquez (d) King Juan Carlos and Queen Sofia

4. Although Fernandez and Fernandez won the gold medal, the Spanish doubles team of Arantxa Sanchez Vicario and Conchita Martinez were the "top-seeded" team, which means that the Spaniards were (a) placed higher in the pre-tournament rankings and expected to win (b) more rested from their previous tennis match and probably stronger (c) allowed to serve first in each of the sets necessary to determine the outcome of the match (d) considered to have an advantage because both live in Barcelona

5. After the arrival of the royal couple, the Spanish partners (a) became so nervous that they lost too many games to recover for the win (b) joined the rest of the audience in singing the national anthem (c) won six games in a row to take the lead in the match (d) played pretty much as they had before

6. Doubles partners ordinarily require months or even years of experience playing together in order to be successful, yet the gold medal championship of partners Fernandez and Fernandez was (a) only their second tournament together and their first-ever win (b) won against amateurs and therefore less demanding (c) the result of speeded-up computerized training at the U.S. Olympic Training Center (d) won against equally inexperienced teams so the lack of practice didn't matter

■ TARGET VOCABULARY

duo	highlight	a sweep
adopted	inspired	accomplishment
Grand Slam	top-seeded	a streak
royal	consecutive	lengthy
major	to regroup	Games

Dictionary Practice

Use each word in a sentence of your own.

1. duo _____

2. adopted _____

3. Grand Slam _____

4. royal _____

5. major _____

6. highlight _____

7. inspired _____

8. top-seeded _____

9. consecutive _____

10. to regroup _____

11. a sweep _____

12. accomplishment _____

13. a streak _____

14. lengthy _____

15. Games _____

Cloze Practice

Fill in each blank with an appropriate word from the target vocabulary list.

For the United States team, one of the _____ of the 1992 Summer Olympics was the _____ play of the women tennis players. That the U.S. women achieved _____ of both gold medals in tennis at the _____ was an especially impressive _____, since the doubles team had never before won a _____ together or a _____ singles tennis championship, although they had won doubles with different partners. The victory of the United States doubles _____, Fernandez and Fernandez, over the _____ Spanish team, Sanchez Vicario and Martinez, was viewed by the _____ couple of Spain, King Juan Carlos and Queen Sofia.

■ CRITICAL READING PRACTICE/TOPICS FOR DISCUSSION

1. During the Barcelona Olympic Games the U.S. women swimmers, gymnasts, and tennis players performed much better, in terms of medals, than their male counterparts. Do you think that there are reasons for this, or do you consider it simply a coincidence? Explain your response.

2. In spite of laws, resolutions, and promises, more than two-thirds of collegiate scholarship money and athletic expenditures go to male

programs. Do you consider this fair? Why do you think that this situation has come about?

3.   What are your favorite participation sports, and why do you enjoy them? What are your favorite spectator sports, and, if they are different from the sports you enjoy playing, why do you enjoy watching them on television or in person?

4.   For Olympic athletes, the line between "amateur" and "professional" was blurred many years ago, and it will soon probably disappear entirely. How do you feel about professionals—whether they play tennis, basketball, or hockey—representing their countries and competing against true amateurs? Explain.

5.   "Day-of-performance" drugs, such as amphetamines, and "training" drugs, such as muscle-building steroids, are both forbidden at the Olympics. But "training" drugs can be masked by still other drugs or avoided for some months before competition, making their detection almost impossible. Do you think that athletes have a personal right to use such drugs? In your opinion, do governments have the right to supply such drugs to athletes or order athletes to take them, in the name of national pride? Why, or why not?

▪ *Life as Navigation, Navigation as Life*

"Life is a journey" is an image used across all cultures and times to describe the passage from birth to death. And on journeys, of course, navigation is crucial.

The following pre-reading essay and article deal with the relatively new sport of "orienteering," which involves the basic steps of figuring out where you are, where you want to go, and how to get there. Athletes compete in wilderness areas by finding a series of pre-set markers and completing the course as quickly as possible, using only a compass and a topographic map (the only markings on which are lines that indicate relative altitudes).

As you read and discuss these pieces, think about the ways in which our lives are indeed "journeys" and subject to all the forces that affect literal journeys from one place to another.

▪ PRE-READING FOR DISCUSSION

There is a lot of "navigation" required in life: We have to figure out where we are, where we want to go, and how we can get there.

Both literally, as when we head out for the nearest available ice cream, and figuratively, as when we decide what work to do with our life, we are all navigators on a daily and life-long basis.

Figuring out where we are, is sometimes called "getting one's bearings" or "orienting" one's self. A familiar street sign or star or mountain or building can each tell us our general location and direction. So can good or bad grades in our course work. So can drinking too much or yelling at children or being depressed all the time in our lives. They're all part of the process of figuring out where we are.

If we want to go somewhere, for whatever reason, we then have to determine how to get there from our present position. Doing this is often trickier than getting our bearings because very few people are able to go in any direction they want, to any destination, without considering the costs (and not just the financial "costs" but also the "expenses" of time and struggle and sacrifice). A poor mark on an exam, for example, is useful information, but it is not good news. A low score says, "Well, it's going to take something more than what you gave last time. More time, perhaps. A new method of studying, maybe. A tutor to help you learn faster. Something. . . ." But time, study techniques, and tutors don't grow on trees; and there are jobs and families and health and a hundred other things to be considered.

School, jobs, marriage, life; all navigation. . . .

Fortunately, our species is designed to solve such problems. Wild geese and salmon may be better at finding the *same* route generation after generation, but we are terrific at finding *new* routes to our destinations, in fact *unique* routes to match each of our unique lives. With patience and courage, we can find ways to get just about anywhere: across oceans, over, around, or under barriers, and even to the moon, if we want the destination badly enough.

Some people say that "Art imitates life." (Art actually does quite a bit more than that.) We can say with certainty, however, that *sports* imitate life, made up of the same basic contests of possession, territory, movement, defense, and navigation through obstacles.

Jane Gottesman's following article on orienteering describes a sport open to women and men of all ages and in all physical conditions. Many orienteering meets even have courses for the disabled. A compass, a map, some checkpoints, and an infinite number of decisions make a great sport. Substitute a sense of right and wrong for the compass, substitute ability and potential for the topographic map, substitute goals and dreams for the checkpoints, and you don't have to be Columbus to discover a great life.

Orienteering—A Test of Flexibility

Jane Gottesman

1   "Oxygen debt" may sound like an awful environmental illness, but it's less noxious and it's not fatal.

2   It's "orienteering" slang, and it's a term used to describe a feeling somewhere between exhaustion and panic. You know you're suffering oxygen debt when trees, rocks and even the sun seem to be deliberately playing tricks on you. The map looks like a watercolor smudge, the compass lies and the only sound in the forest is your own labored wheeze.

3   The affliction is highly curable—catch your breath and let blood flow to your brain—but it takes precious time in an orienteering competition when the objective is to get to the finish line as quickly as possible.

THE COURSE

4   Recently, at the two-day Western States Orienteering Championships held at the Sunol Regional Wilderness, Piedmont's Bruce Wolfe made a navigational error while dashing through the first half of the 18-square kilometer course. As a veteran member of the United States Orienteering Team, Wolfe had the know-how to make up the lapse, and for the third year, win the men's open event.

5   "I was a little mad at myself," Wolfe said. "I circled around for three or four minutes before finding the marker. When I finally saw it, it seemed to be only five feet or so from where I had been looking for it. Maybe sunlight was hitting it, or it was behind a branch. . . ."

6   The elusive marker Wolfe referred to is a prism-shaped, yellow-and-white nylon marker known as a "control point." To successfully complete an orienteering race,

a competitor must prove that he's visited each control point—the proof being a braille-like hole punch in his race card. By the end of a race, a competitor's card is riddled with tiny holes in varying patterns.

7   Control points are tucked away in the landscape—in knolls, beside streams, on fences, next to boulders, hanging from trees. The challenge isn't so much to see where the control points are nestled, it's figuring out how to forge a path to them as quickly as possible, with only a contour map and a compass for reference. Some races have as many as 30 control points.

8   Orienteering is said to be 50 percent physical and 50 percent mental. Cross-country runners tend to excel in the sport because racing up and down steep forested hills is vital. Still, reading the terrain and deciphering a time-saving route off the topographical map are equally important, so pure speed can't win a race. It took Wolfe close to 80 minutes to complete each leg of the race, while some competitors needed more than three hours.

9   Sitting on a grassy slope near the last control point at the Sunol race, meet director Dennis Wildfogel watched as competitors, one by one, emerged out of the shady grove and raced down to the finish line.

10   "Orienteers need to be infinitely flexible," said Wildfogel. "They have to change gears instantly—from thick dark brush to sunny open areas, from soft-packed hills, to muddy streams to rock faces. It's a matter of constantly relocating, because you're always moving and never are sure where you are."

MENTAL GAME

11   Wildfogel says orienteering is liberating, not just because it brings participants

outdoors to wide expanses of undeveloped land, but because it demands intense concentration and clear thinking from start to finish—daydreaming, quite literally, will get you nowhere.

12   "You get so focused you forget about your normal limitations," said Wildfogel. "You hurdle fences, leap over logs, thrash through bushes, jump off cliffs. If you ever thought about it, you'd never be able to do it."

13   Scandinavia is the heartland of orienteering. In the early 1900s, the sport was developed as a modified training regimen for Norwegian and Swedish soldiers. Now, the sport is a favorite form of recreation around Europe and Australia, and it has something of a cult appeal in the United States.

14   Last August, Wolfe and nine other men and women on the U.S. national team trav-eled to Marianske Lazne, Czechoslovakia, to compete in the world championships.

WIDE APPEAL

15   Orienteering via horseback, mountain bike and cross-country skis are modified versions of the footrace, and some competitions are held at night by moonlight.

16   One of the particularly inviting aspects of orienteering is that it's open to all. In each competition there are different divisions for men and women and different age categories.

17   At the Western States Championships, in addition to attracting competitors from all over the United States, including some relocated Swedes, there were shorter and easier courses for beginners. Mulling about in the starting area were people of all ages and ability, from children to senior citizens.

■ EXPLODED VIEW FOR STUDY

Each of the highlighted words should be mastered in the following exercises.

Orienteering—A Test of Flexibility

Jane Gottesman

1   "Oxygen debt" may sound like an awful environmental illness, but it's less noxious and it's not fatal.

2   It's "orienteering" slang, and it's a term used to describe a feeling somewhere between exhaustion and panic. You know you're suffering oxygen debt when trees, rocks and even the sun seem to be deliberately playing tricks on you. The map looks like a watercolor smudge, the compass lies and the only sound in the forest is your own labored wheeze.

3   The affliction is highly curable—catch your breath and let blood

flow to your brain—but it takes precious time in an orienteering competition when the objective is to get to the finish line as quickly as possible.

THE COURSE

4   Recently, at the two-day Western States Orienteering Championships held at the Sunol Regional Wilderness, Piedmont's Bruce Wolfe made a navigational error while dashing through the first half of the 18-square kilometer course. As a veteran member of the United States Orienteering Team, Wolfe had the know-how to make up the lapse, and for the third year, win the men's open event.

5   "I was a little mad at myself," Wolfe said. "I circled around for three or four minutes before finding the marker. When I finally saw it, it seemed to be only five feet or so from where I had been looking for it. Maybe sunlight was hitting it, or it was behind a branch. . . ."

6   The elusive marker Wolfe referred to is a prism-shaped, yellow-and-white nylon marker known as a "control point." To successfully complete an orienteering race, a competitor must prove that he's visited each control point—the proof being a braille-like hole punch in his race card. By the end of a race, a competitor's card is riddled with tiny holes in varying patterns.

7   Control points are tucked away in the landscape—in knolls, beside streams, on fences, next to boulders, hanging from trees. The challenge isn't so much to see where the control points are nestled, it's figuring out how to forge a path to them as quickly as possible, with only a contour map and a compass for reference. Some races have as many as 30 control points.

8   Orienteering is said to be 50 percent physical and 50 percent mental. Cross-country runners tend to excel in the sport because racing up and down steep forested hills is vital. Still, reading the terrain and deciphering a time-saving route off the topographical map are equally important, so pure speed can't win a race. It took Wolfe close to 80 minutes to complete each leg of the race, while some competitors needed more than three hours.

9   Sitting on a grassy slope near the last control point at the Sunol race, meet director Dennis Wildfogel watched as competitors, one by one, emerged out of the shady grove and raced down to the finish line.

10   "Orienteers need to be infinitely flexible," said Wildfogel. "They have to change gears instantly—from thick dark brush to sunny open areas, from soft-packed hills, to muddy streams to rock faces. It's a matter of constantly relocating, because you're always moving and never are sure where you are."

MENTAL GAME

11   Wildfogel says orienteering is liberating, not just because it brings participants outdoors to wide expanses of undeveloped land, but because it demands intense concentration and clear thinking from start to finish—daydreaming, quite literally, will get you nowhere.

12   "You get so focused you forget about your normal limitations," said Wildfogel. "You hurdle fences, leap over logs, thrash through bushes, jump off cliffs. If you ever thought about it, you'd never be able to do it."

13   Scandinavia is the heartland of orienteering. In the early 1900s, the sport was developed as a modified training regimen for Norwegian and Swedish soldiers. Now, the sport is a favorite form of recreation around Europe and Australia, and it has something of a cult appeal in the United States.

14   Last August, Wolfe and nine other men and women on the U.S. national team traveled to Marianske Lazne, Czechoslovakia, to compete in the world championships.

WIDE APPEAL

15   Orienteering via horseback, mountain bike and cross-country skis are modified versions of the footrace, and some competitions are held at night by moonlight.

16   One of the particularly inviting aspects of orienteering is that it's open to all. In each competition there are different divisions for men and women and different age categories.

17   At the Western States Championships, in addition to attracting competitors from all over the United States, including some relocated Swedes, there were shorter and easier courses for beginners. Mulling about in the starting area were people of all ages and ability, from children to senior citizens.

■ READING COMPREHENSION QUESTIONS

1. Like other athletes, orienteering competitors must avoid the dizziness, disorientation, confusion, and other symptoms of (a) extreme dehydration (b) fatigue (c) oxygen debt (d) overtraining

2. Orienteering is an open-country contest in which athletes try to take the least time locating a series of map-indicated (a) control points (b) check-in stations (c) water tables (d) contest representatives with location stamps

3. Regardless of what ratio might be required in other sports, the ratio of physical to mental skills required in orienteering is said to be (a) 75%–25% (b) 90%–10% (c) 25%–75% (d) 50%–50%

4. The most recent world championships of orienteering mentioned in the article took place in (a) Stockholm, Sweden (b) Caracas, Venezuela (c) Marianske Lazne, Czechoslovakia (d) Sydney, Australia

5. Unlike some sports, orienteering is open to all because it uses a system of (a) random pairing of participants (b) gender and age divisions (c) shotgun start (d) handicapping rather like that used in golf

6. The center of interest in orienteering and the area of its creation as a military training exercise is (a) Austria (b) Southeast Asia (c) Argentina (d) Scandinavia

■ TARGET VOCABULARY

noxious	**elusive**	**terrain**
exhaustion	**prism-shaped**	**topographical**
panic	**riddled**	**to emerge**
objective	**knolls**	**cult**
navigation	**nestled**	**inviting**

Dictionary Practice

Use each of the following words in a sentence of your own.

1. noxious _____
2. exhaustion _____
3. panic _____
4. objective _____
5. navigation _____
6. elusive _____
7. prism-shaped _____
8. riddled _____
9. knolls _____
10. nestled _____
11. terrain _____
12. topographical _____
13. to emerge _____
14. cult _____
15. inviting _____

Cloze Practice

Fill in each blank with an appropriate word from the target vocabulary list.

At a time when sports seem _____ with artificiality, an unspoiled countryside of _____ and cool, _____ woods _____ in little canyons may seem an odd "playing field." But _____ victorious, an orienteering champion must overcome _____, and perhaps _____, and meet the goal, or _____, of the sport: successful _____ through an unknown environment, with no aids but a _____ map and a compass. Finding the _____ path from marker to marker, this small _____ of athletes provides useful models for us all.

■ **CRITICAL READING PRACTICE/TOPICS
FOR DISCUSSION**

1. Do you agree with the statements in the pre-reading essay regarding life and "navigation"? Why or why not?

If you agree, explain the "navigation" involved in your career plans. If you do not agree, explain the differences between managing a family on a tight budget and navigating through icebergs.

2. Which of the following games do you think most accurately mirrors the "contest" of day-to-day life, and why do you feel as you do?

    a. chess
    b. baseball
    c. blind man's bluff
    d. hide and seek
    e. soccer
    f. pin the tail on the donkey
    g. basketball
    h. poker

3. Would you like to try orienteering? Why, or why not? What do you think of it as a sport? Should it be included in the Olympics? Why, or why not?

■ *Schools, Athletes, and Responsibility:
Some Unfinished Business*

    Education and athletics have been uneasy companions for over a century. In fact, in the 1890s complaints from college presidents made national headlines in the U.S., citing the familiar charges of professional corruption and lack of academic standards.

    The basic problem, of course, is that both high-level study and high-level athletics make tremendous demands on a person's time. When the demands conflict, as they often do for student-athletes, which set of demands should be met first, the athletic or the academic?

    Attempts to solve this problem through legislation by the National Collegiate Athletic Association (NCAA) and others have only succeeded in making a bad situation worse.

    What do you think of these recent steps to ensure that scholar-athletes attend to the "scholar" side of their role in college? As you read about and discuss these issues, consider how they relate to your ideas of opportunity, professionalism, and hypocrisy.

■   **PRE-READING FOR DISCUSSION**

At its best, the National Collegiate Athletic Association protects the rights of student athletes, fights professionalism, and establishes national standards for athletic departments. At its worst, the NCAA tramples students' rights, winks at *de facto* professionalism, and sets discriminatory standards. Frequently, the NCAA does all these things simultaneously, which makes it a fascinating organization to follow. Good intentions do not guarantee good results.

In the following article, we read of such good intentions: improving the academic preparation and performance of student athletes. We also note, however, the worm in the apple: the lack of adequate preparation many athletes get for college-level studies. This lack of preparation shows up most dramatically in high school records and on national standardized tests, such as the Scholastic Aptitude Test, or SAT.

Coach John Thompson of Georgetown University and many other people have long argued that standardized test scores do not accurately predict student success. Testing agencies are quick to agree, pointing out that tests such as the SAT are designed to show the academic present, not predict the academic future. Critics of standardized tests argue further that the tests aren't "standard" at all, but racially and culturally biased against non-white and non-middle-class students.

Coach Thompson, the testing agencies, and the test critics are all correct. And so is the Presidents Commission of the NCAA. The true problem, however, lies not in the SAT scores or in the number of core courses an athlete takes in high school.

The true problem lies in the "great food chain" of the education system itself, where each successive level consumes the nourishment rising to it from the grades below, without having any control over what happens in those grades. Raising admission standards for college athletes is just fine, so long as *every* athlete in *every* high school has the same opportunity and encouragement to meet those standards from the first grade forward.

The heart of the problem lies in our educational institutions, but in a sense we cannot even blame our schools, since the condition of our school system simply mirrors the condition of our society.

There is where we can see the *real* problem. And only *there* can we find its solution.

Academics Main NCAA Issue

Proposals to Strengthen GPA Requirements, Graduation Progress

Doug Bedell

1   When the chief executive officers from NCAA institutions finally unified last year behind a plan to reform collegiate athletics, resistant athletic directors left the organization's annual meeting in shock.

2   In what Georgia athletic director Vince Dooley called a "presidential blitzkrieg," NCAA delegates for the first time voted by huge margins to trim costs and limit time demands on student-athletes.

3   This year, the 44-member Presidents Commission enters the 86th annual legislative session in Anaheim seeking strengthened academic requirements.

4   And, although NCAA executive director Richard Schultz has warned against complacency, few continue to doubt the power of presidential persuasion.

5   "Their whole focus in this convention is to admit kids who are better prepared earlier and to make sure they graduate within five years once they're in," says Britton Banowsky, Southwest Conference compliance director. "It looks like they're going to do it."

6   After a sound defeat in their first reform efforts three years ago, the presidents have learned to network among themselves and potential opponents.

7   Their efforts to improve academic performance of student-athletes resulted in two major chunks of legislation projected to gain approval during the 1992 convention.

8   The first, Propositions 14–16, would raise the number of core curriculum courses required for entering freshmen from 11 to 13 and boost the necessary high school grade-point average from 2.0 to 2.5.

9   If the convention balks at the strict 2.5 cut-off, the presidents will offer a sliding scale option that allows admission of a 2.0 athlete who scores at least 900 on his SAT or 21 on his ACT.

10   Opponents—led by Georgetown basketball coach John Thompson and other Big East representatives—once again plan to complain that any such use of the standardized test scores should be banned.

11   This perennial argument is backed by the testing agencies themselves, which say their products were never designed to be such strict predictors for academic success.

12   The NCAA's own research into Proposition 48's effects has shown a disproportionate number of minorities are excluded because of tests detractors claim are "racially biased."

13   "We've been told by the experts that the way we're utilizing these standardized tests is incorrect," says Linda Bruno, associate Big East commissioner. "If we're wrong, then continuing to do this is making it more wrong."

14   However, Bruno says her conference may withdraw its alternative legislation in light of an apparent lack of support.

15   "We don't want to bang our heads against a wall, but we are going to get up on the floor and speak to it," Bruno vowed. "We can't just keep coming to these conventions and saying, 'That's fine, let's vote for this!'"

16   The second hunk of presidential reform, Propositions 19–21, makes it tougher to stay eligible once a student-athlete gains admission.

17   One section would force athletes to attain at least 25 percent of their graduation requirements by the end of their third

18   "This is the most significant proposal in the whole book," says Banowsky. "If you are eligible, you would almost have to graduate—unless you just messed around, enrolled in 12 hours and took F's in all of them."

19   Another would mandate similar advancement in an athlete's grade-point average. Athletes entering their third year of college would have to obtain 95 percent of the required graduation GPA in order to participate.

20   Opponents will argue that this will force athletes to select "cake majors"—easier courses of study such as physical education or communications.

21   "But right now," says Banowsky, "kids can kind of float around out there. They

year, then 25 percent more in each of the next two.

may finish their eligibility and still be 60 hours short of graduation.

22   "At least this way you're not only giving the kid a fair chance, but you're requiring him to stay on a graduation track."

23   Perhaps the most divisive proposal in the presidents' package would limit the number of hours a student-athlete could take in summer school.

24   Like many NCAA rules, this one is being spurred on by abuse.

25   Some schools, NCAA leaders contend, are allowing athletes to take a minimum number of hours during the regular academic year. Then, during the summer, they accept 20 or more hours the athlete takes at a local junior college.

26   If passed as expected, all the Presidents Commission legislation would become effective in 1995.

■   EXPLODED VIEW FOR STUDY

Each of the highlighted words should be mastered in the following exercises.

Academics Main NCAA Issue

Proposals to Strengthen GPA Requirements, Graduation Progress

Doug Bedell

1   When the chief executive officers from NCAA institutions finally unified last year behind a plan to reform collegiate athletics, resistant athletic directors left the organization's annual meeting in shock.

2   In what Georgia athletic director Vince Dooley called a "presidential blitzkrieg," NCAA delegates for the first time voted by huge margins to trim costs and limit time demands on student-athletes.

3   This year, the 44-member Presidents Commission enters the 86th

annual legislative session in Anaheim seeking strengthened academic requirements.

4   And, although NCAA executive director Richard Schultz has warned against complacency, few continue to doubt the power of presidential persuasion.

5   "Their whole focus in this convention is to admit kids who are better prepared earlier and to make sure they graduate within five years once they're in," says Britton Banowsky, Southwest Conference compliance director. "It looks like they're going to do it."

6   After a sound defeat in their first reform efforts three years ago, the presidents have learned to network among themselves and potential opponents.

7   Their efforts to improve academic performance of student-athletes resulted in two major chunks of legislation projected to gain approval during the 1992 convention.

8   The first, Propositions 14–16, would raise the number of core curriculum courses required for entering freshmen from 11 to 13 and boost the necessary high school grade-point average from 2.0 to 2.5.

9   If the convention balks at the strict 2.5 cut-off, the presidents will offer a sliding scale option that allows admission of a 2.0 athlete who scores at least 900 on his SAT or 21 on his ACT.

10   Opponents—led by Georgetown basketball coach John Thompson and other Big East representatives—once again plan to complain that any such use of the standardized test scores should be banned.

11   This perennial argument is backed by the testing agencies themselves, which say their products were never designed to be such strict predictors for academic success.

12   The NCAA's own research into Proposition 48's effects has shown a disproportionate number of minorities are excluded because of tests detractors claim are "racially biased."

13   "We've been told by the experts that the way we're utilizing these standardized tests is incorrect," says Linda Bruno, associate Big East

commissioner. "If we're wrong, then continuing to do this is making it more wrong."

14   However, Bruno says her conference may withdraw its alternative legislation in light of an apparent lack of support.

15   "We don't want to bang our heads against a wall, but we are going to get up on the floor and speak to it," Bruno vowed. "We can't just keep coming to these conventions and saying, 'That's fine, let's vote for this!'"

16   The second hunk of presidential reform, Propositions 19–21, makes it tougher to stay eligible once a student-athlete gains admission.

17   One section would force athletes to attain at least 25 percent of their graduation requirements by the end of their third year, then 25 percent more in each of the next two.

18   "This is the most significant proposal in the whole book," says Banowsky. "If you are eligible, you would almost have to graduate—unless you just messed around, enrolled in 12 hours and took F's in all of them."

19   Another would mandate similar advancement in an athlete's grade-point average. Athletes entering their third year of college would have to obtain 95 percent of the required graduation GPA in order to participate.

20   Opponents will argue that this will force athletes to select "cake majors"—easier courses of study such as physical education or communications.

21   "But right now," says Banowsky, "kids can kind of float around out there. They may finish their eligibility and still be 60 hours short of graduation.

22   "At least this way you're not only giving the kid a fair chance, but you're requiring him to stay on a graduation track."

23   Perhaps the most divisive proposal in the presidents' package would limit the number of hours a student-athlete could take in summer school.

24   Like many NCAA rules, this one is being spurred on by abuse.

25   Some schools, NCAA leaders contend, are allowing athletes to take a minimum number of hours during the regular academic year. Then, during the summer, they accept 20 or more hours the athlete takes at a local junior college.

26   If passed as expected, all the Presidents Commission legislation would become effective in 1995.

■ READING COMPREHENSION QUESTIONS

1.   The NCAA has set twin goals regarding the preparation and progress of student–athletes: (a) higher entrance skills and 5 years to graduate (b) lower entrance skills and 7 years to graduate (c) roughly the same entrance skills but 6 years to graduate, counting summer school (d) higher entrance skills and no limit on the number of years to graduate

2.   Research done by the NCAA itself has demonstrated that Proposition 48 in effect excludes a disproportionate number of (a) football players on the defensive line (b) swimmers and divers (c) women basketball players (d) minority athletes

3.   "The most significant proposal" for an NCAA rules change, according to Britton Banowsky of the Southwest Conference, would establish strict requirements for (a) drug testing of all athletes (b) clear progress toward graduation (c) scholarship eligibility (d) athletic facilities and scheduling

4.   The use of standardized tests, such as the SAT, as standards for admission and scholarship eligibility has been heatedly criticized because such tests are (a) culturally biased (b) impossible for student–athletes with learning disorders (c) cold-blooded but infallible predictors of academic success (d) no more accurate than person–to–person interviews

5.   University of Georgia Athletic Director Vince Dooley referred to the recent rules changes as a "presidential blitzkrieg," by which he meant it was a presidential (a) sneak attack under cover of darkness (b) General Sherman-like burning of the past (c) lightning attack (d) slow and methodical grinding down of opposition

6.   The NCAA convention covered in this article was not the first meeting at which the college presidents had tried to make sweeping changes. Three years earlier the presidents had also attempted to make major changes but they were (a) absent when the key votes were taken (b) not able to find language suitable to the NCAA policy committee (c) soundly defeated by those who wanted no changes made (d) declared ineligible to vote at the convention

■ TARGET VOCABULARY

resistant	**opponents**	**proposal**
blitzkrieg	**standardized test**	**eligible**
legislative	**perennial**	**to mandate**
requirements	**to vow**	**divisive**
defeat	**significant**	**legislation**

Dictionary Practice

Use each word in a sentence of your own.

1. resistant _____

2. blitzkrieg _____

3. legislative _____

4. requirements _____

5. defeat _____

6. opponents _____

7. standardized test _____

8. perennial _____

9. to vow _____

10. significant _____

11. proposal _____

12. eligible _____

13. to mandate _____

14. divisive _____

15. legislation _____

Cloze Practice

Fill in each blank with an appropriate word from the target vocabulary list.

For a century _____ have been made to establish clear

_____ for determining whether a college student is truly

_____ to compete in athletics. But attempts _____

such guidelines through _____ have been a _____

source of _____ and angry debate. _____ of such

absolute determinants are _____ to taking _____

action because, at present, no single method of determining eligibility,

such as using a _____, can possibly measure all students

fairly.

■ CRITICAL READING PRACTICE/TOPICS FOR DISCUSSION

1. Based on your experience, do you think that some tests are racially or culturally biased? Being as specific as possible and using your own experience if you can, explain why you agree that such exams can be biased or disagree with that notion.

2. What do you think about the NCAA Presidents Commission's proposal to raise GPA and core curriculum requirements? Whom do you think that this will help, and whom do you think that it will hurt? In what ways? What student athletes do you think will have a better chance of receiving an athletic scholarship under the new rules, and why do you think so?

3. Do you think that athletes at colleges and universities should be allowed to take as many as twenty transfer units at junior or community colleges and still remain eligible to participate in sports programs?

Why do you think that they don't take these courses at the schools for which they compete?

4. Do you generally favor or generally oppose the recent NCAA changes, particularly in terms of their effects on student-athletes who have either attended poor secondary schools or been academically neglected during their high school years? Explain.

■ *Anatomy of a Hero: The Triumph of Russell White*

Courage, skill, NCAA Proposition 48 (dealing with provisional admission for athletes with low grades and test scores), and dyslexia all figure in the next pre-reading essay and article. But the real subject of the unit is a student named Russell White, in whom the four topics come together in a particularly meaningful way.

Fortunately, there is a "happy ending" to this story of a young student with an undiagnosed learning disability. Russell White's dyslexia was eventually identified and treated, and he has done rather well academically since. But such happy endings are not always the case. Had White not been a marvelous athlete . . . well, that's a starting point for a good class discussion.

■ PRE-READING FOR DISCUSSION

Russell White's football talent was well-known long before he entered the University of California at Berkeley. Football coaches and recruiters across the country knew White's 40-yard sprint time, his average gain per carry, his number of carries per game and season, his points scored, his shoe size, his address, his telephone number, and even his high school coach's telephone number.

But not one person, anywhere, knew that Russell White had dyslexia, even though he had been describing its symptoms for years.

Dyslexia is an uncommon way of processing verbal and written information. People who are dyslexic often have difficulty deciphering traditional printed and written forms of ideas, but just as often they see patterns and make connections that only their dyslexia enables them to see and make. Many great thinkers, artists, and writers have exhibited symptoms of dyslexia, and their greatness is, in some measure, due to it.

Russell White was admitted to UC-Berkeley as a "Proposition 48" athlete, so named because of an NCAA provision under which colleges and universities can admit athletes who do not score 700 points or more on the SAT but may not allow them to compete—or even practice—during their freshman year. The goal is for these students to acquire basic college-level skills before they begin to play.

Yet even without practices taking up his time, Russell White found himself in big trouble with the books at Cal. So once again as he had done with teachers and coaches throughout the years, White mentioned that numbers and letters sometimes "appeared backward" to him.

But this time somebody listened: Jo Baker, one of White's academic advisers, immediately began the search that uncovered the dyslexic patterns. And in his first full term following the diagnosis, Russell White pulled a 3.2 GPA.

There are several candidates for heroism in the following *Sports Illustrated* story, "Bear on the Loose," by Austin Murphy. Russell White's mother, Helen, certainly qualifies. So, of course, does Jo Baker. For true heroism, however, I suggest the guy who just *knew* there was something not right, who *knew* deep down he wasn't "on the lame side," who *knew* that schools and learning weren't supposed to be as hard as they were for him, and who *kept saying so year after year*. That's a hero. That's believing in yourself. That's an athlete who truly "competes for the prize."

And should Russell White ever actually put his degree in social welfare to work as a junior high counselor to help others, perhaps others with dyslexia, we'll need a bigger word than "hero."

Bear on the Loose

Austin Murphy

1   At halftime of California's game against UCLA, Golden Bears tailback Russell White had a needle in each arm and a simple request: He wanted his mommy. Despite having rushed for 72 yards and a touchdown before intermission, White wasn't feeling so hot. That much was clear from the way he lunged for the oxygen tank whenever he stepped off the field. The air over the Rose Bowl was the color of Grey Poupon, and White, having been plagued for two weeks by an upper-respiratory infection, couldn't take deep breaths. Further, after 30 minutes of play he was so dehydrated that team doctors stuck *two* glucose-solution IVs in him.

2   With the score tied 14–14, White, who's a junior, could not decide whether to play the second half. But he knew of someone who could decide. A student trainer was sent into the stands to get Helen White. "O.K.," she said upon greeting her son in the dressing room, "what's the matter?"

3   "I get *tired,*" White told her. "I can carry two or three times, then I have to rest."

4   "Go in and give them what you can give them," said Helen.

5   "Don't be a superhero," said Tovi Scruggs, White's girlfriend, who had tagged along with Helen.

6   Scruggs need not have worried. White's second-half contributions were a mortal but important 49 yards rushing—he finished with 121 on 25 carries—and a second touchdown, which tied the score at 24–24 with 4:18 to play. Then, with 30 seconds remaining, Doug Brien's 47-yard field goal tumbled through the uprights to give Cal a 27–24 victory.

7   "These are not the old Cal teams," said UCLA coach Terry Donahue, whose Bruins have lost two straight games to the Bears. Indeed, Cal is 4–0, ranked 13th and headed for an Oct. 19 Pac-10 showdown with third-ranked Washington.

8   Asked to assess White's performance against his team, Donahue chose instead to refer to White's having been a Prop 48 athlete (for failing to score at least 700 on the Scholastic Aptitude Test) and also remarked five times on the Bears' new "commitment to winning." What a shame, Donahue intimated to reporters, that Berkeley, of all places, had accepted such a poor student.

9   Donahue, who is not permitted, by school policy, to sign Prop 48 athletes, did not mention that White is thriving academically at Berkeley. But it is the jabs that have been launched at him closer to home that have most embittered White. He says, "When I'm ready to leave Berkeley, maybe I'll say, 'To all of you who didn't want me here, well, here's my degree, so kiss my ass.'"

10   White was the biggest football recruiting coup in the history of Berkeley—and one of its most controversial admissions decisions. Students, professors and the press demanded to know how the school—home to 15 Nobel Prize winners—could have room for this . . . this *dolt*. "What price glory?" wrote the Riverside (Calif.) *Press-Enterprise,* pointing out that 41% of White's fellow freshmen had 4.0 averages in high school and that the university had rejected another 2,500 applicants with perfect grades.

11   By White's senior season at Crespi Carmelite High in Encino, Calif., his difficulties with the SAT—he took it five times—had become public knowledge. "It

was hell," says White. "I'd sit there thinking, What if I don't pass *this* time? What are people going to think?"

12   That question was easy: They thought he was a dunce. "I walked around like this," says White, nearly touching his chin to his sternum. "It was like I had IDIOT written on my forehead."

13   Even with his afternoons free that first autumn at Cal—as a Prop 48, White was ineligible even to practice his freshman year—he found himself in academic freefall. One day in October 1989, White mentioned to Jo Baker, one of his academic advisers, that numbers and letters sometimes appeared backward to him. He had mentioned this to teachers in his elementary and high schools, but, says White, "They'd say things like, 'Well, maybe it's because you're lefthanded.'"

14   Baker's reaction was different. She had White take a battery of tests. The results were at once gloomy and wonderful: He wasn't dumb, he was dyslexic. "It felt like this incredible weight was lifted," White says. "All my life I'd wondered what was wrong with me. I'd actually gone through life thinking I was on the lame side."

15   Since discovering his dyslexia, White's academic advisers have given him special help. Passages from some assigned texts are explained to him by tutors, and he may be excused from having to fulfill his foreign language requirement. The day he got his grades last spring, White phoned Helen and made small talk. Finally, unable to stand the suspense, she blurted, "Well, how'd you do?"

16   "You know, Mom," he said, milking the moment. "I did pretty damn good."

17   He'd pulled a 3.2. When Russell returned home to Van Nuys, Calif., for the summer, Helen, an accountant, presented him with the keys to a silver-green 1991 Toyota Tercel. "Mom," he said, his eyes misting, "it's too much! I worked hard—I didn't *die*."

18   It is difficult to comprehend how White's learning disability remained a mystery for so long. Helen had enrolled him at Crespi, a parochial school, expressly to prepare him for college. In his first varsity season the Celts went 13–1 and won the California Interscholastic Federation Southern Section Big Five Conference title. The two previous seasons they had been a combined 6–13. In three years White rushed for 5,998 yards and 94 touchdowns, both state records.

19   In the classroom, however, he lagged behind. Since graduating from Crespi, White has criticized his teachers for being too easy on him. "I passed some courses I know I should have flunked," he says. "They call themselves a college preparatory school. Well, they didn't prep me well enough."

20   According to Joel Wilker, a Crespi vice-principal and an assistant football coach, officials at the school deeply regret having missed the telltale signs of White's dyslexia. But with 98% of Crespi's graduates going to college, the school has no special education program. Wilker also points out that White probably would not have gotten into Berkeley had he not attended Crespi. Further, Wilker is of the reasonable opinion that White must bear some responsibility for his academic failures.

21   "I understand some of it's my fault," says White. Then, a moment later he lashes out: "I feel they exploited me. I feel they used me as a piece of meat."

22   When White feels he has been wronged, he files away the injury for keeps. His father, Roosevelt, left home when Russell was six, and Russell has just begun to forgive him. One of Roosevelt's 11 siblings is Charles White, who won the 1979 Heisman Trophy as a tailback at Southern Cal and

spent eight seasons in the NFL. Russell dismisses the mention of his famous uncle with a disgusted wave. "As far as his involvement with me," he says, "there's not much to say."

23   At first White did little to justify the gamble Cal had taken on him. His dyslexia had been discovered too late in the fall semester of 1989 to prevent him from finishing with a 1.96 GPA. Over the Christmas break he told Helen that he was considering quitting Cal and attending a junior college. The suggestion was not well received. "In this family," says Helen, "you start something, you finish it."

24   White returned to Berkeley and, at his request, was given a tutor for each of his spring classes. The help paid dividends in the classroom, but no one knew how he would respond on the football field after having been away from the game for 16 months. Last season, the first time he touched the ball in Cal's Memorial Stadium, White returned a kickoff 99 yards for a touchdown against Miami. All worries were laid to rest. As a backup tailback,

White ended up averaging 5.6 yards per carry. He gained 1,018 yards rushing, was the country's seventh-leading all-purpose back and became the only player in Pac 10 history to be named first team all-conference without having started a game.

25   White should command an enviable position in the NFL draft. But Helen and Russell have markedly different views on life for him after Cal. She speaks of the Plan. "I want him running a 4.2 40," says Helen. "He'll be the best back coming out of college since Gale Sayers."

26   White makes no mention of the Plan. Instead, he speaks passionately of how he will put his degree in social welfare to work as a counselor of junior high students. "Too many of them want to be Magic or Michael," he says. "They should come with me. I can show them a different way. I don't want them getting to 12th grade, sitting in front of some test that's going to influence the rest of their lives and drawing a blank. I can be a positive influence. I really think I can."

■ **EXPLODED VIEW FOR STUDY**

Each of the highlighted words should be mastered in the following exercises.

Bear on the Loose

Austin Murphy

1   At halftime of California's game against UCLA, Golden Bears tailback Russell White had a needle in each arm and a simple request: He wanted his mommy. Despite having rushed for 72 yards and a

touchdown before intermission, White wasn't feeling so hot. That much was clear from the way he lunged for the oxygen tank whenever he stepped off the field. The air over the Rose Bowl was the color of Grey Poupon, and White, having been plagued for two weeks by an upper-respiratory infection, couldn't take deep breaths. Further, after 30 minutes of play he was so dehydrated that team doctors stuck *two* glucose-solution IVs in him.

2   With the score tied 14–14, White, who's a junior, could not decide whether to play the second half. But he knew of someone who could decide. A student trainer was sent into the stands to get Helen White. "O.K.," she said upon greeting her son in the dressing room, "what's the matter?"

3   "I get *tired*," White told her. "I can carry two or three times, then I have to rest."

4   "Go in and give them what you can give them," said Helen.

5   "Don't be a superhero," said Tovi Scruggs, White's girlfriend, who had tagged along with Helen.

6   Scruggs need not have worried. White's second-half contributions were a mortal but important 49 yards rushing—he finished with 121 on 25 carries—and a second touchdown, which tied the score at 24–24 with 4:18 to play. Then, with 30 seconds remaining, Doug Brien's 47-yard field goal tumbled through the uprights to give Cal a 27–24 victory.

7   "These are not the old Cal teams," said UCLA coach Terry Donahue, whose Bruins have lost two straight games to the Bears. Indeed, Cal is 4–0, ranked 13th and headed for an Oct. 19 Pac-10 showdown with third-ranked Washington.

8   Asked to assess White's performance against his team, Donahue chose instead to refer to White's having been a Prop 48 athlete (for failing to score at least 700 on the Scholastic Aptitude Test) and also remarked five times on the Bears' new "commitment to winning." What a shame, Donahue intimated to reporters, that Berkeley, of all places, had accepted such a poor student.

9   Donahue, who is not permitted, by school policy, to sign Prop 48

athletes, did not mention that White is thriving academically at Berkeley. But it is the jabs that have been launched at him closer to home that have most embittered White. He says, "When I'm ready to leave Berkeley, maybe I'll say, 'To all of you who didn't want me here, well, here's my degree, so kiss my ass.'"

10   White was the biggest football recruiting coup in the history of Berkeley—and one of its most controversial admissions decisions. Students, professors and the press demanded to know how the school—home to 15 Nobel Prize winners—could have room for this . . . this *dolt.* "What price glory?" wrote the Riverside (Calif.) *Press-Enterprise,* pointing out that 41% of White's fellow freshmen had 4.0 averages in high school and that the university had rejected another 2,500 applicants with perfect grades.

11   By White's senior season at Crespi Carmelite High in Encino, Calif., his difficulties with the SAT—he took it five times—had become public knowledge. "It was hell," says White. "I'd sit there thinking, What if I don't pass *this* time? What are people going to think?"

12   That question was easy: They thought he was a dunce. "I walked around like this," says White, nearly touching his chin to his sternum. "It was like I had IDIOT written on my forehead."

13   Even with his afternoons free that first autumn at Cal—as a Prop 48, White was ineligible even to practice his freshman year—he found himself in academic freefall. One day in October 1989, White mentioned to Jo Baker, one of his academic advisers, that numbers and letters sometimes appeared backward to him. He had mentioned this to teachers in his elementary and high schools, but, says White, "They'd say things like, 'Well, maybe it's because you're lefthanded.'"

14   Baker's reaction was different. She had White take a battery of tests. The results were at once gloomy and wonderful: He wasn't dumb, he was dyslexic. "It felt like this incredible weight was lifted," White says. "All my life I'd wondered what was wrong with me. I'd actually gone through life thinking I was on the lame side."

15   Since discovering his dyslexia, White's academic advisers have given him special help. Passages from some assigned texts are explained to him by tutors, and he may be excused from having to fulfill his foreign language requirement. The day he got his grades last spring, White phoned Helen and made small talk. Finally, unable to stand the suspense, she blurted, "Well, how'd you do?"

16   "You know, Mom," he said, milking the moment. "I did pretty damn good."

17   He'd pulled a 3.2. When Russell returned home to Van Nuys, Calif., for the summer, Helen, an accountant, presented him with the keys to a silver-green 1991 Toyota Tercel. "Mom," he said, his eyes misting, "it's too much! I worked hard—I didn't *die*."

18   It is difficult to comprehend how White's learning disability remained a mystery for so long. Helen had enrolled him at Crespi, a parochial school, expressly to prepare him for college. In his first varsity season the Celts went 13–1 and won the California Interscholastic Federation Southern Section Big Five Conference title. The two previous seasons they had been a combined 6–13. In three years White rushed for 5,998 yards and 94 touchdowns, both state records.

19   In the classroom, however, he lagged behind. Since graduating from Crespi, White has criticized his teachers for being too easy on him. "I passed some courses I know I should have flunked," he says. "They call themselves a college preparatory school. Well, they didn't prep me well enough."

20   According to Joel Wilker, a Crespi vice-principal and an assistant football coach, officials at the school deeply regret having missed the telltale signs of White's dyslexia. But with 98% of Crespi's graduates going to college, the school has no special education program. Wilker also points out that White probably would not have gotten into Berkeley had he not attended Crespi. Further, Wilker is of the reasonable opinion that White must bear some responsibility for his academic failures.

21   "I understand some of it's my fault," says White. Then, a

moment later he lashes out: "I feel they exploited me. I feel they used me as a piece of meat."

22   When White feels he has been wronged, he files away the injury for keeps. His father, Roosevelt, left home when Russell was six, and Russell has just begun to forgive him. One of Roosevelt's 11 siblings is Charles White, who won the 1979 Heisman Trophy as a tailback at Southern Cal and spent eight seasons in the NFL. Russell dismisses the mention of his famous uncle with a disgusted wave. "As far as his involvement with me," he says, "there's not much to say."

23   At first White did little to justify the gamble Cal had taken on him. His dyslexia had been discovered too late in the fall semester of 1989 to prevent him from finishing with a 1.96 GPA. Over the Christmas break he told Helen that he was considering quitting Cal and attending a junior college. The suggestion was not well received. "In this family," says Helen, "you start something, you finish it."

24   White returned to Berkeley and, at his request, was given a tutor for each of his spring classes. The help paid dividends in the class-room, but no one knew how he would respond on the football field after having been away from the game for 16 months. Last season, the first time he touched the ball in Cal's Memorial Stadium, White returned a kickoff 99 yards for a touchdown against Miami. All worries were laid to rest. As a backup tailback, White ended up averaging 5.6 yards per carry. He gained 1,018 yards rushing, was the country's seventh-leading all-purpose back and became the only player in Pac 10 history to be named first team all-conference without having started a game.

25   White should command an enviable position in the NFL draft. But Helen and Russell have markedly different views on life for him after Cal. She speaks of the Plan. "I want him running a 4.2 40," says Helen. "He'll be the best back coming out of college since Gale Sayers."

26   White makes no mention of the Plan. Instead, he speaks passionately of how he will put his degree in social welfare to work as a counselor of junior high students. "Too many of them want to be Magic or Michael," he says. "They should come with me. I can show them a different way. I don't want them getting to 12th grade, sitting in front of some test that's going to influence the rest of their lives and drawing a blank. I can be a positive influence. I really think I can."

■ READING COMPREHENSION QUESTIONS

1.   The greatest obstacle to Russell White's admission to the University of California at Berkeley, and the subject of widespread criticism following his admission, was White's (a) 40-yard sprint time (b) Scholastic Aptitude Test score (c) high school program and coaching (d) life-long admiration of Stanford University

2.   One of White's academic tutors at Berkeley, Jo Baker, made the discovery that White's academic problems were not related to intelligence but to (a) poor note-taking skills (b) problems organizing his time (c) the Bay Area environment (d) dyslexia

3.   White is critical of some of his high school teachers at Crespi Carmelite High in Encino, California, because they (a) passed him in courses he should have failed and did not investigate his dyslexic symptoms (b) did not prepare him well enough for his college math classes (c) emphasized the sciences over the humanities and arts (d) failed to support the football program

4.   The first full semester following the diagnosis of his dyslexia, Russell White achieved a grade-point average of (a) 2.5 or "C+" (b) 2.0 or "C" (c) 1.75 or "D" (d) 3.2 or "B+"

5.   Russell White's undergraduate major is (a) history (b) economics (c) social welfare (d) anthropology

6.   Russell White and his mother have somewhat different views of his future. His mother's "plan" focuses on a career for White in the National Football League, while he envisions a career as a (a) junior high school counselor (b) coach and P.E. teacher (c) psychologist (d) public defender

■ TARGET VOCABULARY

(to be) plagued	**recruiting**	**to comprehend**
trainer	**a coup**	**disability**
to assess	**freefall**	**telltale**
to intimate	**backward**	**dividends**
to thrive	**tutor**	**counselor**

Dictionary Practice

Use each word in a sentence of your own.

1. (to be) plagued _____

2. trainer _____

3. to assess _____

4. to intimate _____

5. to thrive _____

6. recruiting _____

7. a coup _____

8. freefall _____

9. backward _____

10. tutor _____

11. to comprehend _____

12. disability _____

13. telltale _____

14. dividends _____

15. counselor _____

Cloze Practice

Fill in each blank with an appropriate word from the target vocabulary list.

Winning college athletic programs depend on _____ good female and male athletes. Signing such athletes is considered _____ which will pay significant _____ in the future, if the athlete is not _____ by injuries. Another danger, we know now, is that a learning _____ can make it impossible for some athletes _____ their texts or lectures and send them into an academic _____. The _____ signs of these problems must be _____ early and addressed by _____ and _____. With help, all such students can _____; without it, most will fall _____, losing both athletic and educational opportunities.

■ CRITICAL READING PRACTICE/TOPICS FOR DISCUSSION

1.   Do you think that Russell White's dyslexia might have been diagnosed earlier if he had not been an athlete? Do you think that it might have been diagnosed earlier if he had been a white athlete? Do you think that it might have been diagnosed earlier if he had been a white non-athlete? Explain.

2.   Since he could neither read nor write well, why do you think Russell White was passed from grade to grade in his primary school and, later, at Crespi Carmelite High? Do you think that this could happen again at the same schools? At other schools?

3.   Do you have, or know anybody who has, any type of problem learning in "traditional" classroom ways? If so, what difficulties are connected with such non-traditional learning patterns, for the student as well as the instructor? If not, describe what you think math tests must have been like for the young Russell White.

4.   Do you think that reading the article on Russell White will make you any more aware of and sensitive toward non-traditional learners? Why, or why not?

CHAPTER 7

The Comics Section

The comics, or "funnies," are probably everybody's favorite section of the newspaper. But we should remember that at their best, comics are not just funny but *real news,* as well. The following comics often make us laugh while also making us think about very serious things. Each has some suggested topics for discussion or writing, though each reader will respond to different comics in different ways, and you can probably generate plenty of topics on your own.

It might be useful, though, to remember that humor has four major forms. Perhaps you'll wish to refer to them in the discussions or essays that the comics in this chapter will produce.

THE BASIC FORMS OF HUMOR

Satire

Satire makes you think about very serious subjects by getting you to laugh about them. It's probably the "highest" form of humor, and is certainly a very dangerous one. If a satirist isn't funny *enough,* then people resent being made to think about something uncomfortable.

Irony

Irony uses opposites to create humor. For example, if a race car driver were to get a traffic ticket for driving too slowly, that would be ironic. If an English teacher were to be terrible in spelling, that would be ironic. If a politician were to put the interests of her constituents ahead of getting elected *and then win the election,* that would be not only ironic, but a miracle.

Parody

Parody imitates something well-known, such as a famous actress or a particular writing style or way of speaking. A student can parody an instructor, for example, but should probably be careful doing so.

Sarcasm

Sarcasm stings, cuts, bites, and attacks in a less funny and gentle way than satire. It can get pretty rough, at times, but sarcasm can make some *very* strong points more quickly than the other forms, when it is handled skillfully.

Once again, though, the artist has to be careful. The percentage of our species that may be offended by sarcasm is even greater than the percentage that may be offended by satire, and often more violent.

As you enjoy the comics section, feel free to discuss or write about any aspect of any comic that particularly interests you. Also, you may find it fun to try to identify *why* particular comics are funny, and the above terms may come in handy in such analyses.

THE FAR SIDE   By GARY LARSON

What common human situations does Gary Larson parody in this
cartoon? Have you ever had a similar situation (not involving a pig)
happen to you? How does the picture on the wall add to the cartoon?

© *San Francisco Chronicle*. Reprinted by permission.

This cartoon was drawn *before* the highly publicized rioting that took place in Los Angeles during the spring of 1992, following the acquittal of four police officers who had been filmed beating Rodney King. The cartoon suggests that even the most "surgical" military actions overseas—in this case during the 1991 war in the Persian Gulf—do not provide realistic solutions to social problems here in the United States.

Do you feel that people who want "quick-fix" solutions to social problems are more willing to use force or violence to achieve those solutions than those who believe that social problems result from lack of opportunity and social inequality? What would you do, if you could, to help people in the inner city make their lives better? Why is a picture of jets strafing a jaywalking citizen a particularly powerful image? Explain your responses.

"Whoa! *That* was a good one! Try it, Hobbs —
just poke his brain right where my finger is."

Sometimes, "sick" humor can be very funny indeed. What basic human behavior is being made fun of here? Why is such humor described as "sick"?

© *San Francisco Chronicle*. Reprinted by permission.

"Operation Desert Storm" was the code name for the U.S.-led attack by United Nations forces against Iraq in the 1991 Persian Gulf War. Called the first "video" war because of the extensive use of laser-guided "smart bombs," "suicide-computer" cruise missiles, and "invisible" Stealth bombers, the war is likened in this cartoon to an electronic amusement game.

U.S. and U.N. casualties in the war numbered in the hundreds, while Iraqi deaths numbered tens or hundreds of thousands (no one is sure, and probably no one ever will be). Damage caused by the war undoubtedly led to many more deaths, perhaps even more than those caused by actual combat. Displaced and persecuted refugees of all ages numbered in the millions.

Most people in the West consider having fought the Persian Gulf War absolutely essential, although they violently disagree about its resolution. Regardless of your own opinion concerning the necessity of the war, do you feel that the U.N. or the U.S. has a responsibility to protect the refugees displaced or made vulnerable by the war? If so, to what extent should this protection be given? If not, who must take responsibility for the refugees' displacement and persecution?

© *San Francisco Chronicle*. Reprinted by permission.

The phrase "New World Order" has been used twice in our century: first by Germany before the Second World War and later by the United States following the disintegration of the former Soviet Union.

In what ways is this cartoon's title a sarcastic use of the phrase? Which word is the focus of this sarcasm, and why? What point do you think the cartoonist is trying to make by picturing an exploding globe rather than an "ordered" one?

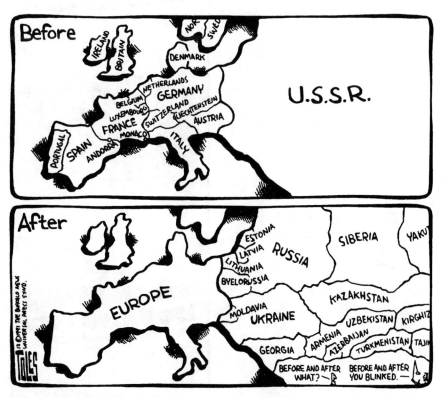

Sometimes the world is more ironic than cartoons. What ironies are being expressed in "Before and After"?

"Gallows" humor is usually reserved for truly grim situations. What basic social attitudes are being examined in "The Argument Against . . ."? What is your opinion of those attitudes? Why do you think that you hold the opinions you do?

© *San Francisco Chronicle*. Reprinted by permission.

Reprinted with special permission of King Features Syndicate.

What basic human trait is the subject of "I Come from a Good Family . . ."? What do you think this cartoon says about politicians in general, if anything? Who do you think the figure on the right might represent, and why do you think so?

DOONESBURY copyright 1992 G. B. Trudeau. Reprinted with permission of Universal Press Syndicate. All rights reserved.

In the 1991–92 Republican primary elections, incumbent President George Bush was challenged by former American Nazi Party member David Duke. Candidate Duke disavowed his former Nazi affiliations and ran as a mainstream, albeit conservative, Republican, much to the discomfort of many in that political party. Duke's bid for the nomination was unsuccessful but his candidacy alone, and the considerable support he actually received at the polls, were the subject of intense national debate.

Symbols are very powerful in any culture. What reactions are triggered in "Not Another Negative Campaign"?

What basic point of view do you think is being presented in this cartoon? How do you feel about such topics being the subject of a comic strip? Being as specific as possible, why do you feel as you do?

The horizontal statue labeled "Lenin" is representative of thousands of statues erected throughout Eastern Europe and Asia by the Communist Party to honor Vladimir Ilich Ulianov (1870–1924), a Russian revolutionary leader who used "Lenin" as his underground name. Such statues were destroyed as symbols of oppression during the collapse of the Soviet Empire.

Unfortunately, terrible civil unrest has followed the loss of central authority in many regions of the former Soviet Union—particularly in the Balkans but in many other areas as well.

Why do you think this has happened? Why have so many groups resorted to violence, and how long do you think that the bloodshed will continue? What solutions can you come up with for these diverse groups to live in harmony? What difficulties do you see in implementing your plan?

© *San Francisco Chronicle*. Reprinted by permission.

When the economy is healthy, politicians, regardless of party, eagerly accept responsibility for low unemployment, rising productivity, and prosperity throughout the land. When the economy goes in the bucket—when unemployment soars, productivity drops, and people are scared—politicians, again regardless of party, very quickly place the responsibility elsewhere. This pattern has existed for thousands of years.

In the early 1990s the United States' economy suffered its most severe recession in half a century. Since the Great Depression things hadn't been so tough for so many for so long. The cartoon "This is the captain speaking . . ." suggests that most people, like the passengers on the airplane, don't care so much who is at fault, but simply that the situation is speedily corrected.

What other situations can you think of in which average people suffer while those in charge argue? How about in your school? Your community? Your job or the job of somebody you know? How much control do you think the government ought to have over the economy? Why?

© *San Francisco Chronicle*. Reprinted by permission.

During his Senate confirmation hearings, Supreme Court Justice Clarence Thomas was accused of sexual harassment by law professor Anita Hill. A former professional associate, Hill made some very shocking allegations concerning Thomas's behavior. The Senate Judiciary Committee, and later the entire Senate, voted to confirm Justice Thomas in spite of Hill's testimony; but many citizens, including many women professionals, believed Anita Hill.

Regardless of one's opinion on the Thomas-Hill situation, the cartoon "Hi! I'm Clarence Thomas . . ." makes it clear that sexual harassment is a humiliating, degrading, criminal activity—and not at all uncommon.

If you have ever been involved in such a situation, or know someone who has, how was the incident dealt with (if at all)? What do you think ought to happen to those who harass others in this way? What do you think needs to be changed in our society in order to eliminate this evil?

Readings from the College Curriculum

In this third part of *Steppingstones,* you will have an opportunity to build on the reading skills you learned in Part I and practiced in Part II. Applying these skills to the following passages from college textbooks will help you achieve the reading level required for typical undergraduate assignments. Of course, these textbook selections are longer and more complex than the news articles you worked with in Part II, so approach them with patience and care. In reading material like this, you'll find that diligence pays off.

Keep in mind that at this level it is assumed you already understand how to use a dictionary to research and define unfamiliar terms and concepts, so no formal vocabulary exercises are included in this part. Keep in mind, as well, that when you work with textbook material, the skills of critical reading, note-taking, and "highlighting" (which refers to marking text with a bright pen and is actually the *ancient* study technique of underlining in a contemporary, fluorescent incarnation) all take on added importance.

To aid your reading and guide you in developing the skills necessary for academic work, each of the following textbook selections begins with a brief introduction that suggests important points to look for. Also, marginal notes have been added throughout each of the selections to help you see items or patterns of particular interest. As in Part II, the first selection, "The Myth of the Moundbuilders" from Kenneth Feder's archaeology text *Frauds, Myths, and Mysteries,* has been "mapped" in order to demonstrate how that useful technique can expand to meet the demands of more difficult readings. You are encouraged to map each of the other sections on your own.

While the work you'll be doing here may seem intimidating at first, remember that you've already mastered most of the concepts and skills necessary for effective reading as you've worked through Parts I and II. "Main ideas" should be old friends by now, "subtopics" should be easy to identify through your mapping practice, and "critical reading" should virtually be a habit at this point based on your post-reading discussion of earlier selections. All that is needed now is practice to help you integrate what you've learned and apply your knowledge to academic material.

■ HIGHLIGHTING, MAPPING, AND NOTE-TAKING

Highlighting, mapping, and taking notes are, in ascending order of complexity, the main methods of reading to study and store what you read. The first of these, *highlighting* (or underlining, which serves the same purposes), simply calls the eye's attention to significant terms, facts, concepts, or relationships within the original text. The second, *mapping,* requires you to identify and then organize for yourself the critical elements of a text. Finally, *note-taking* is a way to structure a text's ideas, as in the mapping process, while simultaneously responding to them personally and for academic purposes.

Each of these techniques is useful, but they have very different functions and, therefore, each serves a very different purpose.

Highlighting and Underlining

For simply remembering data, an important objective in itself and often a crucial means to a scholarly end, highlighting or underlining is probably without equal as a reading trick. For hundreds of years, readers have used underlining to pull their eye back to particular passages, words, or notes; using a "day-glo" pink highlighter is not essentially different. Assuming you highlight carefully, limiting yourself to a text's key points, you will be able to see those points easily and, eventually, remember them just about perfectly.

As Mark Twain might have put it, "When you need that sort of thing, it's *just* the sort of thing you need." Often, however, you must do more with a text than can be accomplished by simply remembering it. As I have had to tell students who faultlessly memorized hundreds of lines of poems and plays without ever troubling over what the lines might actually mean, *remembering* the stuff is often just the first step.

Mapping

The "second step" is figuring out how the text is "constructed" (what Part I described as its "Expository Architecture"). In order to do this, important ideas must be identified, of course, with a highlighter or in some other way. But then these important elements must be grouped together by type and intention, even if they appear in different paragraphs or on different pages or in different chapters. Like a paleontologist working with a roomful of dinosaur bones, you need to reassemble the intellectual skeleton of ideas within a written text, to put the pieces back together, one-by-one, all by yourself—no matter where you find them. Only then will you have an accurate understanding of what the text says.

Mapping is specifically designed to help such reassembling, because its clusters attract related elements and, eventually, the "skeleton" (whether tiny or huge) becomes clear as a Brontosaurus.

For an illustration of how this process works with longer and more complex pieces than those in Part II, note the sample map of the first reading in Part III, Kenneth Feder's "The Myth of the Moundbuilders." (Also keep in mind that mapping can take many forms; you may find that a mapping system you devise for yourself may work better for you.)

Reading Notes

Finally, just as mapping expands highlighting, so taking reading notes expands mapping to encompass critical thinking. Such note-taking fuses your reading and thinking processes (and thereby creates the raw materials necessary for good writing).

Good reading notes must capture the essential points of a text, provide a map or framework of how those points fit together, and *simultaneously* record the reader's thoughts, questions, reactions, opinions, criticisms, comparisons, and any other personal "notes" that occur during the act of reading or after. Such notes not only store and analyze written material, they consider and respond to it in an active, personal way. Basically, if you record the main idea, subtopics, and essential details that support the subtopics, then respond to each of these in a way that captures your questions and opinions along with any possible connections to other such elements in other pieces you may have read, you will have all the notes for studying or writing that you will ever need.

This is when reading is at its most exciting.

This is the deep end of the pool.

What actually takes place in this progression is nothing less than the reader's own evolution from recorder to anatomist to potential writer, bound for the great home sea of words . . . but that's another story.

■ APPLYING YOUR SKILLS

The selections that follow in this part have been taken from college textbooks in the fields of archaeology, religious studies, drama, anthropology, and music. Each of these selections, and indeed each of these disciplines, provides almost endless opportunity for revelation and delight; but each also requires diligence and care on the part of the reader.

Although specific suggestions are included for using these selections to practice and develop your reading skills, you may find it helpful to apply *any* of the basic reading techniques discussed earlier to all or to parts of these selections. And whatever you read, now and in your future studies, keep the following guidelines in mind.

Some Guidelines for Careful Readers

1. When you don't know a word or understand how it is being used, take a minute and look it up. At every level, this is how vocabularies grow and flourish.

2. If you can't summarize the article or chapter you've just read in a sentence or two, you probably don't really "own" it yet. (This does not necessarily apply to fiction, poetry, or drama.)

3. After careful reading, you should be able to recall three or four specific facts, examples, graphs, or illustrations, at least for a few days. (Of course, these will exist in your reading notes too.)

4. Think about any questions that you yourself have, or others have, raised, about what you've read. (Often such questions will be the most interesting things you take from a reading.)

5. Define for yourself anything that seems false, faked, or phoney about the text. Also consider what feels honest and truthful. (Instinct is amazingly accurate in this.)

6. Ask yourself, "What do I know after reading this piece that I didn't know before? How has this knowledge expanded or changed my own thinking?"

CHAPTER 8

Archaeology

"The Myth of the Moundbuilders," from Frauds, Myths, and Mysteries, by Kenneth Feder

"The Myth of the Moundbuilders" has five basic parts: a general introduction that raises the question of why so few Americans know about the ancient Moundbuilders (pages 250–254); a list of the early arguments for a "vanished race" of builders who were not American Indians (254–256); an overview of the archaeological studies of the mounds conducted during the 18th and 19th centuries (256–260); a point-by-point refutation of the original "vanished race" theories; and a survey of present archaeological interpretations of the Moundbuilders' culture (267–269).

Textbook chapters are almost always constructed of such sub-units, each of which becomes a reading challenge itself. The best strategy for understanding and unifying such elements is to adopt some personal form of the following steps:

1. Think about the chapter's or article's title. Then page through the reading, noting graphs, charts, illustrations, maps, and subheadings.

2. Read the piece, highlighting items that seem to be of particular importance and relationships that the author stresses.

3.   Construct your own "map," using the elements that you identified or underlined and any others necessary to answer your questions.

4.   Jot down your personal reactions, responses, questions, opinions, and speculations regarding the material.

Use this process as you read "The Myth of the Moundbuilders," noting as you do the marginal notes commenting on the text's structure.

7

The Myth of the Moundbuilders

In the following
paragraphs, notice
how Feder uses a
personal anecdote to
illustrate the general
principle under dis-
cussion, the almost
universal lack of
awareness regarding
Cahokia's impor-
tance and grandeur.
Always take note of
an academic writer's
use of such personal
incidents because
they are unusual in
scholarship and
often indicate a
point of particular
importance.

Today, the intriguing culture archaeologists know as the *Moundbuilders* is one of the best kept secrets in the study and teaching of American history. That an American Indian civilization with great population centers, power-ful rulers, pyramids, and fine works of art evolved in the midwestern and southeastern United States comes as a surprising revelation, even to those in whose backyards the ruins lie.

Yet the remnants of these ancient inhabitants of North America are nearly ubiquitous. The most obvious manifestation of their culture is their earthworks (Figures 7.1 and 7.2): conical mounds of earth, up to nearly 100 feet in height, containing the burials of perhaps great rulers or priests with fine grave goods in stone, clay, copper, and shell; great flat-topped pyra-mids of earth, up to 100 feet in height, covering many acres, and containing millions of cubic feet of earth and upon which ancient temples once stood; *effigy* earthworks in the shape of great snakes, birds, and bears.

Few of us seem to be aware of the remarkable cultural legacy of this indigenous American civilization. This became sadly clear to me when attending an archaeology conference in St. Louis a few years ago. Much of my excitement about the conference resulted from its location. The largest and most impressive Moundbuilder site, *Cahokia*, an ancient settlement with thousands of inhabitants, sits on the Illinois side of the Mississippi River, just east of St. Louis. Wishing to take advantage of my proximity to the site, I asked the gentleman at the hotel front desk how I might get to Cahokia. The response: a blank stare. He had never heard of it. "You know," I explained, "The big Indian site." "No, no," he responded, "There haven't been any Indians around here for many years."

Figure 7.1 Examples of mounds: Serpent Mound, an effigy earthwork in southern Ohio in the form of a coiled 1,500-foot-long snake [top]. A huge, conical burial mound close to 100 feet high in Miamisburg, Ohio [bottom]. (Serpent Mound courtesy of Museum of the American Indian, Heye Foundation)

Figure 7.2   Aerial photograph of Monk's Mound, an enormous, tiered pyramid of earth at Cahokia in Illinois. Monk's Mound served as a platform upon which a temple once stood. (Courtesy Cahokia Mounds State Historic Site)

The concluding sentences of the third paragraph contain a concise summary of the chapter's basic objective: to make Cahokia known and appreciated. No set of notes should miss these sentences, nor an underlining reader fail to highlight them. Recording personal responses to these observations will capture the reader's basic opinions regarding Feder's argument and scholarship.

No one in the hotel had heard of Cahokia, and even at the bus station people thought I was just another confused out-of-towner. Luckily, I ran into a colleague who knew the way and I finally got to the site.

It was worth the trouble. About 70 of the 120 or so original mounds remain. Several of these demarcate a large plaza where ceremonies were likely held during Cahokia's peak between A.D 1050 and 1250. *Monk's Mound* (Figure 7.2), containing close to twenty million cubic feet of earth, is one of the largest pyramids in the world (including those of Egypt and Mesoamerica). It dominates the plaza. The highest of its four platforms is raised to a height of 100 feet, where it once held a great temple. Surrounding the central part of this ancient settlement was a massive log wall or palisade with evenly spaced bastions.

Cahokia must have been a splendid place with thousands and perhaps tens of thousands of inhabitants, its artisans producing works in shell, copper, stone, and clay. Cahokia was a trading center, a religious center, and the predominant political force of its time. It was, by the reckoning of many, a civilization. And it was a civilization created by American Indians whose lives were far different from the stereotype of primitive, nomadic hunters too many of us envision (Figure 7.3).

From atop Monk's Mound one can peer into two worlds and two different times. To the west rests the modern city of St. Louis, framed by its Gateway Arch of steel. Below rests the ancient city of Cahokia with its monuments of earth, shadows of a long-ignored Indian civilization.

Figure 7.3 An artist's rendition of Cahokia at its cultural peak. With a population estimated as high as 30,000, Cahokia was a virtual prehistoric American Indian city on the Mississippi River more than 700 years ago. (Painting by Richard Schlecht, © 1972 National Geographic Society)

How could people not know of this wonderful place? Suffice it to say that if people twenty minutes from Cahokia haven't heard of it, most New Englanders, Californians, Southerners—in fact, most Americans—are completely unaware of it and the archaeological legacy of the indigenous American civilization that produced it and hundreds of other sites.

Cahokia and Moundbuilder culture, however, were not always an invisible part of the history of this continent. In fact, the remains of their civilization once commanded the attention of the American public and scientists alike. It was not only that the mounds themselves, the fine ceramics, the sumptuous burials, carved statues, and copper ornaments were so impressive, though this was part of the fascination. Unfortunately, much of the intense interest generated by the remains of this culture resulted from a supposed enigma perceived by most; the Moundbuilders clearly lived before Columbus, the Indians were the only known inhabitants of North America before the coming of the Europeans, and it was commonly assumed that the Indians were simply incapable of having produced the splendid works of art and monumental construction projects that characterized Moundbuilder culture. With the rejection of the possibility that American Indians had produced the culture, the myth evolved of an ancient, vanished American race (see especially Silverberg 1970 for a very useful and succinct account of the evolution of the Moundbuilder myth).

The myths of a race of giant men (Chapter 3) and of a human ancestor with a modern brain and simian jaw (Chapter 4) were based on hoaxes, clever or otherwise. People suspended their critical faculties and were

The introduction has told you "who, what, when, and where" in the finest tradition of expository prose. If you are unclear on any of the four, reread the first sub-unit before going on.

fooled by these frauds. On the other hand, the Moundbuilder myth was predicated, not on a hoax (though, as we will see, hoaxes did play a role), but rather on a nearly complete and sometimes willful misunderstanding of genuine data.

The Myth of a Vanished Race

The myth of a vanished race of Moundbuilders was accepted by many Americans in the eighteenth and nineteenth centuries. Five basic arguments were presented to support the notion that American Indians could not have been the bearers of Moundbuilder culture. Let's deal with each in turn.

Highlight each of the five false conclusions regarding the mounds and their creators. Also note the historical justifications for each.

1. *Indians were too primitive to have built the mounds and produced the works in stone, metal, and clay attributed to the Moundbuilder culture.*

    The attitude of J. W. Foster, president of the Chicago Academy of Sciences, was prevalent. Describing the Indian, he states:

    He was never known voluntarily to engage in an enterprise requiring methodical labor; he dwells in temporary and movable habitations, he follows the game in their migrations. . . . To suppose that such a race threw up the . . . symmetrical mounds which crown so many of our river terraces is as preposterous, almost, as to suppose that they built the pyramids of Egypt. (1873, as cited in Silverberg 1970:76–77)

    In his 1872 work, *Ancient America*, J. D. Baldwin is even more direct: "It is absurd to suppose a relationship or connection between the original barbarism of these Indians and the civilization of the mound-builders" (as cited in Thomas 1894:615).

    These arguments can be fairly characterized as racist and unfortunately held sway among many people.

2. *The mounds and associated artifacts were very much more ancient than even the earliest remnants of Indian culture.*

    Though the analysis of soil layering known as stratigraphy was not to become an established part of archaeology until later in the nineteenth century (for example, Dall 1877), in 1820 Caleb Atwater used a simple form of stratigraphic analysis to support the notion that the Moundbuilders were from a period far before the Indians arrived in the New World. He maintained in his book *Antiquities Discovered in the Western States*:

Indian Antiquities are always either on, or a very small distance below the surface, unless buried in some grave; whilst articles, evidently belonging to that people who raised our mounds, are frequently found many feet below the surface, especially in river bottoms. (1820:125)

The evidence of the annual growth rings of trees also was used in the argument that the mounds were quite ancient. In 1786, the Reverend Manasseh Cutler counted the rings on a tree he had cut down on a mound in Marietta, Ohio. He found 463 rings and calculated that the mound must have been built before A.D 1300 (Fagan 1977). Others went further, suggesting that large trees presently growing on mounds must have been preceded by several generations of trees, indicating that the mounds were more than 2,000 years old.

3. *Stone tablets were found in the mounds that bore inscriptions in European, Asian, or African alphabets.*

The best known of such artifacts were those from Grave Creek Mound in West Virginia (Schoolcraft 1854) and the Cook Farm Mound in Davenport, Iowa (Putnam 1886). Because American Indians north of Mexico were not known to have possessed a writing system before European colonization, the presence of writing in the mounds seemed to provide validation of the hypothesis that a non-Indian culture had been responsible for their construction. Where characters from specific alphabets could be discerned, sources for Moundbuilder culture could be, and were, hypothesized.

4. *American Indians were not building mounds when first contacted by European explorers and settlers. When queries were made of the local Indians concerning mound construction or use, they invariably professed complete ignorance.*

Very simply, the argument was presented that if Indians were responsible for the mounds, they should have been building such earthworks when Europeans first came into contact with them. At the very least, living Indians, if no longer building mounds, should remember a time when their ancestors had built them. The supposed fact that Indians were not building mounds when first contacted by Europeans was seen by many as definitive, empirical evidence against any claim of Indian responsibility for Moundbuilder culture.

5. *Metal artifacts made of iron, silver, ore-derived copper, and various alloys had been found in the mounds.*

Historic Indian cultures north of Mexico were not known to use metal other than copper, which could be found in pure veins and nuggets in parts of Michigan, and, on occasion, iron from meteorites. Smelting ore to produce copper or iron and techniques of alloying metal (mixing copper and tin, for example, to produce bronze) were unknown. Therefore, the discovery of artifacts of these materials in the mounds was a further indication that a people other than and more technologically sophisticated than American Indians had been the Moundbuilders.

With these five presumably well-supported "truths" in hand, it was clear to the satisfaction of many that Indians had nothing to do with mound building or Moundbuilder culture. This left open the question of who, in fact, the Moundbuilders were.

Who Were the Moundbuilders?
Identifying the Vanished Race

From our vantage point in the latter part of the twentieth century, it is extremely difficult to imagine how intensely interested many were in the origins of the mounds and Moundbuilder culture. The fledgling Smithsonian Institution devoted several of its earliest publications to the ostensible Moundbuilder enigma. Another government agency, the Bureau of American Ethnology, whose job it was to preserve information concerning rapidly vanishing native American cultures, devoted a considerable part of its resources to the Moundbuilder issue. Influential private organizations like the American Philosophical Society also supported research into the question and published works reporting on such research.

The mystery of the mounds was a subject that virtually all thinking people were drawn to. Books, pamphlets, magazine pieces, and newspaper articles abounded, written by those who had something to say, sensible or not, on the question that seemed so important to answer: "Who had built the mounds?" Though few could agree on who was responsible for construction of the mounds, there was no lack of opinions.

In one of the earliest published conjectures, Benjamin Smith Barton wrote in 1787 that the Moundbuilders were Vikings who had long ago journeyed to the New World, settled, and then died out. Josiah Priest in his 1833 work variously posited that the mounds had been built by wandering Egyptians, Israelites, Greeks, Chinese, Polynesians, or Norwegians

(Silverberg 1970:42). Others suggested that the mounds had been fashioned by Welshmen, Belgians, Phoenicians, Tartars, Saxons, Africans, or even by refugees from the Lost Continent of Atlantis (Donnelly 1882; see Chapter 8 of this book). Even a work believed by Mormons to be the most recent testament of Jesus Christ (commonly called *The Book of Mormon* and first published in 1830) maintains that the mounds were built by Indians who had migrated from the Middle East in the sixth century B.C.

Caleb Atwater was an Ohio lawyer who performed a detailed analysis of the earthworks in his state in an attempt to establish the identity of the vanished race. Though Atwater's conclusions were typical for the time, his methodology was far more scientific than were the speculations of some of his contemporaries. In his work *Antiquities Discovered in the Western States* (yes, Ohio was then considered a "western" state), Atwater divided the archaeological remains found there into three categories: Indian, European Colonial, and Moundbuilder. The last of these he ascribed to "a people far more civilized than our Indians, but far less so than Europeans" (1820:120).

To his credit, Atwater was not an armchair speculator concerning the Moundbuilders. He personally inspected many sites in Ohio and produced detailed drawings and descriptions of artifacts and earthworks. But his myopia about American Indian cultural achievement clearly fashioned his view:

> Have our present race of Indians ever buried their dead in mounds? Have they constructed such works as described in the preceding pages? Were they acquainted with the use of silver, iron, or copper? Did the North American Indians erect anything like the "walled town" on Paint Creek? (Atwater 1820:208)

For Atwater the answer to these questions was a clear "No." American Indians simply were too primitive. He concluded his discourse on the question by suggesting that the Moundbuilders had been "Hindoos" from India.

To be sure, there were a few prescient thinkers on the question of the origin of Moundbuilder culture. Perhaps the first to approach the question objectively was none other than Thomas Jefferson, framer of the Constitution and third president of the United States. Jefferson was curious about the ancient earthworks on and adjacent to his property in Virginia. Not content to merely speculate about them, Jefferson conducted what is almost certainly the first archaeological excavation in North America, carefully digging a trench through a mound that contained many human skeletons (Willey and Sabloff 1980). Jefferson would not hazard a guess as to the authors of the Moundbuilder culture, justifiably calling for more information. As the president of the American Philosophical Society, he later would encourage others to explore this question.

Interest in the mounds and debate over the source of the culture that had produced the tens of thousands of these earthworks continued to increase during the nineteenth century as white settlement expanded into the American Midwest, the heartland of Moundbuilder culture. American archaeology developed as a discipline largely in response to questions about the mounds (as well as to questions concerning the origins of the Indians; see Chapter 5).

In their chronicle of the history of American archaeology, Willey and Sabloff (1980) select 1840 as the benchmark for a shift in American archaeology from a period of speculation to one characterized by research whose goal was description and classification. The work of Ephraim G. Squier and Edwin H. Davis on the Moundbuilder mystery is a good example of this shift in emphasis. Squier was a civil engineer and writer from Connecticut. Davis was an Ohio doctor. Both were interested in the Moundbuilder culture and between 1845 and 1847 carried out intensive investigation of some 200 sites. They conducted excavations and produced detailed maps of the sites and drawings of the artifacts. Their research culminated in a book, *Ancient Monuments of the Mississippi Valley*, which was selected as the first publication of the recently established Smithsonian Institution.

Squier and Davis approached their task without many of the preconceptions and pet theories of their predecessors on the Moundbuilder question: "With no hypothesis to combat or sustain, and with a desire only to arrive at truth, whatever its bearings upon received theories and current prejudices, everything like mere speculation has been avoided" (1848:*xxxviii*).

Ancient Monuments of the Mississippi Valley certainly is a descriptive work, with more than 200 drawings in its 300 or so pages. Squier and Davis were nothing if not systematic in their investigations. Generally, they classified the various kinds of earthworks according to the empirical data of form and content as deduced from their detailed surveys and excavations. However, they also made unwarranted assumptions concerning the function of the different earthwork types.

In any event, they arranged and described the earthworks as follows:

1. *Defensive enclosures*—earth embankments surrounding high flat plateaus

2. *Sacred enclosures*—earth embankments surrounding areas of from a few up to more than 50 acres (Figure 7.4); also, effigy mounds (mounds in the shape of animals; see Figure 7.1 top)

3. *Altar mounds*—tumuli within sacred enclosures, with burned layers showing possible use as sacrificial altars

4. *Sepulture or burial mounds*—conical mounds, six to eighty feet in height overlying human burials that contained grave goods (see Figure 7.1 bottom)

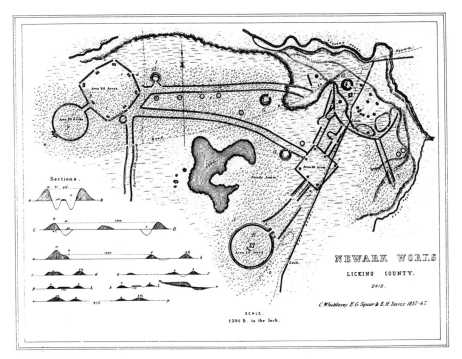

Figure 7.4 Ephraim Squier and Edwin Davis conducted a detailed survey of the mounds of the Ohio Valley and "western" United States in the 1840s, producing beautiful drawings of earthworks like these enclosures in Newark, Ohio. (From *Ancient Monuments of the Mississippi Valley*, AMS Press and Peabody Museum of Archaeology and Ethnology, Harvard University)

5. *Temple mounds*—truncated pyramids, some enormous, with pathways leading to the top where flat platforms, sometimes of a few acres, were found and where temples may have stood (see Figure 7.2)

6. *Anomalous mounds*—oddly shaped or unique mounds

You should be careful to note Squier and Davis's six categories of mounds.

Squier and Davis describe in great detail and depict in beautifully rendered drawings the artifacts that are found in association with the mounds: ceramics, metal implements and ornaments, stone and bone objects, sculptures, and inscribed stones. In a number of places in their book, they compare these objects with those found in other parts of the world, but never attempt to make a direct connection. Nevertheless, Squier and Davis are explicit in maintaining that the quality of art work found in the mounds is "immeasurably beyond anything which the North American Indians are known to produce, even to this day" (1848:272).

Squier and Davis conclude their report by suggesting a "connection, more or less intimate" (p. 301) between the Moundbuilders and the civilizations of Mexico, Central America, and Peru. Ultimately, it seems, they do subscribe to the idea that the Moundbuilders were a group separate from and culturally superior to the American Indians. They refrain, however, from speculating about who they actually might have been and where, ultimately, they came from.

The Moundbuilder Mystery Solved

The late nineteenth century saw a continuation of interest in the Mound-builders. Then, in 1882, an entomologist from Illinois, Cyrus Thomas, was hired to direct a Division of Mound Exploration within the Bureau of American Ethnology. An amendment to a federal appropriations bill in the U.S. House of Representatives directed that $5,000 of the $25,000 B.A.E. budget be devoted solely to the solution of the Moundbuilder mystery. With this funding, Thomas initiated the most extensive and intensive study yet conducted on the Moundbuilder question. The result was a voluminous report of more than 700 pages submitted as an annual report of the Bureau in 1894 (Thomas 1894).

Above all else, Thomas's approach was empirical; he felt it necessary to collect as much information as possible before suggesting hypotheses about mound function, age, origins, and cultural affiliation. And empirical he was. Where Squier and Davis focused on about 200 mounds mostly in Ohio, Thomas and his assistants investigated 2,000 mound sites in twenty-one states. He collected over 40,000 artifacts, which became part of the Smithsonian Institution's collection. And after collecting so much information, Thomas was not afraid to come to a conclusion on the Moundbuilder mystery; where Squier and Davis devote six pages to their conclusions regarding the mounds, Thomas provides a 136-page discussion on the identity of the Moundbuilder culture. The work of Thomas was a watershed, both in terms of answering the specific question of who had built the mounds and also in terms of the development of American archaeology.

For Thomas, the important question to be answered was simple and succinct, "Were the mounds built by the Indians?" (1894:21). He went about answering this question by responding to the arguments against identifying Indians as the Moundbuilders presented earlier in this chapter.

1. *Indian culture was too primitive.*

To the claim that Indians were too primitive to have attained the level of civilization reached by the Moundbuilders, Thomas responded that it was difficult to conceive

Why writers should so speak of them who had access to older records giving accounts of the habits and customs of the Indian tribes when first observed by European navigators and explorers . . . when the records, almost without exception notice the fact that . . . they were generally found from the Mississippi to the Atlantic dwelling in settled villages and cultivating the soil. (p. 615)

For example, in 1539, Hernando de Soto and some 622 men set forth on an expedition of exploration of what is now the southern United States. Their travels lasted more than four years, and they encountered numerous Indian groups. With de Soto was a chronicler known to us only as the "Gentleman of Elvas." He mentions great walled towns of as many as five or six thousand people (1611:122). It is clear from his descriptions of Indian settlements that there was a large, sedentary, "civilized" population in the American Southeast in the sixteenth century.

In another example, William Bartram, a botanist from Philadelphia, began his travels through the Southeast in 1773. In his book enumerating his experiences, he also describes scores of heavily populated Indian towns; in one case he mentions traveling through nearly two continuous miles of cultivated fields of corn and beans (1791:285). He estimates the population of a large town called *Uche* to be as many as 1,500 people (p. 313), and he was very much impressed with how substantially built their structures were.

So, in Thomas's view and in fact, evidence indicated that at least some Indian cultures were agricultural and sedentary, with people living in large population centers. They clearly would have been culturally and practically capable of constructing monumental earthworks.

2. *Mound culture was older than Indian culture.*

In reference to the presumed great age of the earthworks, Thomas denigrates the accuracy of dating the mounds on the basis of tree-ring counts. In fact though, the age of at least some of the mounds may have been more accurately estimated by some of the ancient race enthusiasts. Thomas incorrectly thought many had been built after European arrival in the New World. Ultimately, however, the age of the mounds was only a problem if one accepted the then-current notion that the Indians were relatively recent arrivals. We now know that native Americans first arrived in the New World more than 12,000 years ago (see Chapter 5), and the mounds are all substantially younger.

Figure 7.5 The Davenport tablets were frauds, placed in a mound to take advantage of public confusion in the late nineteenth century concerning the origin of Moundbuilder culture. The tablet shown here exhibits alphabetic characters from a number of European languages. (From Proceedings of the Davenport Academy of Natural Sciences, No. 1)

3. *There were alphabetically inscribed tablets in the mounds.*

Thomas had quite a bit to say concerning the supposed inscribed stone tablets. Though the myth of a vanished race of Moundbuilders was based largely on misinterpretation of actual archaeological and ethnographic data, hoaxes involving inscribed tablets also were woven into its fabric.

For example, in 1838, during an excavation of a large mound in Grave Creek, West Virginia, two burial chambers were found containing three human skeletons, thousands of shell beads, copper ornaments, and other artifacts. Among these other artifacts was a sandstone disc with more than twenty alphabetic characters variously identified as Celtic, Greek, Anglo-Saxon, Phoenician, Runic, and Etruscan (Schoolcraft 1854). Needless to say, translations varied tremendously and had in common only the fact that they were meaningless. The disc was certainly a fraud.

In another case, in 1877, the Reverend Jacob Gass discovered two inscribed slate tablets in a mound on a farm in Davenport, Iowa. One of the tablets had a series of inscribed concentric circles with enigmatic signs believed by some to be zodiacal. The other tablet had various animal figures, a tree, and a few other marks on one face. The reverse face had a series of apparently alphabetic characters from half a dozen different languages across the top, and the depiction of a presumed cremation scene on the bottom (Figure 7.5). Gass discovered or came into possession of a number of other enigmatic artifacts ostensibly associated with the Moundbuilder culture, including two pipes whose bowls were carved into the shape of elephants.

The discoveries in Davenport generated great excitement. However, the fact that such a concentration of apparently conclusive finds regarding the Moundbuilder controversy had been discovered by a single individual within a radius of a few miles of one Iowa town caused many to question the authenticity of the discoveries.

Thomas launched an in-depth investigation of the tablets. Evidence from Gass's excavation indicated pretty clearly that the tablets had been planted only recently in the mound on Cook's farm. Thomas also believed that he had identified the source of the bizarre, multiple-alphabetic inscription. Webster's unabridged dictionary of 1872 presented a sample of characters from ancient alphabets. All of the letters on the tablet were in the dictionary, and most were close copies. Thomas suggested that the dictionary was the source for the tablet inscription (1894:641–42).

McKusick (1970) reports a confession by a Davenport citizen who alleged that the tablets and the other artifacts were frauds perpetrated by a group of men who wished to make Gass appear foolish. Though there are some significant problems with the confession (most notably the fact that the confessor was too young to have been an active participant in the hoax), the Davenport tablets were certainly fraudulent. More recently, McKusick (in press) has discerned the presence of lowercase Greek letters on the Davenport tablet. Lowercase Greek letters were not invented until medieval times. McKusick has also identified Arabic numbers, Roman letters, musical clefs, and ampersands (&) on the Davenport tablet. Their presence is clear proof of the fraudulent nature of the stone. In fact, no genuine artifacts containing writing in any Old World alphabet have ever been found in any of the mounds (see Chapter 6 regarding the authenticity of other supposed ancient inscriptions in North America).

4. *Indians were never witnessed building mounds and had no knowledge of who had built them.*

We next come to the claim that Indians were not moundbuilders at the time of European contact and even did not know who had built the mounds in their own territories. Thomas shows that this is nonsense. DeSoto's chronicler, the

Figure 7.6   The notion that Indians could not have built the mounds was supported by the contention that no historic Indian group had ever been observed building or using earthworks. Yet such a claim was clearly inaccurate. There were a number of written reports and even artistic depictions like this one produced by Jacques Le Moyne in northeastern Florida in the 1560s that bore witness to mound use—here in a burial ceremony—by indigenous tribes. (From *Report on the Mound Explorations of the Bureau of American Ethnology*, by Cyrus Thomas)

Gentleman of Elvas, mentions the construction and use of mounds almost immediately in his sixteenth-century narrative. Describing the Indian town of *Ucita* he writes, "The lordes house stoode neere the shore upon a very hie mount, made by hand for strength" (1611:25).

Garcilaso de la Vega, though not a member of de Soto's expedition, compiled the notes of some of the 311 survivors (de Soto had died during the expedition). He describes how the Indians constructed the mounds upon which temples and the houses of chiefs were placed: "They built up such sites with the strength of their arms, piling up large quantities of earth and stamping on it with great force until they have formed a mound from twenty-eight to forty-two feet in height" (cited in Silverberg 1970:8). Beyond this, sixteenth-century artists depicted Indian burial practices that included the building of mounds for the interment of chiefs (Figure 7.6).

Nearly two hundred years later, at the turn of the eighteenth century, French travelers lived among the Natchez
Indians at the mouth of the Mississippi River. They described
the principal town of these agricultural Indians as possessing
a mound one hundred feet around at its base, with the houses
of leaders located on smaller mounds (Du Pratz 1774). William Bartram, at the end of the eighteenth century, mentions
the fact that the houses of chiefs are placed on eminences.
Even as late as the beginning of the nineteenth century, the
explorers Lewis and Clark noted:

> I observed artificial mounds (or as I may more justly term graves)
> which to me is strong evidence of this country being once thickly
> settled. The Indians of the Missouris still keep up the custom of
> burying their dead on high ground. (Bakeless 1964:34)

There clearly was ample historical evidence of Indians
building and using mounds. The ironic reason for the demise
of at least some of the mound-building cultures of the Southeast was that de Soto accidentally introduced smallpox into
these populations. Exposed to this deadly disease for the first
time, the indigenous people had no immunity to it and died in
great numbers. Large mound sites were abandoned as a result
of the tragic consequences of this deadly epidemic.

5. *There were metal objects found in the mounds beyond the metallurgical skills of the Indians.*

   Thomas carefully assessed the claim that some mound
artifacts exhibited a sophistication in metallurgy attained only
by Old World cultures. Not relying on rumors, Thomas actually examined many of the artifacts in question. His conclusion: all such artifacts were made of so-called *native copper*
(Figure 7.7). Certainly this implied extensive trade networks.
Michigan was the source of the raw material for the metal
artifacts found as far away as Florida. There was no evidence,
however, for metallurgical skills the Indians were not known
to have possessed.

Thomas clearly had marshalled more evidence on the Moundbuilder
question than had anyone before him. In a rather restrained fashion, he
comes to this conclusion: "It is proper to state at this point, however, that
the author believes the theory which attributes these works to the Indians
. . . to be the correct one . . ." (1894:610).
With the publication of Thomas's *Report on the Mound Explorations of*

**Note how each of
the original points
has been refuted in
order, and each ar-
gument systemati-
cally overturned.**

Figure 7.7 Moundbuilder metallurgy was restricted to the use of naturally occurring, pure copper without smelting, casting, or alloying. This photograph shows a hammered copper sheet depicting what may be a shaman or priest in a bird costume. This artifact was found at a well-known mound site, Etowah, in Georgia. (Smithsonian Institution)

the Bureau of American Ethnology, Moundbuilder archaeology had come of age. Its content was so detailed, its conclusions so reasonable that, though not accepted by all, the myth of a vanished race had been dealt a fatal blow.

Rationale for the Myth of a Vanished Race

The myth of a non-Indian, vanished race of moundbuilders was predicated not on a hoax or series of hoaxes, but on ignorance and selective acceptance of the data. Silverberg's thesis that the vanished race myth was politically motivated is well-founded; it was, as he says, "comforting to the conquerors" (1970:30).

Perhaps if the Indians were not the builders of the mounds and the bearers of a culture that impressed even the rather ethnocentric European colonizers of America, it made wiping out the presumably savage and primitive natives less troublesome. And, if Europeans could further convince themselves that the Indians were very recent interlopers—in fact, the very invaders who had savagely destroyed the gentle and civilized Moundbuilders—so much the better. And if, finally, it could be shown that the Moundbuilders were, in actuality, ancient European travelers to the Western Hemisphere, the circle was complete. In destroying the Indian people, Europeans in the eighteenth and nineteenth centuries could

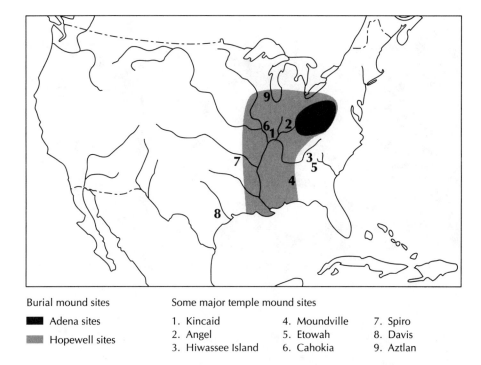

Burial mound sites

■■■ Adena sites

▨▨▨ Hopewell sites

Some major temple mound sites

1. Kincaid	4. Moundville	7. Spiro
2. Angel	5. Etowah	8. Davis
3. Hiwassee Island	6. Cahokia	9. Aztlan

Figure 7.8   Location of Adena and Hopewell heartlands and some of the better known temple mound sites in the United States. Clearly, the geographical focus of Moundbuilder culture was the river valleys of the American Midwest and Southeast.

rationalize that they were only giving back to the Indians what they had meted out to the Moundbuilders and, in a sense, merely reclaiming territory once held by ancient Europe. The Moundbuilder myth was not just the result of a harmless prank or a confusing hoax. It was part of an attempt to justify the destruction of American Indian societies. We owe it to them to set the record straight.

𒊹𒊹𒊹𒊹 CURRENT PERSPECTIVES 𒊹𒊹𒊹𒊹
The Moundbuilders

An enormous amount of research has been conducted on the Moundbuilder culture in the last hundred years. We now realize that there was no one Moundbuilder culture but several, separated geographically and chronologically (Figure 7.8). The conical burial mounds are earlier and have been divided into two cultures: the *Adena* and the *Hopewell*. These both involved burial cults, long-distance trade, and the production of fine crafts and art

Figure 7.9 The primary burial at Mound 72, Cahokia. Laid out on a bed of some 20,000 drilled shell beads, the young male who was laid to rest here was likely an important person, perhaps a ruler of Cahokia. This sort of burial bears witness to a level of social stratification associated with complex civilizations. (Courtesy Illinois State Museum)

work. Both possessed mixed economies relying on wild plants and animals as well as domesticated crops, which eventually included corn. Their focus on life after death was made possible by the food surpluses such an economy produces.

Cahokia is part of a later culture of Moundbuilders. Here, large towns developed with substantial populations; Cahokia is certainly the largest, but others like Etowah in Georgia and Moundville in Alabama had populations in the thousands.

Old World civilizations like those of ancient Egypt and Sumer and New World civilizations like the Aztec and Maya are marked by stratified social systems. Kings, emperors, or pharaohs ruled with the help of noble and priestly classes. The nature of social stratification is exhibited quite clearly in the archaeology of their deaths; the tombs of pharaohs and kings are large and sumptuous with concentrations of finely crafted art work, rare or exotic (and presumably expensive) materials, and even the presence of retainers—people killed and buried with the ruler to accompany him or her to the afterlife.

Cahokia too has evidence of just such a burial (Fowler 1974:20–22, 1975:7–8). Mound 72 represents the interment of members of a royal family of Cahokia. A young man was laid out on a platform of thousands of perforated shell beads that had, perhaps, been woven into a burial cloak (Figure 7.9). Nearby, three women and three men were buried, accompanied by stone weapons made from materials imported from Oklahoma and Arkansas as well as by sheets of mica from North Carolina. A two-by-three-foot sheet of copper from Michigan had also been included in their burial.

Another part of the mound contained the burials of four men, decapitated and with their hands cut off. Close by were the remains of fifty women, all in their late teens and early twenties. These likely were all individuals whose lives were sacrificed for the presumed needs of the rulers in their lives after death.

The evidence at Cahokia and other temple mound sites, as well as at sites of the Adena and Hopewell cultures, is clear. American Indians produced cultures of great sophistication and complexity. The only mystery that remains is why more Americans are not aware of the legacy of these indigenous civilizations.

Sample Map for "The Myth of the Moundbuilders"

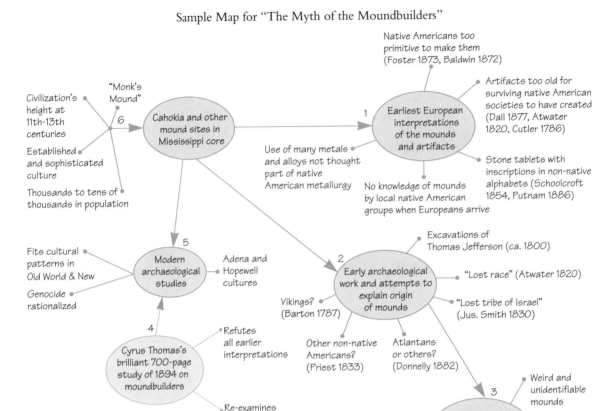

Note: For each of the following readings in Part III, you are encouraged to draw maps of your own like this one, applying the mapping skills you learned in Part I.

■   **READING COMPREHENSION AND DISCUSSION QUESTIONS**

1.   Feder notes that "Willey and Sabloff (1980) select 1840 as the benchmark for a shift in American archaeology from a period of speculation to one characterized by research whose goal was description and classification. The work of Ephraim G. Squier and Edwin H. Davis on the Moundbuilder mystery is a good example of this. . . ."

In what specific ways and on what specific points does the work of Squier and Davis in *Ancient Monuments of the Mississippi Valley* (1848) differ from that of Barton, Priest, and the "others" cited in Donnelly (1882)?

2. Why is the work of Caleb Atwater in *Antiquities Discovered in the Western States* (1820) representative of both the "old" and "new" schools of archaeology? Do you imagine that there is any connection between Atwater's training as an attorney and his revolutionary archaeological methodology? Why, or why not?

3. What impresses you most about the truly monumental work of scholarship published by Cyrus Thomas in 1894? Is it the number of sites he visited, the volume of artifacts he collected, his ability to rise above common prejudices, or something else? Explain your choice.

CHAPTER 9

■ *Religious Studies*

■ *"The Writings: Wisdom Literature,"* *from* Understanding the Bible *by* *Stephen Harris*

"The Writings: Wisdom Literature" is also divided into manageable study units, each focusing on a book of the Hebrew Bible—Proverbs, Job, and Ecclesiastes—that falls under the heading of "Wisdom Literature." Note how each unit has been divided into sub-units, as well ("Key Themes" and "The Role of Wisdom," for example). Your highlighting, underlining, mapping, and reading notes should reflect and capture these organizational elements.

Also note the thorough bibliographies at the end of each main unit. Each of the works listed on these bibliographies would further discuss and clarify the unit's main ideas, as well as provide the reader with another set of valuable reading notes.

Harris has also included a useful vocabulary list and a set of discussion and review questions (page 288). After reading this selection, see how well you recall the "Terms and Concepts to Remember" and the points raised in the "Questions for Review and Study."

P A R T

5

❀ ❀

The Writings

Wisdom Literature

In ancient Israel, people belonging to three callings or professions could speak with authority—the priest, the prophet, and the sage. According to Jeremiah (18:18), the priest's business was to instruct in covenant law (the Torah), the prophet's to convey Yahweh's "word," and the sage's to provide wise advice (see also Ezek. 7:26). The "wise," including both men and women, held positions of public respect and commonly served as counselors to kings (2 Sam. 14:21; 16:23; 20:14–22). Prophets were sometimes critical of the professional class of sages— as they were of priests—but the wisdom movement ultimately outlasted the prophetic line and produced some of the greatest books in the Bible.

The origins of Israel's wisdom tradition are unknown, but archaeological discoveries have revealed that long before Israel came into existence, thinkers in Egypt, Mesopotamia, Edom, and Phoenicia had produced astute guides to the "good life." Among Hebrew writers, however, wisdom material acquired a new tone and emphasis: "The fear of Yahweh is the beginning of knowledge" (Prov. 1:7). Although the writers of many proverbs—short, memorable sayings summarizing insights about life—stressed observation and experience as a source of knowledge, they regarded wisdom as much a divine gift as the prophetic word (Prov. 2:6). Wisdom, rather than the Torah, was envisioned as Yahweh's first creation and, personified as a gracious divine woman, acted as a liaison between the Deity and humanity (Prov. 8). This theme of Wisdom as a creative spirit linking humanity with a primary attribute of the Creator is most fully developed in a late apocryphal work, the Wisdom of Solomon (7:22–9:18).

Renowned for his shrewd judgments, King Solomon—the reputed author of 3000 proverbs—stood at the head of Israel's wisdom tradition (1 Kings 3:1–28; 4:29–34). Later ages, honoring Solomon's role in establishing a national institution of wise government counselors and other sages, attributed a large body of wisdom writings to him. These include the canonical books of Proverbs, Ecclesiastes, and Song of Solomon, the apocryphal Wisdom, and the pseudepigraphal poetry collections known as the Psalms and Odes of Solomon.

In Hebrew literature, wisdom was expressed in many different literary forms. Early types include riddles, fables, and proverbs (Judg. 9:18–15; 14:14; 1 Kings 4:32). In later times, anonymous sages produced far more complex and sophisticated works, such as the Book of Job, where subtle theological arguments are sustained through lengthy debates about divine justice and the meaning of human suffering. Works like Ecclesiastes contain an amalgam of the sage's personal reflections on life's futility and meditations on death, as well as paradoxic maxims, proverbs, and expressions of skeptical pessimism.

The author of only one wisdom book is known—Jesus Ben Sirach, who compiled the observations, teachings, and experiences of a lifetime in Ecclesiasticus. This weighty volume, the longest of its kind in the Bible, reveals the existence of "wisdom schools" at which young people were educated by a recognized wisdom authority. One of the last-written books of the Apocrypha, the work entitled Wisdom of Solomon (about the first century B.C.E.) is the only Old Testament work that specifically links the righteousness born of wisdom to hopes of personal immortality (Wisdom 1:12–3:9; 5:4–24; etc.).

Besides these works, certain psalms also contain wisdom motifs (Pss. 1, 8, 16, 17, 19, 34, 37, 49, 73, 92, 104, 112, 119, and 139) as do the prose tales of Joseph and Daniel, wise men loyal to their Jewish heritage who rose to power in foreign nations (Gen. 39–41; Dan. 1–6). Both of these figures are depicted as recipients of a divine gift, the wisdom to interpret dreams foreshadowing the future. The greatest **wisdom literature**, however, is based on the authors' profound reflections on the significance of ordinary life, with its unequal distribution of good and evil fortune, unexpected calamities, and the ambiguity of its ethical "message."

Because of its diversity in outlook, thought, and form, wisdom material defies easy classification. Its characteristic themes are strikingly different from those in the Torah and the Prophets, Wisdom books typically make no references to the covenant relationship that bound Israel to Yahweh. Neither Job nor Ecclesiastes even mentions the Mosaic Torah; but both agree that many religious assumptions, such as a divinely favored "right side's" winning in life's battles, are unjustified by human experience. The deuteronomic thesis that Yahweh directs human history, of which individual lives are a part, is also conspicuously absent.

Evaluating the ethical quality of human life from a variety of perspectives, the wisdom authors typically come to rather seditious conclusions. Their observations and analyses of experience tend to subvert some other Bible writers' interpretation of Israel's history. The prophetic tradition held that Yahweh observed all people's actions, inevitably punishing the bad and rewarding the good, an assumption shared by the Deuteronomistic historians, who interpreted Israel's growth and destruction as the consequence of keeping or breaking

Note the paragraph beginning "Because...." Harris is being polite and scholarly, but this is a real bombshell and the actual introduction to his coming analysis of the Book of Job. The Wisdom Writers' view of Yahweh as "beyond" or "above" the human ideals of rewarding good and punishing evil is quite shocking to many people even now, thousands of years later. The Wisdom Writers eloquently and disturbingly contend that the Creator is not bound by any human concepts of good and evil, right and wrong, fair and unfair.

This excellent chapter introduction, properly highlighted and noted, should give you a framework that organizes and clarifies the complex relationships among all of the chapter's subsequent units: Proverbs, Job, and Ecclesiastes. Be sure that you have mastered Harris's basic points regarding the Wisdom Writers before you move on. Rereading is always better than getting lost or confused—and much more time-efficient in the long run.

covenant laws. Among the Hebrew thinkers who vigorously disputed this simplistic view of life was the anonymous poet who wrote Job.

RECOMMENDED READING

Brueggemann, Walter A. *In Man We Trust: The Neglected Side of Biblical Faith.* Richmond, Va.: John Knox Press, 1972.

Bryce, Glendon E. *Israel and the Wisdom of Egypt.* Lewisburg, Pa.: Bucknell University Press, 1975. Analyzes the influence of Egyptian wisdom on the book of Proverbs.

Crenshaw, James L. *Studies in Ancient Israelite Wisdom.* New York: KTAV Publishing House, 1976.

———. *A Whirlpool of Torment: Israelite Traditions of God as an Oppressive Presence.* Philadelphia: Fortress Press, 1984.

Humphreys, W. Lee. *The Tragic Vision and the Hebrew Tradition.* Philadelphia: Fortress Press, 1985.

Lambert, W. G. *Babylonian Wisdom Literature.* Oxford, Eng.: Clarendon Press, 1960.

Murphy, Roland E. *Seven Books of Wisdom.* Milwaukee: Bruce, 1960.

———. *Wisdom Literature and Psalms.* Nashville, Tenn.: Abingdon Press, 1983.

Scott, R. B. Y. *The Way of Wisdom in the Old Testament.* New York: Macmillan, 1971.

Proverbs

KEY THEMES

Although ascribed to Solomon, traditional founder of Israel's wisdom schools, the Book of Proverbs contains practical advice drawn from diverse sources, ranging from ancient Egypt through many generations of Israelite thought. Besides "Solomonic" maxims (Chs. 10–22), the book's highlights include reflections on the value of wisdom (Chs. 1–6), personifications of Wisdom and Folly (Chs. 7–9), and a portrait of the "perfect wife" (Ch. 31).

Yahweh created me [Wisdom] when his purpose
first unfolded,
  before the oldest of his works.
From everlasting I was firmly set,
  from the beginning, before earth came into
  being.

> Proverbs 8:22–23

Whereas examples of speculative wisdom, such as Job and Ecclesiastes, deal with theological inquiries about the nature of God and the purpose of human life, the Book of Proverbs is devoted to advocating practical wisdom and with guiding readers to find their proper place in the social and religious order. *Proverb* translates from the Hebrew term *mashal,* which means "a statement of truth" or "standard of appropriate behavior." The biblical proverbs are typically based on observation and experience rather than on divine revelation and are commonly nonreligious in tone. Thus,

> The rich man's wealth is his stronghold,
> poverty is the poor man's undoing.
>
> Proverbs 10:15

is simply an observed fact of life: Riches give security and poverty the opposite.

Like much wisdom literature, Proverbs is not peculiarly Jewish; most of its admonitions could apply equally well in a pagan society totally different from Israel's theocracy:

> The generous man is his own benefactor,
> a cruel man injures his own flesh.
>
> Proverbs 11:17

It is not surprising, then, that archaeologists have found almost word-for-word parallels of biblical proverbs in Mesopotamia and Egypt; indeed, a whole passage from the wisdom book of the Egyptian sage Amenemope has been taken over almost verbatim in Proverbs 22:17–23:11. Scholars now realize that proverbs and other wisdom writings were produced in many New Eastern cultures and that Israel's sages in some cases borrowed from older literary collections.

Proverbs Attributed to Solomon   Because King Solomon, who was credited with more than 3000 proverbs (1 Kings 4:29–33), has been traditionally associated with the production of adages or wise sayings, the superscription ascribing Proverbs to Solomon (Prov. 1:1) may mean no more than that these proverbs are written in the "manner" of Solomon. Other writers, in fact, are specifically cited. Agur, son of Jakeb, is the author of Chapter 30; Lemuel, king of Massa, of Chapter 31; and various unnamed sages of 24:23–24. Like the Psalms, Proverbs grew from many different sources over a span of centuries.

The Role of Wisdom

Value of Wisdom   What principally distinguishes some of Israel's proverbs from those of Edom, Babylonia, or Egypt is the theme that true wisdom promotes loyalty to Yahweh and sensitivity to the divine will. The wise person makes his or her behavior accord with divine law (Prov. 3; 19:16); the wise person is the righteous person who harmonizes his or her conduct with Yahweh's will (Prov. 16:1, 9; 19:21, 23). Proverbs also affirms the orthodox theme that in this world the righteous are rewarded and the wicked punished (Prov. 11:17–21; 21:21). Fearing Yahweh, observing the commandments, and behaving discreetly will ensure a long and prosperous life. Only the fool rejects admonition and suffers accordingly.

Proverbs's emphasis on the pragmatic "getting ahead" in life endeared it to Israel's middle and upper classes. The directive to "study the ant, thou sluggard" (Prov. 6:6–11) is one of several that attribute poverty to laziness (see also Prov. 24:30–34). Considerable proverbial wisdom is aimed at young people who wish to establish themselves at court and become the counselors of kings. Others offer advice on table manners and how to behave in the company of rich and powerful persons whom one

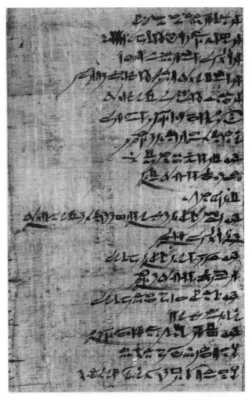

An ancient Egyptian papyrus recording the Wisdom of Amenemope (c. 1200 B.C.E.) contains sage advice that was later incorporated into the Book of Proverbs (Prov. 22:17 to 24:22). The wisdom movement permeated virtually the entire ancient Near East, creating an international legacy shared by Egypt, Mesopotamia, and Israel. (Courtesy of the Trustees of the British Museum)

wishes to impress favorably. The sages point out that achieving these ambitious goals requires self-discipline, reverence for Yahweh, and the special combination of humility and penetrating insight that enables the wise to perceive the cosmic order and attain one's place in it.

Wisdom and Folly   The writer of Proverbs characteristically assumes the role of a father advising his son against bad company in general and seductive women in particular (Prov. 1–2). Folly (lack of wisdom) is likened to a harlot who corrupts youth, whereas Wisdom is personified as a noble woman who seeks to save young men from their own inexperience and bad judgment. In Chapter 1, Wisdom is pictured as calling from the streets and housetops, promising rich treasure to those not too ignorant to appreciate her. The theme of "Lady Wisdom's" supreme value climaxes in Chapter 8, in which she is presented as nothing less than Yahweh's associate in creation:

> Yahweh created me when his purpose first
>   unfolded,
>   before the oldest of his works.
> From everlasting I was firmly set,
>   from the beginning, before earth came
>   into being.

* * *

> I was by his side, a master craftsman
>   [alternatively, "darling child"],
>   delighting him day after day,
>   ever at play in his presence,
> at play everywhere in his world,
>   delighting to be with the sons of men.
>   Proverbs 8:22, 23, 30, 31

This passage, which shows Yahweh creating the world with Wisdom, a joyous feminine companion at his side, seems to have influenced such later Jewish thinkers as **Philo Judaeus**, who lived in Alexandria, Egypt, during the first century C.E. Philo's attempt to reconcile Greek philosophy with Hebrew revelation included his doctrine of the **Logos** ("Word") by which God created the universe. (*Logos*, a masculine term in Greek, became more acceptable to Hebrew patriarchal thinking than *Sophia*, "Wisdom," which is feminine.) The Hymn to Logos with which John opens his Gospel is derived from Philo's (and ultimately Proverbs's) assumption that a divine mediator stands between God and the world.

The Perfect Wife   The book closes with a famous alphabetic poem on the perfect wife. Although promiscuous women and domineering wives receive considerable censure throughout Proverbs, the wife who works hard and selflessly to manage her husband's estate and increase his wealth is praised as beyond price (Prov. 31).

RECOMMENDED READING

Bryce, Glendon E. *Israel and the Wisdom of Egypt.* Lewisburg, Pa.: Bucknell University Press, 1975.

Camp, Claudia. *Wisdom and the Feminine in the Book of Proverbs.* Sheffield, Eng.: Almond Press, 1985.

McKane, William. *Proverbs.* Philadelphia: Westminster Press, 1970.

Scott, R. B. Y. *Proverbs. Ecclesiastes.* Anchor Bible, Vol. 18. Garden City, N.Y.: Doubleday, 1965.

Whybray, R. N. *Wisdom in Proverbs: The Concept of Wisdom in Proverbs 1–9.* Studies in Biblical Theology, No. 45. London: SCM Press, 1965.

Job

KEY THEMES

A supreme masterpiece of religious thought, the Book of Job dramatizes the plight of a representative human whose tragic sufferings inspire him to question the ethical nature of a god who permits evil and the unmerited pain of sentient creatures. The prose prolog (Chs. 1 and 2) features two scenes in Yahweh's heavenly court in which the Deity and humanity's Adversary agree to test Job's loyalty. In the long poetic central section (Chs. 3–31), the author exposes the inadequacy of conventional religious explanations about divine–human relationships, expressly discrediting the deuteronomic thesis that God is pledged to protect and reward the righteous, a position taken by Job's three friends who argue that suffering is an inevitable result of sin. After Elihu's interpolated discourse

(Chs. 32–37), Yahweh delivers two speeches emphasizing cosmic wonders beyond human comprehension (Chs. 38–41). The prose epilog recounts Job's restored fortunes (42:7–17).

> It is all one, and this I dare to say:
>   innocent and guilty, he [Yahweh] destroys all
>   alike.
> When a sudden deadly scourge descends,
>   he laughs at the plight of the innocent.
> When a country falls into a tyrant's hand,
>   it is he who blindfolds the judges.
>   Or if not he, who else?
>
> Job 9:22–24

The Bible's prime example of *speculative wisdom*—the kind of intellectual activity that questions the principles and assumptions commonly accepted by society—the Book of Job is a profound exploration of the issue of God's responsibility for evil and the extent to which he is morally bound, by the intrinsic goodness of his own nature, to protect sentient creatures from unmerited pain. It is also concerned with the psychological relationship between humanity and God, as well as with the intellectual honesty of a righteous person whose integrity does not allow him to evade the dilemma by falsely confessing to sin in order to justify his god's harsh treatment of him. The author's rejection of conventional explanations and his unorthodox demand that Yahweh meet Job on equal terms to explain his (Yahweh's) questionable morality undoubtedly shocked pious readers when the book was new, as it may still shock some readers today. Because the questions it raises have never been satisfactorily resolved, the book is as provocative now as it was 2500 years ago.

Scholars do not agree on when Job was written. Although Hebrew tradition ascribed the book to Moses, both its language and theological outlook are later than the Mosaic period. The book seems to be the product of a troubled age when the moral assumptions of the deuteronomic thesis had lost much of its former authority. The Book of Deuteronomy

The cuneiform script on this clay tablet narrates a Sumerian variation of the Job story. Like the Book of Job, this text records the humiliating ordeals of a righteous man who nonetheless clings to his faith and is at last delivered from his undeserved sufferings. The problem of evil, with its conflict between the concept of a good God and the fact of unmerited human pain, was a perplexing theme explored in Egyptian, Babylonian, and Israelite literature. (Courtesy of the University Museum, University of Pennsylvania [Neg. #S8-68052b])

had argued that the good person, obedient to Yahweh's regulations, would automatically enjoy security, prosperity, and long life, but the history of Israel did not support this comfortable belief. After the Babylonians under

Be sure to make note of the plot's sub-units, such as "Jahweh's Heavenly Court" and "The Central Poetic Drama," as well as the author's comments on each.

You should also be aware that some scholars believe the prose-poetry-prose design of Job is intended to move the reader through obvious traditional literary artifice into a horribly painful but glorious reality and then back into comfortable illusion, thereby replicating the religious experience through art. Stephen Mitchell's translation and study of Job is especially recommended for further reading.

Nebuchadnezzar had demolished both Yahweh's sanctuary and the Israelite state—acts involving the suffering and deaths of hundreds of thousands of people—it was necessary to rethink Israel's traditional philosophy of history.

During the Babylonian exile, then, Israel's wisdom writers had to grapple with troubling questions. How could Yahweh allow such a disaster to afflict his chosen people? How could he permit his holy Temple to fall into pagan hands? The prophets had answered that Israel suffered defeat because the Israelites had, by sinful disobedience to the Mosaic covenant, forfeited their privilege of divine protection. Because it is unthinkable that Yahweh does wrong, individuals must deserve whatever evils befall them.

The anonymous author of Job, writing sometime after the exile, probably in the fifth century B.C.E., could not agree that Israel's oppression was justified either by Deuteronomy's simplistic system of rewards and punishments or by the prophets' insistence that the people had earned their miseries. Combining the traditional reverence for Yahweh with an acutely critical intelligence and demand for moral logic, he uses an old folktale of the legendary patriarch Job to illustrate his conviction that neither the God-fearing person nor the blasphemer receives what he or she deserves in this life. But if God is in control of the universe, why is this so? The writer's attempt to probe this mystery leads him to reexamine the basic concept of divinity.

While most of Job is in poetry, the prolog and epilog are in prose, and most scholars believe that the prose sections represent an old fable that the author used as a framework for his central poetic drama.

Yahweh's Heavenly Court

Prolog   The prolog presents Job as a thoroughly upright and godly man who in no way deserves the evils inflicted on him. Described as "sound and honest," one "who feared God and

shunned evil" (Job 1:1 and 2:3), he is meant to represent a universal type, the person of good will found everywhere throughout history. For this reason the writer does not make him a Jew but a native of Uz (perhaps the south of Edom) who lived long before Israel's birth. So scrupulous is Job about not offending God, however, that he offers sacrifices for his children in case they, even in thought, have sinned. No wonder Yahweh declares that "there is no one like [Job] on the earth" (Job 1:8).

Ironically, Job's outstanding righteousness attracts the interest of "the satan," a heavenly being who acts as Yahweh's prosecuting attorney. Appearing among "the Sons of God" before Yahweh's throne, he suggests that Job will not remain loyal if deprived of family, property, and reputation. For reasons known only to himself, Yahweh accepts this challenge, withdrawing the protective "wall" with which he had previously shielded Job from misfortune. Job now experiences the power of chaos—the sudden injection of violent change into his formerly stable environment. Predatory nomads sweep away his flocks and herds; "the fire of God" consumes his sheep and shepherds; a fierce wind demolishes the house where Job's children are feasting, killing them all. Stripped of everything he holds dear by chaotic forces of earth, air, and sky, Job still blesses Yahweh's name (1:1–2:21). As if tempting God to doubt further the integrity of his human creation, "the satan" next persuades Yahweh to infect his faithful worshiper with a painful and disfiguring disease, although Yahweh protests such persecution is unjustified, "without cause" (2:1–10). In contrast to Yahweh, who yields to his Prosecutor's suggestions, Job rejects his wife's despairing plea to "curse God and die."

The Central Poetic Drama

Sufferings and Complaints   In Chapter 3, the action shifts from the heavenly court to Job's dungheap, where, in a long monolog he prays to have the process of creation reversed, asking for a return to the primeval darkness that shrouded all before God illuminated the cosmos (see Gen. 1:1–2). If light and life are mere vehicles for pain, it is better not to exist or, once born, to sink quickly into the oblivion of Sheol, the dark subterranean realm where the human dead remain in eternal nothingness (see also Eccl. 9:5, 10). The lack of moral meaning in Job's fate is such that he evokes **Leviathan**, the mythical dragon of chaos, "the fleeing serpent," embodiment of the darkness and disorder that Yahweh subdued—but apparently did not annihilate—when creating the world (cf. Job 3:8; 26:10–14; 40:20–41:25; Pss. 74:12–13; 89:9–10; Isa. 27:1; etc.). Leviathan's significance is crucial to the problem of evil explored in the Book of Job, for Yahweh's reply to Job's accusations about divine injustice climaxes in a final evocation of Leviathan's chaotic role in the universe (Ch. 41).

The Central Debate   The hero is joined by three friends, **Eliphaz**, **Bildad**, and **Zophar**, who, following the comfortable assumptions of conventional wisdom, insist that Job's present misery must be the result of some vile but unknown sin. Each friend gives a speech, and Job in turn replies, refuting his contention. As the debates become more heated, Job's early patience gives way to a realization of two unorthodox truths: (1) that his humanity entitles him to certain moral rights, which Yahweh seems to ignore in permitting him to suffer undeservedly; (2) that if he is guiltless, who is responsible for the evil that he and all other people endure?

In Chapters 9 and 10, Job challenges Yahweh to appear before him as a human being so that their conflict may be settled in terms of human justice. Anticipating Yahweh's appearance in the whirlwind, however, he realizes that he has no chance to present the justice of his cause before so formidable an opponent. A human is no match for the strength of God. Furthermore, the power that afflicts him is the same that will judge him.

> Suppose I am in the right, what use is my
>   defense?
> For he whom I must sue is judge as well.
> If he deigned to answer my citation,
>   could I be sure that he would listen to my
>   voice?
> He, who for one hair crushes me,
>   who, for no reason, wounds and wounds
>   again,
> leaving me not a moment to draw breath,
>   with so much bitterness he fills me.
> Shall I try force? Look how strong he is!
>   Or go to court? But who will summon *him*?
>   Job 9:15–19 (italics added)

With courage born of his honest recognition that good people can be more compassionate and moral than their gods seem to be, Job suggests that Yahweh must learn what it is like to be human, to bear the sorrows of mortality.

> I shall say to God, "Do not condemn me.
>   but tell me the reason for your assault.
> *Is it right* for you to injure me,
>   cheapening the work of your own hands
>   and abetting the schemes of the wicked?
> Have *you* got *human eyes*,
>   do *you see as mankind sees*?
> Is *your* life *mortal* like man's,
>   do your years pass as men's days pass?
> You, who inquire into my faults
>   and investigate my sins,
> *you know very well that I am innocent*,
>   and that no one can rescue me from your
>   hand."
>   Job 10:2–7 (italics added)

Reversing the traditional wisdom that asks us to look at things from the Deity's perspective, Job boldly demands that God try to see the world from the vantage point of pain-ridden, mortal humanity. In his famous essay *Answer to Job*, the psychologist Carl Jung suggests that Job's challenging Yahweh to abandon his icy distance from human suffering had an enormous impact on the development of religious thought. Many centuries later, as a branch of first-century Judaism evolved into early Christianity, the concept of a remote, omnipotent Deity was radically transformed into the notion that Israel's God assumed human shape to suffer as the man Jesus.

No longer conceived as utterly distinct from humanity, God—through the Incarnation—placed himself amid the human predicament, subject to the pain and evil that had afflicted Job. (See the discussion of John's Gospel, Part 8.)

Elihu's Speeches   Most scholars believe that the lengthy words of **Elihu**, a young man who suddenly appears in Chapter 32, are a later addition to the Book of Job. Except to sharpen the accusations against Job—of self-righteousness, pride, or secret sin—Elihu adds little to the discussion, although he claims to resolve the entire theological problem Job's case presents. Verbose and overconfident, Elihu betrays his absurd pretentiousness in speaking "on God's behalf":

> I will range far afield for my arguments
> to prove my Maker just.
> What I say to you contains no fallacies,
> I assure you,
> you see before you an enlightened man.
>   Job 36:2–4

After six chapters of Elihu's rehashing the friends' arguments, readers may well feel that the opening question in Yahweh's first speech applies to him rather than Job: "Who is this obscuring my designs with his empty-headed words?" (38:2).

Yahweh Reveals His Universe

Yahweh Speaks   As Job foresaw in Chapter 9, when Yahweh appears it is not in human form to debate the cause of injured innocence but in a superhuman display of power that ignores the mental anguish and disillusionment in divine goodness that are the principal source of Job's suffering. Speaking from the whirlwind as if to underscore the untractable, amoral energy of the natural world he has created, Yahweh emphasizes the enormous distance between divinity and humanity. His first speech (38:1–39:30) parades images of cosmic grandeur before Job's dazzled eyes, sardonically demanding that Job inform God about the miracle of creation, astronomical phenomena, and the curious habits of wildlife. Note that Yahweh invites Job to share his creative pride in the world of animal violence, such as the fearless warhorse that delights in battle (39:19–25). In his final horrific example, Yahweh describes the eagle or vulture that "feeds her young on blood," feasting on the bodies of dying humans, oblivious to their pain (39:27–30).

Job did not need to be told about Yahweh's cosmic might, of which he was already thoroughly aware (9:1–10), but he had hoped for reassurance about God's intrinsic goodness, compassion, and paternal concern for suffering humanity. Instead, Yahweh recites a catalog of impersonal natural wonders and a pitiless survey of predatory nature, "red in tooth and claw."

When Yahweh asks if Job, now deluged with examples of the savage and inexplicable, is ready to give up, Job merely replies that he will speak no more. Yahweh has refused to answer any of humanity's questions about the ethical principles by which he rules the universe and has arbitrarily limited the debate to a display of omnipotence that avoids addressing the real issue—his questionable moral character. As many readers have observed, Job's silence before God's self-disclosure is not reverent submission but the numbness of moral shock.

Apparently unsatisfied with Job's half-hearted acquiescence, Yahweh then launches into a second long speech in which he strikes at Job's deepest fear: that in the absence of a recognizable divine ethic, humans will have to create—out of emptiness—their own meaning of life. When Yahweh asks "Do you really want to reverse my judgment, and put me in the wrong to put yourself in the right?" (Job 40:8), Job's response must be no, for it is the necessary function of an omniscient God, not fallible man, to enforce a recognizable moral order. Faced with the total failure of the prophetic or deuteronomic attempts to explain human loss and pain in terms of an ethical Creator, Job is next compelled to stare even more deeply into the magnificence—and horror—of the universe Yahweh has fashioned.

Yahweh begins by inducing Job to examine the sphere of human activity, asking him if he can duplicate the divine thunder that (when it chooses) can obliterate the wicked. But Yahweh does not linger over his strangely inconsistent enforcement of justice in human society; instead, he demands that Job consider the untamable **Behemoth**, "the masterpiece of all God's work," a monster so powerful, so grotesque, and so removed from any possible relation to human experience that God's admiration of the creature forces Job to realize that the world is not a place designed for human welfare. The universe Yahweh unveils is God-centered, frightening in its vast indifference to human needs. (Compare the Genesis tradition of humanity's position as the pinnacle of creation [Gen. 1:26–31].)

Scholars used to think that Behemoth and Leviathan were, respectively, the hippopotamus and crocodile, but since the discovery of Ugaritic texts referring to Baal's defeat of Lothan, the primeval sea monster, it is known that Leviathan is a mythological beast representing the chaos that existed before creation. The Canaanite Lothan and Hebrew Leviathan are variant forms of **Rahab**, the chaotic beast that Yahweh subdued when bringing order to the cosmos (Ps. 89:9–10). Note that Yahweh describes Leviathan in mythological terms, as a dragon belching fire and smoke (41:10–12) from whom the ocean waves flee (41:14, 17).

Whereas Yahweh's might has tamed Leviathan, the monster still has power to disrupt the world order, spasmodically returning the world, at least in part, to the primordial watery chaos described in Genesis 1.

> When he stands up, the waves themselves
>   take fright,
>   the billows of the sea retreat.

* * *

> He churns the depths into a seething caldron,
>   he makes the sea fume like a scent burner.

> Behind him he leaves a glittering wake—
>   a white fleece seems to float on the deeps.
> He has no equal on earth,
>   being created without fear.
> He looks the haughtiest in the eye;
>   of all the sons of pride he is the king.
>   Job 41:16–17, 22–26

Yahweh's climactic reference to Leviathan's supreme "pride" recalls the beginning of his speech in which the Deity described his ability to overthrow "the haughty" and the "proud" (41:6–14). Although Yahweh crushes human pride, he does not annihilate Leviathan, the embodiment of chaos that lies coiled like a serpent around the visible cosmos, primal energy unassimilated into the stable order, that periodically rears its head to shatter the peace of both nature and humanity.

In Job, Yahweh seems to tolerate the chaotic forces that still permeate creation, but in Isaiah he is represented as vowing to destroy Leviathan—on the last day when he fully imposes his universal sovereignty.

> That [final] day, Yahweh will punish,
> with his hard sword, massive and strong,
> Leviathan, the fleeing serpent,
> Leviathan, the twisting serpent:
> he will kill the sea dragon.
>   Isaiah 27:1

The final overthrow of the chaotic principle inherent in creation, as in human experience, began with Yahweh's initial ordering of the cosmos but will not be complete until Yahweh's Day of Judgment, when his righteousness ultimately defeats the dragon of chaos. (Compare Yahweh's promised overthrow of Leviathan with the mythic image of the Dragon, "the serpent of old that led the whole world astray, whose name is Satan, or the Devil" in Rev. 12:3–9.)

Job's total submission after Yahweh's Leviathan speech is commonly understood as a recognition of humanity's puny insignificance when confronted with Yahweh's irresistible power or a simple case of Job's moral right trampled under God's implacable might:

I know that you are all-powerful;
   what you conceive, you can perform.
I am the man who obscured your designs
   with my empty-headed words.
I have been holding forth on matters I cannot
   understand,
   on marvels beyond me and my knowledge.

                              Job 42:2–3

When Job hears Yahweh's acknowledgment of Leviathan's continuing power, he recognizes that his earlier questions about the God's ethical character are irrelevant. The universe is as it is, an unfolding process in which Light and Dark, Gentle and Violent, and Good and Evil are intrinsic components. "The satan," who (unknown to Job) attends Yahweh's heavenly court as one of "the Sons of God," and the primordial sea beast Leviathan, whom Yahweh has reduced to a plaything, are perhaps manifestations of the same mysterious, seditious force that Yahweh tolerates as part of the cosmic whole.

Job's reconciliation to the God who had permitted his unspeakable misery arises from a new understanding of divinity:

I knew you then only by hearsay;
   but now, having seen you with my own eyes,
I retract all I have said,
   and in dust and ashes I repent.

                              Job 42:5–6

Job's concept of God and of the divine–human relationship is radically altered by Yahweh's self-revelation, particularly the Deity's climactic invocation of Leviathan. The chaotic monster's very presence suggests God's ongoing struggle to shape and maintain the created order—a struggle in which Job places himself on Yahweh's side. Although Job's unqualified submission suggests that he has attained a more profound understanding of his God, questions about the insights that motivate him abound.

Because Yahweh is eternal, having neither beginning nor end, the origin of chaos remains problematic. If cosmic violence did not precede Yahweh's emergence as Creator, it must bear some relationship to the Deity himself, an ex-pression of the divine nature—a concept suggested by Second Isaiah:

I am Yahweh, unrivaled,
I form the light and create the dark.
I make good fortune and calamity,
It is I, Yahweh, who do all this.

                              Isaiah 45:7

As strict monotheists, do Second Isaiah and the author of Job imply that a single universal Being encompasses all opposites, including what humans call Good and Evil, Order and Chaos?

Does Job "see" Yahweh embodying all things, including a counterforce inimical to the order he has created, a chaotic element represented by his "shadow," "the satan"? Or does Job perceive that Yahweh's power is somehow limited by the persistence of chaotic forces—from violent mass extinctions of species on earth to exploding suns in distant galaxies—the erratic outbursts of "Leviathan" that randomly disrupt an evolving universe? Perhaps, as Carl Jung suggests, Job's challenge has caused Yahweh to become aware of hitherto unconscious aspects of his character, to acknowledge the link between the vast, inhuman complexities of the cosmos and the suffering of intelligent beings whom he had fashioned in his image.

At the least, the author of Job demonstrates the intellectual and ethical inadequacy of the deuteronomist theory of history. Eliphaz, Bildad, and Zophar argue passionately that God is just and that everyone gets exactly what he deserves. By contrast, the God-centered world Yahweh describes is *not* based on retributive justice, and human misery is *not* consistently the result of wrongdoing. Conventional moral logic is contradicted by Job's experience.

To some commentators, the prose epilog in which Job becomes wealthier than before and begets more sons and daughters to replace those Yahweh had allowed to be killed seems a tacked-on fairy-tale ending that undercuts the main thrust of the poetic dialogs. Note, however, that in this prosaic conclusion Yahweh condemns the three friends who had so ardently defended God's justice, declaring that they had not spoken "truthfully about me as my servant Job has done" (42:7). Yahweh prefers Job's honest doubts about the divine character to the friends' doubtful orthodoxy. God's restoration and double blessing of Job do not resolve the perplexing issue of evil and undeserved suffering, but to Job—who has come to an understanding with his God—this divine goodness may foreshadow the time when Yahweh will permanently expel Leviathan, "the fleeing serpent," from our universe.

RECOMMENDED READING

Crenshaw, James L., ed. *Theodicy in the Old Testament.* Philadelphia: Fortress Press, 1983.

Dhorme, Edouard P. *A Commentary on the Book of Job.* Translated by H. Knight. London: Thomas Nelson, 1967. Reprint of a major study of Job, first published in 1926.

Gordis, Robert. *The Book of God and Man: A Study of Job.* Chicago: University of Chicago Press, 1965.

Hone, Ralph E., ed. *The Voice Out of the Whirlwind: The Book of Job.* San Francisco: Chandler, 1960. Includes King James Version of text of Job and a collection of interpretive essays.

Kallen, H. M. *The Book of Job as a Greek Tragedy.* New York: Moffat, Yard, 1918. A stimulating comparison of Job to the tragedies of Aeschylus and Euripides.

Levenson, Jon D. *Creation and the Persistence of Evil.* San Francisco: Harper & Row, 1988. A lucid study of divine omnipotence and the problem of evil.

Pope, Marvin H. *Job.* Anchor Bible, 5th ed. Garden City, N.Y.: Doubleday, 1978. An up-to-date translation with many useful notes.

———. "Book of Job." In G. A. Buttrick, ed., *The Interpreter's Dictionary of the Bible,* Vol. 2, pp. 911–925. New York and Nashville, Tenn.: Abingdon Press, 1962.

Sanders, Paul S., ed. *Twentieth-Century Interpretations of the Book of Job: A Collection of Critical Essays.* Englewood Cliffs, N.J.: Prentice-Hall, 1968. A variety of viewpoints.

Terrien, Samuel L. "Introduction and Exegesis to Job." In G. A. Buttrick, ed., *The Interpreter's Bible,* Vol. 4, pp. 877–1198. New York and Nashville, Tenn.: Abingdon Press, 1954. A valuable introduction to the study of Job.

———. *Job: Poet of Existence.* Indianapolis: Bobbs-Merrill, 1958.

von Rad, Gerhard. *Wisdom in Israel.* Translated by J. D. Martin. Nashville, Tenn.: Abingdon Press, 1973. An excellent theological study.

Ecclesiastes

KEY THEMES

The Bible's finest example of skeptical wisdom, the book of Ecclesiastes is ascribed to King Solomon but is actually the work of an anonymous Israelite sage who calls himself Koheleth (Qoheleth), one who presides over a circle of learners. Delighting in paradox, Koheleth denies the possibility of knowing anything for sure, except the inescapable facts of death and the ultimate futility of all human effort.

> The race [of life] does not go to the swift, nor battle to the strong; . . . all are subject to time and mischance.
>
> Ecclesiastes 9:11–12

If life is a tragedy to those who feel, as an English novelist once remarked, it is a comedy to those who think. The Book of Ecclesiastes is, like Job, an example of speculative wisdom in which the author unflinchingly faces the world's moral anarchy and attempts to find a pattern of meaning that might reveal God's purpose in permitting good to go unrewarded and evil to flourish. Whereas the author of Job presents an emotionally charged inquiry into God's connection with cosmic violence and human injustice, the author of Ecclesiastes adopts an emotionally neutral position of coolly ironic detachment. An aloof observer of human folly, he derives a certain dry amusement from his ivory-tower perspective on the human predicament.

An element of Proverbs's practical wisdom also permeates the work. Having experienced much, the writer has found that there is "nothing new under the sun" that has not been seen,

As with the book of Job, be sure that your notes reflect the thematic components of Ecclesiastes.

said, or felt a thousand times before. He therefore advises his readers not to be taken in by the world's sham innovations. True wisdom lies in observing everything, knowing how little has genuine value, and refusing to become committed to the hopeless pursuits to which most people blindly devote their lives.

Although the superscription to the book attributes its authorship to Qoheleth or **Koheleth**, "son of David, king in Jerusalem"—presumably Solomon—most scholars regard this as merely a literary device that offers the writer an elevated position from which imaginatively to experience everything enjoyed by Israel's wealthiest and wisest monarch (Eccles. 1:12–2:12). The Solomon persona is soon dropped and not referred to after the second chapter.

Koheleth means "one who presides over a congregation," a term the Septuagint translators rendered as "Ecclesiastes," from the Greek *ekklesia* ("assembly"). But Koheleth was not a preacher as some English translations call him; he was a professional sage living in Jerusalem who may have assembled a circle of student-disciples about him. Because the author seems familiar with various strands of Greek philosophy, including that of Heraclitus, Zeno the Stoic, and Epicurus, experts tend to place the book's composition sometime during the Hellenistic era, after the campaigns of Alexander of Macedonia had brought Greek culture to Palestine. In its present form, the book resembles a somewhat rambling essay studded with aphorisms, short poems, and meditations on the futility of existence. An epilog (Eccles. 12:9–14) preserves some later editorial reactions to Koheleth's unorthodox teaching.

The Impossibility of Finding Meaning in Life

Futility of Human Aspiration Most of Ecclesiastes' principal ideas are stated in the first two chapters. The remaining ten mainly illustrate

and elaborate the basic perception that the rewards of humanity's customary activities are either short-lived or nonexistent. The book opens with a description of the eternal cycle of nature, in which all things—sun, rivers, seas—are seen as moving in endless circles and eventually returning to their place of origin to begin the same cycle again. It is merely society's bad memory that causes people to imagine that anything new ever occurs. Individual observers simply are not around long enough to recognize that, in the long view, all that is repeats itself without essential change.

Aware that knowledge is a burden because wisdom makes the illusion of happiness impossible, Koheleth nonetheless determines to sample the various pursuits that are commonly believed to provide fulfillment in life. He first tries pleasure, a deliberate savoring of "folly." Although he enjoys being able to "deny his eyes nothing they desired" and "refuse his heart no pleasure" (Eccles. 2:10), he finds the experiment in hedonism empty. He next tries "great" enterprises, such as elaborate building programs, but finds these endeavors equally unsatisfying. He then concentrates on amassing wealth but concludes that this, too, is meaningless. Koheleth acknowledges some valid pleasure in hard work but cautions that all effort is ultimately "vanity" and a "chasing of the wind" (Eccles. 2:1–11).

The author offers several reasons for his negative view of human activity:

1. No matter what he achieves in life, he must ultimately die and leave everything to someone else, perhaps an unworthy heir who will waste it all.

2. Regardless of his successor's conduct, time itself will destroy whatever he builds or creates.

3. No matter how hard he labors or how wisely he plans, life can never compensate him for the toil and sacrifice expended to achieve his goals.

4. Death will inevitably frustrate all his intentions and hopes.

What arguments can you make against the four points at the bottom of the second column? Try writing a point-by-point refutation of these assumptions, giving specific examples of why you disagree. Refuting any single point of these four at length would likely make a respectable lower-division paper. Try sketching such a paper by generating 3–5 sub-topics that would be of interest to you in a project like this.

Sheol Lurking behind the author's pessimism is a conviction that death is the absolute end to life, that there is no conscious existence beyond the grave (**Sheol**) to which all will descend without reaping either rewards or punishments that the present world does not offer. He has no hope that the Deity will distinguish between human and animal lives, let alone between virtue and sin.

> Indeed, the fate of man and beast is identical; one dies, the other too, and both have the selfsame breath; man has no advantage over the beast, for all is vanity. Both go to the same place (Sheol); both originate from the dust; and to the dust both return. Who knows if the spirit of man mounts upward or if the spirit of the beast goes down to the earth?
>
> Ecclesiastes 3:19–21

In view of the traditional Old Testament belief that *all* the dead are indiscriminately housed in the grim underworld of Sheol, the author's question here should be understood as purely rhetorical, emphasizing the inequitable fact that the righteous worshiper fares no better after death than an animal. Indeed, it is better, the writer ironically continues, to be a "live dog" (living Gentile) than a "dead lion" (deceased king of Judah), for "the living know at least that they will die, the dead know nothing; no more reward for them, their memory has passed out of mind. Their loves, their hates, their jealousies, these all have perished, nor will they ever again take part in whatever is done under the sun" (Eccles. 9:5–6).

The dead in Sheol are eternally oblivious, without hope of future resurrection. Hence, Koheleth advises the living to live fully now (Eccles. 9:7–9), for "there is neither achievement, nor planning, nor knowledge, nor wisdom in Sheol where you are going" (Eccles. 9:10). Such counsel resembles that of the Epicurean philosophy, which held that humans are a chance collection of atoms that disintegrates at death. The consciousness or "soul" is as physical as the body and, like the body, perishes utterly. Like the Roman poet Horace, Koheleth

advises the wise person to seize the day and wring from it whatever pleasures are possible.

The writer also entertains some typically Stoic ideas. Chapter 3, which begins with "there is a season for everything, a time for every occupation under heaven," seems to imply that a providence directs all things. Because the author is a Hebrew, he probably regarded Israel's God as the enforcer of the cosmic timetable. But Koheleth's God is apparently interested only in enforcing natural laws, not in giving meaning or order to human lives. Even the Stoic idea of a providentially managed universe is modified by Epicurean warnings that chance typically determines one's fate: "The race [of life] does not go to the swift, nor the battle to the strong; there is no bread for the wise, wealth for the intelligent, nor favor for the learned; all are subject to time and mischance" (Eccles. 9:11). It would be almost impossible to make a declaration more at variance with Israel's Prophets or the Deuteronomistic historians.

Paradoxes The author's love of paradox is a characteristic of the book that troubles some readers; he seldom makes a statement that he does not somewhere else contradict. Advising one to savor life and to drink wine with a joyful heart (Eccles. 9:7), he also states that it is better to frequent the house of mourning than the house of feasting (Eccles. 7:3). The day of death is better than the day of birth (Eccles. 7:1), but he would rather be a "living dog" than a "dead lion" (Eccles. 9:4). All people are "in the hand of God" (Eccles. 9:1) and should live righteously (Eccles. 8:10–13); but it is as much a mistake to behave too virtuously (Eccles. 7:16) as it is to be excessively wicked (Eccles. 7:17).

These paradoxic views are among the book's chief strengths, however, for the writer is not contradicting himself but asserting that life is too complex for absolute certainties. Just as there is a time to live and a time to die, there are occasions when radically different attitudes and behaviors are appropriate. Koheleth refuses to be confined to any single philosophical position. Whereas many Greek thinkers made logical consistency the test of truth, Ecclesiastes' author perceives the irrational elements in life and refuses to omit observable variety in the interests of theoretical coherence. In a world where the Deity does not seem to act (and it is significant that Yahweh, the Lord of history, is mentioned by name nowhere in the work), illogic and absurdity must be acknowledged. Koheleth's admonition is to be aware and take no chances.

Try your hand at identifying the vocabulary terms and answering the discussion questions. The third and fifth questions are particularly interesting.

Postscripts   The book closes with a poignant allegory of old age and death (Eccles. 12:1–8), but later writers added a series of brief postscripts. In the first, a disciple praises Koheleth for his wisdom and "attractive style" and adds a proverb extolling the value of wise teachers (Eccles. 12:9–11). A later editor, perhaps scandalized by the author's human-centered philosophy, warns the reader that writing and studying books is exhausting (Eccles. 12:12). It was perhaps a still later redactor who appended the final admonition to "fear God" and keep the commandments (Eccles. 12:14). The presence of this orthodox advice—inserted elsewhere into Koheleth's text as well (e.g., Eccles. 5:6b)—could have been partly responsible for the eventual admission into the biblical canon of this deeply skeptical, religiously uncommitted book.

RECOMMENDED READING

Blank, Sheldon H. "Ecclesiastes." In G. A. Buttrick, ed., *The Interpreter's Dictionary of the Bible*, Vol. 2, pp. 7–13. New York and Nashville, Tenn.: Abingdon Press, 1962.

Crenshaw, James L. *Ecclesiastes*. Philadelphia: Westminster Press, 1987.

Gordis, Robert. *Koheleth: The Man and His World*. New York: Jewish Theological Seminary of America Press, 1951. A translation with interpretative notes.

Rankin, O. S. "Introduction and Exegesis to Ecclesiastes." In G. A. Buttrick, ed., *The Interpreter's Bible*, Vol. 5, pp. 3–88. New York and Nashville, Tenn.: Abingdon Press, 1956.

Scott, R. B. Y. *Proverbs and Ecclesiastes*. Anchor Bible, Vol. 18. Garden City, N. Y.: Doubleday, 1965.

Wright, Addison G. "The Riddle of the Sphinx: The Structure of the Book of Qoheleth." In L. Crenshaw, ed., *Studies in Ancient Israelite Wisdom*, pp. 245–266. New York: KTAV Publishing House, 1976.

TERMS AND CONCEPTS TO REMEMBER

Behemoth	Philo Judaeus
Bildad	Rahab
Eliphaz	Sheol
Koheleth	wisdom literature
Leviathan	Zophar
Logos	

QUESTIONS FOR DISCUSSION AND REVIEW

1. What diverse kinds of documents do we find in the third major division of the Hebrew Bible, the Writings? In what ways—subject matter, themes, and theological concerns—do these books differ from the Torah and the Prophets?

2. Describe some of the major differences between the "practical" wisdom of Proverbs and the speculative wisdom of Job and Ecclesiastes. In what ways does Wisdom challenge the assumptions of the Torah and Prophets?

3. A profound questioning of the conventional view of God, the Book of Job dramatizes the problem of Evil, particularly God's responsibility for undeserved suffering. The author uses none of the traditional explanations—sin inherited from Adam, a demonic rebellion against the Deity, or a future immortality to compensate for earthly pain—to excuse Yahweh's permitting humanity's torment. In keeping his integrity, why must Job refuse to put himself in the

wrong? What revelation about his universe does Yahweh make from the whirlwind?

4. In what ways does Koheleth delight in collecting proverbs that contradict each other and challenge assumptions about the possibility of understanding God's world? How do his beliefs about the utter finality of death differ from those of conventional religion? Why do you suppose that "subversive" books like Job and Ecclesiastes found their way into the biblical canon? Do they ask questions that religion must try to answer?

5. Do you think that the Wisdom books can help people cope with the violence and injustice that millions of people endure every day? Are the questions that Job poses about the character of God intensified by historical events like the Holocaust, in which 6 million Jews were deliberately annihilated? Do natural catastrophes over which we have no control and the terminal illnesses of children keep the Jobian issues alive? What advice would you give to victims of chaotic Evil?

■ READING COMPREHENSION AND DISCUSSION QUESTIONS

1. Absolutely undimmed as a piece of art after thousands of years, the Book of Job has no equal in literature. As theology, however, it raises some interesting and perhaps troubling points, as Stephen Harris carefully points out to the reader (page 284):

[T]he author of Job demonstrates the intellectual and ethical inadequacy of the deuteronomist theory of history. Eliphaz, Bildad, and Zophar argue passionately that God is just and that everyone gets exactly what he deserves. By contrast, the God-centered world Yahweh describes is *not* based on retributive justice, and human misery is *not* consistently the result of wrongdoing. Conventional moral logic is contradicted by Job's experience. . . .

Yahweh condemns the three friends who had so ardently defended God's justice, declaring that they had not spoken "truthfully about me as my servant Job has done" (42:7).

In what ways does God's confirmation that evil is not punished, nor good rewarded, run counter to generally accepted Christian, Jewish, and Islamic opinion? How do you feel about this issue, and why do you feel as you do? How can such a statement exist in sacred texts?

2. Apply the teaching of Koheleth (Qoheleth), author of Ecclesiastes, to your student career. If it is true that there is "nothing new under the sun" that has not been seen, said, or felt before, then what is the purpose of scholarship, learning, and research? What are their objectives?

Are your personal conclusions on these topics supported by the text of Ecclesiastes or contradicted by it? What do you think Koheleth would have to say about your opinions? What do you think he'd have to say about the New York Stock Exchange, the World Series, a perfectly baked blackberry pie, and urban riots in poverty blighted neighborhoods?

CHAPTER 10

Drama

"What Is a Play?" from Theatre *(Brief Version), 2nd Edition, by Robert Cohen*

Robert Cohen's "What Is a Play?" is a gold mine of useful terms, concepts, and relationships, as well as an excellent example of keen-eyed analytic writing. First explaining the traditional ways of classifying plays, then analyzing the components that make up plays, Cohen concludes this chapter by producing a kind of theatre within the reader-as-audience's imagination. Aristotle himself would approve of Professor Cohen's performance.

Texts as lively and personal as this one almost require the reader to record personal, on-the-spot emotional reactions in order to accurately capture the spirit of the piece. Careful readers should develop some technique or identifying symbol that "flags" such personal reactions, whether through highlighting and notes written in the margin of a text or through notes made on cards or in a notebook. Often, the very best ideas for papers or essay exams are to be found in such responses.

WHAT IS
A PLAY?

A play is, essentially, a unit of theatre. It is not a "thing" but an event, taking place in real time and occupying real space. It is identified by some sort of title, and it has a recognizable order of presentation calculated to engage the attention of an audience. It is through the play that we experience the theatre.

Plays are customarily classified in two ways: by duration and by genre. Although these classifications have been emphasized more in the past than they are today, they still play a part in theatre understanding.

DURATION

A "full-length play" is one that lasts about two to four hours. This duration has been fairly standard since Renaissance times. It is long enough to afford sufficient significance and entertainment value to bring people out of their homes and short enough to be squeezed into the period between lunch and dinner, or between dinner and bedtime, and still allow time for travel to and from the theatre.

A "short play" lasts about twenty minutes to an hour. Usually it is either combined with one or two others to make a "bill" of sufficient duration to attract a conventional theatre audience, or else it is presented in some other setting, such as a lunch-time theatre, a dramatic festival, a classroom, a street entertainment, or a cabaret.

Occasionally, plays much shorter than twenty minutes' duration or much longer than four hours' are presented with high artistic impact. Samuel Beckett's *Breath*, for example, lasts a minute or so; several celebrated productions of the 1980s—Trevor Nunn's *Nicholas Nickleby* in London, Peter Brook's *The Mahabharata* in Paris, Peter Stein's *Oresteia* in Berlin, and Robert Wilson's international production of *The CIVIL warS*—have durations of nine to eleven hours. Indeed, Wilson's *Ka Mountain* has been performed for anywhere between 24 and 168 continuous hours. These extremes, however, demand such drastic accommodation on the part of audiences, actors, and behind the scenes personnel that it is highly doubtful they will be commonplace in the future.

GENRE

Genre is a more informative means of classifying plays, even though (or perhaps because) it brings into discussion more subjective criteria. Indeed, dramatic criticism for many centuries seemed to concern itself primarily with defining precise standards for various dramatic genres and then assessing plays in terms of how they measured up to these standards.

Two genres have dominated dramatic criticism since ancient times: *tragedy* and *comedy*. To Aristotle, the Greek philosopher generally recognized as the father of dramatic criticism, tragedy and comedy were not genres, but wholly separate art forms, derived from entirely unrelated sources. Tragedy, to Aristotle, was an outgrowth of certain prehistoric religious rituals, whereas comedy was a secular entertainment developed out of bawdy skits and popular revels. Aristotle strove to create a poetics (poetic theory) that would define these dramatic forms and that would create standards for their perfection. Unfortunately, only his poetics for tragedy has survived.

Today, aestheticians and scholars recognize a number of generic classifications. In addition to the original tragedy and comedy (now more narrowly defined than in Aristotle's day), the interlude, cycle play, history play, tragicomedy, dark comedy, melodrama, farce, documentary, and the musical have been identified as major genres into which modern plays (and, retroactively, older plays) can be classified.

A *tragedy* is a serious play (although not necessarily devoid of humorous episodes) with a topic of universal human import as its theme. Traditionally, the central character, often called the *protagonist*, is a person of high rank or stature. During the play, the protagonist undergoes a decline of fortune, leading to suffering and death. Integral to tragedy is the protagonist's period of insightful recognition or understanding. The effect of a tragedy, Aristotle claimed, was to elicit both pity and terror in the audience, which were resolved in a *catharsis*, or purging, of those aroused emotions.

The insightful recognition of the protagonist, his or her struggle against decline, and the consequent catharsis of the audience's aroused feelings, are central to the tragic experience, which is not to be confused with a merely sad or pathetic experience. Tragedy is neither pathetic nor sentimental; it describes a bold, aggressive, human attack against huge, perhaps insurmountable odds. Tragic protagonists are often flawed in some way (indeed, classical tragic theory insists that they must be flawed or at least acting in ignorance), but they are leaders, not victims, of the play's events. Indeed, their leadership of the play's action and their discoveries during the course of that action bring the audience to deep emotional and intellectual involvement.

The notion of *protagonist* (Greek: "carrier of the action") is complemented by a notion of *antagonist* ("opposer of the action"), which gives tragedy its fundamental conflict and character struggle. The protagonists of tragedy often go forth against superhuman antagonists: gods, ghosts, "fate," or else the hardest of human realities. Such protagonists are *heroes*—or tragic heroes—because their supreme struggle, although perhaps a doomed effort, takes on larger-than-life proportions. Then, through the heat of supreme conflict, the tragic heroes themselves assume a superhuman force and draw us into the full magnitude of their thoughts and actions. Thus tragedy offers us a link with the divine and puts us at the apex of human destiny.

A tragedy should ennoble, not sadden us. Characters that we admire may fall, but not before heroically challenging the elements, divinity, and death. Tragic heroes carry us to the brink of disaster—but, finally, it is their disaster and not ours, or at least not ours yet. Seeing a tragedy is to contemplate and perhaps rehearse in our minds the great conflicts we may still have ahead of us.

There are only a few universally acknowledged tragedies of this sort. Sophocles' *Oedi-*

Be careful to record and master all of the dramatic terms and concepts presented in this section. They are essential if you are to profit from Cohen's subsequent text, but also indispensable to study in many other disciplines, which routinely use vocabulary from theatre.

Lena Nyman plays the protagonist, Medea, in the 1986 production of Euripides' tragedy at Sweden's Royal Dramatic Theatre in Stockholm. The protagonist is here shown, typically, surrounded by the chorus.

pus Tyrannos was Aristotle's model of a great tragedy; most critics also class that author's *Electra* and *Antigone;* Aeschylus' *Oresteia* and *Prometheus Bound;* Euripides' *The Trojan Women, Medea,* and *The Bacchae;* Racine's *Phedre;* and Shakespeare's *Hamlet, King Lear, Othello,* and *Macbeth* as among a dozen or so true tragic masterpieces. The question is often raised as to whether a modern play can be such a tragedy. Arthur Miller's *Death of a Salesman* (1947) is often the play for which this question is posed, for Miller deliberately challenged the traditional notion of a high-ranking protagonist by naming his principal character "Willy Loman," (that is, low man). Furthermore, the antagonists Willy challenges are faceless bureaucrats, insensitive children, and an impersonal capitalistic economic sys-

tem—not gods, fates, or ghosts. Most critics today, if they approach this question at all, deny Miller's play the tragic dimension on the grounds that the struggle is human, not superhuman, and that tragedy demands a larger-than-life context. If that is the case, tragedy probably belongs to an earlier world, one where audiences could be expected to accept without dissent the presence of divine forces mixing in with everyday human affairs.

Comedy began, according to Aristotle, as an improvised entertainment that combined satirical skits, bawdy jokes, erotic singing and dancing, and uninhibited revelry. The first known written comedies were those of Aristophanes, a playwright of brilliantly funny wit and savagely penetrating political acumen. Writing in Athens in the late fifth century, Aristophanes set the general pattern, although not the structure, for comedies to come: interpersonal conflicts, topical issues, witty dialogue, physical buffoonery, verbal and sexual playfulness.

Comedy is not a simple amusement, however, nor is comedy simply entertaining; comedy is always about a serious human conflict. The passionate pursuit of love, ambition, social status, and money are age-old comic themes. Indeed, the themes of many comedies are often hard to distinguish from those of tragedies; the plot and the style of comedies, not the theme, assure that the dramatic experience will avoid sustained pity or terror and will elicit more laughter than cathartic shock. The comic plot requires a generally happy ending; the comic style includes characters drawn on human scale, often in an exaggerated manner, who face the kinds of everyday problems we know well in our own lives. Gods, fate, suffering, and death rarely figure significantly in comedies, and the problems of the characters are social rather than cosmic, interpersonal rather than metaphysical.

The best comedies are often those in which characters foolishly overreach themselves and are hilariously shown up for their foolishness. Not only are Aristophanes' plays (*The Birds, The Frogs, The Clouds, The Acharnians,* for example) masterpieces of this format, but so are the great comedies of Shakespeare (*As You Like It, Twelfth Night, A Midsummer Night's Dream*) and Molière (*The Miser, The Bourgeois Gentleman, The School for Wives*). In these plays, excesses of romantic love, intellectual pretension, physical braggadocio, or financial greed turn on their perpetrators' heads, to the delight of the spectators in the audience—who can also recognize the germs of such behaviors in themselves. In this fashion, comedy seeks to advise as well as to entertain. The Roman poet Horace coined the term *utile dulce,* or "sweet instruction," to denote this deeper purpose of the comic drama.

There are many modern authors of dramatic comedy: George Bernard Shaw, Jean Giraudoux, Simon Gray, Alan Ayckbourne, and Neil Simon are only a few of the twentieth-century playwrights who have succeeded in this genre. Because they are topical, comedies are usually less long-lasting than tragedies. Because they generally probe less profoundly into the matter of human destiny, they offer less fertile ground to academic scholarship. Hence, relative to tragedies, comedies are usually less frequently published in play anthologies, less frequently examined in critical literature, and less frequently studied in most academic institutions. Nevertheless, comedy's place in the theatre is every bit as secure as is tragedy, and its impact on audiences is no less strong now than it was in Aristophanes' day.

Comedy and tragedy remained the two "official" dramatic genres through the seventeenth century, when neo-classic French critics attempted to formalize them into absolutely rigid classifications. But from the Renaissance onward, playwrights and critics began to develop new dramatic genres or to dispense with genres altogether.

The medieval theatre, for example, brought to the stage *interludes,* comic entertainments presented between courses at state banquets (from *inter* = between and *ludus* = play), and *cycle* plays, short biblical plays performed in a series (cycle), often in procession through a town.

Shakespeare's editors divided his plays into the traditional genres of tragedy and comedy, plus a newly defined genre: the *history,* which is a play purporting to dramatize the key events in the life of a king or head of state. Shakespeare seems to have invented this genre; and his great series of nine history plays, covering English royal history from 1377 to 1547 (inaccurate as they may be as historical documents) provides the bulk of what most people ever remember of the English kings Richard II, Henry IV, Henry V, Henry VI, and Richard III. Shakespeare's histories combine serious scenes, brilliant poetry, battlefield pageants, and hilarious comic moments. None of the plays, however, seeks to attain the classical catharsis of tragedy or the sustained humor of comedy. The history play thus seems to have been a mixed genre whose only suc-

Notice this "transition paragraph," which summarizes what has come before and introduces what is to follow. Such transitions, whether presented as independent paragraphs or as parts of paragraphs (usually the first or last sentences), are crucial cues to the material's organization.

Melodrama, an exaggerated seriousness, is evident in this moment from American Conservatory Theatre production of The Tavern, *an early twentieth-century theatrical piece by showman George M. Cohan.*

cessful proponent was its originator, Shakespeare himself.

More long-lived are two other mixed genres, *tragicomedy* and *dark comedy,* which also have both tragic and comic components.

Tragicomedy, as the name implies, is a form that deliberately attempts to bridge the two original genres. It maintains a serious theme throughout but varies the approach from serious to humorous and relaxes tragedy's larger-than-life scale. The problems of tragicomedy are solvable, and the antagonists are not divinely insuperable; tragicomedies, despite their rousing speeches and sentiments, conclude without the violent catharsis that its audience has been led to expect. It has been called "tragedy that ends happily." *Amphitryon,* by the Roman playwright Plautus, is generally considered the first tragicomedy (the play has been revised by subsequent authors into both tragic and comic versions). Many of Shakespeare's tragedies were in fact turned into tragicomedies by rewrite men in the tragicomedy-prone seventeenth century: Nahum Tate's 1687 revision of *King Lear,* for example, concludes with Lear and Gloucester retiring to "calm reflections on our fortunes past" and with Cordelia installed as Queen of England; all are dead at the close of Shakespeare's original.

Dark comedy is the obverse: a generally comic play that ends ironically, or at least very strangely, leaving the impression of a less-than-cheery universe surrounding the play's characters. Although the term "dark comedy" is fairly recent, there are dark endings to many of Shakespeare's plays classed at the time of their initial publication as comedies, including *The Merchant of Venice, Measure for Measure,* and *The Winter's Tale.* Modern dark comedies have proven an extremely popular genre, particularly with playwrights such as Samuel Beckett, Joe Orton, Edward Albee, John Guare, Christopher Durang, Jean Anouilh, and Harold Pinter.

If histories, tragicomedies, and dark comedies are mixed genres, then *melodramas* and *farces* are pure extremes, carrying the notion of dramatic genre as far as it can be taken.

Some of the essence of farce is captured in this production photograph from Georges Feydeau's Hotel Paradiso, *as presented by the American Conservatory Theatre in 1978. Actors' exaggerated expressions and postures, as well as multiple-door setting, are standard features of farcical plays.*

Melodramas are plays that purport to be serious but that are in fact trivial entertainments, often embellished with spectacular stagings, sententious dialogue, and highly suspenseful—and contrived—plotting. Melodrama presents a simple and finite confrontation between good and evil rather than a complex exposition of universal human aspirations and sufferings. Plays in this genre cannot sustain unpleasant endings or generate catharsis, but can indeed provoke a deeply emotional outpouring of audience sentiment—always a powerful theatrical response. A pure creation of the theatre, melodramas employ every possible theatrical device to generate audience emotion (the name "melodrama" reveals the function music originally played in the melodramatic experience) and tend to reflect reality, or real human issues, only on the most superficial and sentimental level. Melodrama in its pure form rarely exists today—the melodramas that are occasionally produced these days are parodies, played for laughs—but melodramatic elements frequently find their ways into dramas of every sort.

Farces are similarly pure creations of the theatre. In farce, one finds a wildly hilarious

In the Belly of the Beast: Letters from Prison *documents life in prison.*
Adapted by Adrien Hall from letters by Jack Henry Abbot, the play is
here seen in the 1985 production at the Wisdom Bridge Theatre,
Chicago.

treatment of a trivial theme, ordinarily one of the various stock themes—mistaken identity, illicit infatuation, physical dissolution, monetary scheming—that have come down from ancient times. Plot components of farces are also drawn from a set of stock situations and events; identical twins, lovers in closets or under tables, full-stage chases, switched potions, switched costumes (often involving transsexual dressing), misheard instructions, and various disrobings, discoveries, and disappearances characterize this age-old and perennially durable dramatic genre. Elements of farce exist in almost all comedies, but pure farce makes no pretense toward Horace's *utile dulce;* the motto instead is "laugh 'til you cry," and in a well-written, well-staged farce the audience does just that. Michael Frayn's *Noises Off,* a pure farce set in a provincial English theatre, had audiences collapsed in hysteria on both sides of the Atlantic in the 1980s; every couple of years a new "laugh-riot" tends to appear—just as we are beginning to lament the demise of this popular dramatic genre.

Many minor genres have been usefully described in the contemporary theatre; the *documentary* and the *musical* are of particular importance.

Fiddler on the Roof, an internationally famed American musical by Jerry Bock and Joseph Stein, here seen in East Berlin production (1971) at the Komische Oper (Light Opera) theatre, under direction of Walter Felsenstein. Singing, dancing, acting, spoken dialogue, comedy, sentiment, and a touch of violence are mingled in this composite theatrical form.

The *documentary* is a genre of fairly recent development, in which a great deal of authentic evidence is used as a basis for portraying relatively recent historical events. Trial transcripts, news reports and pictures, personal and official records are marshaled as documentation to bring alive a particular issue and point of view. Famous court trials—those of J. Robert Oppenheimer, John C. Scopes, Adolph Eichmann, the "Zoot Suit" gangs, and Leopold and Loeb, for example—have been a prime source of material for documentary dramatizations.

The *musical* genre is defined by its extensive musical score, particularly by its vocal score. Operas and operettas are, of course, examples of musical theatre but are generally considered more music than theatre. The musical exists as a dramatic genre, however, in such popular and stage-oriented forms as musical comedy (a comedy with songs and dances, such as *A Chorus Line*), musical documentary (such as the World War I–inspired *Oh, What a Lovely War!*), or a musical melodrama (Stephen Sondheim's *Sweeney Todd, the Demon Barber of Fleet Street*). The musical play has often been considered America's greatest contribution to the theatre, particularly owing to the great post–World War II musicals by Cole Porter (*Kiss Me Kate*), Frank

Cohen's cautionary two-paragraph summary of the "Genre" section and his introductory note on "Structure" are relatively rare examples of an academic writer encouraging the reader to maintain a healthy skepticism regarding the literal uses and applicability of the writer's own analysis. Arguing about trees rather than seeing the forest is always a scholarly danger, and not uncommon even in textbooks. Cohen's advice here—to remember that "the theatrical experience (is) always . . . greater than the sum of its parts"—is wise, useful, and relevant to just about every discipline.

GENRE–LY SPEAKING

Shakespeare has brightly parodied the division of plays into genres, a practice which in his time was already becoming almost an affectation. In *Hamlet,* he has Polonius describe an acting company as "The best actors in the world, either for tragedy, comedy, history, pastoral, pastoral-comical, historical-pastoral, tragical-historical, tragical-comical-historical-pastoral, scene individable, or poem unlimited."

Loesser (*Guys and Dolls*), Alan J. Lerner and Frederick Lowe (*Brigadoon, My Fair Lady*) and Richard Rodgers and Oscar Hammerstein (*Oklahoma, South Pacific, The Sound of Music, The King and I*). Today, however, the musical is at least a binational dramatic genre, with much of the newest work originating from Stephen Sondheim in America (*Company, A Little Night Music, Follies*) and Andrew Lloyd Webber in England (*Cats, Evita, Starlight Express, Phantom of the Opera*). The musical is considered more fully in the discussion of modern theatre.

Potentially, of course, there are as many theatrical genres as the diligent critic wishes to define. No system of classification should obscure the fact that each play is unique, and the grouping of any two or more plays into a common genre is only a convenience for purposes of comparison and analysis. We in the twentieth century have certainly learned that past formulations of tragedy and farce have had little bearing on the long-range assessment of the importance, quality, or worth—on the staying power—of any individual play; and critics who today dwell inordinately on such questions as "Is *Death of A Salesman* a true tragedy?" are doubtless spending too much time deciding what box to put the artistic work in and too little time examining and revealing the work itself.

On the other hand, genre distinctions can be useful if we keep their limitations in mind. They can help us to comprehend the broad spectrum of purposes to which plays may be put and to perceive important similarities and differences. For the theatre artist, an aware-ness of the possibilities inherent in each genre—together with a knowledge of the achievements that have been made in each—stimulates the imagination and aids in setting work standards and ambitions.

STRUCTURE

Plays can be analyzed structurally in two ways: by their components (that is, plot, character, theme, etc.) and by their order of organization (exposition, development, climax, etc.). Both methods are used by most persons who find it worthwhile to analyze dramatic art, and both will be used in this book. However, it must be clear from the outset that a drama which is taken apart in the classroom inevitably loses something. The individual components and the sequential aspects of any given play are never in fact isolated in the theatrical experience, and any truly useful dramatic analysis must end with a resynthesis of the studied portions into a living whole. The complexity of the theatrical experience and its multi-sensual impact decree that we see it always as greater than the sum of its parts.

The Components of a Play

The division of plays into components is an ancient analytical practice. Aristotle in his *Poetics* (325 B.C.) described the components of a tragedy (by which he meant a serious play) as plot, character, theme, diction, music, and spectacle—in that order. Aristotle's list, with some modification and elaboration, still serves as a pretty fair breakdown of what theatre is all about, although the relative importance of each of the components has been a matter of continuing controversy.

PLOT

The *plot* of a play is the means by which most people know and describe it; perhaps that is why Aristotle listed it first. Essentially, plot is the mechanics of dramatic storytelling. More than merely conveying a story line, plot determines the structural development of a play's action: entrances, inquiries, recognitions, physical behaviors, and other communications of a kind that can be readily summarized in narrative form. Plot embraces both outer actions (such as Romeo stabbing Tybalt) and inner ones (such as Romeo falling in love with Juliet); the sequence and arrangement of these actions, in a series of scenes and acts punctuated by intermissions, is one of the most difficult and demanding tests of a playwright's skill.

Traditionally, the primary demands of plot are logic and suspense. To satisfy the demand for logic, the actions portrayed must be plausible, and events must follow one upon another in an organic rather than arbitrary fashion. To sustain suspense, the actions portrayed must set up expectations for further actions, drawing the audience along in a story that seems to move inexorably toward an ending that may be sensed but is never wholly predictable. Melodramas and farces tend to rely heavily on intricate and suspenseful plots. The "well-made plays" of the late nineteenth century reflect an attempt to elevate plot construction to the highest level of theatrical art; today, murder mysteries and "whodunits" are likely to be the most plot-intensive works to be seen on the stage.

CHARACTERS

The *characters* of a play are the human figures—the impersonated presences—who undertake the actions of the plot. Their potency in the theatre is measured by our interest in them *as people*. The most brilliant plotting in the world cannot redeem a play if the audience remains indifferent to its characters; therefore, the fundamental demand of a play's characters is that they make the audience *care*. To this end, characters cannot be mere stick figures, no matter how elaborately detailed. The great dramatic characters of the past—Hamlet, Masha, Amanda, Iago, Vladimir, Peer Gynt, Phaedra, to name a few—bring to an experienced theatregoer's or playreader's mind personalities as vivid and memorable as those of good friends (and hated enemies); they are whole images, indelibly human, alive with the attributes, feelings, and expectations of real people. We can identify with them; we can sympathize with them.

Character depth is what gives a play its psychological complexity, its sensuality, and its warmth. Without it, we cannot experience love, hate, fear, joy, hope, despair—any of the emotions we expect to derive from theatre; and a theatre devoid of those emotions that stem from the humanness of the characters portrayed would be a theatre without an audience in a matter of days. For this reason many playwrights have scoffed at the notion of primacy of plot and at the often mechanical contrivances of the well-made play. Indeed, several playwrights have fashioned plays that were quite arbitrarily plotted, with the story line designed simply to show various aspects of a fascinating character.

THEME

Theme is the abstracted intellectual content of a play. It may be described as the play's overall statement: its topic, central idea, or message, as the case may be. Some plays have obvious themes, such as Euripides' *The Trojan Women* (the horrors of war) or Molière's *The Bourgeois Gentleman* (the foolishness of social pretense). Other plays have less clearly defined themes, and the most provocative of these have given rise to much scholarly controversy. *Hamlet, Oedipus Tyrannos*, and

Careful readers might suspect that a writer confident and straightforward enough to have made such an observation is a personality well worth listening to with particular attention. In textbooks, as in life, unusually good advice ought to prompt gratitude and trust, and Cohen seems to be giving the reader just that sort of guidance.

Waiting for Godot all suggest many themes, and each has spawned a great many debates among adherents arguing fiercely about which theme is central.

Nothing demands that a play have a single theme, of course, or even that it be at all reducible to straightforward intellectual generalization. Indeed, plays that are too obviously theme-intensive are usually considered too propagandistic or too somberly academic for theatrical success: "If you want to send a message," one Broadway saying goes, "go to Western Union." What is more, although the themes of plays address the central questions of society and mankind, their theatrical impact hinges always on audience engagement in plot and characterization.

The importance of theme is that a play must have something to say, and that something must seem *pertinent* to the audience. Further, the play must be sufficiently focused and limited to give the audience at least some insight into that something within its two- to four-hour framework. Plays that try to say nothing or, conversely, plays that try to say everything, rarely have even a modest impact, no matter how entertaining or well plotted they may be. Thus, from the beginning, playwrights working in every genre, be it tragedy, comedy, melodrama, or farce, have recognized the merit of narrowing their field of intellectual investigation when crafting a play.

DICTION

Diction, which Aristotle listed fourth, relates not only to the pronunciation of spoken dialogue but also to the literary character of a play's text, including its tone, imagery, cadence, and articulation, as well as its use of literary forms and figures such as verse, rhyme, metaphor, apostrophe, jest, and epigram.

The theatrical value of poetry has been well established from the beginning; until fairly recent times, as a matter of fact, most serious plays were written largely in verse. Today, comedies as well as more serious plays still make liberal use of carefully crafted dialogue, although the verse form is relatively rare. Many plays succeed on the basis of brilliant repartee, stunning epigrams, poetic language, witty arguments, and dazzling tirades. Other, quite different, sorts of plays feature a poetry of silences and inarticulate mutterings: these, as fashioned by Anton Chekhov or Harold Pinter, for example, can create a diction no less effective than the more ostentatiously crafted verbal pyrotechnics of a Bernard Shaw or a Tom Stoppard (see the chapters on modern drama).

The diction of a play is by no means the creation of the playwright alone. It is very much the product of the actor as well, and for that reason throughout the history of Western theatre an effective stage voice has been considered the prime asset of the actor. Even today, the study of voice is a primary and continuous obligation at most schools and conservatories of classical acting. The chief aim of these schools is to create an acting voice capable of dealing in quite spectacular fashion with the broad palette of dramatic diction demanded by the works of the world's most noted playwrights.

MUSIC

Any discussion of *music*, Aristotle's fifth component of theatre, forces us to remember that in Aristotle's time plays were sung or chanted, not simply spoken. That mode of presentation has all but disappeared, and yet the musical component remains directly present in most plays performed today, indirectly present in the rest.

Music is directly present in the large number of plays that call for actual music in their presentation. This music takes many forms. Songs are common in the plays of Shakespeare, as well as in the works of modern writers, such as Bertolt Brecht, who feature "direct" performance techniques. Many naturalistic writers have found occasion to work familiar songs into their scripts, sometimes by having characters play records on stage.

A GOOD PLAY

What's the difference between a poor play and a good one? I think there's a very simple way of comparing them. A play in performance is a series of impressions; little dabs, one after another, fragments of information or feeling in a sequence which stir the audience's perceptions. A good play sends many such messages, often several at a time, often crowding, jostling, overlapping one another. The intelligence, the feelings, the memory, the imagination are all stirred. . . . Shakespeare seems better in performance than anyone else because he gives us more, moment for moment, for our money. This is due to his genius, but also to his technique. The possibilities of free verse on an open stage enabled him to cut the inessential detail and the irrelevant realistic action: in their place he could cram sounds and ideas, thoughts and images which make each instant into a stunning mobile.

Peter Brook

Chekhov and Tennessee Williams both make extensive use in their plays of off-stage music—for example, a military marching band can be heard in Chekhov's *The Three Sisters;* and Williams provides for music from a nearby dance hall in *A Streetcar Named Desire* and from a cantina in *Night of the Iguana.* Directors also frequently add incidental music to play productions—sometimes to set a mood during intermissions or before the play begins, sometimes to underscore the play's action itself. The power of music directly present in the theatre is well known, and its effectiveness in moving an audience to ever deeper feeling is one that few playwrights or directors wish to ignore.

Indirectly, music is present in every play. It is in the rhythm of sounds that, while not specifically tuneful, combine to create a play's "score," its orchestration of sound. Vocal tones, footsteps, sighs, shouts, off-stage railroad whistles, the shrilling of a telephone, muffled drumbeats, gunshots, animal cries, conversations in the next room, and amplified special effects (heartbeats, respiration, otherworldly noises, for instance) are frequently employed by authors and directors to create a symphony of the theatre quite apart from, though supportive of, the plot, characters, dialogue, and theme. Moreover, the spoken word creates, in addition to its semantic impact (its meaning and connotation), an aural impact: it is an integer of pure sound, and it can be appreciated as pure musical vibration. Under the guidance of a skilled director, all of a play's sounds can be orchestrated to produce a performance of such dramatic force that it can thrill even persons wholly unacquainted with the language of the dialogue.

SPECTACLE

Spectacle, Aristotle's last component, encompasses the visual aspects of production: scenery, costumes, lighting, make-up, properties, and the overall *look* of the theatre and stage. It would be wrong to infer that "spectacle" is synonymous with "spectacular," for some productions are quite restrained in their visual artistry. Rather, it is spectacle in the sense that it is something seen. If this point seems obvious, it is also crucial. Theatre is a visual experience every bit as much as it is an aural, emotional, or intellectual one: the ancient Greeks clearly had this in mind when they chose the name "seeing place" to designate the site of their performances.

When an author includes an aside, quote, or extended note, such as this one from Peter Brook, and sets it off from the body of the text in a "box" or different type, it's always a good idea to make a note of the addition. Just as the aside or box clarifies or amplifies a point for the author, it may well be able to do the same for you in a paper or on an examination.

This box, by the way, is different from the note on page 300, which is Cohen's own introduction to a quotation from *Hamlet* pointing to the difficulty of categorizing plays by genre.

Laura and Jim O'Connor, the 'gentleman caller," admire a glass unicorn in one of the central moments of Tennessee Williams' The Glass Menagerie. *Here the stage prop symbolizes the transparency and fragility of the shy young heroine. Arizona Theatre Company, 1977.*

Germaine Montero, as Mother Courage in Brecht's play of that name, pulls her wagon in a celebrated French production at the popular theatre festival in Avignon.

Much as the cinema has been called the art of "moving pictures," so the theatre might be called the art of fluid sculpture. This sculpture is fashioned in part from the human body in motion and in part from still or moving scenery and props, natural and manufactured items of both dramatic and decorative importance, all illuminated by natural or artificially modulated light. It is a sculpture that moves in time as well as in space; and although it is generally considered to be primarily a support for the plot, characters, and theme of a play, it has an artistic appeal and an artistic heritage all its own. Certainly some ardent patrons of the theatre pay more attention to settings and costumes than to any other aspect of a play, and in many a success-

ful production dramatic visual effects have virtually carried the play.

Memorable visual elements can be both grand and prosaic, imposing and subtle. Nineteenth-century Romanticism, which survives today primarily in the form of grand opera, tends to favor mammoth stagings featuring processions, crowd scenes, palaces, animals, triumphal arches, and lavish costumes. Twentieth-century movements are more likely to go in for domestic environments and archetypal images: Jimmy and Cliff reading newspapers while Alison irons a shirt in John Osborne's *Look Back in Anger* and Laura playing with her glass animals in Tennessee Williams' *The Glass Menagerie;* or Mother Courage pulling her wagon in Brecht's *Mother Courage* and

The ashcans of Endgame, *by Samuel Beckett, are home for the parents of Hamm (seated). Nagg, Hamm's father, comes up to ask for "more pap," while Clov, standing, mocks his pleas. From original Parisian production, 1957.*

Nagg and Nell in the ashcans of Samuel Beckett's *Endgame.* In the long run, conceptual richness and precision in a play's visual presentation are far more telling than grandeur for its own sake.

CONVENTION

To these six components of every play we should add a seventh which Aristotle apparently never saw reason to consider as a discrete component: theatrical *convention.* The agreement between audience and actor includes a whole set of tacit understandings that form the context of playwatching—conventions such as "when the curtain goes up, the play begins; when the curtain goes down, the play is over." Many of these conditions are so imbedded in the fabric of the theatregoing experience that we tend to forget about them altogether unless something happens that casts them into relief. Our theatre conventions are most visible when we see them from afar—in contrast to the practices of theatres of other cultures. For example, the conventions of the Japanese Noh Drama decree that major characters enter on a gangway, that choruses sing the lines of characters who are dancing, that hand-held fans are used in certain ways to indicate wind, water, rain, or the rising moon. Patrons of the Noh Drama accept these conventions as unquestioningly as we accept the convention that, when the stage lights dim, we are to ignore the scurrying about of actors and stagehands during a scene change.

Each play sets up its own system of conventions, but in most cases they accord with the traditions of their times and therefore go largely unnoticed (doubtless that is why Aristotle, familiar with no drama other than his own, made no specific mention of them). In modern times, with playwrights and directors becoming increasingly aware of other traditions and possibilities, more and more play productions seek to employ conventions of ancient times or foreign cultures and even to establish new ones. Peter Shaffer's *Black Comedy*, which supposedly takes place in the dark, utilizes a convention which Shaffer attributes to the Chinese: when the lights are on they are "off," and when they are off they are "on." Eugene O'Neill's *Strange Interlude* gives us to understand that when the actors freeze and speak, we in the audience—but not the other characters in the play—hear their thoughts. Jean Anouilh's *Antigone* uses a variation on the Greek device of the chorus: a single man speaks with the author's voice as the characters on stage freeze in silence. Lanford Wilson, in *The Rimers of Eldritch*, presents a story in more than a hundred tiny scenes that jump back and forth in time, and only at the play's end do we get any real sense of story line. Arthur Miller's *After The Fall* places an imaginary psychiatrist in the midst of the audience, and the play's protagonist repeatedly interrupts the action of the drama to address his analyst in highly theatrical "therapy" sessions. And so it goes. There is no formal requirement for the establishment of theatrical conventions, except that the audience must "agree" (which it does, of course, unconsciously) to accept them.

These seven components of every play— with the seventh more or less framing Aristotle's six—are the raw material of drama. All are important, and certainly the theatre could not afford to dispense with any one. Some plays are intensive in one or more; most great productions show artistry in all. The *balancing* of these components in theatrical presentation is one of the primary challenges facing the director, who on one occasion may be called upon mainly to clarify and elaborate a theme, on another to find the visual mode of presentation that best supports the characters, on another to develop and "flesh out" the characterizations in order to give strength and meaning to the plot, on another to heighten a musical tone in order to enhance sensual effect, on another to develop the precise convention—the relationship between play and audience—that will maximize the play's artistic impact. For as important as each of these components is to the theatrical experience, it is their combination and interaction, not their individual splendor, that is crucial to a production's success.

The Order of a Play

Plays can also be looked at in terms of their temporal (time) structure. Here again, Aristotle affords some help. He tells us that drama has "a beginning, a middle, and an end," and here and there in his *Poetics* he proffers a little detail about the nature of each of these elements. We can expand Aristotle's list somewhat, for by now some fairly consistent features can be distinguished in the organization in time of any theatrical experience.

THE GATHERING OF THE AUDIENCE

Theorists often either ignore the audience in considering the crucial elements of the theatre or else dismiss it as a "paratheatrical" (para meaning "only somewhat") concern. The gathering of the audience is, however, an extremely important consideration in the presentation of a play, and it entails a process that is not without its artistic and cultural significance. The chief concerns in that process have to do with publicity, admission, and seating. Each of these concerns has given theatre producers much food for thought since ancient times.

Going to theatre in Shakespeare's London meant, for most patrons, a trip across the Thames to Bankside, for the large public theatres of the day were not permitted inside the city proper. Here, flags atop theatre buildings indicate where performances are scheduled today.

For how does the theatre attract its audience in the first place? Theatregoing, after all, is not a need of mankind in the same way that eating is a need; the population of a society does not spend half its waking hours trying to supply itself with theatre in the way it strives to secure food, shelter, and physical security. Rather the theatre, if it is to survive, must go out and recruit attention; in every era, theatre has had the responsibility of gathering its audience.

Therefore, the goal of every theatre producer is to make his or her theatre accessible, inviting, and favorably known to the widest possible public—and also, in many eras, to the *richest* possible public—and to make theatre as an art form as thrilling and spiritually *necessary* as it can possibly be.

One of the oldest known ways of publicizing the theatre is by means of a procession. The circus parade, which still takes place in some of the smaller towns of Europe and the United States, is a remnant of a once universal form of advertisement for the performing arts that probably began well in advance of recorded history.

The Greeks of ancient Athens opened their great dramatic festivals with a *proagon* (literally, "pre-action") in which both playwrights and actors were introduced at a huge public meeting and given a chance to speak about the plays they were to present on subsequent days. Today, similar conclaves—usually via television talk shows in this global village of ours—are often used to promote theatrical events to the public at large. The

A priest is about to take his designated place in a stone seat in the first row of the ancient theatre of Athens.

Elizabethans flew flags atop their playhouses on performance days, and the flags could be seen across the Thames in "downtown" London, enticing hundreds away from their commercial and religious activities. The lighted marquees of Broadway theatres around Times Square and of London theatres in the West End are a modern-day equivalent of the flags that waved over those first great English public theatres.

Developments in the printing and broadcast media have spurred the growth of theatre advertising until it is today a major theatrical craft in its own right. Splendid posters, illustrated programs, multi-color subscription brochures, full-page newspaper advertisements, staged media events, articulate press releases, and flashy 30-second television commercials have been employed to summon us out of the comfort of our homes and into the theatre. For premieres or for openings of new playhouses, giant searchlights are often used to beckon the public to the theatrical location. Far from being an inconsequential aspect of theatre, publicity today occupies a place of fundamental impor-

tance in the thinking of theatrical producers and commands a major share of the budget for commercial theatrical ventures.

Procedures for admitting and seating the audience are usually straightforward and conventional; however they can have important—and occasionally decisive—effects on the overall theatrical presentation.

Ordinarily, theatre is supported at least in part by fees charged the audience. These fees make up what is called the "box office revenue." For commercial theatres, box office revenue provides the sole means of meeting production costs and providing a profit to investors. The admission charge dates from ancient Greek days, and since then only a few amateur or civic productions (such as the religious pageants of medieval England or the free Shakespeare performances in contemporary New York City) have managed to survive without it.

Seating is frequently determined by the price of admission: the best seats cost the most. What determines "best" and "poorest" seating, however, depends on many things. In modern Broadway and West End theatres, the most costly seats are in the orchestra (known in the West End as "the stalls"), which is the ground-level seating area; balcony seats ordinarily cost less, and the higher the balcony, the smaller the price. In the public theatres of Elizabethan London, however, the ground level (which was standing room) provided the cheapest space, and the "gentlemen's rooms" in the balcony—where one could be seen and visited—commanded up to twelve times as much. In the Restoration period, seats on the stage itself brought the highest prices of all, assuring their purchasers the widest possible personal recognition (but affording a ridiculously poor view of the play's action).

Seating is not always scaled according to price, however. In the Greek drama festivals of ancient Athens, the front row seats were reserved for priests, and members of the lay audience sat in sections of the *theatron* reserved for their particular tribe. In many noncommercial theatres today, the best seats go to those patrons willing to wait longest in line to get them. The National Theatre of England has experimented with a seating system designed to reward the most eager of its fans, not the richest; this practice is common in East European countries. In racially divided countries, audiences are segregated according to the color of their skin. This regrettable practice persisted well into the twentieth century in the United States, and indeed in the 1960s was occasionally revived by "Black Theatre" companies. Perhaps the most radical seating experiments occurred in the "New Theatre" movement of the early 1970s, in which audiences were often led one by one to seats determined in an impromptu interview with one or another of the cast members acting as ushers. What is more, patrons were sometimes ordered to leave their assigned seats in mid-performance to make room for actors!

THE TRANSITION

Gathered, admitted, and seated, the audience remains a collection of individuals preoccupied with their daily concerns. Now the theatre must transform them into a community devoted to the concerns of the play and enmeshed in the actions of imaginary characters. The theatre, in other words, must effect in their awareness a transition from real life to stage life, and it must do so in a smooth and agreeable fashion.

The written program is one modern device (modern in the sense that it dates from the eighteenth century) which helps to prepare the audience for the fiction they are about to see. It gives them the locale and time of the action, the names of the characters and of the actors who impersonate them; in these ways it allows the audience to preview the general scope of the play's environment—spatial, temporal, and personal—and to accept the actors as valid impersonators of the play's characters. Having read that Kevin Kline is playing Hamlet, for example, we don't spend playwatching time trying to figure who the lead actor is.

Often music is used, in the contemporary theatre, to set the mood or tone of a play, particularly when the action is set in a certain period in the past. For a musical production, an entire orchestral piece—called the overture—usually precedes any action on stage.

Lobby displays are sometimes used to supplement the written programs, featuring either pictures of the actors or other pictures and documents relevant to the play, its period, its author, and its critical reception. Occasionally the seating area is altered to aid in this transition, sometimes by the addition of wall posters, sometimes by other ornamentation. When no curtain is used, the scenery may be "warmed" by "pre-show" lighting that eases the audience into an expectation of the performance to follow—in some productions that "scenery" includes actors sitting, standing, or lying motionless on the set or engaging in quiet, understated movement. Sometimes slide presentations, songs, or improvised activities take place on stage before the play begins, and the patrons may be asked to participate in some way as they find their way to their seats. Many of these methods date from ancient times; all of them have been used to introduce modern plays to an audience and to

The effect of recreating the theatrical experience in the reader's imagination mentioned in the introduction begins with the section "The Transition" and continues to the end of the chapter. As you read, notice how the author involves you in the actual experience of a theatrical performance.

When you finish "What Is a Play?" write several sentences describing how this concluding section illustrates the elements described earlier in the chapter.

prepare the audience to enter the world of the stage.

Finally, a swift new transition to stage life occurs: the play begins. Most often this is a shared moment. The houselights dim and a curtain rises or stage lights come up to reveal a scene. Occasionally this transition is more subtle, and each member of the audience glides into the play at his or her own moment of discovery; a "pre-show" improvisation begins to take on a more pronounced, attention-demanding character, or perhaps some small but seemingly significant alteration galvanizes the consciousness to full attention. Either way the transition is complete. The thinking of the audience shifts from workaday concerns to the characters of the play and their story. This, to use a familiar theatrical term, is "magic time."

THE EXPOSITION

No important play has ever begun with a character dashing onstage and shouting "The house is on fire!" At best, such a beginning could only confuse the audience, and at worst it could cause them to flee in panic. For at that point they would have no way of knowing what house, or why they should care about it. Most plays, whatever their style or genre, begin with dialogue or action calculated to ease us, not shock us, into the concerns of the characters with whom we are to spend the next two hours or so.

"Exposition" is a word not much in favor now, coming as it does from an age when play structure was considered more scientific than it is today. But it is still a useful term, referring to the background information the audience must have in order to understand "what's going on" in the action of a play.

In the rather mechanical plotting of the "well-made" plays, the exposition is handled with little fanfare, with a few characters, often servants (minor figures in the action to follow), discussing something that is about to happen and enlightening each other (and of course the audience) about certain details around which the plot will turn. Consider

these lines from the opening scene of Henrik Ibsen's 1884 classic, *The Wild Duck*:

PETTERSEN, in livery, and JENSEN, the hired waiter, in black, are putting the study in order. From the dining room, the hum of conversation and laughter is heard.

PETTERSEN: Listen to them, Jensen; the old man's got to his feet—he's giving a toast to Mrs. Sorby.

JENSEN: (*pushing forward an armchair*) Do you think it's true, then, what they've been saying, that there's something going on between them?

PETTERSEN: God knows.

JENSEN: He used to be quite the lady's man, I understand.

PETTERSEN: I suppose.

JENSEN: And he's giving this party in honor of his son, they say.

PETTERSEN: That's right. His son came home yesterday.

JENSEN: I never even knew old Werle had a son.

PETTERSEN: Oh, he has a son all right. But he's completely tied up at the Hoidal works. In all the years I've been here he's never come into town.

A WAITER: (*In the doorway of the other room*) Pettersen, there's an old fellow here . . .

PETTERSEN: (*mutters*) Damn. Who'd show up at this time of night?

After a few more lines, Pettersen, Jensen, and the waiter make their exits and are seen no more. Their function is purely expository—to pave the way for the principal characters. The conversation they are having is a contrivance intended simply to give us a framework for the action—and the information they impart is presented by means of a conversation among servants only because a convention of realism decrees that words spoken in a play be addressed to characters, not to the audience.

The exposition of non-realistic plays can be handled more directly. It was the Greek custom to begin a play with a prologue preceding the entrance of the chorus and the major play episodes; the prologue was some-

times a scene and sometimes a simple speech
to the audience. Shakespeare also used pro-
logues in some of his plays. In one particularly
interesting example, Shakespeare's *Henry V,*
each of the five acts begins with a character
called "Chorus" directly addressing the audience and setting the scene for the act:

CHORUS: O for a Muse of fire, that would
ascend
The brightest heaven of invention!
A kingdom for a stage, princes to act,
And monarchs to behold the swelling
scene!
Then should the warlike Harry, like
himself,
Assume the port of Mars, and at his heels
(Leash'd in, like hounds) should famine,
sword, and fire
Crouch for employment. But pardon,
gentles all,
The flat unraised spirits that hath dar'd
On this unworthy scaffold to bring forth
So great an object. Can this cockpit hold
The vasty fields of France? Or may we
cram
Within this wooden O the very casques
That did affright the air at Agincourt?
O, pardon! since a crooked figure may
Attest in little place a million,
And let us, ciphers to this great accompt,
On your imaginary forces work.
Suppose within the girdle of these walls
Are now confin'd two mighty
monarchies,
Whose high, upreared, and abutting
fronts
The perilous narrow ocean parts
asunder.
Piece out our imperfections with your
thoughts;
Into a thousand parts divide one man,
And make imaginary puissance;
Think, when we talk of horses, that you
see them
Printing their proud hoofs i' th' receiving
earth;
For 'tis your thoughts that now must
deck our kings,

Carry them here and there, jumping o'er
times,
Turning th' accomplishment of many
years
Into an hour-glass: for the which supply,
Admit me Chorus to this history;
Who, Prologue-like, your humble
patience pray,
Gently to hear, kindly to judge, our play.

This justly famous prologue establishes setting, characters, and audience expectation of
plot in an utterly straightforward manner,
and begs the audience's indulgence for the
theatrical conventions they will be called
upon to entertain.

THE CONFLICT

Now is the time for the character to enter
shouting "The house is on fire!"

It is a truism that drama requires conflict;
in fact the very word "drama," when used in
daily life, implies a situation fraught with conflict. No one writes plays about characters
who live every day in unimpaired serenity; no
one, quite certainly, would ever choose to
watch such a play. Conflict and confrontation
are the mechanisms by which a situation becomes dramatic.

Why is this so? Why are conflict situations
so theatrically interesting? The reasons have
to do with plot, theme, and character. Plot can
hold suspense only when it involves alternatives and choices: Macbeth has strong reasons
to murder King Duncan and strong reasons
not to; if he had only the former or only the
latter, he would project no real conflict and
we should not consider him such an interesting character. We are fascinated by a character's actions largely in light of the actions he
rejects and the stresses he has to endure in
making his decisions. In other words, plot
entails not only the actions of a play but also
the inactions—the things that are narrowly
rejected and do *not* happen. A character's
decision must proceed from powerfully
conflicting alternatives if we are to watch his
behavior with empathy instead of mere curi-

osity. In watching a character act, the audience must also watch him *think;* a playwright gets him to think by putting him into conflict.

Conflict can be set up between characters as well as within them; it may be reducible to one central situation or it may evolve out of many. Whatever the case, conflict throws characters into relief and permits the audience to see deeply into the human personality. To see a character at war with himself or in confrontation with another, is to see how that character *works,* and this is the key to our caring.

The theme of a play is ordinarily a simple abstraction of its central conflict. In Sophocles' *Antigone,* for example, the theme is the conflict between divine law and civil law; in *Death of a Salesman* it is the conflict between Willy's reality and his dreams. Conflicts are plentiful in farces and comedies as well—the conflicts inherent in the "eternal triangle," for example, have provided comic material for dramatists for the last two millennia. Many of the more abstract philosophical conflicts—independence versus duty, individuality versus conformity, idealism versus pragmatism, integrity versus efficiency, pleasure versus propriety, progress versus tradition, to name a few—suggest inexhaustible thematic conflicts that appear in various guises in both ancient and contemporary plays.

The playwright introduces conflict early in a play, often by means of an "inciting incident" in which one character poses a conflict or confrontation either to another character or to himself. For example:

FIRST WITCH: All hail, Macbeth, hail to thee,
　　　　Thane of Glamis!
SECOND WITCH: All hail, Macbeth, hail to thee,
　　　　Thane of Cawdor!
THIRD WITCH: All hail, Macbeth, that shalt be
　　　　King hereafter!
BANQUO: Good sir, why do you start, and
　　　　seem to fear
　　Things that do sound so fair?

In this, the inciting incident of Shakespeare's *Macbeth* (which follows two brief expository scenes), a witch confronts Macbeth with the prediction that he will be king, thereby posing an alternative that Macbeth has apparently already considered, judging from the startled response that elicits Banquo's comment.

Once established, conflict is intensified to crisis, usually by a series of incidents, investigations, revelations, and confrontations which the playwright creates. Sometimes even nonevents serve to intensify a conflict. Such is certainly the case in the modern classic, *Waiting for Godot,* in which two characters simply wait, through two hour-long acts, for the arrival of a third who never comes. Indeed, with this play, Samuel Beckett virtually rewrote the book on playwriting technique by showing how time alone, when properly managed, can do the job of heightening and developing conflict in a dramatic situation.

THE CLIMAX

Conflict cannot be intensified indefinitely. In a play as in life, when conflict becomes insupportable, something has to give. Thus every play, be it comic, tragic, farcical, or melodramatic, culminates in some sort of dramatic explosion.

Aristotle described that dramatic explosion, in tragedy, as a *catharsis,* or purification. Aristotle's conception is susceptible to various interpretations, but it has been widely accepted and broadly influential for centuries. According to Aristotle's system, the catharsis is the crucial axis in the structure of tragedy, evolving out of the tragic hero's recognition (*anagnorisis*) of some fundamental truth and his consequent reversal (*peripeteia*) of some former ignorance, such as a horrific deed unknowingly performed (*pathos*). The catharsis releases the audience's pity, and thereby permits the fullest experience of tragic pleasure, washing away, as it were, the terror that has been mounting steadily during the play's tragic course. Such catharsis as accompanies Oedipus' gouging out his own eyes as he recognizes his true self illustrates the extreme theatrical explosion of which the classical Greek tragic form is capable.

For any dramatic form, the climax is the conflict of a play taken to its most extreme; it is the moment of maximum tension. At the climax, a continuation of the conflict becomes unbearable, impossible: some sort of change is mandated. Climaxes in modern plays do not as a rule involve death or disfiguration (although there are exceptions: Peter Shaffer's celebrated *Equus* reaches its climax with the blinding of six horses, and Edward Albee's *The Zoo Story* climaxes with one character impaling himself on a knife held by another); however, they inevitably contain elements of recognition and reversal if not of catharsis, and usually the major conflicts of the play are resolved by one or more of these.

THE DENOUEMENT

The climax is followed, and the play concluded by a denouement, or resolution, in which a final action or speech or even a single word or gesture indicates that the passions aroused by the play's action are now stilled and a new harmony or understanding has been reached.

The tenor of the denouement tends to change with the times. In the American theatre of the 1950s and 1960s, for example, the sentimental and message-laden denouement was the rule: in Robert Anderson's *Tea and Sympathy*, a teacher's wife prepares to prove to a sensitive boy that he is not homosexual; in Dore Schary's *Sunrise at Campobello*, a future American president makes his way on crippled legs to a convention platform. In the current theatre, in this existential age that looks with suspicion on tidy virtues and happy endings, more ironic and ambiguous denouements are to be expected. The current theatre also provides less in the way of purgation than do more classical modes; that is doubtless because the conflicts raised by the best of contemporary drama are not amenable to wholesale relief. But a denouement still must provide at least some lucidity concerning the problems raised by the play, some vision or metaphor of a deeper and more permanent

understanding. Perhaps the final lines of *Waiting for Godot* best represent the denouement of the current age:

ESTRAGON: Well, shall we go?
VLADIMIR: Yes, let's go.
 They do not move.

THE CURTAIN CALL

The last staged element of a theatrical presentation is the curtain call, in which the actors bow and the audience applauds. This convention, which has been customary in the theatre at least since the time of the Romans, plays an important but often overlooked role in the overall scope of theatrical presentation.

The curtain call is *not* simply a time for the actors to receive congratulations from the audience, although many actors today seem to think it is. Historically, it is a time in which the actors show their respect for the audience that patronizes them. And aesthetically, it is a time in which the audience allows itself to see the other side of the "paradox of acting." The curtain call liberates the audience from the world of the play, and when there is no curtain call audiences are palpably distressed and often disgruntled. For it fulfulls the last provision, so to speak, in the mutual agreement that characterizes the theatre itself—the agreement by which the audience agrees to view the actors as the characters the actors have agreed to impersonate. It is at the curtain call that actors and audience can acknowledge their mutual belonging in the human society, can look each other in the eye and say, in effect, "We all know what it is to experience these things we've just seen performed, we must all try to understand life a little better, we have enjoyed coming this far together, we are with you, we like you." In the best theatre, this communication is a powerful experience.

THE AFTERMATH: CRITICISM

What follows the curtain call? The audience disperses, of course; but the individual audience members do not die, and through them the production enjoys an extended afterlife both in talk and in print—in late-night postmortems at the theatre bar; in probing conversations and published reviews over the next few days; and sometimes in formal classroom discussions, television talk shows, letters to the editor in the local newspaper, and scholarly articles and books seen weeks, months, or years later. For the theatre is a place of public stimulation, both intellectual and emotional, and it should be expected that the stimulation provided by a provocative production would generate both animated discussions and illuminating commentaries.

Both of these we may call *dramatic criticism*, which is the audience's contribution to the theatre. Criticism is as ancient as Aristotle, and as contemporary as the essays and lectures that are presented daily in newspapers, journals, books, and academies all over the world. But criticism is not solely an expert enterprise; criticism—which combines analysis and evaluation—is everybody's job. We shall look further at this key aspect of the theatre's art in Chapter 3.

■ READING COMPREHENSION AND DISCUSSION QUESTIONS

1. In what ways do Robert Cohen's definitions and illustrations of "tragedy" and "comedy" contradict, modify, or mirror your own conceptions of those terms when applied to art? According to Cohen's definitions, are television situation comedies true comedies? Why, or why not? In which episodes of which shows do you find support for your opinion?

2. Cohen writes, "Character depth is what gives a play its psychological complexity, its sensuality, and its warmth. Without it, we cannot experience love, hate, fear, joy, hope, despair—any of the emotions we expect to derive from theatre." If you have seen a play, of any kind, do you agree with Cohen about the function and importance of character depth? Do you think that this principle holds true when applied to motion pictures? Why, or why not?

3. Beginning with the section called "The Transition" (page 309), the reader experiences a kind of play in the imagination as the chapter concludes. Compare this experience to the act of dreaming. Consider the effect of the dimmed house lights, the "willing suspension of disbelief" and its relationship to sleep, the immediacy yet unreality of the experience.

What parallels and differences of interest do you find in this comparison? Do you think that there could be biological or physiological similarities in these experiences (the author does) in addition to more obvious psychological similarities?

In what ways are plays "scripted dreams"?

CHAPTER 11

◼ *Anthropology*

◼ *"On the Origin of Our Species," from* Human Antiquity *by Kenneth L. Feder and Michael Alan Park*

Accurate and useful notes for "On the Origin of Our Species" should contain not only the usual highlighted elements but also the scholarly references enclosed in parentheses. True college reading demands this ability to identify sources, or "references," by author and publication date. Note-taking skills function in exactly the same way as we have practiced them throughout this book: The reader simply adds an author's name and a year, usually in parentheses, in order to be able to find or refer to the original work. All subsequent scholarship, including writing, depends on mastery of this simple but essential skill. You may recall having studied such material in "The Myth of the Mound-builders," by Kenneth Feder. Now it is time to master this type of academic prose, and fortunately the process is quick and easy.

For example, "(Harmon et al. 1980)" is inserted into the final paragraph on page 323 to show the reader the source of the author's information. This parenthetical documentation follows the statement "A minimum age of 228,000 B.P. has been calculated. . . ." and informs the reader that the study *establishing* this age (228,000 years before the present) was conducted by "Harmon and others" in 1980. The surname "Harmon" can be located in the textbook's bibliography, where a reader can find the information necessary to look up the original study, paper, or book.

As you progress through school, you'll find taking such notes increasingly important for your own research. *All* scholarship, you'll discover, depends on getting by with a little help from your friends.

10

ON THE ORIGIN
OF OUR SPECIES

For the last century and a half our species has been exploring its origins, as well as the origins of life itself on our planet and the birth of our universe. The following chapter is essentially a summary of the scientific work of several generations regarding our species, *Homo sapiens sapiens* (we have dubbed ourselves "the really smart thinking person," with characteristic modesty). Take special note in working with this material to record each of the sub-unit headings within the larger sections of the chapter—for example the "Steinheim," "Swanscombe," and "Petralona" sub-units of "Archaic *Homo Sapiens* Fossils" beginning on page 196. These headings will help you quickly organize your final notes for review or writing.

We saw in the last chapter that the evolutionary bush had been pruned from at least three, highly variable twigs—*Australopithecus africanus/robustus, Australopithecus boisei,* and *Homo habilis*—to a single, rather homogeneous species, *Homo erectus*. As we are about to see, however, about 400,000 years ago our evolutionary bush branched again after a punctuational event. In other words, the single twig of *Homo erectus* seems to have sprouted a new twig. We call the fossils who made up this twig on the evolutionary bush **archaic *Homo sapiens*** (Figure 10.1). One of the later populations, the Neandertals, are probably the best known of the archaics and have generated the greatest amount of controversy.

Remember our discussion of biological nomenclature in Chapter 6: Calling a fossil species *Homo sapiens* is not an arbitrary act. It means we believe the species was so similar to our own that it shares all our biological designations—it lived, in other words, at practically the same evolutionary address as we do. Technically, modern people are *Homo sapiens sapiens*—the second *sapiens* designating our subspecies. Subspecies designations are based on even finer distinctions than the species label. There is only one recognized human subspecies today and, as we

Figure 10.1 *Fossil localities of archaic* Homo sapiens.

will see in Chapter 15, all people belong in it. The archaics, on the other hand, are thought to represent an ancient and extinct subspecies of the human species. According to the rules of biological nomenclature, all the different groups of people alive today, no matter how different their appearances, are more similar to each other than any of us are to these extinct members of our species.

THE FIRST MEMBERS OF OUR SPECIES

As mentioned at the end of the last chapter, the one consistent difference between the archaics and *Homo erectus* in general is the larger cranial capacities and, therefore, bigger brains of the archaics. The mean cranial capacity of a small sample (six) of preserved brain cases of archaic *Homo sapiens* (not including the Neandertals, to be discussed separately) is just over 1200 cc (Rightmire 1985a). Compare that to the mean for *Homo erectus,* about 1000 cc. Just as in the comparison between the skulls of *Homo habilis* and *erectus,* however, the brains of the archaic *Homo sapiens* were not just larger than those of previous hominids, they appear to reflect a different arrangement, with greater similarity to modern humans.

We can generalize that the brains of the archaics were differently proportioned than those of earlier hominids, with a greater emphasis on the front or forebrain, and a resulting higher forehead, though the latter is not nearly as steep as in modern humans. The size of the face, relative to the rest of the head, is reduced; and the overall degree of prognathism is less than in *Homo erectus.* The bones that make up their skulls, at least in some of the archaics, are thinner than in older fossils and more similar to modern humans with our quite thin cranial bones. In some specimens the brow ridges, though still spectacular by modern standards and as clearly defined as in *Homo erectus,* do not dominate the face to the degree seen in earlier hominids. The postorbital constriction, so prominent in *erectus,* is greatly diminished. This is a result of the expansion of the front of the brain case to accommodate the increasing size of the frontal part of the brain.

ARCHAIC *HOMO SAPIENS* FOSSILS

The archaic members of our species are a varied lot. They share in common a brain larger than that of *erectus,* and within the normal human range. Beyond that there seems to be quite a bit more variation than that seen in *Homo erectus.* Several famous fossils show these contrasts quite clearly.

Steinheim

In 1933, the cranium of an archaic *Homo sapiens* was found in a gravel pit adjacent to the Murr River, in the town of Steinheim, just north of Stuttgart, West Germany (Howell 1960; Figure 10.2). The skull was found along with the fossil remains of several extinct species, including straight-tusked elephant, wild ox, cave bear, and cave lion. The gravel bed in which the hominid skull was found was probably laid down at the end of an interglacial or the beginning of a glacial stage. We know that the straight-tusked elephant was adapted to life in woodlands. This suggests an interglacial or relatively mild early glacial rather than a full-blown glacial period. Though dating of the skull has been problematic, a recent

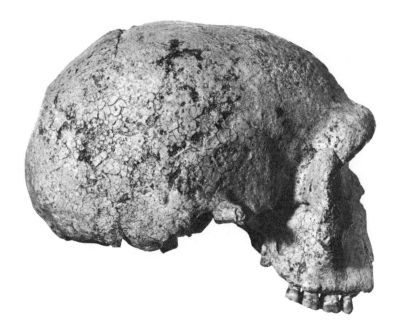

Figure 10.2 *The nearly intact cranium of an archaic* Homo sapiens *from Steinheim, West Germany. Note the more rounded appearance of the skull and the higher forehead than in* Homo erectus. *However, also note the large brow ridges.* (State Museum for Nature, Stuttgart, Federal Republic of Germany)

electron spin resonance date indicates that it is probably between 200,000 and 240,000 years old (Ikeya 1982). No artifacts were found with the hominid remains.

The skull is long and relatively narrow. Though the brow ridges are substantial, they are smaller than in most *Homo erectus* specimens. The face is flat and rather small, as in modern humans. There is no occipital torus, giving the rear of the skull a modern appearance. The bone of the skull is thinner than in *Homo erectus* but thicker than in modern humans. The cranial capacity has been estimated at just below 1200 cc, toward the small end of the modern human range but large for *Homo erectus*.

Swanscombe

Another probable example of archaic *Homo sapiens* was found in Swanscombe, England in 1935 (Howell 1960; Ovey 1964). The Swanscombe find includes three major skull fragments: the back (occiput) and both sides (parietals). Remarkably, the three fragments that fit together so perfectly were found over a period of more than 20 years and were located as much as 50 feet away from each other.

The base of the skull as well as the face was missing, so it is difficult, if not impossible, to judge brow ridge size or the degree of prognathism. What was recovered of the skull, however, is informative. The bone itself is quite thick, as in older specimens. Additionally, in a detailed analysis of

17 cranial measurements (Weiner and Campbell 1964), it was concluded that in many respects the skull is quite similar to *Homo erectus*.

A few of the characteristics of the Swanscombe skull, though, are more modern. As in Steinheim, the occiput shows little sign of a torus. Beyond this, the skull is quite large, with an estimated cranial capacity of over 1300 cc. This places the brain size of "Swanscombe Man" well within the modern human range, though, it must be said, its general appearance is a mosaic of primitive and modern traits.

The skull fragments were found in a gravel deposit along with the fossilized remains of wolf, lion, straight-tusked elephant, horse, ox, deer, and rhinoceros. A radiometric date (uranium series) for this associated material was calculated at 326,000 B.P. (Szabo and Collins 1975). The margin of error for this date, however, is large, and the skull could be 100,000 years older or 50,000 years younger. Flint tools, including hand axes and flakes, were found in the same deposit.

Petralona

A cavern at Petralona, southeast of Thessalonika, Greece, was investigated in 1959. Initially only fossilized animal bones were discovered, but in 1960 an ancient-looking and very well preserved hominid skull was found encased in a stalagmite deposit (Poulianos 1971-72).

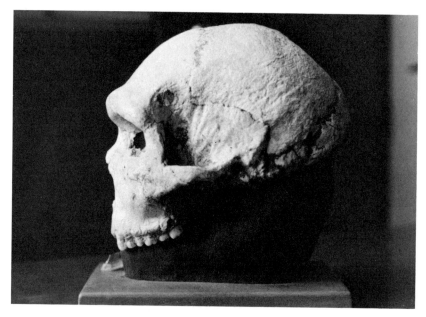

Figure 10.3 *The Petralona skull from Greece is clearly that of an* archaic Homo sapiens. *Discovered in a cave near Thessalonika, the rest of the skeleton was, apparently, lost.* (Christopher B. Stringer)

The Petralona skull possesses very large brow ridges, but it is rounder and the face is flatter than in *Homo erectus* (Figure 10.3). The cranial capacity is judged to have surpassed 1200 cc.

A detailed statistical analysis (Stringer 1974a) of 50 cranial measurements comparing Petralona to a large number of other fossil hominids including Steinheim, *Homo erectus,* and the Neandertals unfortunately shows that the Petralona skull cannot be easily categorized. Though its cranial vault is similar to that of the later Neandertals, some of its cranial measurements are reminiscent of *Homo erectus* from Zhoukoudian. To complicate matters further, its face is more like Steinheim, with the upper part being relatively flat and the lower jutting out. Stringer concluded from his analysis that Petralona represents an early form of *Homo sapiens* even though it possesses a mixture of traits.

Animal bones found in the cave included cave bear, lion, several kinds of deer, wolf, and rhinoceros. The mix of animals indicates a possible contemporaneity with the Steinheim skull, suggesting an interglacial date corresponding to stage 7 on the oxygen isotope curve (see Figure 9.3). The skull, however, could be much older or much younger because it may have washed into the cave from somewhere else. Electron spin resonance performed on an encrustation on the skull resulted in a date of between 160,000 and 240,000 years ago (Henning et al. 1981).

Other European Archaics

Several other examples of archaic *Homo sapiens* have come from Europe. Material associated with a small occipital fragment found in Vértess-zöllös, Hungary has produced a uranium series date of between 250,000 and 475,000 years ago (Gamble 1986). The bone is rather thick and there is an indication of an occipital torus, but the extrapolated cranial capacity is larger than in *erectus*. At Arago, near the village of Tautavel, France, the fragmentary remains of at least four adult and three juvenile hominids were found (Cook et al. 1982). The best preserved of these is a distorted face with large, thick brow ridges (Figure 10.4). The Arago fossils appear to represent archaic *Homo sapiens* dating to more than 250,000 years ago (Gamble 1986).

In the German Democratic Republic, the Bilzingsleben site produced two occipitals, two frontal bones, and a molar. These were found together with about 60,000 flint flakes reflecting a range of scraping tools, awls, points, and chopping tools (Gamble 1986). A minimum age of 228,000 B.P. has been calculated (Harmon et al. 1980). An adult skull fragment was also found in Ehringsdorf, East Germany, and dated to 225,000 B.P. (Cook et al. 1982). Bifacially worked points and scrapers were also found at this site.

Figure 10.4 *The postdeposition-ally deformed Arago skull from France shows the typical array of archaic characteristics. Note the very large brow ridges.* (The Institute of Human Paleontology, Paris. H. deLumley)

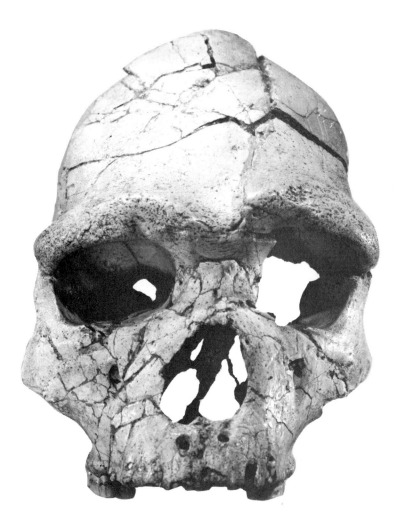

African and Asian Archaics

Outside Europe a growing number of specimens has been found that, based on cranial capacity, seems to fit in the archaic *Homo sapiens* category (Rightmire 1984; Brauer 1984). The Broken Hill or Kabwe site in Zambia produced an ancient skull with brow ridges larger than many of the *Homo erectus* specimens. Its cranial capacity (just under 1300 cc), however, and the roundness of the skull are similar to archaic *Homo sapiens*. Unfortunately, dating the fossil has been a problem; estimates ranging from 250,000 to 40,000 years have been suggested.

In East Africa, the Ndutu skull has a cranial capacity of over 1100 cc and is more rounded in profile than in *Homo erectus*. Also from East

Africa, the Bodo fossil probably fits into the archaic human category. Ndutu and Bodo are both likely to be more than 200,000 years old; the latter may be as much as 400,000 years old. Interestingly, it has recently been suggested that the Bodo cranium shows evidence of cannibalism, or at least defleshing for some unknown purpose. Paleoanthropologist Tim White (1986) identified 13 areas on the skull where scanning electron microphotographs show clusters of what appear to be cut marks made by stone tools. White is currently examining a series of other fossil hominid bones to assess evidence for similar behavior.

In Ngandong on the island of Java, so-called "Solo Man" included fragments of seven skulls whose estimated cranial capacities ranged from just over 1000 to just under 1300 cc (Wolpoff, Wu, and Thorne 1984). The skulls are thick boned, somewhat rounded, with sharp occiputs and large brow ridges. Though their cranial architecture is reminiscent of *Homo erectus,* the cranial capacities of these fossils place them closer to modern humans.

ARCHAIC HUMAN CULTURE

Having introduced you to a sample of archaic *Homo sapiens,* it must be admitted that, beyond knowing what they looked like, we are certain about little else. Several of the discoveries were accidental and made by nonscientists with no training in proper techniques of excavation. We have little in the way of habitation remains dating to the period 400,000 to 100,000 years ago that could enlighten us about their culture.

One aspect of their culture, however, is fairly well represented, and that is stone tool technology. It is clear that many aspects of earlier Middle Pleistocene technology continued among these hominids. They continued making Acheulian hand axes and using the larger flakes that resulted from the hand axe manufacturing process.

About 200,000 years ago, however, these archaic *Homo sapiens* were responsible for a great advance in toolmaking. They invented a technique of preparing stone cores according to a regular pattern that ensured a certain degree of consistency in the proportions of the stone flakes to be removed. In other words, they did not simply rely on accidentally well-shaped flakes to make tools but developed a technique for controlling the shape of the flakes. The new technique is called **Levallois** after the French suburb where it initially was recognized.

Before Levallois, stone tools were either core tools like the Oldowan choppers of *Homo habilis* or the Acheulian hand axes of *Homo erectus* or else were made on flakes that came off cores and happened to meet the needs of the tool maker; undoubtedly, a certain amount of luck was involved in this process. With Levallois, in contrast, we see a great deal of forethought in the preparation of the stone core to ensure that a number

Notice that the emphasis in this section shifts from natural and naturally occurring artifacts to the first evidence of the "great advance in toolmaking" brought about by the artificial shaping of stone. This working of stone for technological purposes, or *Levallois,* separates two major components of this chapter since it reflects a huge archaeological leap by archaic *Homo sapiens.*

Figure 10.5 *The Levallois technique has been described by experimental archaeologist Bradley (as quoted in Gamble 1986:19) as involving a series of steps including: (a) producing a margin along the edge of the core, (b) shaping the surface of the core, (c,d) preparing the surface to be struck (the striking platform), (e) removing the flake, and either returning to step b for additional flake removal or, if the core had become too small, discarding the core.* (after Bordaz 1970)

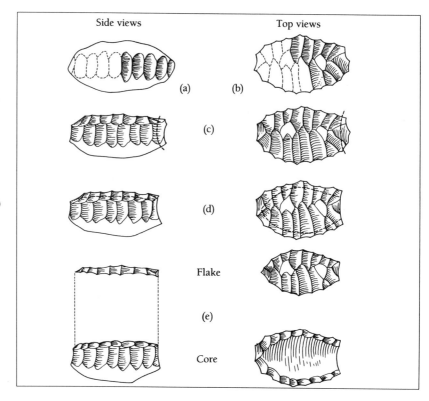

of flakes of the desired shape would ultimately be produced (Figure 10.5). The core reduction process involves more work in the beginning but results in better flake "blanks," which can then be made into specific cutting, scraping, or piercing tools. The technique was also more efficient, getting more sharp edge for the amount of stone started with.

In an archaeological experiment designed to analyze the Levallois technique, Bradley (1977, as cited in Gamble 1986) produced 20 Levallois cores on flint blocks. He found that he could usually strike off four or five similarly shaped flakes from a core before the core became too small to use. Preshaping the core was the key to controlling and standardizing the shape of the flakes. The Levallois technique was clearly a more complex way of producing stone flake blanks for tools, and also more effective and efficient, than any previously used method.

Beyond their stone tool technology, we see little else in the way of cultural innovation among the archaics. This is perplexing considering the increase in their brain size compared to *erectus*. But perhaps we can suggest something else about these earliest members of our species. In Europe they managed to survive during a period of great climate change, with the ending of an interglacial (isotope stage 7) and the beginning of a glacial (isotope stage 6). In all likelihood, glacial periods came on slowly relative to the length of a human generation. The ability of a *culture* to change over several generations, however, reflects a flexibility that is an identifying mark of humanity.

Archaic humans were faced with substantial changes in their environment. Animal species on which they relied became extinct or migrated. Plants on which they depended for food, fuel, and construction materials changed in response to the fluctuations in climate. Seasonal duration and intensity shifted, with longer, deeper winters and shorter, cooler springs and summers. Scheduling of subsistence activities would also have necessarily been shifted to meet the demands of nature's shift in seasons.

Whereas other species, biologically adapted to specific environments, were forced to move or die, archaic humans with their *cultural* adaptations were able to change their way of life. This flexibility allowed for their continued existence under new, drastically different circumstances.

THE NEANDERTALS: A SPECIAL CASE

Neandertal. The name itself has entered our language as an insult. People use the term to describe someone who is stupid, violent, brutish. Yet what we now know about so-called "Neandertal Man" and his culture shows that he bore little similarity to this caricature.

The fossil that gives us the name was discovered by workmen in the Neander Valley in the Rhine Province of Germany in 1856 (Figure 10.6). Only the top of the skull was recovered, but this fragment was enough to make the Neandertal fossil an enigma. It was a relatively large skull, with a probable cranial capacity even larger than the modern average, but flattened and with enormous, thick brow ridges. These characteristics gave the skull a primitive look. It was not at all what people in the nineteenth century expected a human ancestor to look like. People were just getting used to the general notion of biological evolution and its specific application to our own species. The Neandertal skull looked simply too primitive for most to accord it a place in the human lineage.

Those who accepted the notion of human evolution had expected the discovery of a "missing link," a creature part ape, part human, like Piltdown. As mentioned in Chapter 7, because what most clearly distinguishes us from other animals is our intelligence, the assumption was that the brain had evolved first. Those looking for a missing link expected it to be primitive from the neck down but to have an advanced, almost modern head. The Neandertal skull did not meet that expectation.

Though a few similar-looking skulls had already been discovered in Europe, these had not generated great interest. In comparison, the find in the Neander Valley produced a large amount of publicity and public attention (Kennedy 1975). Scientists pondered the significance of the

What follows is an interesting summary of a particularly violent collision between social assumptions and scientific discoveries. There was no shortage of such head-on clashes during the 19th and early 20th centuries (Darwin, Marx, Pasteur, Curie, Freud, Einstein), and this is representative of them at their best. One probably must return to the generations just after Copernicus to find such earth-shaking battles between sincerely held beliefs of this magnitude.

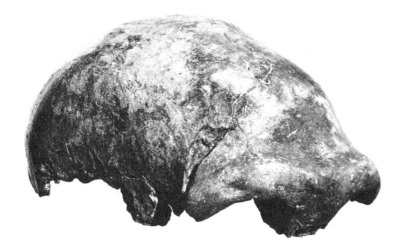

skull in terms of human evolution. Many decided that it could not have been a human ancestor but was, instead, a pathological oddity—a relatively recent, deformed individual. One well-known anatomist, Rudolf Virchow, even suggested that the large brow ridges were the result of blows to the head.

As more Neandertals (what all similar fossils were called in Europe) were found, however, it became impossible to ignore their evolutionary significance. Many specimens were discovered, especially in caves. Geological and paleontological evidence indicated that they inhabited Europe during the latter part of the Pleistocene, from sometime before about 100,000 to after 40,000 years ago. Nevertheless, even with its acceptance as an ancient, primitive variety of human, biases and preconceptions (and, as it turns out, misconceptions) colored scientific interpretations of Neandertal's place in the human family.

In 1913, the French anthropologist Marcellin Boule produced one of the most important and influential reconstructions of Neandertal Man (Boule and Vallois 1923; Figure 10.7). Unfortunately, his model was riddled with errors. Most of the mistakes stemmed from Boule's preconception that the Neandertals did not fit into the human evolutionary mainstream. Having already decided that they were very primitive, he exaggerated their differences from modern humans and ignored their points of similarity. His reconstruction had the Neandertals barely upright, with their heads so far forward they could hardly stand, shoulders hunched, and knees bent. He even gave the Neandertals an opposable big toe similar to that of the apes.

It has been thought that Boule's reconstruction of a stooped-over individual resulted from the fact that the skeleton he was working with,

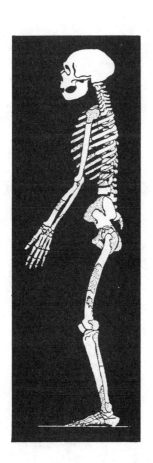 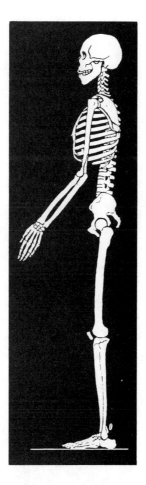

Figure 10.7 *Marcellin Boule's reconstruction of the skeleton of the so-called "Old Man" of La Chapelle-aux-Saints (left) compared to that of a modern human. Boule regarded the Neandertals as primitive and reconstructed this skeleton in a way that made it appear to be ape-like with bowed legs and head thrust forward.* (From *Fossil Men* by Marcellin Boule and Henri Vallois, Dryden Press (CBS Educational and Professional Publishing))

from the French cave of La Chapelle-aux-Saints, was actually an aged man crippled by arthritis. We now know that this was not the case and Boule did not make an accurate reconstruction that was based on a pathological specimen (Trinkaus 1985). Though the individual did suffer from degenerative bone disease, those areas of the skeleton most directly involved would not have affected his ability to walk to any great degree. Beyond this, Boule had two other perfectly normal Neandertal specimens (La Ferrassie 1 and 2) in his lab at the time and also used them in his reconstruction. It is much more likely that Boule simply reconstructed the "typical" Neandertal as apelike because that is how he expected it to look. After Boule, even reconstruction of facial characteristics emphasized the primitive; in most of these, Neandertal has a vacuous and rather stupid expression on his face — certainly not something indicated by the actual fossil skulls.

NEANDERTALS: NOT BRUTES, BUT NOT US

When we examine the evolution of the Neandertals, we cannot help also considering the evolution of our thinking about them. Since Boule's time, researchers have drastically revised their opinions of the Neandertals to the point where recently these archaics were considered to be quite advanced and, in fact, virtually modern in appearance and behavior (Figure 10.8 and see, for example, *The Neandertals* in the Time-Life series, *The Emergence of Man*). Their physical appearance was reassessed and reconstructions of the face became much more humanlike. Often,

Figure 10.8 *In the last few decades, reconstructions of Neandertal physical features and cultural practices have emphasized similarities to modern humans. Here, a painting by Rudolph Zallinger depicts Neandertals conducting a ceremony, much in the same manner of modern human hunters.* (Courtesy of R. F. Zallinger and Life Magazine)

merely choosing to depict the Neandertal face as shaven and clean did wonders for its appearance (see, for example, the cover of the October issue of *Science 81*). The opinion has shifted so far that until recently the Neandertals have been considered by just about all researchers to be an archaic subspecies of *Homo sapiens,* specifically, **Homo sapiens neander-thalensis**. In fact, by 1957, Straus and Cave could generate little disagreement when they said: "If he could be reincarnated and placed in a New York subway—provided that he were bathed, shaved, and dressed in modern clothing—it is doubtful whether he would attract any more attention than some of its other denizens" (1957:359).

We now know that just as Boule and other researchers at the turn of the century exaggerated alleged primitive features of the Neandertals, some more recent scientists and writers have exaggerated the degree of similarity these archaics show to modern humans. In fact, though they were by no means primitive brutes, the Neandertals did differ in some important ways from modern humans in their cranial as well as post-cranial characteristics.

Some of these differences have been ascribed to Neandertal physical adaptation to the cold climate maximum of the last glacial stage. For example, Neandertal bodily proportions, with relatively short distal limb segments (i.e., the lower arms and lower legs), were probably adaptive (Trinkaus 1983). Such a configuration is common in cold-adapted mammals because body heat loss increases with the surface area of the organism and limbs expose a proportionally large amount of surface to the elements. Among modern people, those living nearest the Arctic have proportionally the shortest lower limbs and those living nearest the equator have the longest.

On the other hand, there are some much more basic differences between the skeletons of the Neandertals and those of modern people. For example, Neandertal skulls are immediately recognizable as different from those of modern humans. Though their cranial capacity ranged from about 1300 cc to 1640 cc, well within the modern span, the front part of their skulls was rather flat, so the Neandertals had little or no forehead. The back of their skulls was broad and the sides were bulging. Their brow ridges were not straight, as in earlier *Homo sapiens,* but were rounded over each eye orbit. The ridges were thick, long, and protruding, though not as large as in some of the earlier archaics. The Neandertal face was large and prognathous, with broad cheeks, a wide nose, and widely set eyes. The mandible showed little development of a chin. So their heads and faces are clearly distinguishable from those of modern people (Figure 10.9).

Below the neck, Neandertals were also significantly different from modern humans. Certainly they were fully bipedal and we need not resurrect Boule's image. On close inspection, however, almost all of the bones of Neandertal show a robustness and enlargement of the areas of

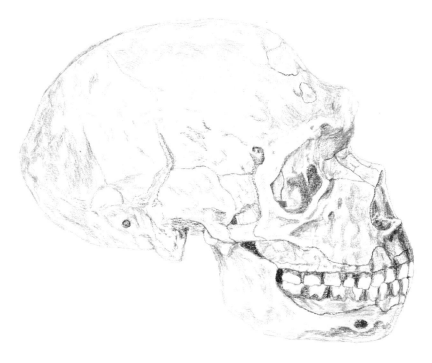

muscle attachment that are either at the limit or outside the range of modern human variation (Trinkaus 1983). Their ribs display a thickness and heaviness that reflect the great size and strength of shoulder and back muscles. Neandertal shoulder blades also reflect the great size of the attached muscles, and their proportions would have resulted in great arm strength. The bones of the arm itself also show larger areas of muscle attachment and even architectural features not seen in modern humans. Even in the hands, the Neandertal skeletons display evidence of strength rare or absent in modern humans; their thumbs and fingers would have been able to exert impressive grips. It seems likely that Neandertal stone toolmakers may have been able to perform actions that both earlier and subsequent hominids could not.

Neandertal leg bones exhibit the same pattern of size and strength. When Lovejoy and Trinkaus (1980) subjected three Neandertal tibia and a sample of modern American Indian and European tibia to a test of twisting and bending strength, they found the Neandertal bones to be twice as strong as the modern human examples. Neandertal stamina for walking must have been impressive.

Recent analysis of Neandertal pelves also shows significant differences from modern humans. Whereas the Neandertal pelvis is, in many respects, just like ours in those features related to locomotion, it is different in the length and configuration of the pubic bones, possibly indicating a larger birth canal. It has been estimated by Trinkaus (1983, 1984b), in an analysis of the preserved pubic portions of seven fossils, that the Neandertal pelvic outlet could have accommodated the birth of a baby's head of up to 25 percent greater volume than what can pass through the birth canals of modern human females (1984b:510). This suggests to Trinkaus that Neandertal gestation length might have been up to or even more than 12 months, implying that their newborns would have been more physically developed than ours. Compare a 3-month-old baby to one just born and you can see what an enormous difference that would have made.

There is some disagreement on this issue. Trinkaus was dealing with a small sample of fragmentary pelves. Recently an intact right side of a 60,000-year-old Neandertal pelvis was excavated in Kebara Cave on Mt. Carmel, Israel by Rak and Arensberg (1987). They identified this specimen as belonging to a male, a not unimportant fact when you consider the sexual dimorphism in pelvic outlet shape among modern humans. These researchers maintain that the pelvic outlet in this specimen was differently shaped but not larger than it is in modern humans. Rak and Arensberg feel that this difference, along with a difference in the configuration of the acetabulum, the bony socket in which the top of the femur rests, indicates differences not in gestation length but in how the Neandertals walked when compared to modern humans.

On a related issue, Dean, Stringer, and Bromage (1986) analyzed the cranial remains of a Neandertal child from Gibraltar. They concluded that the child died at the age of 3 and that his cranial development was advanced when compared to a modern human's of the same age. They suggest that Neandertal gestation was the same length as in modern humans. They believe instead that Neandertal children were probably more developed at birth than are modern humans and that Neandertals developed more quickly after birth.

If Trinkaus is correct, then there might have been some selective advantage to a shorter gestation period in the evolution of modern humans. He suggests that it might allow for a greater number of births during a female's reproductive years because less time is spent gestating each child. This might be advantageous, particularly when infant mortality is high. Also, being exposed to the world at an earlier stage in brain development, might have hastened neurological development, up to a point. Whatever the case, this possibility would mark a significant difference between Neandertals and modern humans.

If, on the other hand, Rak and Arensberg are correct, there was no significant difference between the Neandertal and modern human gestation length. Their analysis suggests, however, that there were significant differences between the Neandertals and modern humans in the biomechanics of their locomotion.

What follows is a classic scholarly debate regarding the interpretation of data. Using your notes, see if you can sketch out the two theories advanced regarding Neandertal gestation. Compare the two sides, and see if one seems more likely to be true than the other. Then, explain why, or why not. This basic puzzling out of problems is one origin of useful (and fun) scholarship in every field.

If Dean, Stringer, and Bromage are correct, then Neandertal gestation length was the same as ours, but Neandertal children were more fully developed at birth and matured more quickly than we do.

Whoever is right here (and they all might be, in part) we can conclude that the Neandertals and modern humans were, in some important ways, physically quite different from each other. Reconstruction of Neandertals as virtually identical to modern humans turns out to be almost as much a caricature as Boule's image of the primitive brute. As a result of the now recognized differences between the Neandertals and modern humans (and other extinct archaics), it has recently been suggested that the Neandertals do not belong in the species *sapiens* at all, but deserve the status of a separate species, **Homo neanderthalensis** (Gould 1988). The irony here is that this is what Boule suggested more than 70 years ago. Though he had the wrong reasons, he may have been right about Neandertal's place in human evolution after all.

THE NEANDERTAL FOSSILS

Hominids with Neandertallike skulls first begin to turn up in the archaeological record during isotope stages 5 and 6 (Figure 10.10; Cook et al. 1982). The Fontéchévade skull fragments, for example, are possible early Neandertals dating to this period. Found in a cave in France, they were recovered under a stalagmite layer and may be more than 100,000 years old (Gamble 1986). Though the remains are fragmentary, cranial capacity has been estimated at just under 1500 cc. The Neandertal fossil from La Chaise, France has been associated with a thermoluminescence date of 126,000 B.P. (Cook et al. 1982). Another isotope stage 6 Neandertallike hominid from France comes from Biache Saint-Vaast.

The Krapina finds in Yugoslavia consist of the fragmentary remains of at least 45 and as many as 65 individuals (Trinkaus and Thompson 1987). Though very broken up, they appear to have large brow ridges and fairly rugged occiputs; cranial capacity estimates range from 1200 cc to 1450 cc. They appear to reflect an isotope stage 5 date.

A number of rather more modern-looking specimens from Africa exhibiting a mixture of Neandertallike and modern traits probably date to the early part of isotope stage 5 (Rightmire 1984; Brauer 1984). Among these we can include the fossils from Jebel Irhoud in Morocco (though the dating is uncertain), Florisbad in southern Africa, and Ngaloba from Tanzania.

Also in Africa, two skulls found about a kilometer apart near the Omo River in Ethiopia are important. The layer in which the Omo 1 skull was recovered has been radiometrically dated to about 130,000 B.P. Omo 2

Combe Grenal
Roc de Marsal
Peche de l'Aze
La Ferrassie
La Chapelle-aux-Saints
Fontechévade
La Chaise
Le Moustier
La Quina
Regourdu

ASIA

Arctic Ocean

Spy   Neandertal
Biache St. Vaast
Saccopastore
Krapina
Gibraltar
Monte Circeo
Amud
Tabun
Shanidar
Jebel Irhoud
Haua Fteah
Teshik Tash

Pacific Ocean

AFRICA

Omo

Ngaloba

Atlantic Ocean

Indian Ocean

AUSTRALIA

Florisbad
Saldanha

Figure 10.10 *Neandertal fossil localities. This distribution shows quite clearly that the Neandertals were essentially a European-Southwest Asian population.*

was found some distance away and may be from the same stratigraphic level, but it cannot be dated with certainty. The Omo skulls have cranial capacities of about 1400 cc but are quite different in appearance. Omo 2 exhibits a mixture of primitive and modern characteristics and, in fact, seems to be intermediate between Neandertal and modern. Omo 1 is surprisingly modern looking and is discussed in Chapter 11.

It was isotope stage 4, however, in Europe and Southwest Asia that witnessed an apparent flowering of Neandertal population and culture (Trinkaus 1986). Neandertal sites dating to between 80,000 and 40,000 years ago are abundant in these areas. Sites include Le Moustier, La Chapelle-aux-Saints, La Qunia, Regourdu, La Ferrassie, Pech de l'Aze, Roc de Marsal, and Combe Grenal, all in France; Monte Circeo and

Figure 10.11 *A Neandertal skull from La Ferrassie, France, exhibits many of the typical Neandertal features. The skull also shows the degree of variation among Neandertals since it is relatively rounded, with a high forehead.* (Courtesy Museum of Man, Paris)

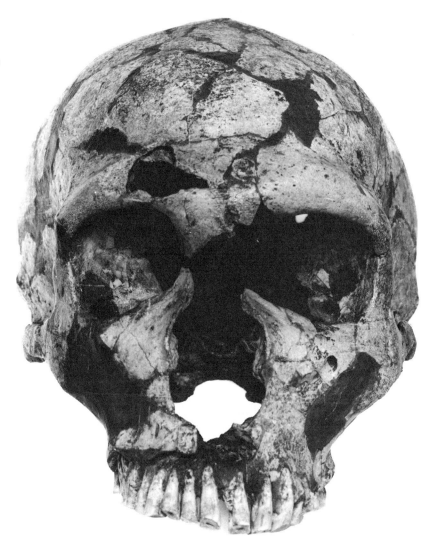

Saccopastore in Italy; Spy in Belgium; Gibraltar on the southern tip of the Iberian Peninsula; and Neandertal in Germany (Figure 10.11). Outside Europe, examples of fossils similar to the European or "Classic" Neandertals have been recovered in: Shanidar in Iraq; Teshik-Tash in the Soviet Union; Haua Fteah in Libya; Saldanha in southern Africa; and Amud and Tabun in Israel (Figure 10.12). An additional group of even more modern-looking fossils that still exhibit some Neandertal traits is known from the Middle East. This last group will be discussed in more detail in Chapter 11.

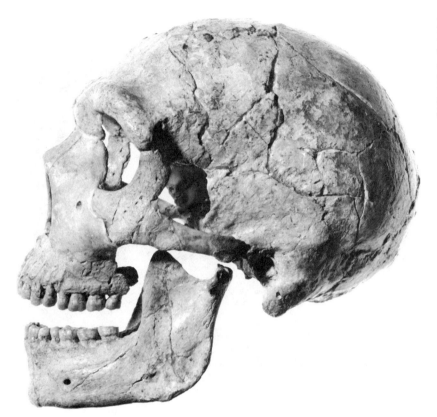

Figure 10.12 *The Amud Neandertal cranium from Israel is quite similar to those from Europe, indicating, at least in part, the geographic range of this variety of archaic* Homo sapiens. (Department of Antiquities and Museums, Jerusalem)

NEANDERTAL CULTURE

Just as our reconstruction of the physical appearance of the Neandertals has drastically changed, so too has their behavior been rehabilitated. Here again we see a pattern of the initial verdict of brutishness and savagery replaced by the other extreme, seeing them as kind and gentle souls. Neither of these views accurately describes Neandertal behavior.

The European Neandertals were certainly highly intelligent and adaptive hominids who faced the extreme climate of a glacial maximum. During such extended cold periods, large portions of the forested land of central Europe were transformed into arcticlike tundra — virtually treeless expanses covered by ground-hugging bushes, mosses, and lichens (Figure 10.13). Those trees that survived in this climate were all cold-loving conifers, grouped in bunches, few and far between. Into this environment moved great numbers of woolly rhinoceros and mammoth, bison, horse, reindeer, and musk ox (Kurtén 1968).

Figure 10.13 *Modern Alaskan tundra resembles parts of Europe as they appeared during glacial stages of the Pleistocene.* (M. Banks)

The following passage on technological development depends on, and expands upon, the information introduced on page 325. A note referring to the earlier section is very useful in such cases because connections like these are easily forgotten, particularly when you are working with several sources and texts.

(If you are putting your notes on a computer disk, such

The Neandertals of glacial Europe flourished in this seemingly forbidding climate. They became supremely adapted to life on the windswept tundra, scavenging and perhaps hunting large game animals, collecting what vegetable foods they could in season, and controlling fire. Though these Neandertals may have possessed some physical adaption to the cold, it was truly their culture that enabled them to survive in the freezing world of Europe during the last glacial period.

Tool Technology

The Neandertals continued the Levallois technique of flake removal observed in earlier archaics and elaborated on it. The stone tool tradition of the Neandertals, called **Mousterian** after the French site of Le Moustier, is technically characterized as a retouched flake technology. This means that the Neandertals removed flakes from cores that they then proceeded to sharpen and/or shape by precise additional flaking, usually on a single face or side of the flake, but occasionally on both faces. Using this method, the Neandertals produced cutting, scraping, and piercing tools (Figure 10.14). They also continued the tradition of making bifacially flaked hand axes in some areas.

The Mousterian industry exhibits a much greater level of variation than did the earlier Acheulian. One of Europe's preeminent prehistorians, François Bordes, identified 63 tool types and 21 hand axe forms in a detailed analysis of the Mousterian (Bordes 1972). He notes that these different tool categories do not all co-occur at all sites. Instead, Bordes maintains that at least five different groupings of the 63 categories can be recognized in Europe. He interprets these as representing the toolmaking traditions of five and possibly more distinct Mousterian cultures who "co-existed in the same territory but influenced each other very little" (1972:146).

A contrasting view of this situation has been offered by Lewis and Sally Binford (Binford and Binford 1966; S. Binford 1968). Using a statistical approach called factor analysis, they found that there were indeed five discernable groupings of the 63 artifact types Bordes defined, but that these could be explained on functional grounds. They suggest that the groupings do not reflect the different traditions of coexisting, noninteracting Mousterian people. Instead, they believe that these clusters reflect different tool kits used for different functions like hunting, bone and antler tool manufacture, and plant processing, by the same people in different places.

Archaeologist Harold Dibble has suggested a third possibility for one of the tool categories (1987): that different types of scraping tools defined by Bordes reflect different stages in the use histories of these tools. According to Dibble, single-edged, double-edged, and converging-edged scrapers do not reflect different styles of separate groups of people, nor do

related passages are very handy if placed in their own file as you come across them in different places or works.)

Figure 10.14 *Unifacially retouched Mousterian flint flakes from sites in France.*

they represent different functions. He proposes that when scrapers with a single edge got dull, a second edge was sharpened; as more edge was sharpened, the edges converged.

Subsistence

The precise meaning of the different Mousterian tool types is still a point of contention among European prehistorians. In any event, with such tools the Neandertals developed a way of life dependent on the animals that flourished in Europe during the height of the final glacial stage, including reindeer, ibex, horse, woolly rhinoceros, bison, bear, and elk.

There is no question that Neandertal existence was largely dependent upon animal resources; Europe during glacial maxima offered little else. But were the Neandertals great hunters, as is sometimes suggested? Lewis Binford examined the faunal assemblages of a number of Neandertal sites and concluded that there is little evidence to support such a claim.

Binford conducted an ethnoarchaeological study among the Nunamiut Eskimo of Alaska, focusing on their hunting, butchering, and disposal practices (1978). He compared his findings among these living people with archaeological evidence from the French Mousterian site of Combe Grenal (Binford 1981). Binford found a patterned distribution of cut marks on the bones from France that were similar in some ways to those he saw in the ethnographic sample. For example, characteristic marks on aurochs (wild ox), horse, and reindeer mandibles from Combe Grenal matched those the Nunamiut made on caribou jaws in order to extract the animals' tongues. There were also cut marks on the joints of the long bones found at Combe Grenal, indicating butchering. Cut marks Binford noticed on the antler bases of the Combe Grenal reindeer skulls matched those the Nunamiut made on young caribou when they were skinning the animals for winter clothing.

Cut marks that would reflect butchery of the choice cuts of meat were not abundant, however. It may be that the cut marks on mandible and leg bones represent scavenging practices, not hunting behavior. In this reconstruction, cut marks are abundant at Neandertal sites on mandibles and legs, because that is where the meat was left on animal carcasses after the carnivores were through with them.

That the Neandertals were capable of producing effective tools and of surviving in a rigorous climate is undeniable and reflects their great intelligence and ability. It has also been suggested that in other spheres of behavior they were indistinguishable from modern human beings. Specifically, the Neandertals have been characterized as being altruistic to their comrades, as having engaged in burial ceremonialism, and of having practiced the first religion. Let us consider these cultural activities in turn.

Altruism: Were the Neandertals Their Brothers' Keepers?

Commonly, the fossil of the "Old Man of La Chapelle-aux-Saints" is cited as evidence that the Neandertals possessed the human quality of altruism by caring for their sick and aged (Strauss and Cave 1957; Constable et al. 1973).

The remains in question are said to be those of an old man who probably suffered from arthritis. This would imply that he could not have contributed much to the subsistence of the group — he was long past the point where he could have hunted or even gathered much in the way of food. He also was missing most of his teeth and, it is often said, may even have needed some help chewing.

A recent reexamination of the "Old Man" has shown that this was not the case (Tappen 1985). In fact, much of the presumed tooth loss in this individual occurred after death, not before. Toward the end of his life, he still had five matching upper and five lower teeth on the left side; he also might have had teeth on the upper right. The only teeth certainly missing were those on the right side of the mandible, where a tumorous growth destroyed the bone, leading to tooth loss. But even this event probably occurred close to the end of this individual's life. In all likelihood, the "Old Man" was perfectly capable of chewing his own food.

Beyond this, we are uncertain how bad his arthritis really was. As stated before, Trinkaus and Thompson (1987) maintain that the locations of the disease were not those that would have significantly affected locomotion. Characterizing this person as a helpless cripple who survived to old age only because of the selfless assistance of his comrades is also wrong.

Finally, it is ironic to note that the so-called "Old Man" who, if not a toothless cripple, at least is evidence for care and nurturing of the elderly, was probably less than 40 when he died (Trinkaus and Thompson 1987), based on tooth wear and cranial suture closure. Trinkaus and Thompson have used this misinterpretation to approach the entire question of Neandertal longevity. Does the evidence support the scenario of altruistic Neandertals caring for the aged? Is the image of a society very much like our own, where the elderly are nurtured and where they can share the knowledge of their experience with the group, supported by the Neandertal data? Trinkaus and Thompson say no.

In most animal species, they point out, survival beyond the years of reproduction is rare. From an evolutionary perspective, there is little selective pressure for survival beyond the reproductive years for noncultural animals. In humans with our cultural adaptations, however, there are advantages to having older individuals survive. Their greater knowledge, expertise, and experience can greatly improve the chances of group survival and more than make up for whatever burden they might impose if they become physically hampered.

Note well, as the following section demonstrates, that what people *wish* to see is constantly being superimposed on what they *actually* see. Scientists are just like everybody else in this respect, regardless of their time and place, as science writer Stephen Jay Gould has pointed out in so many of his wonderful essays (excellent reading practices, by the way). This pattern of subjective interpretation, at least in initial discoveries, would seem to be the rule rather than the exception and seems highly likely to continue.

It is therefore significant that in a sample of 246 individual Neandertals, Trinkaus and Thompson found that nearly 40 percent died before reaching adulthood (1987:126). Of the 152 adult Neandertals in the sample, only 8.6 percent show a skeletal age at death of 40 years or more (1987:127). For the Neandertals, death in their twenties was common; in their thirties, it was the rule.

So the case for Neandertal care and nurturing of the old as in modern human societies is simply not supported by the data. The image of altruistic Neandertals is not possible to prove.

Burial Ceremonialism

The reconstructed scenes are certainly evocative: At Teshik-Tash, in Soviet Asia, a young Neandertal boy, dead in the flower of his youth, was carefully laid out in a shallow grave. Around the grave were placed six pairs of Siberian mountain goat horns as a memorial for the dead child (Movius 1953). At La Chapelle-aux-Saints in France, the "Old Man" had been placed in a shallow trench, surrounded by tools, and even accompanied by a bison leg—perhaps as food thought necessary for use in the afterlife (Bouyssonie 1908). In the Shanidar cave in Iraq, pollen analysis has been used to construct a scenario of a recently deceased young man, placed on a bed of pine boughs and then covered with wild flowers: bachelor's buttons, hollyhock, and grape hyacinth (Solecki 1971). At La Ferrassie in France, six Neandertal burials occur together. A man, a woman, two children, and two infants had been placed in trenches. Five were laid out east to west. The woman was placed in the fetal position (Figure 10.15); the man had a flat stone slab placed over his chest (Heim 1968).

It seems undeniable that Neandertals buried their dead. But detailed scenarios are often difficult to assess and the precise meaning of the burials is even harder to evaluate. Many of the burials were excavated in the late nineteenth and early twentieth centuries. Archaeological methodology was not as advanced as it is today, much information was lost, and the taphonomy of the many of the claimed burial sites is impossible to resolve.

Was the bison leg at La Chapelle-aux-Saints intended to be food for the next life, or were the Neandertal and bison bones merely dragged into the cave by carnivores? Is the site at Teshik-Tash evidence of Neandertal ceremonialism or simply carnivore activity? (Actually, only the skull lay within the circle of goat horns; the rest of the bones were dispersed.) Were the flowers at Shanidar intended as symbols of life, were they used for their medicinal qualities, or is the pollen intrusive, brought in later by rodents? To some, the meaning of these Neandertal "burials" is clear. They see in them evidence of the origins of belief in an afterlife. That may well be, but the specific meaning is lost to us.

Figure 10.15 *An undisputed Neandertal burial from La Ferrassie, France. Here, the individual was interred in the fetal position with knees drawn up to the chest.* (Museum of Man, Paris, M. Lucas, photographer)

Anthropologist Frank Harrold (1980) has analyzed a sample of pre-sumed Neandertal interments and found 36 where the evidence strongly indicated intentional burial. In these, there was clear evidence of the digging of a grave, special positioning of the body (as in, for example, a fetal position), and/or the presence of indisputable grave offerings. These burials had ages of between 75,000 and 35,000 years. When they were compared to 96 burials of anatomically modern humans dating from 35,000 to 10,000 B.P., some obvious differences became apparent. In those cases where the data could be used, almost 90 percent of the burials of modern humans contained grave goods, including such objects as stone and bone artifacts, mollusc shells, coloring materials, and items of personal adornment such as necklaces (1980:205). On the other hand, only about 40 percent of the Neandertal burials contained grave goods, and these were restricted to objects like stone tools and animal bones.

It seems that the Neandertals indeed buried their dead, though such burials are generally not as elaborate as those of later periods involving anatomically modern humans. Whether Neandertal burials were in-tended to assure the deceased the necessities for life in the hereafter or were simply part of ceremonies to comfort his or her companions left behind is impossible to determine, though ultimately, perhaps, not so important. Whatever their actual intent, these burials show that the Neandertals treated the dead and death in a ceremonial way, and that is a uniquely human trait. They were conscious of their own mortality, recog-nized the enormity of that fact, and treated death in a way that reflected that recognition.

Cave Bears

Neandertals are commonly credited with the worship of a now extinct species of bear that inhabited the caves of Europe (see Figure 10.8). A closer look at the data, however, does not support the dramatic picture of a prehistoric cave bear "cult."

We know that the European Neandertals used caves. We also know that they competed for such natural shelters with bears that were up to 50 percent larger than the largest living bears, the Alaskan Kodiak. When a Kodiak stands on its back legs, it can be as much as 9 feet tall. When a cave bear stood up, it could surpass 12 feet. Needless to say, people have been fascinated by the suggestion that Neandertals killed such enormous animals and then paid special attention to the remains.

At a cave in Drachenloch, Switzerland, Neandertals are alleged to have made chests of stones more than three feet on a side. Inside these chests were several cave bear skulls. Deeper in the cave six more cave bear skulls had been placed in niches in the cave wall. Other caves supposedly show similar treatment of cave bear remains. For example, Regourdu in

France has 20 cached skulls housed in a cubicle topped with an enormous stone slab.

Did Neandertals worship the cave bears? Did they collect their skulls as a part of that worship? Did the Neandertal hunters collect the heads of slain bears and keep them in stone chests much in the way modern trophy hunters collect the heads of animals they have killed and then mount them on their walls? These are all thought-provoking possibilities, but they are unsupported by the data.

Anthropologists Philip Chase and Harold Dibble (1987) have reassessed Neandertal ceremonialism, pointing out that the excavations at Drachenloch and Regourdu were not as carefully conducted as we would have hoped. When original field notes were examined, their descriptions did not always correspond to later, far more dramatic reconstructions. For example, the so-called stone chests at Drachenloch were far less well defined than most people realize; they appear instead to be natural clusters of rock. Beyond this, no butchering marks have been found on the bear bones. One would expect cut marks of some kind if Neandertals had really killed the animals and then removed the bears' heads. The stone slab covering the "cubicle" at Regourdu weighs 850 kg and was far more likely the result of a cave-in than any intentional construction by Neandertals or anyone else.

As our understanding of cave taphonomy has become more sophisticated, we have come to recognize that there are many natural processes by which the specific bones of animals may accumulate. It seems that, at least at present, the accumulation of cave bear bones in European caves was the result of natural processes. They do not show that Neandertals worshipped cave bears or practiced a cave bear "cult."

THE PLACE OF THE ARCHAICS

We ended Chapter 9 by saying that the appearance of archaic *Homo sapiens* may have been a punctuational event, a sudden surge in evolution. In this chapter we have shown that the data present a complicated picture. Apart from their brain size, the archaics, including the Neandertals, are a varied lot indeed. Some of the crania look highly advanced in the sense that they are more similar to the modern form than to *Homo erectus*. Others possess a mosaic of traits, some primitive, some modern. The most recent of the archaics and the one about which we possess the most information, the Neandertals, have been shown here to differ in some very significant ways from modern humans.

The false abstraction of evolutionary ladders has not helped our understanding of the place in the human lineage of the Neandertals and the other archaic *Homo sapiens*. The "ladder" model of development causes us to interpret fossil species as distinct points on a directional evolutionary continuum. But the archaics do not fit neatly on any particular rung of our evolutionary ladder.

The Neandertals, for example, though more recent than the other specimens of archaic *Homo sapiens* discussed in this chapter, appear more primitive in some cranial characteristics, particularly in the size of the face and brow ridges. Their brain size, on the other hand, indicates a great degree of modernity — yet again, it fits no neat continuum because they are even larger than some modern humans.

The Neandertals and most of the other archaics should be viewed not as rungs on a ladder but as a twig on the human evolutionary bush, parallel to our own. The Neandertals appear more significant than they actually are to human evolution in general because we have the bones of so many of them. But they are so abundant in the archaeological record simply because they lived in caves and buried their dead.

Stringer and colleagues (1979) proposed a series of "grades" of archaic humans, from those most like *Homo erectus* to those possessing intermediate appearance to the most modern looking. Brauer (1984) has added to, and modified, this list of grades (Table 10.1). Importantly, the grades do not represent the gradual evolution of archaic *Homo sapiens* after the punctuation that defined them. Though our dating of individual fossils is not as firm as we would like it, it seems clear that some of the specimens in different grades were contemporaries and equally that some of the more modern-looking ones are actually older than some of the less modern. It remains for us to discuss how one of these populations of archaic *Homo sapiens* gave rise to modern humanity (Grade 4).

Table 10.1 *The Evolutionary Grades of* Homo sapiens.

Grade 1:	Arago, Bilzingsleben, Petralona, Vértesszöllös, Bodo, Broken Hill/Kabwe, Ndutu
Grade 1/2:	Steinheim, Swanscombe, Omo 2, Laetoli 18, Florisbad
Grade 2:	Biache-St-Vaast, La Chaise, Ehringsdorf, Fotechévade, Saccopastore
Grade 3:	Jebel Irhoud, Haua Fteah, Neandertal, La-Chapelle-aux-Saints, Monte Circeo, La Ferrassie, Krapina
Grade 3/4:	Amud, Tabun
Grade 4:	Omo 1, Klasies River Mouth, Border Cave, Cro-Magnon, Jebel Qafzeh, Skhul

The different grades have no chronological implications and merely convey similarities and differences in various fossils. (Stringer et al. 1979; Brauer 1984; Gamble 1986)

FOR MORE INFORMATION

For capsule descriptions of many of the fossils discussed in this chapter, see Clark Spencer Larsen and Robert M. Matter's *Human Origins: The Fossil Record* and, especially, Michael H. Day's *Guide to Fossil Man*. Kenneth A. R. Kennedy's *Neanderthal Man* provides an excellent discussion of the history of scientific thought on the Neandertals. In the Time-Life *Emergence of Man* series, the volume *The Neanderthals* has some terrific artwork reconstructing the environment of glacial Europe but presents a rather outdated view of the archaics. The October 1981 issue of *Science 81* has a cover story (Boyce Rensberger, "New Face for the Neandertals") on our current understanding of the place of the Neandertals in human evolution.

■ READING COMPREHENSION AND DISCUSSION QUESTIONS

1. Briefly but thoroughly, identify the key variations among the Steinheim, Swanscombe, and Petralona finds, and compare these with the other European, African, and Asian *Homo sapiens* archaics.

2. Consider the differing views of Bordes, the Binfords, and Dibble concerning Neandertal tool technology. Which interpretation strikes you as the most likely explanation of the flake technology artifacts? Why does this view seem more probable to you than the other two?

3. Do you think that the ethnoarchaeological study conducted by Lewis Binford among the Nunamiut Eskimo of Alaska has relevance to, or sheds any light on, hunting and butchery practices at the early Combe Grenal site? Why, or why not?

4. Theories of Neandertal altruism and spiritual practices involving the cult of the cave bear have been largely dismissed because the archaeological record simply doesn't seem to verify them. However, even the most steely-eyed interpreter sees evidence of ritual ceremonial burial among the Neandertal, and none doubt that Neandertal's brain was several hops away from the other primates' standard models. What do these observations suggest to you regarding the species' potential for spiritual thought? When does such thought begin, what sort of thinking ability does it require, and why does it separate us from other organisms?

CHAPTER 12

■ *Music*

■ *"The Age of the 'isms'*
(1900–1940)," from Encore!
A Guide to Enjoying Music
by Jack Boyd

Jack Boyd's chapter intersperses three kinds of material simultaneously: a general historical narrative; reproductions of musical scores,
with analysis ("Listening Guides"); and biographical sketches of influential musicians. Such a style presents challenges to the reader, but the
rewards are also great.

Trying to map the whole chapter at once would be a daunting enterprise, so, whether mapping or highlighting, try to *group* similar material: historical with historical, musical with musical, biographical with
biographical. What results should be an extremely useful 3-track set of
notes that would make studying for an exam very easy (although the
text certainly does not give that impression at first glance). Charting the
biographies, for example, is relatively simple: Ravel, Schoenberg, Stravinsky, and so on. Similarly, the musical examples can be highlighted
("Pavane for a Dead Princess," "Mondestrunken," and so forth), as can
the various historical movements and schools, providing in each case a
sharply defined "skeleton" for review or use in one's own work.

THE AGE OF THE "ISMS" (1900–1940)

12

A Burst of Musical Languages

he twentieth century is your century. No matter how young or old you are, it is the century that formed you. It began as the age of the airplane and the telephone — incomprehensible technological marvels to the people of that time. Electricity was a new, fearful force, but the idea of traveling a mile a minute by car, flying a mile up in the air, or speaking across the ocean simply boggled people's minds. To be honest to their time, the art forms had to represent both the technological advances and the fears of their new users.

The twentieth century is also the era when the stream of Western musical tradition divides, and divides again. For three centuries, the basic sound in the music of all the Western countries came very close to matching the same ideal. Though each country might emphasize a different aspect, the fundamental language of music was the same. It translated easily and traveled well. Suddenly, however, shortly after the turn of the century, we find several musical vocabularies beginning an uneasy coexistence, like small, angry countries, each with a different language.

Thus, the twentieth century is the age of the *isms* — Impressionism continues as Post-Impressionism, Expressionism arises, Primitivism springs up briefly, and Futurism and Neoclassicism attract an audience that is still with us. Several other *isms* flourish for a time, then drop back into the history books. One important point to remember: These new movements in music did not appear end to end — that is, Impressionism did not die just as Expressionism was

Paul Cézanne began his career as an enthusiastic Romantic artist. He turned to a disciplined investigation of form and color, where brush techniques were of paramount importance, much as the sounds and colors of individual instruments fascinated the Impressionist composers. The distinctive shape of Mont Sainte-Victoire became the almost obsessive subject of a series of paintings. Mont Sainte-Victoire *(1902–1904), although blocky and forbidding, is a seething sea of movement and energy, much like compositions such as Debussy's* La Mer *(The Sea) or* Jeux *(Games). (See Color Plate 14.)*

At this point it is probably a good idea to begin three "parallel" sets of notes for the movements, biographies, and listening guides. A simple method of doing this is to indicate each with a symbol of abbreviation (MOV-BIO-LG for example) at the margin or center of the page on which you are recording the notes. This way all notes under a heading can be studied sequentially and quickly scanned for references.

If you prefer note cards, abbreviations or simple "corner"

appearing, and Expressionism did not fade to be totally replaced by Primitivism. Rather, each style appeared gradually as another was beginning to wane, overlapping one another, sometimes unexpectedly.

IMPRESSIONISM REVISITED

Late in the nineteenth century the French, with their characteristic desire for elegance and diversion in the arts, threw out the suffocating German artistic profundity (they called the Germans "the *Profondateurs*"). As we saw in Chapter 11, many French composers replaced the German sounds with Impressionism, a pleasing but transitory style without the staying power of a more dynamic music. This is not to say that Impressionism was a useless sound or that it has never been heard from since its heyday. Rather, it was a style that lived its life and then faded, to be used sparingly by later composers for certain effects or flavor, much like a spice in a casserole.

Movements in music generally lag some years behind parallel movements in the visual arts. Impressionism in painting began, as we saw, with the famous Paris Exhibition of 1874, but musical Impressionism came at least a decade later. For convenience, we will give the dates of 1885–1915 for Impressionism in music, or about fifteen years before and after the turn of the century. Though this is a simplistic framework and many exceptions can be found, nonetheless for the bulk of Impressionistic music this was the time, France was the place, and Debussy was the top—but by no means the only—composer.

Frederick Delius and Charles Griffes, the "Foreign" Impressionists

Frederick Delius (1862–1934), an Englishman of German parents, studied in Leipzig, then spent several years in both Florida and France. His harmonies and melodies were extremely personal and fall into no easy categorization. Delius's motivating force was a unique view of French Impressionism mixed with shifting Wagnerian harmonies. His melodies were fragmentary but beguiling, giving his works the appearance of mosaics. Many of Delius's compositions use descriptive titles such as *On Hearing the First Cuckoo in Spring* or *Summer Nights on the River.* American listeners might like his *Appalachia,* "Variations on an old slave song with final chorus."

The American Charles Tomlinson Griffes (1884–1920) also brought a Germanic education to his strikingly personal style. After studying four years in Berlin, Griffes returned to New York State to teach music at a boy's school. Despite his training in Berlin, he was fascinated by the exotic sounds of both the new French style and the mystical compositions of the Russian Alexander Skryabin. Griffes's best-known instrumental works are two tone poems, *The White Peacock* and *The Pleasure Dome of Kubla Khan,* and a *Poeme* for flute and orchestra. Griffes also produced a set of atmospheric songs for voice and piano or orchestra titled *Three Poems of Fiona MacLeod,* the best of the three being "The Lament of Ian the Proud." In this song Griffes shows himself at the peak of his artistic power. The text—which is actually by the poet and biographer William Sharp but written under a pseudonym—imitates the style of an ancient Celtic epic recounting the inner thoughts of an old Celtic warrior who hears songs others do not hear.

numbers can tell you which set is which or you can use cards of different colors.

On a computer, of course, simply dump the notes in appropriately titled files and print the files for study.

Without any such organizing system, however, even the best reader will become quickly confused when reviewing notes from this chapter.

LISTENING GUIDE

CHARLES T. GRIFFES • "THE LAMENT OF IAN THE PROUD," FROM *THREE POEMS OF FIONA MACLEOD* (orchestral version) (1918)

Introduction — Oboe paraphrases a storyteller's voice, over a dronelike orchestral murmuring.

(continued)

Recording the whole text of this and the following songs isn't practical, although you should note all of the titles and composers. But recording an image or two in order to help you recall each lyric is probably a good idea. An image such as "A whirling leaf about the grey hair/of me/who am weary and blind" could prove very useful on an exam or in a paper.

A

What is this crying that I hear in the wind!
Is it the old sorrow and the old grief
Or is it a new thing coming,
A whirling leaf about the grey hair
of me
who am weary and blind?

Upward-reaching lament. Oboe enters briefly.

B

I know not what it is,
but on the moor above the shore
There is a stone
which the purple nets of heather bind,
And thereon is writ: she will return
no more,

Agitation at remembered visions.

Slower, introspective.

A'

O blown whirling leaf, and the old grief
And wind crying to me who am old
and blind!

The oboe returns to introduce explosive anger, followed by quiet resignation.

Conclusion

The work ends with the oboe/storyteller returning over the orchestral drone.

Maurice Ravel, the French Craftsman

Maurice Ravel, an enigmatic, unpredictable, and thoroughly enjoyable French composer, is living proof that it is possible to be too inventive. Three times he lost the *Prix de Rome* because his progressive tendencies irritated the traditionalists on the panel of judges. On his fourth try for the prize, he was eliminated in the preliminaries. Fifteen years later, he refused to accept the *Légion d'Honneur* because of the earlier rebuffs.

Ravel tried every genre except religious music, writing piano works, songs, chamber music, gemlike choral pieces, ballets, orchestral works, concertos, and two small operas. In all his works Ravel was a precise craftsman, prompting Stravinsky to give him the nickname "Swiss watchmaker." Some of this precision came from his study of and love for the harpsichord works of French Baroque composers. His immersion in the works of this period eventually led him away from the imprecise pastels of Impressionism toward a more witty, ironic style based on traditional forms.

In 1899, Ravel composed a simple and placid rondo for piano titled *Pavane pour une Infante défunte* (Pavane for a Dead Princess). Over a decade later, he orchestrated the gentle, ethereal work. The princess of the title was imaginary, but the piece recalls the royal Spanish custom of performing a stately, solemn dance during a time of mourning. Despite this fanciful explanation, Ravel is said to have chosen the French title because he liked the sounds of the words themselves.

Maurice Ravel (1875–1937) experimented in a wide variety of styles. His earlier piano works such as *Jeux d'eau* and *Miroirs* are in the tradition of Liszt's spectacular keyboard flourishes. The three songs in *Scheherezade* (not to be confused with the similarly named tone poem by Rimsky-Korsakov) were Impressionistic. The suite for piano *Le Tombeau de Couperin,* an homage to the eighteenth-century French composer, was much more Neoclassical in its forms and approach.

Of Ravel's orchestral works, *Boléro* leads the pack. This 1928 set of variations produces a constant crescendo of volume and color. Other favorites are *La Mère l'Oye* (Mother Goose Suite, for piano duet, later orchestrated) and *Rapsodie espagnole*. Ravel's *String Quartet* of 1903 is often paired with Debussy's quartet. His jazz-inspired *Concerto for Left Hand* was written for Paul Wittgenstein, the Austrian pianist who lost his right arm in World War I.

MAURICE RAVEL

 ISTENING GUIDE   & CD

MAURICE RAVEL · *PAVANE FOR A DEAD PRINCESS*
(orchestral version) (1899)

A   Horn over *pizzicato* (plucked) strings. Two phrases divided by a harp glissando.

B   Two phrases, the first featuring the woodwinds, the second muted strings.

A   Similar to the first **A** section, with woodwinds playing the melody.

C   In minor, with various instruments on an upward-reaching melody.

A   Similar to the second **A** section, with added harp accents.

Ravel is often thrown into the general pile of Impressionistic composers, but his styles were far too wide ranging for such simplistic pigeonholing. Although he was a child of the twentieth century, Ravel never strayed far from traditional harmonies and forms. His inspirations were often poetic, his vision always personal.

THE FIST-WAVING EXPRESSIONISTS

If at first you don't succeed, yell louder. This has become the bumper sticker for many twentieth-century artists. The **Expressionists** concerned themselves with presenting reality in a distorted form to communicate their inner visions of a world gone mad. The general time frame of the Expressionists is 1905–1925, although this description, as with most others, has many exceptions. It began, predictably, with the painters—and a new wish to express the inexpressible. Sigmund Freud's investigations into the unconscious and nightmares laid a groundwork for artists of all stripes to explore the inner universe. The very ruthlessness of Freud's hypotheses appealed to artists fed up with both the

Georges Rouault mirrored both the passion and morbid quality of the Expressionist fervor in his painting Head of Christ *(1905) (See Color Plate 15) and the more mature* The Old King *(1916–1937) here, whose brilliant colors and black-edged details remind us of Gothic church windows. Expressionistic composers used similar techniques to portray a world in turmoil.*

traditional Germanic intellectual approach to music and the prettified French Impressionistic reaction. Expressionism is in many ways a (mostly) German reaction to a French reaction to the nineteenth-century German dominance in music. Keep all the reactions straight and your century will make much more sense.

Certain visual artists led the Expressionistic charge into battle. Georges Rouault (1871–1958), Oskar Kokoschka (1886–1980), and Vassily Kandinsky (1866–1944) used psychological tension, distorted forms, and the shock of pure color to grab the attention of a jaded and often confused audience. Because, in their own view, the Espressionists inhabited a disturbed world, their artistic works must also disturb. This was not a new concept; Bosch in the sixteenth century, El Greco in the seventeenth century, and Goya in the early nineteenth century all used distortion and shock as primary devices. Young painters whose early works were influenced by the "decadent" styles of the 1890s found this new freedom intoxicating. Their first public exhibition in 1905 earned them the nickname *Fauves* (Wild Beasts), a label that delighted them.

The new literature, as exemplified in the works of Franz Kafka (1883–1924) and James Joyce (1882–1941), also revolted against realism and naturalism, seeking instead to depict spiritual or psychological truths. The world was represented as part reality and part dream, with modern people carrying the double burden of guilt and anxiety as they mounted a futile search for happiness and "salvation," whatever that might mean. Theirs was not a pretty point of view.

Given these deliberately distorted visions, it is small wonder that the new art seemed to the traditionalists to be gaudy parodies of what had come before. Viewers, readers, and listeners found themselves thrust into a new world with each exhibition, play, or concert, and with each new world came the necessity for learning a new language. Now each concert required total concentration as a new vocabulary and syntax was unleashed on listeners. There was nothing soothing about the new art works; they demanded effort.

Arnold Schoenberg, the Rule Maker

One voice in the new century's music began to outsing all the rest. Arnold Schoenberg (originally Schönberg) was almost entirely self-taught, and his early works were in the late Romantic style. Shortly after the turn of the century, Schoenberg began experimenting with music that expressed his inner compulsions. He also began dabbling in painting in the Expressionistic style. A Jew, he converted to a nominal form of Christianity when he was eighteen, then returned to Judaism in 1933 at age fifty-nine, when the Nazis dismissed him from the Prussian Academy. Schoenberg emigrated to America the same year.

About 1907, Schoenberg turned out several influential musical works that eventually led to his devising a (supposedly) brand new method for writing music. This principle of "composition with twelve notes," which he solidified about 1921, was essentially a return to a complex polyphonic style not too far from some medieval and Renaissance music — though considerably more problematic for its listeners.

Note that Schoenberg emerges as the first dominant figure in the chapter. Some indication of this should appear in your notes here and with your notes on subsequent figures of such stature.

Schoenberg's new method presented the twelve notes of an octave (the individual notes between a tone and the same note twelve notes above) in an unvarying sequence. Though these twelve tones could be presented as a theme, they were more important in that they served as a reservoir of ideas for further development. The notes could be presented in a sequence; two or three could be sounded together as a sort of chord; they could be turned upside down or played backward — or upside down *and* backward — the notes strung out with vast distances between them; or they could be arranged according to a huge number of other possibilities. Because these notes were presented as an unvarying series, the style quickly came to be called **serialism**.

Serialism originated as a means of restoring order to an art form that had, according to some, degenerated into a formless mush. Some called this new style **atonality**, meaning there was no perceivable tonality or traditional harmonic basis. Schoenberg preferred the term *pantonality*, meaning all tonalities were available at any given time. He considered his work as the logical extension of what had come before and saw no conflict between his work and that of Beethoven, Wagner, and Brahms. Some consider serialism a mechanical method of composition in which a device tells the composer what note comes next as opposed to a more intuitive selection. As with most art forms, quality in serialism depends entirely on the talent and inventiveness of the artist. At its best, atonality is a singularly difficult style for casual listening; a tune seldom remains with a listener after leaving the concert hall. This seemed to bother Schoenberg very little. He said, "My historic duty is to write what my destiny orders me to write." Later in life he returned to a form of traditional tonality.

Pierrot lunaire (Moonstruck Pierrot), a strange, spooky tale of moon madness, is a unique Expressionistic fusion of words and music. Five instrumentalists support a female reciter who uses a technique called *Sprechgesang* or *Sprechstimme*, an intense vocal style halfway between singing and speaking. The story is divided into three sets of seven songs each (the three of the Trinity, the seven of Perfection?). The twenty-one songs touch on Moonstruck Pierrot's

---

ARNOLD SCHOENBERG

Although the works of Arnold Schoenberg (1874–1951) are studied more often than they are performed, they were highly influential to other composers during the 1920s, 1930s, and 1940s. Besides the sprawling tone poem *Verklärte Nacht,* (Transfigured Night), written in a lush late Romantic style reminiscent of Wagner or Mahler, his most performed pieces are *Five Pieces for Orchestra* (1909); *Pierrot lunaire* (1912), a set of twenty-one songs for reciter and small ensemble; and occasional piano works and songs. Schoenberg's most enduring influence has been in his teachings and the students whose work is based on his theories.

drunken view of the world that surrounds him. The opening song, "Mondes-trunken" (Moondrunk), speaks poetically of the wine poured nightly by the moon that we drink with our eyes.

ISTENING GUIDE   ●● & CD

ARNOLD SCHOENBERG · "MONDESTRUNKEN" (MOONDRUNK), FROM *PIERROT LUNAIRE*, OP. 21, for flute, violin, cello, piano, and reciter (1912)

Den Wein, den man mit Augen trinkt
(The wine that only eyes can drink
Giesst Nachts der Mond in Wogen nieder,
Pours nightly in waves from the moon,
Und eine Springflut überschwemmt
And a Springtide flood inundates
Den stillen Horizont.
The quiet horizon.

Gelüste schauerlich und süss,
Desires, dreadful and sweet,
Durchschwimmen ohne Zahl die Fluten!
Swim through flutes without measure!
Den Wein, den man mit Augen trinkt,
The wine that only eyes can drink,
Giesst Nachts der Mond in Wogen nieder.
Pours nightly in waves from the moon.

Der Dichter, den die Andacht triebt,
The poet, under the impulse of piety,
Berauscht sich an dem heilgen Tranke,
Gets befuddled on the holy drink;
Den Himmel wendet er verzückt
He tilts backward toward heaven
Das Haupt und taumelnd saugt und schlüret er
His head, and sucks and sips
Den Wein, den man mit Augen trinkt.
The wine that only eyes can drink.)

Light, dancelike piano and flute, then other instruments, all in their upper register.

A sudden accent on "Springtide flood."

Flute and violin introduce the second stanza. All instruments still in the upper register.

Suddenly louder and more agitated with the piano pounded.

Lighter on "heaven," ending with light, ethereal mistlike sounds.

Schoenberg's Disciples: Berg and Webern

Paul Gauguin's Mahana No Atua (Day of the Gods, 1894) *shows the deliberately flat, two-dimensional "carved" quality that would inspire many of the later Primitives in their search for purity and innocence. Paul Gauguin, French (1848–1903). Oil on canvas, 1894, 68.3 × 91.5 cm. Helen Birch Bartlett Memorial Collection, 1926.198. Photograph © 1990, The Art Institute of Chicago. All rights reserved.*

Although many other composers, notably Pierre Boulez (b. 1925), Karlheinz Stockhausen (b. 1928), Luigi Dallapiccola (1904–1975), and even Igor Stravinsky, used serialism in highly personal ways, Schoenberg's two main disciples were Alban Berg (1885–1935) and Anton Webern (1883–1945). Berg's style, though still difficult at times, could also be lyrical and engaging. Several of Berg's compositions, such as the *Lyric Suite* for string quartet and parts of his opera *Wozzeck*, border on a Romantic style. Berg's outlook on the world was much more positive than Schoenberg's, and his works mirror this optimism. Anton Webern reduced music to the barest essentials. He preferred unusual combinations of solo instruments presenting intense, poetic sounds that were as condensed as music could become. *Five Pieces for Orchestra* contains a mere seventy-six measures for the entire five movements, and the *Six Bagatelles* for string quartet last a total of just over 3½ minutes.

PRIMITIVISM: LOOKING FOR
THE FOUNDATIONS

Throughout the nineteenth century, artists admired whatever seemed to show the unsophisticated side of humankind. This **Primitivism** could be seen both in English gardens, with their studied carelessness and irregularities, and in the simplicity and naivete of folk art. The eighteenth-century idea of the "Noble Savage" gave Western artists permission to glorify peasants and tribal peoples all over the world. In the nineteenth and early twentieth centuries this idealization (at a safe distance, of course) came to include the notion that the lower classes were more in touch with sensuality and natural instincts than "civilized" Westerners. Now it was not so much the Noble Savage as pagan sensuality that was being glorified.

The twentieth century provided new access to the "primitive." The new invention of the phonograph allowed folk song collectors and other musicians the great advantage of studying the unique sounds of ethnic music from across the world. Musicians found dissonance, angular melodies, and off-center rhythms pervading the indigenous music of the Near East, India, Asia, America, and other "exotic" locales. Further, the texts often contained far more violence and anger than that found in familiar folk songs and carols. Because violent, primal instincts were obviously an important part of both the primitive and the modern world, it was logical to assume that violence should also be a major part of art. This new obsession with exposing the turbulent fury lying just underneath civilized society shocked many who wanted art to be placid and calming, or at the very least show an orderliness that was familiar. Several composers saw the artistic possibilities in this savagery, but two men, one a displaced Russian, the other a nationalistic Hungarian, led the rest.

Igor Stravinsky, the Russian Visionary

As a youth, Igor Stravinsky studied piano and composition. He was a student of Rimsky-Korsakov but also absorbed the influences of Skryabin, Tchaikovsky, and even Debussy. In 1910, at the age of twenty-eight, Stravinsky traveled to Paris, where the prominent ballet impresario Sergei Diaghilev immediately commissioned the score to the ballet *The Firebird* (Russian: *Zhar'-ptitsa*) for his Ballet Russe in Paris. With its fiery music, folktale plot, spectacular sets, and exotic costuming, *The Firebird* was a direct descendant of the fairytale operas and ballets of Rimsky-Korsakov, and it was an immediate hit. Diaghilev demanded a second score for the next year. *Petrushka*, the earthy 1911 sequel, is the story of a puppet that comes to life during the pre-Easter Shrovetide Fair in St. Petersburg. The ballet's rhythmic verve, brilliant orchestration, and obvious tone painting made it an enduring favorite.

Diaghilev, his impresario's keen nose smelling popular success, asked for a third ballet score. Stravinsky dipped once more into his storehouse of Russian tales for *The Rite of Spring*, a ferocious study of human sacrifice in primitive Russia. The two parts of the work, "The Adoration of the Earth" and "The Sacrifice," were choreographed by Nijinsky and produced by Diaghilev in Paris

Boyd is introducing a new "school" here, artists who were drawn to the "primitive" as a means of escaping the artificiality they felt surrounded them. You should record a brief definition of each aesthetic school as you meet it, then identify and group the artists who worked within the schools.

Igor Stravinsky's 1913 ballet, The Rite of Spring, *with its subtitle "Scenes of Pagan Russia," caused a riot at its opening performance. Audiences weren't ready for scenes of human sacrifice in a ballet. This scene comes from the Joffrey Ballet's 1989 reconstruction of the ballet.*

in 1913 to one of the stormiest receptions ever given a musical work. A riot broke out that trashed the theater.

The cause of all the commotion was the work's unrelenting pounding rhythms and abrasive discords, which went against all previously established rules of music. Moreover, for an audience used to watching delicate ballerinas in tutus or couples waltzing in regal ballrooms, the sight of a young girl dancing herself to death to propitiate a harvest god, accompanied by frenetic pagan rhythms, was just too much to stomach. Now, of course, all the musical devices introduced in *The Rite of Spring* have become common coin through film scores. In 1913, it was cause to question the musical judgment, if not the actual mental stability, of Stravinsky and anyone who defended this music.

For the "Introduction" that opens Part 1, Stravinsky uses a sad, almost despairing Lithuanian folk song played by a straining bassoon in its upper reaches. A gradually thickening texture is dominated by the woodwinds. Stravinsky interrupts the anguished opening dance by a sudden return of the folk song. Then a quiet, sinister rhythmic thunking by *pizzicato* (plucked) violins heralds the "Dance of the Youths and Maidens." This urgent, insistent rhythm is, in turn, destroyed by the loud, savage, off-center rhythmic pounding of a single dissonant chord. Where audiences expected the regularly recurring **1** 2 3 — **1** 2 3 stresses of the waltz or the **1** 2 3 4 — **1** 2 3 4 of the march — both a feature of Western music since the Renaissance—Stravinsky placed his accents in unexpected and often incomprehensible places: **1** 2 3 4—**1** 2 3 4—**1** 2 3 **4**—**1** 2 3 **4**—**1** 2 3 4—**1** 2 3 4. That could translate as: a nine-beat introduction—**1** 2—**1** 2 3 4 5 6—**1** 2 3—**1** 2 3 4—**1** 2 3 4 5—etc. Harmony (the chord) was being used as rhythm, but not a rhythm that could be anticipated. Further, the chord itself was a dissonant, unpleasant (to its first audiences) sound that mirrored perfectly the primitive fertility rites of the plot. It was just too much change; the audience short-circuited into a riot.

 ISTENING GUIDE

IGOR STRAVINSKY · "AUGURS OF SPRING—DANCE OF THE YOUTHS AND MAIDENS," FROM *THE RITE OF SPRING* (1913)

Interlude

- Plaintive bassoon cry in the upper register.
- *Pizzicato* violins.
- Three clarinets interrupt, then strings interrupt.
- *Pizzicato* violins again.

Tempo giusto

- Sharp, dissonant chords by the strings, accents by eight horns, rhythms only, no melody.
- Short melodic explosions almost like folk song fragments from the woodwinds and brasses, repeated many times with only slight modifications, very loud.
- Sudden repetition of sharp, dissonant chords.
- Abrupt downward pairs of notes from piccolo to trombone, violin 1 repeats its *pizzicato* figure, except bowed, and woodwinds play melodic fragments as the texture gradually thickens and the volume increases. The music proceeds straight into the next section, "The Game of Abduction."

IGOR STRAVINSKY

The international career of Igor Stravinsky (1882–1971) began with these three early ballets, *The Firebird, Petrushka,* and *The Rite of Spring,* and they show his progress from Russian nationalism to a thoroughly twentieth-century idiom. Always atuned to the problems of the world, Stravinsky was to change both his styles and his homeland several times.

By the mid-1920s, Stravinsky had embarked on his Neoclassical phase, which climaxed with his opera *The Rake's Progress* (1951). By now a resident of California, Stravinsky finally came to terms with serialism. He turned out a series of master-works in his old age, the best known of which are *Threni* (1958) for soloists, chorus, and orchestra, and *Movements* for piano and orchestra (1959).

Throughout his life Stravinsky retained his interest in the Russian Orthodox church. Works influenced by his faith are the *Symphony of Psalms* (1930); the *Mass* (1944–1948), for winds and chorus; *The Flood* (1962), which used a text from English mystery plays; and the *Requiem Canticles* (1966), with nine extremely compact movements in 15 minutes.

Béla Bartók, the Hungarian Nationalist

Two years before Stravinsky wrote *The Rite of Spring,* the Hungarian Béla Bartók produced an energetic and percussive piano work he called *Allegro barbaro* (loose translation: "Fast and Barbarically"). It was an outgrowth of his tours of the Hungarian provinces collecting strongly accented folk songs and dances. Although composed in 1911, the piece was not performed in public for almost

Béla Bartók collecting folk songs in Transylvania, a historic region in central Rumania that was also his birthplace. The free, nonsymmetrical rhythms and bright melodic touches of these folk songs influenced many of his best-known works, such as the Allegro barbaro *and his 153 teaching pieces for piano,* Mikrokosmos.

BÉLA BARTÓK

Two influences formed the music of Béla Bartók (1881–1945): the works of Beethoven and Bach, and the folk music of his native Hungary. From the intense pounding of *Allegro barbaro* to his final "American" works, he utilized the freedom of both the sounds and forms of folk music allied with the control of the great German composers.

Bartók's best-known works are the *Music for Strings, Percussion and Celeste* (1937), the anguished cry for his embattled homeland in the *Concerto for Orchestra* (1943), his series of graded piano works titled *Mikrokosmos,* and the six string quartets that are considered keystones of twentieth-century chamber music and the greatest works in that genre since Beethoven.

a decade, and then only by Bartók himself. The rhythmic energy caused a scandal of sorts, but there was no denying that the strict ABA form and recognizable harmonic structure bound *Allegro barbaro* with the past. Although it was still startling, Primitivism was being tamed.

Other Russian Perspectives

Other Russian composers were also experimenting with strong rhythms and nontraditional approaches. Sergei Prokofiev (1891–1953) composed his hard-driving *Toccata* for piano in 1911 (the same year Bartók wrote *Allegro barbaro*) and the *Scythian Suite* in 1914, drawing his inspiration, like Stravinsky, from pagan Russia. Alexander Skryabin (1872–1915), a pantheistic mystic, composed a series of three tone poems between 1905 and 1910, the last being *Prometheus: The Poem of Fire,* which used a "mystic chord" in the music and featured a "color organ" to project certain colors on a screen to match the psychological transformations in the music.

NEOCLASSICISM: BACK TO THE FUTURE

About 1920, a new, somewhat self-conscious and ironic musical style surfaced that is now called **Neoclassicism**. It is just what the name implies, a new viewing of the ideals of the Classical era of Haydn, Mozart, and early Beethoven. Lightness, a clear texture, and a respect for traditional forms and the counterpoint of the late eighteenth century infused these works. The style is particularly attached to the name of Stravinsky, but other composers also fell under its influence.

Stravinsky's rearrangements of some early eighteenth-century music attributed to Giovanni Battista Pergolesi became the ballet *Pulcinella*. Much Neoclassical music was intended for chamber ensembles or small chamber orchestras of two dozen or so players, again mirroring the size and sound of musical performance of the time of Mozart. That does not mean the music sounded like Mozart; the harmonies were definitely twentieth century, the melodies often angular and unpredictable. Schoenberg was a sworn enemy of Neoclassicism because he saw it as destroying what he considered the logical progression of nineteenth-century music into his own serial style. Paul Hindemith's (1895–1963) Neoclassical works from the 1920s have a vigorous and lively shine that belie his staid Germanic upbringing.

The French, with their historic delight in music for diversion, took readily to the Neoclassical concept. Ravel, in particular, used older forms, as in his delightful suite *Le Tombeau de Couperin* (Tombstone, or Monument, to Couperin), a rewriting of six eighteenth-century keyboard pieces originally by François Couperin. The "Minuet" is just that, a slow, stately antique dance entirely at odds with the stridency of modern life. Other movements include "Fugue," "Forlane" (a lively Italian dance), and "Rigaudon" (a French dance). Francis Poulenc (1899–1963) and George Auric (b. 1899) also wrote in this so-called "Back to Bach" style featuring transparent textures, light orchestrations, and a deliberate movement away from the profundities of the Expressionists.

Giacomo Balla's 1912 oil painting, Dynamism of a Dog on a Leash *(oil on canvas, 35⅜ × 43¼". Albright-Knox Art Gallery, Buffalo, New York. Bequest of A. Conger Goodyear and gift of George F. Goodyear, 1964), used cartoon techniques to show the tiny dog straining for freedom. Such paintings led to the action paintings of Jackson Pollock and the mobiles of Calder, where motion was real, not implied.*

FUTURISM AND FANTASY

In the times when it took two or three generations to see visible change in a political or artistic system, there was less interest in the future; both artists and laypersons tended to be more concerned with the present and its problems than in what might or might not come to pass. But when violent aesthetic changes began happening every decade or so, artists, worried that their works would become outdated or their messages passé, looked into the future for inspiration. In the first third of the twentieth century more and more composers, painters, dramatists, and poets attempted to picture a future based on what they could see at that time. Basically, what they anticipated was technology gone wild—and they loved it.

The painters, as usual, were already immersed in this **Futurism** trend. In 1912, two works appeared, one French, one Italian. In *Nude Descending a Staircase, No. 2*, Marcel Duchamp (1887–1968) attempted to reproduce motion on a static plane, almost like the images reproduced by multiple-exposure photography. Giacomo Balla used comic strip devices in his *Dynamism of a Dog on a Leash*, which, again, attempted to portray motion in a static form. This was not a new concept; Joseph M. W. Turner, the early nineteenth-century English painter, pictured the dramatic power and movement of a steam locomotive in his *Rain, Steam and Speed*. All three of these paintings were paeans to technological progress.

The Futurists

Musicians became fascinated with the noises that were the natural by-products of industry everywhere. In 1923, Arthur Honegger (1892–1955), a Swiss composer who also happened to be a steam train enthusiast, composed *Pacific 231*, a highly pictorial work giving the "visual impression and physical sensation of a train." (At that time, the Pacific 231 was the largest and most powerful intermountain steam locomotive in the world.) Honegger pictured the opening sounds of the steam escaping, the towering driver wheels screeching along the tracks, the train gathering momentum, and then the trip itself. Finally, the train slows and pulls into the station. Even today it is a haunting and impressive work.

Two years later, in 1925, George Antheil (1900–1959), a U.S. composer residing in Paris, wrote the notorious percussion work *Ballet méchanique*. Originally composed for a 1923 abstract motion picture, this work gave Antheil the opportunity to develop a new means of musical construction based on rhythms alone; the score used many traditional percussion instruments plus four pianos, electric bells, and airplane propellers. Antheil insisted that *Ballet méchanique* was not meant to glorify the beauty and precision of machines but was designed rather to escape the "iron grip of the tonal principle" and the limits of traditional forms. On the other hand, he also described this work as his interpretation of the "barbaric and mystic splendor of modern civilization." Make your own judgment.

& CD

GEORGE ANTHEIL · *BALLET MÉCHANIQUE* (1924, revised 1954)

0:00   Strict rhythm in tympani, followed immediately by the piano introducing the main "melodic" and rhythmic material.

0:25   Tympani and xylophone develop the main musical material.

0:55   Tympani roll into strong piano accents, xylophone dies away.

1:25   Piano alone, strong rhythms, nonmelodic.

2:35   Xylophone added to mostly piano material.

2:50   Xylophone, tympani dominate, then other instruments added.

3:35   Over a tympani roll, nonpredictable rhythms by other instruments.

4:05   The work continues with similar sounds.

Antheil, as a species of Renaissance Man, wrote two books on glandular
criminology, another book on military history, and for pocket money produced
a regular advice-to-the-lovelorn newspaper column.

Edgard Varèse, the French Visionary

If an American like Antheil could write a revolutionary piece in Paris, then a
Frenchman could do the same in New York. Edgard Varèse (1883–1965) attended the riotous 1913 premiere of Stravinsky's *The Rite of Spring* and thought
it "very natural." When his health failed under the strain of World War I, he
emigrated to America, became a citizen, and in 1921 helped establish the International Composers Guild, which promoted experimental music. Varèse's experiments helped him establish his own concept that musical "density" was
of greater importance than harmony or form. *Ionisation*, his work for 40 percussion instruments, was premiered in New York in 1931 to wildly varying
critical responses. Many of Varèse's works use quasiscientific titles such as
Hyperprism for wind and percussion orchestra, *Density 21.5* (the density of the
platinum used in a new flute) for solo flute, *Intégrales*, and *Arcana*. He also
pioneered in the use of electronics as the music of the future, the best known
being *Poème électronique,* written for the 1958 Belgian World's Fair and using 425
loudspeakers.

TRADITIONALISM

With all the experiments in music and art described in the past several pages, the first four decades of the twentieth century may seem to have been nothing but a jungle of outrageous new sounds. This was not the case, however. Audiences, like all human groupings, change very slowly. In fact, for any new art it is usually a case of growing a new audience rather than changing the old one.

The young audiences of the 1880s and 1890s had been beguiled with the sounds of those newcomers Mahler, Tchaikovsky, Puccini, and Dvořák. Although these and others were "different" (meaning not exactly like Schumann and Mozart), they were close enough to traditional music to be acceptable. As these listeners grew older in the opening decades of the twentieth century, they wanted to hear music that was "the same but different." To this traditional audience, Schoenberg, Stravinsky, Bartók, and the rest of the young iconoclasts presented sounds that were not only unconventional, they weren't even musical.

Several composers decided — possibly subconsciously — to compose in a style that was a continuation of the Romantic century. For these writers it was not a matter of finding a new voice, only of refining a voice that already existed. Previously in Western music, this had been the situation for any composer: Take what has been handed to you, then give it your own voice. Several highly talented composers decided that if the Romantic style was good enough for Schumann, Liszt, and Wagner, it was certainly good enough for them.

Such composers often came from outside the mainstream countries of Germany and France. Italy, with its traditional emphasis on opera and vocal music, stayed firmly in the traditional vocal paths. Puccini's operas plowed very little new ground, and Puccini's heir-apparent, Gian Carlo Menotti (b. 1911), still uses virtually the same musical vocabulary. Menotti's best-known work, *Amahl and the Night Visitors* (1951), is Puccinian to the core.

One of the most determined Romantics was Sergei Rachmaninov (1873–1943). His studies in the St. Petersburg and Moscow conservatories grounded him in the sounds of Tchaikovsky and the forms of the Germans. Although he composed excellent pieces into the final year of his life, Rachmaninov never left that basic late-nineteenth century sound. Part of his music's charm is its nostalgic brooding for his native Russia, which was present even in his early works but more pronounced after he emigrated to America in 1917. Rachmaninov's music has great emotional intensity, particularly the symphonies and the four concertos. His *Rhapsody on a Theme by Paganini* (1934) is a perennial favorite, as are the *Preludes* (1904) and other works for solo piano.

Jean Sibelius, Finland's Nationalist

Jean Sibelius (1865–1957) is Finland's only composer with a worldwide reputation. Although Sibelius spoke with an individual voice, his works were still recognizably within the main flow of European music. Sibelius's best-known work by far is the 1899 tone poem *Finlandia*, a soaring piece whose love-of-homeland theme transcends national boundaries. Although the melodies in *Finlandia* appear to be folk songs, they are, in fact, all original with Sibelius.

You might wish to note some contrasting attitudes between the schools of "Traditionalism" and "Neoclassicism" and those of "Futurism" and "Fantasy." You might also wish to compare some of the representative products and champions of each movement.

The Romantic vision was not dead, but its darker, more mysterious side was showing. For some painters and composers, the means of communication was often ambiguous or troubling. Giorgio de Chirico's paintings employ a steep perspective, empty space, and forms out of their normal context. Even the title of this work, Gare Montparnasse (The Melancholy of Departure) is disquieting. (1914. Oil on canvas, 55⅛" × 6'⅝". Collection, The Museum of Modern Art, New York. Gift of James Thrall Soby.)

Other international favorites of Sibelius are the four *Legends* based on the Finnish epic *Kalevala* (of which *The Swan of Tounela* is the best known), incidental music to Shakespeare's *The Tempest,* a fine violin concerto, and several pieces of chamber music.

Gustav Holst, England's Mystic

Gustav Holst, despite his Swedish name, was thoroughly English. After a traditional musical upbringing, he developed a profound interest in mystical Sanskrit literature and Asiatic melodies. Although his various works, particularly choral, occasionally appear on concert programs, he is best known for a single work, *The Planets* (1916), a seven-movement tone poem describing the astrological associations of the planets in our solar system. The work uses a large orchestra, pipe organ, and (in the final movement) a women's chorus. Each of the movements has its own individuality and charm. "Mercury, the Winged Messenger" (Mvt. 3) is actually an orchestral *scherzo* (a rapid, spritely work), a quicksilver flash of notes conveying the traditional view of Mercury as both the messenger of the Greek gods and also the patron of thieves. The upper strings and woodwinds predominate as the fey elflike imp whizzes across the musical heavens accompanied by some double-tonality passages.

ISTENING GUIDE

GUSTAV HOLST · "MERCURY, THE WINGED MESSENGER," MVT. 3
FROM *THE PLANETS*, OP. 32 (1916)

A   Woodwinds and plucked strings bubble upward with repeated short
fragments of melody.
The celeste (orchestra bells) interrupts, then downward motives with
the same bouncy and fragmented instrumentation.

B   Solo violin and solo oboe with an Oriental-like melody.
Other instruments added in a *crescendo*, again repeating short fragments of melody.

A'   Similar to the first **A** section, with fragments of sound bouncing from
one instrument to another.

Coda   Roll on the tympani, the celeste sounds the **A** theme, the solo violin
plays the **B** motive, everything bubbles up again, under a high violin
drone.

Throughout its history, England has always shown both conservative tendencies and unique traits in the arts, possibly as a result of being an island
kingdom. England had its own style of Reformation, its own church music, a
peculiar Renaissance that was a generation behind the Continent's, dramatic
traditions that obstructed its development of opera, and a strong folk music
tradition that influenced all "serious" music.

Ralph Vaughan Williams, England's Folkist

From 1903 until 1912, Ralph Vaughan Williams—the last name is Vaughan
Williams, without a hyphen—trudged the hills and lanes of England, collecting and analyzing the folk songs of his homeland. In 1904, he was invited to
become the musical editor of a new hymn book, *The English Hymnal*, into
which he managed to slip some folk tunes. These two varieties of folk music—
most of our hymns are a type of folk music—would eventually flavor many of
Vaughan William's compositions. In addition, he loved and performed the great
English religious choral works from the late sixteenth century, the sounds of
which can be heard in his own choral pieces.

Possibly Vaughan Williams's ramblings through the English countryside collecting folk songs gave him his positive but honest outlook on life. Even as he
was taking these walking tours, he composed music reflecting the sedate villages and winding lanes. In 1904, he made settings for piano and voice of nine

Grant Wood's painting Midnight Ride of Paul Revere *(1931), like Vaughan Williams's music, reflects a nostalgic yearning for country life and open spaces.*

of the poems from Robert Louis Stevenson's *Songs of Travel*. Such titles as "The Roadside Fire" and "Whither Must I Wander?" reflect this attitude of ambling freedom. One of the most popular of the set, "The Vagabond," praises the freedom of the out of doors; and still, Vaughan Williams wrote the work in minor. Listen for the nostalgic sadness in the piano part, the courageous marchlike sounds that seem to say, "Enjoy this freedom now, for civilization will take it from you soon enough."

RALPH VAUGHAN WILLIAMS

Vocal music was central to Ralph Vaughan Williams's (1872–1958) output. From the early choral setting of Whitman's *Toward the Unknown Region* and the song cycle *On Wenlock Edge* to his six operas and the beautiful *Flos Campi* (Flowers of the Field) for solo viola, chamber orchestra, and wordless chorus, the voice set the style of his works.

Vaughan Williams's symphonies contain many elegiac passages as well as spots of great power and even brutality. Those wishing to understand Vaughan Williams should start with the *Sea Symphony*, the *Fantasia on a Theme of Thomas Tallis* (both from 1910), and, of course, the "Fantasia on Greensleeves" from his opera *Sir John in Love* (1929). Later, listen to the chamber music and the choral music, particularly *Flos Campi*, the *Mass in G* and *Hodie*. The beguiling melodiousness and honesty are immediately apparent. (For the purists among us, Vaughan Williams's first name is usually pronounced *Rafe*, rhyming with *safe*.)

ISTENING GUIDE

RALPH VAUGHAN WILLIAMS · "THE VAGABOND," FROM *SONGS OF TRAVEL* (1904)

Give to me the life I love,
let the lave go by me.
Give the jolly heaven above,
and the byway nigh me.
Bed in the bush with stars to see,
Bread I dip in the river—
There's the life for a man like me,
There's the life for ever.

Let the blow fall soon or late,
Let what will be o'er me;
Give the face of earth around,
And the road before me.
Wealth I seek not, hope nor love,
Nor a friend to know me;
All I seek, the heaven above,
And the road below me.

Open, buglelike minor chord for the head motive.
Similar, but higher and in major.

Two similar half-phrases.

High and exuberant, but ending meditatively with the opening minor chord head motive.
[Same music as the first stanza.]

THE RISE OF THE STAR CONDUCTOR

When the Renaissance, Baroque, or Classic composer presented a work it was assumed he would be the leader (**conductor**). If the composer did not conduct, then the job generally fell to the principal violinist, the one we now call the *concert-master*. This worked as long as the music was relatively uncomplicated. But in the nineteenth century, musical scores, not to mention operas, became extraordinarily complex. Some leader with an overall view of the music had to be in charge, and one important requirement for this somebody was a strong personality that could mold divergent musical ideas into one vision.

Hector Berlioz, Carl Maria von Weber, and Felix Mendelssohn were the first star conductors. By the late nineteenth century, Richard Wagner, Hans von Bülow, and Hans Richter traveled widely conducting various orchestras and opera companies. In 1869, Wagner wrote a thinnish book titled *Über das Dirigieren* (Concerning Conducting), in which he stated that the conductor's two

MUSIC CRITICISM:
WRITERS ON MUSIC

The first time one of our human ancestors banged two rocks together in what he considered an attractive rhythm, without doubt somebody else yelled, "That's terrible! Cut it out." Thus was born the first music critic.

Music criticism began as a branch of aesthetics; in Greek thought they were basically the same. Then, about 1600, the Florentine Camerata began discussing how Greek music should *really* be performed. Throughout the 1700s, music journals flourished and died, writers presented critical papers for encyclopedias, and such works as Charles Burney's 1789 multivolume *A General History of Music* contained an "Essay on Musical Criticism."

Music criticism came into its own in the nineteenth century, led by several German periodicals, the best known being Robert Schumann's *Neue Zeitschrift für Musik* (New Journal for Music). About the same time, the new scholarly discipline of **musicology** arose to give some order to the investigation of music. Critics were divided into two camps or goals: (1) those who wished to instruct unlettered music appreciators concerning what to listen for in music, and (2) those investigating everything from acoustics to proper historical performing style. All found that attempting to translate music into a verbal mode was difficult if not impossible.

Nevertheless, music critics are valuable in that they give multiple viewpoints from (hopefully) educated musicians concerning the role of music in society. Such musicologist-writers as Ernest Newman and Alfred Einstein (Albert's brother), as well as composers like Aaron Copland and Igor Stravinsky, have provided valuable insights into the psychology and physiology of music. Of course, some critics are more impulsive. When Margaret Truman (a singer of modest ability and the daughter of then President Harry S Truman) received an uncomplimentary review following one of her recitals, the President invited the critic up to the Oval Office. Wisely, perhaps, the critic chose not to accept the invitation. Though possibly not the best judge, the amateur is always the most impassioned critic.

main problems are "setting a proper tempo" (speed) and "finding the melody," meaning discerning which of the main parts in a complicated score is the most important, then balancing the rest of the parts against that main melody.

As the size of the orchestras increased and complexities were layered on each other, demands on the conductor increased. Only an extraordinary musician could keep all the musical balls up in the air, and those who could handle the job became the conducting superstars. By the beginning of this century, a handful of men — all, predictably, Europeans — were able to demand extra rehearsal time to refine performances until they glistened. These conductors were often megalomaniacal tyrants. Felix Weingartner, Wilhelm Furtwängler, Fritz Reiner, and particularly Arturo Toscanini terrorized orchestral players and concert organizers alike. There were no established female conductors until well into the twentieth century.

Because of the unbelievable costs in maintaining a group of musicians, conductors quickly devised methods for cutting down on rehearsal time. In 1820, Ludwig Spohr introduced the modern baton to London audiences, who saw it as a silly novelty. But when Mendelssohn began using a baton in Leipzig in 1835, it entered general use. Baton techniques improved and a school of conducting arose with a more or less uniformity of meaning in each gesture.

Modern star conductors seldom spend their careers or even a full season with the same orchestra. Instead, the best ones travel the world, rehearsing for a week to conduct a set of two or three identical concerts, then jetting to another city to do the exact same concert two or three more times. Some conductors specialize in a certain repertoire, such as music of the Baroque or the early twentieth century, limiting themselves to polishing a certain style far beyond that allowed a "generalist" conductor.

KEY TERMS

Expressionist
serialism
atonality
Primitivism

Neoclassicism
Futurism
conductor
music criticism
musicology

Each of these terms should be familiar to you, and you should be able to use them comfortably. If not, review problem areas until the concepts are mastered. Then continue on to the Reading Comprehension and Discussion Questions.

■ READING COMPREHENSION AND DISCUSSION QUESTIONS

1. Although the musical terms, artists, and movements of Boyd's text may have been new to you, the processes of musical evolution remain the same in our time as they were in the late 19th and early 20th centuries. Beginning with your favorite "type" of contemporary music—that is, the "name" usually given to the music you most enjoy—try to identify the "type" of music that came before it. Who are some representative artists in each group? What do you know about their lives or careers? How many "types" of music can you identify working backwards from the present? How many works and artists?

2. People were shocked at much of the music and other art described in "The Age of the 'isms'" and many were angered by it. Can you think of parallels to their reactions regarding the arts, particularly music, in the years since 1920? How about 1930? 1950? The 60s? The 70s, 80s, and 90s? What forms did such anger and opposition take? Why do you think that people reacted in so hostile a way to art?

3. What instances of Primitivism do you see in the arts with which you are familiar, including music? Do you sympathize with the desire to flee artificiality, to become—as Boyd describes the motivation (359)—"more in touch with sensuality and natural instincts" with "simplicity and naivete"? Do you think that this desire is likely more common now than a century ago, less common, or about the same? Why?

Index

Text Credits

Page 27, Copyright © 1991 by The New York Times Company. Reprinted by permission.

Pages 34, 108, Copyright © 1991 The Washington Post. Reprinted with permission.

Page 49, Copyright © 1992 The Baltimore Sun Co. Reprinted with permission.

Page 74, This essay by Page Smith is reprinted by permission of Chronicle Features, San Francisco, California.

Page 101, Reprinted by permission of Cox News Service.

Page 115, Copyright © 1991 Los Angeles Times. Reprinted by permission.

Pages 122, 139, 161, 201, © 1991 San Francisco Chronicle. Reprinted by permission.

Page 146, Reprinted with permission from The Atlanta Journal and The Atlanta Constitution.

Page 153, Copyright © 1991 Creators Syndicate and Joe Bob Briggs. Reprinted by permission.

Page 168, Copyright © 1991 Chicago Tribune Company, all rights reserved. Used with permission.

Page 184, Reprinted with permission of The San Francisco Examiner.

Page 209, Reprinted with permission of The Dallas Morning News.

Page 218, "Bear on the Loose" by Austin Murphy is reprinted courtesy of SPORTS ILLUSTRATED from the October 14, 1991 issue. Copyright © 1991 The Time Inc. Magazine Company. All Rights Reserved.

Text selections in Part III: *Frauds, Myths, and Mysteries,* Kenneth L. Feder, © 1990 Mayfield Publishing Company; *Understanding the Bible,* Third Edition, Stephen Harris, © 1992, 1985, 1980 Mayfield Publishing Company; *Theatre* (Brief Version), Second Edition, © 1988, 1981 Mayfield Publishing Company; *Human Antiquity,* Kenneth L. Feder and Michael Alan Park, © 1989 Mayfield Publishing Company; *Encore! A Guide to Enjoying Music,* Jack Boyd, © 1991 Mayfield Publishing Company.

Photo Credits

Page 294, Bengt Wanselius

Page 296, Act - William Ganslen

Page 297, Act - William Ganslen

Page 299, © Arvid Lagenpusch

Page 304, (left) Tim Fuller; (right) French Cultural Services

Page 305, © Photo Pic

Page 350, Paul Cezanne, *Mont Sainte-Victoire,* Philadelphia Museum of Art

Page 353, The Bettmann Archive

Page 354, Giraudon / Art Resource, New York

Page 356, The Bettmann Archive

Page 360, The Joffrey Ballet, *Le Sacre Du Printemps,* members of the Joffrey Ballet, choreography by Millicent Hodson. Photo by Herbert Migdoll.

Page 362, (top) The Bettmann Archive; (bottom) Courtesy the Bartók Archivum and the Béla Bartók Memorial House, Budapest

Page 370, (top) Grant Wood, *The Midnight Ride of Paul Revere,* The Metropolitan Museum of Art, Arthur H. Hearn Fund, 1950. (50.117), © Grant Wood / VAGA, New York, 1990; (bottom) The Bettmann Archive